DREAMS TO REMEMBER

DREAMS TO REMEMBER

Otis Redding, Stax Records, and the Transformation of Southern Soul

MARK RIBOWSKY

LIVERIGHT PUBLISHING CORPORATION

a division of W. W. Norton & Company

New York | London

For information about permission to reproduce selections from this book,
write to Permissions, Liveright Publishing Corporation, a division of
W. W. Norton & Company, Inc., 500 Fifth Avenue, New York, NY 10110

For information about special discounts for bulk purchases, please contact
W. W. Norton Special Sales at specialsales@wwnorton.com or 800-233-4830

Manufacturing by Courier Westford
Book design by Chris Welch Design
Production manager: Julia Druskin

Library of Congress Cataloging-in-Publication Data

Ribowsky, Mark.
 Dreams to remember : Otis Redding, Stax Records, and the transformation
of Southern soul / Mark Ribowsky. — First edition.
     pages cm
 Includes bibliographical references and index.
 ISBN 978-0-87140-873-0 (hardcover)
 1. Redding, Otis, 1941–1967. 2. Soul musicians—United States—Biography.
3. Soul music—History and criticism. I. Title.
 ML420.R295R53 2015
 782.421644092—dc23
  [B]

                    2015009097

Liveright Publishing Corporation
500 Fifth Avenue, New York, N.Y. 10110
www.wwnorton.com

W. W. Norton & Company Ltd.
Castle House, 75/76 Wells Street, London W1T 3QT

1 2 3 4 5 6 7 8 9 0

In loving memory of my mother,

Frances Ribowsky

CONTENTS

INTRODUCTION

The Big O

If one looks back at the 1960s through a high-magnification lens and with a healthy sentience of culture and the innate role popular music played within it, two songs might very well reveal everything there is to know about the nature and meaning of that decade. Indeed, within this book's covers, the argument can and will be made that these two recordings—Aretha Franklin's cover of Otis Redding's "Respect" in the spring of 1967, and Redding's posthumously released "(Sittin' On) The Dock of the Bay" early in 1968—rise above all other three-minute, 45-RPM, vinyl-backed symphonies derived from those turbulent and terrifying times. One reflects the need for generational outcasts to find a place among new societal norms, the other the need to find sanctuary in that new place.

Unlike "Sgt. Pepper"/"Incense and Peppermints" entreaties to tune in and drop-out, or "Blowin' in the Wind"/"Eve of Destruction" vetoes of hubristic war and group-think intolerance, "Respect" and "Dock of the Bay" provided the thread and threnody of the most uproarious and portentous of decades. Performed not incidentally by the "king" and "queen" of soul, they helped seed social change that, alas, never came to fruition in Redding's time and was in fact smacked down metaphorically in the decade's dying days by the literal deaths on a motel balcony in Memphis—mere blocks from where Otis Redding recorded most of his songs—a hotel kitchen in Los Angeles, and a speedway in Altamont.

Both of these priceless, timeless, chart-topping capsules of an America at war with itself, were so perfectly timed, just months apart, that they stand as a cause and effect. With them, Otis Redding found his own calling, not as musician, but as a prophet and a poet. In other words, Redding—simply the most overpowering and electrifying soul stage performer of his time, and just as profound an influence behind the scenes—became the nerve and conscience of soul music about to be fully integrated into the rock and roll arc.

"Respect" was clearly much larger in overall meaning than its individual verses, which were meant to add dynamite to the emotional ammunition of Redding's raspy, open-wounded wailing, which was perfectly coordinated with the edgy call-and-response horn blasts and soul-deep back beat that stamped the jazzy, sweaty funk of the "Memphis sound." But because it was recorded in 1965, the year of the Voting Rights Act, a year after the Civil Rights Act, and two years after the March on Washington, such a demand by a black man—to be appreciated for his hard work and the sacrifices he made—transcended the song's narrow trope of a man looking to be respected by his woman after a hard day. Civil rights anthems were not necessarily tightly and obviously focused on the cause; during the march, when Dr. Martin Luther King delivered his "I Have a Dream" peroration, Little Stevie Wonder's raucous "Fingertips (Part 2)" was the top song on the *Billboard* Hot 100 chart, a major crossover step for a black artist, and for no easily discernible reason was a sort of quasi-anthem for the event, wafting as it did on transistor radios through the crowds on the Mall between the Washington Monument and Lincoln Memorial.

In the same way, the songs of Motown and Stax/Volt were heard often on Armed Forces Radio in the jungles of Vietnam, offering American GIs who didn't want to be there the familiarity of life back home, a hint that such music soldered civil rights to anti-war protests and another prompt to question why they were indeed there.

•

REDDING'S "RESPECT," cut on July 9, 1965, in a converted movie theater in Memphis that would become the center of popular music a few years later, was just another day at the office for the staff at Stax. It was produced by Steve Cropper and anchored by the best house band known to man, the inimitable Booker T. and his MG's— Cropper, Donald "Duck" Dunn, Al Jackson, and their leader, Booker T. Jones. When it was released on August 15, 1965, the song only made it to number 35 on the pop chart. Yet its impact was felt within the well of black pride. It was Top 5 on the Black Singles Chart, a category soon changed in favor of the more politically correct R&B Chart. But, like "Fingertips (Part 2)," its grooves and that sweeping title of pride against prejudice were important cultural markers, for inner-city America a command to keep fighting the de facto segregation of Jim Crow, to not sit at the colored lunch counter or follow the signs to the "Colored Only" bathroom.

Still, it's one of the threads of the Redding story that he would nurse his aversion to being labeled and interpreted instead of merely heard. Yet even neutrality was reflexively criticized by some in a black cognoscenti impatient to present "their" stars as patriotic equals of white performers who knew enough to pay lip service to men in war. "Why won't top Afro-American entertainers go to Vietnam and entertain the troops there? It's a sore subject, and one they do not like to talk about," asked the venerable black newspaper of Harlem, the *New York Amsterdam News*, in 1967.[1] Needless to say, standing against the war would have been far out on a limb, indeed.

When Otis in 1965 cut a cover of Sam Cooke's posthumous 1964 release "A Change Is Gonna Come"—as brilliant a landmark as ever there was among sixties soul "message" songs—Redding's intent was less urgent than Cooke's, who came of age in the 1950s when black men were paid not to make a ruckus anywhere but onstage. Cooke's conscription of protest into an ingredient of his bombastic stage show was enough of a leap forward. Change wasn't here, but it was going to come—in time. For Redding's prime influences— Little Richard and James Brown—there never was such a revelatory transition; indeed, Brown's political coming-out (as opposed to his racial coming-out in such anthems as "Say It Loud I'm Black and I'm Proud") was, confusing to many, as a *Republican*, his statement made almost tragicomically, wearing a flag-draped jumpsuit while performing "Living in America."

It was only logical, then, that Redding's version of "Respect" was not as successful or earthmoving as Aretha Franklin's cut, arguably one of the greatest recordings in modern music history. Although each version was recorded under entirely different conditions and protocols—Franklin's a technical marvel made in New York under the watch of uber engineer Tom Dowd, and Redding's in Memphis, the product of nearly impromptu jams, one or two takes, all live— both had the benefit of some of the most talented session musicians ever born.

But Aretha also had the benefit of two more years of cultural give and the progression of inner-city norms into a hip white society that was just now learning to respect the talent and contributions of black men and women. Redding had provided the groove and beat of a song so infectious it has been covered by literally dozens of artists from every idiom. In the maw of the '60s, it could be interpreted any number of ways—indeed, when Franklin verbally spelled out *R-E-S-P-E-C-T*, she also had the advantage of a yearning for respect that was being echoed by a fledgling women's rights movement. And when she told her man, "Take care . . . TCB," a line she added to the song, this command from a strong woman to take care of business cut in a million directions: political, sexual, generational, and all in between. Little wonder that Otis, as ambivalent as he was about being one-upped on his own song, began using the line in his own renditions of it.

Jerry Wexler, the grand doyen of Atlantic Records' soul music empire, produced the Franklin version, a symbolic and sonic connection between the Memphis sound and the company that muscled in as its Northern overlord and creative partner. He once remarked that "Respect" was "global in its influence, with overtones of the civil rights movement and gender equality. It was an appeal for dignity."[2] In a great leap forward for the song's marketability, such an appeal, and the impudence of a woman making it, broadened the implicit significance of the deceptively ingenuous lyrics. As a result, Wexler and Franklin took the song to number 1 on both the pop and R&B charts. This meant that even assassination and conditioned opposition could not stop what was now the developing lay of the land in American culture.

●

OTIS REDDING was many things—in the coolly autobiographical "Love Man" he sang, about being "six feet one" with "fair skin"— and his performances multi-flavored. He preened, he pouted, he strutted, and he bled. And if his work didn't appear to be overtly political in nature, it was because he was canny enough to know the most trenchant messages always were up to the listener to realize. Like the song masters who came before him, Redding wrote and performed to allay the pain lurking in the folds of three-chord pop music. Redding could neither read nor write music, nor did he really know how to dance. But as he reached his apogee, cornering the market on its emotion and sincerity, he practically carried black music on his back.

His rise from the son of a preacher man in Macon, Georgia, to a preacher of three-minute soul sermons on vinyl discs was, in every way, the final stage in the maturation of African-American music as an idiom and an industry. Given its ticket to the big dance of emerging soul, Stax/Volt, encouraged and financially stoked by the biggest of the Northern soul–driven record companies, Atlantic Records, impudently but accurately called itself "Soulsville U.S.A." in pointed contrast to "Hitsville U.S.A.," Motown's founding father Berry Gordy's consciously less racially identifiable persona. And Redding was its vulnerable soul, laying out a full-on emotional release that flowed from what he defined as a pain in his heart. His musical palette, a cosmic alloy of gospel and blues, hammered into a gritty but elegant template by both black and white musicians, remodeled soul and rock and anchored the most infectious native music America had heard since the big bands.

The allied and alloyed Stax/Volt and Atlantic Records roster didn't last long, but it was profound—Booker T. and the MG's, Wilson Pickett, Sam and Dave, Percy Sledge, Eddie Floyd, and Solomon Burke, among others. Their sonic resonance was heard in 167 songs that made the top 100 on the pop chart, 250 songs on the R&B chart. Even novelties like Redding's Christmastime duet with Carla Thomas, "New Year's Resolution"—which, with his version of "White Christmas" can be found on the greatest and most underrated holiday album ever, Atlantic Records' 1968 *Soul Christmas* (guarantee: You ain't never heard "Silver Bells" the way Booker T. and the MG's did it)—are like mined gold today. Considering all this occurred at a time when the cultural hurdles were many for a place in the South calling itself Soulsville, it is no surprise that Stax/Volt became far more celebrated in review than in its currency, and in England more than America.

Within the music world, the South was always like Mecca. Seeking to glean some of the magic within the region's hallowed studio walls, the biggest musical acts in the world would beat a path to Nashville and Muscle Shoals. Still, there was no replicating what they were doing in Memphis, though even Elvis Presley, when he needed a shot of rejuvenation in the '70s, came to Soulsville to record. Saddest of all, however, despite Redding's high influence, it required his untimely death for him to sell records in large numbers in the United States. For that reason, "(Sittin On') The Dock of the Bay" is a metaphor for much in Redding's life. Its ode to lonely longing is a somber refrain indeed, and one he may well have intended to be taken in a mournful context.

Indeed, there is an unmistakable resignation to it, his voice far softer and more quaveringly vulnerable than it ever had been; when he sang of "watching the tide roll away," it is evident that he was watching not just the waters of San Francisco Bay roll away but also his optimism, his achievements, even his own life. Unsure of whether the song would be succor for his legacy or be stillborn, he spent much time during an introspective sabbatical after throat surgery obsessively playing *Sgt. Pepper's Lonely Hearts Club Band*, seeking clues to what pop music demanded in a postmodern world.

•

NOT INCIDENTALLY, in between the releases of "Respect" and "Dock of the Bay" Redding enjoyed his greatest moment of triumph. On June 18, 1967, the second day of the three-day Monterey Pop Festival, during the wistful ideological apogee of the rock era known as the Summer of Love, an idyllic twilight beneath the northern California bluffs served as his backdrop. This was the first grand ritual of rock and roll's post–teen idol evolution. The marquis featured some of the biggest mainstream acts on the globe. And while, for many, the breakout stars of this epochal bash were the sublime Janis Joplin and Jimi Hendrix—a white Texas woman who sang soul and a black man from Washington State who played white rock and roll—Redding was essentially reborn, a Deep South black-as-night soul man who for a decade dragged himself from stage to stage, turning himself inside out extracting the blackness of each word he sang.

Even on this stage, and at the age of twenty-six, he braved the trend of a culture given to leather, spangled jeans, long hair, and headbands. An imposing, well sculpted, beautiful looking man, Redding normally performed while looking ready for a *GQ* photo shoot, in leisure tops, cardigans, open-necked shirts and sport jackets, and neatly pressed slacks. On this night, he was dressed to kill, chitlin'-circuit style, all eye candy in a turquoise suit, not a hair of his close-cropped Afro and manicured mustache out of place.

"This is the love crowd, right?" he teased at the beginning of his set, betraying his tenuous connection to the new ethos. He needed no lines though, only a song to sing. When he broke into one of his hypnotic, ultra-sensuous trademark ballads, "I've Been Loving You Too Long (To Stop Now)," the song built to sonic bliss. Then, as he stalked the laser-and-strobe-lit stage, he fell to his knees as if pain had kicked his knees out, breathing fire, oozing sex. His raspy-throated bellowing and honey-coated purring blended seamlessly into the wailing horns of his backup band, the peerless Stax house musicians, and the effect wasn't rock but pure, unapologetic, uncompromising soul.

If there is only one clip that could be viewed, it would be the one from 1967, when he performed "Try a Little Tenderness" at Monterey, writhing and then exploding. He would remain onstage milking every last drop out of it, spitting out a machine gun–like barrage of "got-a, got-a, got-a, got-a," arms and legs conducting their own separate tribal dances. The very stoned audience of record industry lice and mainly white, middle- and upper-class teenage hippies on summer vacation, was left stunned and damp, turned incredulous by a black man singing a 1932 big band tune by Bing Crosby that had been refashioned into a soul standard.

Redding made his point. Loud and clear. Not entirely incidental was that everyone went home from the festival with Redding on their minds and in their ears, as much as they did Joplin and Hendrix, the festival's other big breakout stars. The Stax/Volt idiom now carried immense cachet, at least as important as was Motown in the public eye. At last, Redding stood as the cynosure of a new rock order that venerated African-American music but sublimated African-American artists. But he had precious little time to enjoy the air up there.

●

IT WAS no wonder that, after Monterey, Redding could sit back and ask for a little time before heading back to the cultural battlefront. He was a different breed than many in the rock and roll vanguard; projecting a traditional hip-to-be-square brand of cool, eschewing beads, bangles, robes, Beatle-esque lyrics that pimped a drug lifestyle, though he was hardly a bluenose in these matters. He took to the stage at Monterey somewhat or fully stoned, fueling himself with weed. Still, while few examined the lyrics of his songs closely, it was clear that his drug of choice was writing the perfect song and banging it out in the studio.

On December 10, 1967, just as he had put "Dock of the Bay" in the bank, time ran out. He died in perhaps the most tragic of the litany of small plane crashes that have sundered some of contemporary music's most promising and brilliant talent—from Buddy Holly/ Ritchie Valens/J. P. Richardson (a.k.a. the Big Bopper) to Patsy Cline to Lynyrd Skynyrd to Jim Croce. All were grievous losses;

none perhaps more cruel than the one that took Redding from the new order of music he had already begun to define—though he would continue to do that, anyway, having shaped the landscape in so many ways. He was only twenty-six when his plane went down but already had seen the tidal wave of America's civil rights struggle and the liberation of the music industry that mirrored its halting progressions, already had achieved exalted status as a singer, songwriter, producer, and record company executive. But it was the genuine undercurrent of open-wound vulnerability and grim fatalism in those pastoral images that sold "Dock of the Bay" and still does; by one measure, "Dock of the Bay" is the fifth biggest jukebox hit in history, behind "Hound Dog," "Don't Be Cruel," Patsy Cline's "Crazy," and "Rock Around the Clock."[3]

Few have ever cut the same sort of broad swath in transmitting statements that even years later contain equal currents of glory and tragedy. Not for nothing has Robert Hilburn, the venerable *Los Angeles Times* music critic and witness to Redding in the context of his time, written that "Dock of the Bay" and "I've Been Loving You Too Long (To Stop Now)" "conveyed marvelously the tenderness and heartache that rests at the foundation of soul music."[4]

It's no easy thing to verbalize the tragic components of life—all life, good, bad, and worse—so clearly that it physically makes you feel joy or pain. When Redding sang, every inch of him seemed to resonate in hallelujah celebration or woebegone anguish; hearing him sing "Mr. Pitiful" was to climb inside his heart and count its scars from being broken. That this was a primary trait was evident early; his first album, in 1964, was titled *Pain in My Heart*. That kind of deeper-than-deep soul can find its way into many contexts—for example, Redding's 1966 song "My Lover's Prayer" was on a 2001 soundtrack album of music used in *The Sopranos* TV series, along with the likes of Vivaldi, Frank Sinatra, Lorenzo Jovanotti, Keith Richards, and Henry Mancini. And, in retrospect, Redding's rare ability to make a heart hurt can only have been because his own was so breakable.

This sadness made Redding's joy even more joyous, those being the moments when he could ignore all the prophesies of impending doom, even if not for long. What he really feared was that a lurking scythe, one marking time until it could drop on him, making all the work he had done for naught. Of course, he was wrong about that; as with Caruso, Sinatra, and Lennon, Redding's death meant perpetual renewal.

•

AND WITH death emerged a kind of sainthood, something few deserve, and certainly not Redding for anything beyond his music. His prim but hardy wife, Zelma, knew that when she married him at the age of sixteen. Ever since, she has had to endure gossip, much of it falling into the realm of craziness. Pushed beyond her limits by a 2001 Redding biography with more than a little dirty laundry, she up and sued the author for $15 million.[5] Though she settled short of victory, it was because of her objections that the book was banned throughout Macon, Georgia—the hometown Redding never left—in many bookstores and in the library of the now-defunct Georgia Music Hall of Fame.[6] To be sure, misinformation has always pervaded the Redding legend. Upon his death—when, unlike for any of the other famous rock and roll plane-crash victims, stunningly bad-taste pictures of his corpse, still strapped in the copilot's seat, were published—*Esquire* ran an article that nonchalantly and wrongly posited that he had been at the pilot's controls when the flight went down, a fable many still believe. Questions are still asked about odd aspects of his death, some legitimate due to inconsistencies in the police reports, including that a mysterious missing attaché case supposedly full of cash and marijuana either was or was not found in the wreckage—and, in one print story, cocaine and opium.[7]

Redding's life can fairly be, and has been, called a "riddle."[8] But whatever else it is, the soundtrack has churned away as a profitable enterprise. Zelma Atwood Redding, in her seventies and still hardy even on one leg, the other amputated a few years ago because of diabetes, sits atop the legacy, zealously trying to cleanse and protect her husband in death from interlopers and despoilers. She mulls over projects including potential movies of his life, all of which have thus far failed to pass muster with her. A few years ago, she took back her husband's personal papers that she had once donated to the Macon public library, rather than having them available to any prying eyes. Having never remarried, her memories have only been partially for sale; the rest can be classified by the title of the one song she wrote with her husband—"I've Got Dreams to Remember." All the songs he ever wrote are personal to her. "I always thought everything he sang," she says, "he sang for me."[9]

•

IN TRUTH, Redding was not in the same league of depravity that his biggest influence, Little Richard Penniman, was. Although Redding became a hugely wealthy man, the bread never drove him—he would have been the first to nod in agreement with the John Lennon line "You don't take nothing with you but your soul." As stable and clean an image as he created for himself, the cruelest irony was that, while both Joplin and Hendrix derailed themselves with drugs and personal weakness, Otis—the strong one, the clear-eyed ballast against the wind—had less time left than they did riding that dangerous wind.

Redding's conflicted state of mind was helped neither by his difficulty assimilating into a white-dominated industry or the tangled web that the industry was, and is. The record game, to be polite, is one of the most venal and soulless entities ever known, and a bane to creatively inclined people easily manipulated by power brokers with a fast line and legal levers to rip them off. This was of course a trap that a generation of black performers fell into. Redding did much to alter that evil equation, but not nearly enough to suit him or make the industry cower, or even stop abusing *him*. Indeed, some have even wanted to avoid the pressures Redding had in establishing a conveyor belt of crossover soul without compromising the fundamental bedrock of his own inner soul, which was always translated through his sound and style.

On the other hand, Otis learned valuable lessons from his church deacon father—who tried mightily to nip Otis's singing in the bud when Otis was a teenager and in possession of an ungodly voice and a "Jazz Singer's"–style obsession—about living modestly and purely but with ferocious commitment. Otis willingly and voraciously craved more and more hegemony, and kept so true to his roots that many of his own songs, meant not to be commercially winsome as much as a kick to the gut, were not made-to-order pop hits. His mission was to make soul the overarching musical format of his generation, with himself as the gatekeeper. His loyalty thus was to his art, his craft, and not necessarily his wallet, and he wanted everyone to know that about him, every time he cleared his throat.

Even so, he parlayed his ambition and talent, with a tempered personality that was irresistible—a "soulful force of nature," as one chronicler of music history called him, or "a magic potion," to Stax/Volt co-founder and Rock and Roll Hall of Fame member Jim Stewart.[10] Although Stewart was not normally open to the adaptations that an artist with fiercely independent ideas like Redding insisted on, and there were times they butted heads, both always understood that such "magic" would be conceived and actualized on Redding's terms. Those adaptations after all were what put Stax/Volt, that onetime speck on the music map, into a position of inordinate power in the mid-1960s.

While Gordy built the first black-owned music empire at Motown, Redding did something at least as impressive: converting one of the whitest bastions of the post-Confederate South into the vital core of *black* music. America's musical evolution had been redirected to and refashioned in the South, taken there by black artists whose immediate ancestors had been shunted aside by the big labels, their work cribbed and covered in antiseptic pop for a ride up the charts. Then Redding came along and suddenly it was more common for black artists to cover Rolling Stones and Beatles' songs, stripping them down to their soulful components. And when whites covered the songs that had come out of Memphis and Muscle Shoals, the difference was that the songs had already been massive hits. It was an inversion of the highest order, and with the utmost . . . respect.

Redding's whole career was a matter of building and flexing his muscle, with music, with women, with rivals, but with a gentleness that belied that side of his ambition. But he knew early on that he was God's chosen vessel of transition, from lounge act to corporate player, cutting a common path through the shrubbery of soul, funk, and R&B compatible with acid rock. The fruits of this labor are heard today—as were, for a time in the '80s, the fruit of his loins, his sons Dexter and Otis III, fronting the funk/dance band the Reddings. Few had any idea that the Black Crowes' 1989 hard rock hit "Hard to Handle" was a 1967 Redding song. In this way, Otis never really dies, no more than Sinatra or Louis Armstrong or Sam Cooke does.

There is of course endless repackaging of his albums and an argosy of literature about Stax/Volt. Then, every once in a while, the name will leap from the gene pool of pop music for another go-round. There was George Faison's *Suite Otis*, the choreographer's ballet set to six Redding songs, performed by the Alvin Ailey American Dance Theater in 1986. Of more recent vintage was Kanye West and Jay-Z's 2011 *Watch the Throne* album—one of its tracks, "Otis," noted as "Featuring Otis Redding," sampled Redding's vocal on "Try a Little Tenderness," helping sell over a million copies.[11] In 2014, the classic rocker Paul Rodgers covered three Redding songs on his album *The Royal Sessions*. And on and on it goes.

•

TRUE STORY: There is a man in Italy named Graziano Uliani, whom Memphis Horn trumpeter Wayne Jackson swears is "the biggest Otis Redding fan on the planet." A record producer and president of the Otis Redding Appreciation Society of Italy, he lives on Via Otis Redding, overlooking the quaint town of Porretta. He speaks English haltingly, but every word he knows he learned from listening to Otis Redding records.[12] Another true story: In a quaint little railway station in Rochelle, France, one of the station walls bears a gigantic art deco mural with the images of two people: Ray Charles and Otis Redding.[13]

Then there is this. The Al Jazeera America website recently carried a news story from civil-war-torn Liberia. At one point, the story quotes a Liberian army general who "sits in a dim powder blue bunkerlike room with two other aging servicemen as Otis Redding's 'I've Got Dreams to Remember' plays from a large speaker on the street."[14]

This is all part of the enduring dominion built by Otis Redding, who, taken merely as a performer, was one of the most enduringly passionate and tragic icons music has ever witnessed. He earned the postage stamp that bore his image in 2003, having stood at the top of the heap of consistent and consistently good artists and live performers of the sixties. For what it's worth, contemporary retro-rankings by *Rolling Stone* a decade ago placed him eighth among the "100 Greatest Singers of All Time"—Aretha was number one, with Marvin Gaye, Sam Cooke, and Ray Charles just ahead of him in the soul subset[15]—and twenty-first among the "100 Greatest Artists of All Time" topped by the Beatles.[16] But of course, all the others had time. Much more time.

It only takes a listen to his records or a glimpse of him onstage, always a revelatory experience, to be left breathless; and thank the heavens for film and videotape of some typically wondrous performances through his career. Big, manly, emotional, and full of piss, vinegar, and heart, the man never cheated his audience. Each of his songs was calculated for maximum stage bang. Up there, a three-minute interlude of "Fa-Fa-Fa-Fa-Fa (Sad Song)," "Try a Little Tenderness," or his riotous cover of "Satisfaction" were, and still are, like, weightless, free falling emotions unabridged. Many of Redding's live performances are available on DVD and the Internet, and if there is only one that could be viewed it should be a choice between the 1967 clip of him belting out "Tenderness" at Monterey or during the legendary Stax/Volt tour of Europe. To watch him nearly collapsing in his fervor at these venues is to see a man who *was* soul music in the sixties, the clues to the DNA of that era endless and fascinating; and even a few minutes can teach one *something* about his art and his times.

•

THROUGH REDDING we can trace a lineage, a heritage, dating back to Jelly Roll Morton and Lead Belly. Drawing on the sound and fury of the early R&B-cum-rock-and-roll acts like Billy Ward and the Dominoes, the original Drifters, Little Richard, Chuck Berry, Etta James, and the first wave of doo-wop harmonizers, Redding had carefully crafted a sturdy, transformative, postmodern epoxy of the bombast of James Brown and Jackie Wilson, the heaving emotional R&B kick of Ike and Tina Turner, and the shale-smooth gospel pop-soul of Ray Charles and Sam Cooke. Even in pain, his songs are odes to the joy of full-on emotion, something lacking from the grooves of music since his death. For the 2003 *Soul Comes Home* DVD, recorded at the Celebration of Stax Records concert at Memphis's Orpheum Theater that year, Solomon Burke sang not any of his soul standards but rather "Try a Little Tenderness." Such deference is reserved only for a scant few.

But it sure wasn't as easy as Redding made it look. If "Dock of the Bay" came about as a reflection of his own growing visions of personal apocalypse and mortality, one can imagine that his fatalism wasn't limited to his own life. Within the cauldron of a decade gone to hell, he had no idea where the madness might end. As it happened, the song hit the market less than three years after the assassination of Malcolm X, three months before that of Martin Luther King Jr., five months before Robert Kennedy. Sadly, he had only a little while himself, and would find no real serenity. During his final months on Earth, he was back again in the mortal beehive, squabbling with industry canons over intra-industry pettiness, so much so that he intentionally spent more time with his protégé, Arthur Conley, a Stax reject, writing and producing a number 2 pop and soul hit for him, "Sweet Soul Music."

What's more, when he came in with "Dock of the Bay," no one at Stax/Volt, Atlantic, or even his own manager thought it up to snuff; they said—and Jerry Wexler was the most adamantly critical—that the vocal was lost, it was too stark, too subtly soulful, too quirky. Otis had to threaten to walk away from everyone involved if the song wasn't released as it was recorded. This demonstrated how innately soulless this ever-corrosive industry was, and still is, if even a man like Otis Redding could be asked to do the bidding of men who should have just let him do his thing and not get in his way. This was the way of the industry, yet in this case it seemed punitive to black men even like Redding who had earned their cachet but apparently not quite in America.

Not uncommon for black stars, he was far more cherished in England, where appreciation for black American musical idioms was a revelatory experience not clouded by guilt or denial. Not that Britain was free of racist contamination—it took until the mid-1960s proliferation of pirate radio ships to lift a longtime BBC ban on African-based rock music—but in a world where no one was conditioned to accept a plantation society and a century of de facto segregation, Redding, in the year he died, was voted the world's number one male vocalist in the *Melody Maker* Pop Poll, ahead of James Brown. Otis, who had no doubt about it himself, played it humble. Wilson Pickett, he said, should have won.[17]

•

THE REDDING story is one of great conquest and, sadly, a requiem, which can seem like a short story with endless significance. Not just was his life briefer than it needed to be, just five years of prime time, he was also a soul man unhappier than he had a right to be—his best album, the remarkable 1965 breakout *Otis Blue*, was well named. As far as he came, he lived with considerable unease about an industry that refused him full appreciation—and never awarded him a Grammy until he was in his grave. Out on the road, away from the Georgia clay that always brought him back down to earth, he was not the affable, big-hearted gentleman the PR material painted him to be. He was impulsive—once risking his career by shooting through a window and wounding a man in the leg, an incident that curiously went unreported—and had a decidedly broad view of marital fidelity. But even with the endless tap of his influence, he deserved better. In retrospect, if the loss of any one man mattered to the perpetuation of what Southern soul had become, it was Otis Redding.

Not by coincidence, his death left the entire idiom without a broad back to ride on. It was almost as if what had been built in a decade fell to the ground with that plane. The unlikely union between Memphis and Broadway, which had made for strange bedfellows but sweet soul music, was dashed within a year of Redding's demise when Atlantic sucker-punched Stax, breaking the partnership and looting it of its biggest resource, its precious song catalog.

With little sentimentality, soul re-created itself, its center of gravity shifted from the streets of Memphis to the history-rich studios of Philadelphia. Stax itself was raised from the dead, the horns and hooks of the '60s transformed into a politically acute and impolite conveyor of '70s funk and "badass" black stereotypes, its main man now "soul man" Isaac Hayes, its anthem his "Theme from *Shaft*," its Woodstock the 1972 Wattstax concert. Surely this rephasing, and re*phrasing*, of soul would have happened, regardless; that is the nature of musical evolution. But if Otis Redding could never have been a "badass" or sing of a black private dick who's a sex machine to all the chicks, neither would he likely have faded away quietly. He would no doubt have found a way to hold the pins of Southern soul to the sacred ground on which it was built. A likely scenario is that his own record company would have churned out crossover soul that itself would have evolved into a Ray Charles–style pop bent while still retaining the sweatier roots of soul. Still, at an eternal twenty-six, Redding survives in far more tangible ways than he ever could have imagined, as a fix for an American culture that has become diluted of soul in so many ways since his death. Redding in the end was bigger than the music he sang, because of how he sang and interpreted it during the most traumatic, metamorphic decade in history. And, given how little soul has survived him, Lord how we could use him now.

DREAMS TO REMEMBER

PROLOGUE

"It Was Music*"*

Wayne Jackson, a diminutive but spry and wiry seventy-two-year-old horn man with a perpetually young way about him, takes his strides with a typical cool. On this day he wears shades, a black lizard-banded Stetson and leather vest and jacket, a stylish yet functional way to deal with mid-January in Memphis. From under the hat flows a mane of long silver hair matching his neatly trimmed beard and mustache. His lizard-skin cowboy boots have just made tracks down McLemore Avenue, arguably the most famous byway in South Memphis, which happens to be in one of the town's worst neighborhoods, and was so even when Jackson spent most of his days there. His destination: 926 East McLemore—under a marquee that reads SOULSVILLE, USA, beneath a neon-lit, bright red STAX and fluorescent curlicues shaped like records stacked on top of one another like pancakes.

This of course was where American pop culture was transformed, where Otis Redding recorded all of his records. The theater and the sign are not original but a re-creation of the kingdom of soul that carried America through its most exhilarating and awful decade. Wayne Jackson was there from the very beginning, from the day a Memphis banker named Jim Stewart bought the abandoned Capitol Theater and made it the Stax Records office and studio. That was in 1961. And here it stood for nearly four decades before, in 1989, the Southside Church of God in Christ bought the once-again abandoned property from the Union Planters Bank and tore it down.

That desecration was supposed to be part of a neighborhood beautification project, but was in truth a mortal insult to the company and its black heritage. More insultingly, the project never developed and all that remained of Stax was a rubble-and-root-strewn lot, all the way until 2010. In that year, Bell helped arrange a revival whereupon a donor that the Stax publicists identify only as "an anonymous philanthropic Memphis businessman" donated $30 million to reanimate the famous face of the theater that, with Graceland, exists as the dual sine qua non of this most musically rooted of American cities.

And so Soulsville U.S.A. rose again, not as an active record company—it had lain dormant since 1981 as such, before its revival in 2004 mainly as a means to reissue repackaged product from the golden age—but as a sacred memory carved in brick and stone. Rebuilt from the ground up as a museum and gift shop, it faithfully restored every inch and detail as it was in the 1960s, including even the art deco exterior of the old Satellite record store next door. Because of the glittery lights that sparkle again here, it is as if the sun always shines on Stax, and, after the rebuilding of the landmark, the neighborhood finally began getting a facelift. While it has a long way to go, Stax plays a big part in the "new" Memphis, including the creation of the Stax Museum Academy, which funds stay-in-school programs. This is just one of many examples how Stax and Motown differ; those who built Stax still live in Memphis, while only trace matter of Motown is left in Detroit. And even the ghosts of Stax are undying.

The streets of the neighborhood around it—an area semi-officially known as Soulsville—are not the battlefields they were only a few years ago. The traffic to 926 East McLemore is also constant, with tours given almost around the clock, for many an introduction to this golden age of soul.

Wayne Jackson can talk all day about *that*. A native of Tennessee, he made his living in the sixties blowing hard into his trumpet as one of the founding members of the Memphis Horns, the trio of brass players who spun off from the Mar-Keys and backed up Redding and other great Stax/Volt singers on nearly every recording they made. This alliance was so organically perfect that, upon the 1987 release of the three-CD *Otis Redding Story* box set, the *New York Times'* Robert Palmer, reviewing it as the "pop album of the week," wrote, "[They] just may have been the greatest rock-and-roll band of all time."[1] The Horns were quite a sight, too, almost like a comedy act: Jackson a slight, white dynamo with beach-boy-golden hair and two black bookends, lanky Floyd Newman on alto sax and the muscular, round-faced Andrew Love on tenor sax. But their horns blew in perfect meter and tone with the voices they burnished. They did it for years at sixty-five dollars per three-song session. And they couldn't have cared less about what the going rate was. It was the cheapest investment Stewart made, getting in return what Wayne Jackson uses as his email handle: sweet medicine.

"We did it because we loved music, and loved the performers," Jackson says, as he walks through the front lobby of the museum toward the studio. "I can say I loved Otis Redding. I never met anyone like him, as real, as . . . good."[2]

Looking around the interior of the mock studio, which has some of the instruments, cables, and other detritus from the original studio realistically strewn about, one senses the ghost of Redding in the air. The chords of "Respect" or "Try a Little Tenderness" are somewhere within the walls, as if they held the same spot even after the originals were torn down and then found a place in the new ones. Jackson, who has in the intervening years after Stax's demise continued playing his magical trumpet for rock and roll acts as diverse as Elvis Presley, Rod Stewart, Billy Joel, Al Green, the Doobie Brothers, and Sting, can still get a bit dewy-eyed recalling the Stax sessions.

"I can see him now, running around the floor barking out what he wanted to the musicians," he says. "During the rehearsals he would grab this little old guitar he kept at Stax. It was tuned to 'open E,' which means you don't have to play chords, you just hold down the strings and all you had to do was move your finger up or down and you'd have a chord. He couldn't read music, but that's how he'd know where to go with a song. He'd run all over during the take, he was a live wire. We'd tell him, 'Take it easy, big boy, slow down.'

"But that's how we got to know how to play for him. He'd sing something then clap and point to us and say, 'Yo turn!' And we'd just play. Every one of those sessions were done live, on a four-track tape machine. No overdubs, no separate vocal tracks. It wasn't the way recording was supposed to be done, but it wasn't a product, it was . . . righteous. It was *music*."

The visitor with Jackson offers a thought. "People say about the great blues singers that they make you feel what they feel. When they hurt, you hurt. When they're joyful, you're joyful. I was a teenager when Otis Redding became hot, but I can remember feeling those things when I heard him."

"You know what, playing behind him, we could feel that, too, all the pain and the joy. He made us better musicians that way. We're only human. A guy starts singing like that and you know it's more than a song. It was like that with every one of 'em, but for Otis it was like the gospel, he was like a preacher. He was in the pulpit, the world was his congregation."

"He was the son of a preacher," the visitor needlessly reminds him.

"Right. And he took a lot from him. I met his father. He used to hang out at Otis's place, the Big O farm out in the country. Nice man. Strict man."

"I hear they had their ups and downs."

"I don't know. That's not my business. But that emotion had to come from somewhere. Otis was a very sensitive man. You could hear it in his songs. He had to have had moments when he hurt. We all do." Then, "He was just a real guy. When he was feelin' good, he'd show it. He'd get fried chicken down the block and flirt with the gals at the drive-in window. He'd love being Otis. That's what he was—Otis. You didn't need the last name. Of course, he wasn't always carefree. Some shit started happening around here, on the business side. There was a time when the Black Panthers started trying to muscle in on Stax. It got a little hairy. We had to make a stand, all of us, black and white. And then after Otis died, you could feel it dying around here."

He moves to the spot where in the great old studio Redding would pour soul into a microphone. "I loved the guy, we all did. He was never a jerk, arrogant. At least I never saw that. He just laid it all on the line, every song. He did that the first time I saw him, right here in this room." To Wayne Jackson on this day, one ghost of Soulsville was very much there.

•

NOT EVERYONE has been so eager to hang with the ghosts. Jim Stewart, for one, has rarely been to the place he used to own, and, in his eighties, has been for the most part unwilling to speak about his triumphs that became almost pyrrhic, and certainly tragic, when his own company's song catalog was ripped from his hands. And few of Stewart's surviving heaven-sent artists and studio musicians have even set foot in the place. The visitor, encountering Tim Sampson, the Stax publicist for two decades, wonders about one particular survivor, Carla Thomas, whose 1967 album with Redding, *King &*

Queen, gave Marvin Gaye and Tammi Terrell a run for their money on soul duets. Sampson, sitting in his office, doesn't bother to spoon any pablum. "Man, that is another *looooong* story." How so? "Carla does not have a phone, by choice. Well, she has many, but she has never activated one of them. She just shows up when and where she wants to. But don't hold your breath."[3]

And then there is Zelma Redding. Nearing seventy, she has chosen not to venture far from the Big O Ranch, the enormous three-hundred-acre estate her husband had built in the mid-sixties out in bucolic Round Oak, Georgia, marinating in much resentment from years of being either bypassed or, as she sees it, ripped off in literary or filmed accounts of her husband's life. Having battled with the skeletal remains of Stax Records in court over the years for control of any old masters left in the vaults, Zelma has excommunicated even Stax. "Zelma is a total recluse," Sampson says. "For years she was angry at Donn Pennebaker, who was more responsible than anybody for making Otis Redding a huge star. [Pennebaker's documentary of the Monterey Pop Festival was an epiphany of late-sixties pop culture.] Donn used that unforgettable footage of Otis at Monterey the way he did with Jimi Hendrix and Janis Joplin in later documentaries, and apparently Zelma had some sort of problem with it.

"Zelma wants to protect Otis's legacy. That's not a bad thing. And she has done many things in her life, for charities, the museum, a lot for Macon's business district. But the last few years, she's shut herself off."

Indeed, she has also refused to participate in most public tributes to him, mawkish as they can be, such as those on the anniversaries of his death, once explaining, "You don't celebrate people's death. That's so stupid."[4] Apparently, isolation is the price she has exacted for enduring a lifetime of either real or perceived slights and stories about Otis and other women that have made the rounds of the Internet and gossip rags. Says Sampson, laughing, "Loretta

Williams came here recently. She was a singer who was called Otis's protégée back in the day. He even wrote a couple of songs for her and recorded her on his own label. And she wrote one of those self-published books claiming that Otis was a thief, that he hit on her, that he was basically a bully, a bad guy. She was trying to get publicity and showed up for a Stax function like she was a VIP. After a while she said, 'Okay, I'm ready for the cameras.' It was like Gloria Swanson in *Sunset Boulevard*.

"How's that for irony?" Sampson muses. "Otis Redding was the most big-hearted, lovable guy in the music business, a guy who reeked of joy, a guy who was king, larger than life. And now his legacy is kept tightly under control and all around it is a kind of circus atmosphere with characters running around soiling his name. And I guess it's the price for being as oversized a figure as he was. You can't live in peace even when you're dead almost fifty years. That's the kind of thing that happens to men like Otis Redding. They're *too* big."

1

Son of a Preacher Man

Macon, Georgia would not seem to be much of a breeding ground for artistic eminence. Life doesn't rock and roll here as much as it simply unwinds in its own good time and speed. Stretching out fifty-six square miles, with a population of around ninety thousand, it squats approximately ninety miles southeast of Atlanta, roughly equidistant between the latter and the port city of Savannah in "the heart of Georgia," as the city brochures say. There really are two Macons, the rural-urban core downtown attached by a nexus of bridges—including the one on Fifth Street called the Otis Redding Bridge, which one can get to by taking the Otis Redding trolley down Cotton Avenue, past a building housing the Otis Redding Foundation. Beyond the Ocmulgee River, reaching to the north, can be seen the Old Red Hills of the Piedmont Plateau, while the washboard-flat, pine-treed forests proliferate to the east and south as far as the eye can see. Under those hills are copious deposits of kaolin, the clay-like mineral used in the manufacture of porcelain, cosmetics, toothpaste, paper, and Pepto-Bismol.

Caught between progress and tradition, with superhighways crisscrossing serene neighborhoods where clean white colonial homes rub up against drab brown housing projects and abandoned warehouses, Macon suggests at once the courtly, honeysuckle Old South and modern urban decay. The wonder is that a city of not particularly intellectual standing like Macon is home to two superb colleges, the Baptist-affiliated Mercer University and Wesleyan College, a Methodist women's school. Today, scattered towers of concrete and glass carve a nice, tightly bunched smoky skyline. For longtime Maconites, there is much to be proud of—nothing more so than the town's standing as perhaps the greatest incubator of American soul music there has ever been.

While Macon had bred an intriguing array of famous and semi-famous—including the stately actor Melvyn Douglas, racism-spouting Atlanta Braves relief pitcher John Rocker, and John Birch, the curious missionary whose name was subsumed after World War II by the extreme right-wing "society" that bears his name—all anyone need know about the city is that Little Richard and Otis Redding were raised and perfected their craft here, on the streets of downtown Macon, at the center of what the postcards once called "the prettiest and busiest city in Georgia." On the streets of the historic district, running along the wide expanse of College Street, there is still the pulse and a scent that sixty years ago drew Little Richard, James Brown, and Otis Redding into a grid of nightclubs within this corridor.

The music that made Macon a cultural cornerstone can be traced as far back as to when African-Americans began to settle here. Most of those were sharecroppers who came from the rural farmlands after years of breaking their backs for too little in return. Indeed, the plight of the sharecroppers was a regional disgrace that went too long unnoticed, another end-run around racial equality developed in the aftermath of Reconstruction. In theory, sharecropping seemed an ideal way to cut blacks in on the economic pie, by giving them a part of the same plantations that whipped their forebears into obedience. The old plantations were divvied up for freed slaves to be given "forty acres and a mule" and live and work for the same bosses, but at barely livable wages, and the crops owned by the bosses. With nowhere else to go, the freedmen, and their succeeding generations, were no more than virtual slaves.

•

ONE OF those Georgia sharecroppers was Otis Ray Redding Sr., a crisply articulate, proper, fanatically religious man. The grandson of a slave, he lived and worked on a 1,500-acre farm in Dawson, down in rural Terrell County, tilling peanuts, picking cotton, slopping hogs, whatever put some cash in his pocket. He also preached at the local Baptist church and, after marrying a sharecropper's daughter named Fannie, had four daughters of his own, Debra, Darlene, Christine, and Louise. Then they had their first son, Otis Ray Redding Jr., on September 9, 1941. He did not come out crying "fa-fa-fa-fa-fa" instead of "ma-ma-ma-ma-ma," but even in the crib there seemed something melodic about this baby's whining, though all it meant to Otis Sr. was another mouth he had to feed, and his pay at a farm owned by a man named Lang wouldn't cut it.

So shortly after the birth of their son, the Redding family followed the same path as thousands of black families just like them, moving to where there was a future. That usually meant the road to Atlanta. Years before, for example, another family man that made it out of Dawson, Ben Davis Sr., worked his way up to become editor of a black newspaper and a prominent Republican in Atlanta, something he would never have been able to accomplish in his hometown.[1]

Otis Redding Sr. set out for Atlanta, but, like many others in that caravan, he first found Macon to his liking and stopped right there. The Redding brood settled into a four-bedroom apartment in a newly erected public housing project in Tindall Heights on Plant Street just east of the Mercer University campus, a mile south of the same Gateway Park where Otis Redding can be found as a seven-foot bronze statue strumming a guitar not on the dock of a bay but on the bank of the Ocmulgee.

Just after the Reddings' move to Macon, Pearl Harbor was attacked and many of the men of the city enlisted, the blacks of course shunted into segregated units. While Otis Sr., deferred because he had a large family—another son, Luther Rodgers Redding, was born in 1943—he could nonetheless be proud that he served, as a janitor at Robbins Field, the Air Force installation south of Macon. To supplement his income, he also helped out on a farm just outside of town. Fannie also worked, as many black women did, as a maid, at the Woolworth's a few blocks from the apartment. War and work did not keep Otis Sr. from his higher calling. He became the deacon at Vineville Baptist Church, a mile to the north up Pio Nono Avenue.

The living was easier and the pay better in Macon. The complex sat on one of many of the Jefferson Hills overlooking the bustling highway now called Eisenhower Parkway and the flatlands to the east. The complex was a big step up. There were electric refrigerators, hot-water heaters, gas stoves, and, as the ads for apartments boasted, "a complete bathroom indoors."[2] There were, too, plenty of fresh air and the faint scent of pine when the wind was blowing right. All in all, residents had the feeling that they lived in luxury. But those clean walls were paper-thin and the units cheaply constructed. Soon Fannie Redding was stuffing rags into cracks in the walls to keep the cold out, and gangs were running around the streets making trouble.

Reflecting his parents' sensibilities, Otis Redding Jr. kept his distance from gang activity. Adhering to the deacon's stern requisites, he was a fixture in the church pews when Otis Sr. delivered his sermons and a very noticeable presence in the choir. Indeed, if not for his father's avocations and expectations, it is unlikely that Otis Redding Jr. ever would have found the magic elixir of singing. Not incidentally, it was the only real bond he had with the deacon, and thus was a solidifying force between them even as the son began to drift from the family. As such, despite the dissension between the two when Otis Sr. realized his boy was adopting the wrong kind of music, Otis Jr. would still deposit himself in church—that much he always believed he owed to the father whose love was unconditional, even if his words seemed to betray it. The trips they would take together, to the fishing hole, to hunt, to ride horses in the country, to the deacon's friends' homes, to other church socials where Otis Sr. would be invited to do some fire and brimstone, each was an occasion for father and son to learn about the other, for the son to obey and conform, if with the unspoken understanding that a clash was sure to arise soon enough.

The complicated dynamics between them were implicit, yet both maintained the ligature. Otis, for all the seductions of modern pop music, earnestly kept a flag raised for gospel and its tangible roots in the new music of the 1950s. Without actively seeking a music education, he was imbued with an ability to feel out music that he would sing, understand it, *feel* it. This was the essence of the blues, of evolving soul, and the debt he had to that enlightenment was directly traced to Otis Sr., a man who ironically couldn't sing a note but heard in his son's voice nothing less than the sound of the Lord. This continuing tuition stretched for over a decade as the boy grew into a man earlier than most of those his age would. He had the swagger and sensibility of an adult, maybe too much so for his own good, and certainly in the eyes of the deacon, who may have wished his son would have tarried just a little longer in adolescence, to be able to decipher good from bad.

There was, to be sure, a certain dichotomy to the Redding who careened from child to manchild under the watchful gaze of a father who never quite knew if his boy was a man or a boy on any given day. Sometimes, having the characteristics of both could serve the young man well. As he grew up, he could defend himself with his fists, though his game was to get along and he seemed to know the punks by name. His younger brother Luther, who called himself by his middle name, Rodgers, said Otis could charm a snake and that there was no one on the block who disliked him.

When the complex finally deteriorated into a tenement, Otis Sr., who had become a dad again with the birth of another daughter, Christine, began checking out the better neighborhoods where a black family could live. He found one several miles to the northeast that seemed an aerie, high on Sugar Hill in the Bellevue section near Azalea Park, on Pike Street. With only four homes to the block, a dead end street at one side, and a dirt road called Log Cabin Drive on the other, the complex sat across from miles of green glades and undeveloped valleys known as "the Bottom."

The deacon wanted this peaceful, if still segregated, habitat to be an idyll for his good Christian family and so they moved there in 1954, when Otis was fourteen. To his father's relief, Otis Jr. finally found something besides singing to occupy his time. Here were fishing holes and hiking trails. Just down Log Cabin Road was a white section, with stately colonial houses and an ice skating rink, the closest that most blacks in Macon could come to a transitional neighborhood one step away from integration. Otis and his new buddies, testing the limits, would cross over the boundary and go ice skating or get into football and baseball games with the white boys. Sometimes it got dicey for them; seeing them intermingling, rednecks in pickup trucks would roll in, the cue for Otis and his friends to have their feet start walkin', though when the trucks rolled out they'd go back again and resume the game.

If this all seemed like an innocuous game, the grave seriousness of those trucks was underlined when Otis and a friend named Benny Davis, whom he took to after learning that his brother Richard had played drums in Little Richard's band—a very impressive credit once Little Richard broke out big in the mid-1950s and owned Macon—were hiking through the Bottom and saw a noose dangling from a tree, a sight that gave him his first real understanding of what racism meant, and how perilous it was to be out alone, walking black.[3] That hanging tree would give him a cold chill from then on, a reminder of that thin line. Even as he achieved a level of adoration in his life, there seemed a haunted look deep in his eyes and a defensive skepticism about whether the races could truly mix.

As serene as life could be in Bellevue, it was a fleeting respite. The area also deteriorated into a colloquial "Hellview." The Reddings learned that the four-room cottage they had bought was built on the cheap and after a year required too much work and was too much of an expense to maintain. It also turned out to be a potential death trap. One day when the family was out, something caught on fire and the place burned to the ground. Fortunately the deacon had insurance and with the settlement money he bundled whatever was salvaged and hired movers again, determining that it was best to retrace his steps and head back for Tindall Heights. But then again, wherever they could have gone at that point would be a rough go. They were black and this was the Deep South. And if any reminder was needed, a short walk from the Heights to the closest avenue took you to signs that read: JEFF DAVIS STREET. That would be Jefferson Davis, president of the Confederate States of America.

•

THE BEST any black family could reasonably expect in Macon was an uneasy, tenuous peace. They lived with awareness that the KKK was growing strong in the town. Furthermore, Macon's racial history was mixed, at best. This could be seen in ambivalence to integration even by some of the city's most prominent African-American statesmen, most notably Harry McNeal Turner, who during the Civil War was the first black chaplain of the United States Colored

Troops, fighting his native region's Confederate soldiers. During Reconstruction, Turner, having settled in Macon, was elected to the Georgia state legislature and named the first Southern bishop of the American Methodist Church. Yet, outraged by the rise of Jim Crow, Turner, who preached that God was black, became an advocate of the Back to Africa movement, and remained so until his death in 1925. The law, he once remarked, "has made the ballot of the black man a parody, his citizenship a nullity and his freedom a burlesque."[4] Turner also was appointed by President Ulysses S. Grant as the first black postmaster, his domain being Macon, and it was in the post offices of Georgia where some early signs of racial comity arose, with many white postal officials resisting demands from their towns to fire their black clerks—sometimes appealing to their congressmen and senator.[5]

As in most cities under the yoke of Jim Crow, blacks in Macon had their own neighborhoods—Pleasant Hill, Unionville, Fort Hill, Tybee, Bellevue—and were expected to stay in them, at great risk otherwise, including the real chance of being lynched. Tindall Heights was another safe harbor, not that Otis Redding Jr. would accept being chained to it. Still, until the mid-1960s, when he was well into his twenties, he never saw a day in Macon when segregation wasn't common law, a sticking point that was addressed by Martin Luther King Jr. when he gave a speech at the Steward Chapel African Methodist Episcopal Church on Forsyth Street in 1957.[6] At Redding's early shows at the clubs, blacks were herded into separate lines and tables inside; later, *whites* would be prohibited from entering some of these juke joints, per the "separate but equal" doctrine.

The proverbial stains of Jim Crow—the colored drinking fountain and bathrooms, and lunch counters barred to Negroes—were inured into quotidian life. High society dances at the Armory Ballroom were off limits. Terminal Station had a colored waiting room. A Confederate monument stands beside the county courthouse. Even so, Macon congealed into something like a model of incipient post–Jim Crow urbanism without demonstrations or marches. For example, the town's newspaper, the Macon *Telegraph*, was overseen by some remarkably brave and progressive editors. What's more, there were two black-owned papers, the *Voice* and the *World*, where black readers could go for reinforcement. There was also a steady growth in NAACP membership. Macon's colleges had opened their doors to African-Americans a century before those in Alabama and Mississippi were ordered to do so by the attorney general of the United States.

Not that the cleft between black and white didn't exist, and adamantly, nor, as Otis could attest with a shiver, the hanging tree unseen. But as one scholar has put it, racial relations in Macon were something like an "unutterable separation."[7] For the times, it was progress enough. And today, the mixed racial flavor of Macon is such that Little Richard Penniman Boulevard runs right into an intersection with Jeff Davis Street, and Martin Luther King Jr. Boulevard runs parallel to it. The man for whom the former was named, who washed dishes at the Greyhound bus depot in Macon before hitting it big, always had a riposte for racists who heckled him during concerts in the 1950s, saying that when he heard the common heckle of "Go back to Africa where you came from," he would reply, "Africa? Who told you I was from Africa? I'm from Macon, Georgia. I am a peach."[8]

●

MUSIC WAS a crucial component in the art of simple survival and simple ambition. In days before rock and roll, or a civil rights movement to speak of, nothing perhaps save the Bible could soothe and promote optimism in the face of pain like the salve of rhythm and blues. Not that everyone was so quick to make that concession. For Otis Redding Sr., however, the Bible had no alternatives. While many other hardworking black laborers waited for Friday night to head to the black and tan speakeasies in downtown Macon to drink in some jazz and blues along with Scotch and gin, Redding's father actually called it the devil's music—and there were few exceptions, even Lena Horne singing "Stormy Weather" crossed over into an evil place.

For the stern, proper deacon, acceptable music was played on the church organ and an occasional piano recital. Indeed, reversing the normal pattern, the father was introduced by the son to the blues that had been born on plantations like those he had tilled in Dawson. Otis Jr. spent almost all his allowance and money from odd jobs on blues and R&B records. As a result, when Otis Sr. walked past his boy's bedroom, he heard the emotive sounds of the earliest lineup of the Drifters, stamped by the honey-glazed voice of Clyde McPhatter, spilling off Otis Jr.'s secondhand phonograph. That would be cause for another lecture about the devil and his ways. To get his ten-year-old boy's mind off singing, the deacon would haul him and his younger brother to the farm, where the boys would ride around on horses and breathe in clean country air.

But the old man never went as far as to forbid such music in his home. He was not a martinet of a father, allowing his children some slack to find their own way, hopefully to God. It was also a matter of pride to him that his namesake son had singing talent, which came in handy at the church on Sunday mornings when Otis Jr., as young as three, was draped in robes wailing gospel songs as Otis Sr. played the pipe organ. The deacon didn't have any problem boasting about his boy's voice. Indeed, when an eight-year-old Otis had to have his tonsils out, he fretted. "I remember him saying, 'Will I be able to sing again?'" his brother Rodgers recalled. "And my father said, 'Sure. Probably you'll be able to sing better.'" Indeed, not long after the surgery, his brother said, "He started getting into piano and trying to write." That was, he added, "around the eighth grade."[9]

The deacon and his wife, who were friends with seemingly everyone in the congregation and neighborhood, had a crucial, if passive, effect. The couple often went to sedate parties. During these functions, which normally took place in their neighbors' homes, Otis Sr. played the piano himself, though he played safely anodyne music. He would occasionally take his boy with him, hoping to show him what sort of songs he should be singing. What he didn't realize was how much any given song could teach a kid whose antennae could find the beat to any tune.

"We used to go out to a place called Sawyer's Lake," Otis once recalled. "There was a calypso song out then called 'Run Joe.' My mother and daddy used to play that for me all the time. I just dug the groove."[10]

When young Otis sang for the parishioners, adding a bit of that good old gospel emotion for effect, the deacon sat beaming, quietly tapping a foot to the beat. He could be proud, for sure, that even as a teen, his son was not only handsome and tall, but always mannerly and solicitous, keeping a tenacious sense of family as the fulcrum of his life. That and singing, which Otis began doing outside of church, at talent shows he often won at the segregated Ballard-Hudson High School—the only high school for black children in Macon. He sometimes played drums to keep occupied between his songs, and in time he had stepped up from school talent shows to actual nightclubs with the devil's brew and real blues singers, joints where laws against children being allowed onto the premises were almost never enforced.

One such club was owned by a guy from the neighborhood, Claude Sims, whose son Earl called himself "Speedo," after the 1955 doowop song of the same name by the Cadillacs. Speedo knew more than a teenager should have about the nightclub lifestyle and had his own group, the Peppermint Twisters. After Otis began singing at the club, Speedo was leading him on tours of other clubs, introducing him to owners and much older, wicked women who passed their time away on bar stools. The changing times and the atmosphere of Macon were Otis Jr.'s biggest lures, and Otis Sr.'s biggest enemies. There was something enticing about singing in Macon, especially in the early 1950s. Like most Deep South cities, it had a music tradition dating back to men in varying degrees like Reverend Pearly Brown, known to some as "the last great street singer." Born blind in 1915, Pearly Brown would tread downtown Macon, a cup attached to his guitar, a sign around his neck reading I AM A BLIND PREACHER. PLEASE HELP ME. Brown sang what he called "slave songs" with a bottleneck-style slide guitar that would be a staple of country and country rock by the time he was finally heard on records in the early 1960s.

It is said that several generations of Macon-bred musicians and singers were given an education by Pearly Brown, and that included Otis Redding. But one need not have been African-American to drink that elixir. Also born here was Emmitt Miller, a white man who ingested the same blues sources but skewed them to the nascent genre of country music—no stretch given that Pearly Brown was also the first black performer to play the Grand Ole Opry theater in Nashville. Miller, a minstrel act early in his career, in mandatory blackface, fronted a group called the Georgia Crackers, and their jazzy, western-swing records on the Okeh label had an immediate impact on rising big band acts such as Tommy and Jimmy Dorsey, Texas swing leader Bob Wills, and yodeling cowboy troubadours like Hank Williams and Jimmie Rodgers.

Like New Yorkers and their bagels, they like to say in Macon that its rich musical history is explained by there being something in the water. But it's more like something in the blood. Once it got into Otis Redding's blood, it would never seep out.

2

Heebie Jeebies

The conditions that finally set the stage for Otis Redding had been brewing since the Eisenhower years. Conventionalism, like that practiced by Reverend Redding, was fighting a losing battle with new norms fueled by angst and alienation, much of it unfocused but seemingly made clearer by both the rebellious young faces on movie screens and voices on vinyl records. Using Marlon Brando, James Dean, Elvis Presley, motorcycle gangs, long sideburns, short shorts, beehive hairdos, jeans, leather, and sex, lots of rarely seen but heavily panting thoughts of sex bouncing around the culture, the American entertainment industry captured its target demographic, teenagers born just before or during the war. And among this gallery was a black face or two, the most recognizable being another Macon native who by now had found fame for himself, while rewriting the playbook of pop music.

This was the inimitable and madly inscrutable Richard Penniman. Born in 1932, Penniman grew up in the Pleasant Hill section wailing gospel in church, his ambition as raw as his nerve. His singing became a means of escape from his father Charles "Bud" Penniman, who walked the line between being a moonshiner, a Pentecostal minister, and a nightclub owner, all the influences of which were invested in his son, who was never quite, well, normal. Richard once said his father "put me out of the house. He said he wanted seven boys, and that I had spoiled it, because I was gay." When Richard was nineteen, Bud Penniman was shot to death outside a Macon bar by one of his son's friends, although the circumstances remain a mystery.[1]

By then Richard was professionally and otherwise "Little Richard," a larger-than-life pastiche full of sexual confusion and gender-bending manifestations, with a touch of Bible-thumping thrown in. Having cut his teeth in the downtown clubs like the Tick Tock, teaching himself how to play boogie-woogie piano, he put together his own bands, had several record deals, and by 1955 was signed up with Specialty Records, working with a big-time producer, Bumps Blackwell. Little Richard, of course, had an enormous impact on an entire generation being shaped by his music. As a performer he was over the top, bounding around, mounting his piano, lifting his leg onto the keyboard while he played. He even had a light show, with neon bulbs flickering on and off. It was all about showmanship now; you couldn't just stand there with a microphone.

Otis Redding would always pay homage to the man, especially during times when Richard was struggling. Typical was a 1966 encomium that "if it hadn't been for Little Richard, I would not be here . . . Richard has soul, too. My present music has a lot of him in it. . . . Yes sir, Little Richard has done a lot for me and my soul brothers in the music business."[2]

No doubt, Richard Penniman was the ideal avatar of a musical idiom bold and daring yet conventionally spiritual enough to wear the label derived from a centuries-old religious conceptualization of the immortal essence of the human spirit and its undying connection to a higher power. That was the connector that permitted an entire race to survive bondage, and songs derived from Negro spirituals and church hymns surely had dibs on the term "soul music," which was not yet common in the 1950s but clearly on the way considering that "soul brother" and "soul food" entered the American vernacular in 1957.[3] Other performers had plumbed the sexual nature of the more widely used "race music," but no one did it as strenuously, or with the androgyny of Richard, who slathered on mascara and makeup and dressed in glittery zoot suits and dangling watch fobs, hair piled high in a pomade-slicked pompadour. To boot, his lyrics were brazenly raunchy—one of the first songs he wrote, "Tutti Frutti," included leering references to "good booty." And, in what would be a rock tradition, the scatted verbalization of a musical instrument, in this case a drum line that went "a-whomp-bomp-a-loom-a-mop-a-lomp-bam-boom" (which in today's translation is "boinka-doink-a-doink"), became something like a new generation's mating cry.

That path had been cleared by some early R&B/rock and roll acts, most notably on the L.A.-based Federal Records, the only label that would have dared release the Dominoes' "Sixty Minute Man"—which told of "fifteen minutes of kissin'" leading to "fifteen minutes of blowin' my top"—in 1951 and Hank Ballard and the Midnighters' openly suggestive "Work With Me, Annie" three years later. The latter, one of the first records to use an electric bass, which, along with the electric guitar line, formed the essential recipe for all rock and roll to come, sold one million copies, even though it was banned by the FCC as too dirty for radio play.

Little Richard, however, took the suggestion of perversity seriously, even deliriously. In his personal life, he went from bed to bed, with women or men, with mounting angst about how to fit his lifestyle in with his religious fundamentalism. But he had the gift of timing, too. Seeing him, it was evident why parents worried so much about rock and roll—which of course only made their kids want to embrace it even more. This was music of their own, not handed down from their parents' old collection of 78-rpm records. That yearning, to find a collective identity all their own, did more than anything else to propel rock and Little Richard to the top of the charts. Such was evident when, after "Tutti Frutti" went to number 2 on the R&B chart and top 20 pop, Little Richard pumped out a string of others in the same throbbing vein, including "Long Tall Sally," "Good Golly Miss Molly," "Ready Teddy," and "Rip It Up." Two went to number 1 R&B and "Sally" top 10 pop.

Soul music had arrived.

•

JAMES BROWN was the first to prosper in Richard's image. Of African, Chinese, and Native American ancestry, Brown was born in South Carolina, living at one point in his aunt's brothel, but after his family moved to Augusta, Georgia, when he was young, he began singing gospel music. After a three-year stretch in juvenile detention for armed robbery at age sixteen, he formed his own group, the Famous Flames, playing frequently in Macon and living with his band in a flat above the Two Spot nightclub. Brown's bombastic gospel version of Little Richard gained the group the services of Richard's manager, Clint Brantley, who once recalled how "four or five little niggers walked through the door" of his office. "I had some little niggers out of Jacksonville, the Speeds. They'd come to Macon and I'd recorded them and then I never did hear no more from them. So I didn't want to be bothered."[4]

In its time frame, such a vernacular of nonchalant racism was taken as an innocuous side effect of growing up a Southern white man. In fact, Brantley was well respected as a guy who could make things happen, and powerful enough to terminate his business relationship with Little Richard and sic lawyers on him to get back money he'd advanced Richard. Brantley was able to book acts and make record deals, as he did for Brown and the Flames with Federal

Records' boss Syd Nathan. In 1956, Brown's first single, the emotively yearning "Please Please Please," sold a million copies, and he followed Little Richard out onto the inner-city chitlin' circuit—which contrary to the phrase, put acts like Brown, Ray Charles, Etta James, John Lee Hooker, and Ike and Tina Turner on some major stages, such as Harlem's Apollo Theater, the Howard Theater in D.C., the Regal in Chicago, the Uptown in Philadelphia, the Fox in Detroit, and the Royal Peacock in Atlanta.

At the age of fourteen, Redding heard the same calling, but the difference was that the traditionalism of the deacon would keep him from maturing as a singer using anything but his voice. He never would present himself in a way that would make Otis Sr. wince; he would not for a minute don zoot suits and baggy seersucker pants with white buck loafers. Makeup? Mascara? He would sooner have worked in the rock quarry. Ironically, this conventionalism better prepared him for the kind of soul that would be right for the 1960s, when black entertainers saw less need to act out and tone up, no more playing up their blackness but playing it *down*, prideful, dignified, not standing out but among the crowd. He would wear his natty but fashionable suits and ties, keep his hair short and free of pomade and a pompadour, and sing the songs that grabbed him by the gut, that he could *feel* claiming his soul and anatomy.

Hanging trees aside, the pain and agony of life as a black man in the Deep South was something he could only imagine, and he had no conception that anything he sang was any sort of social commentary, though that kind of music could not help but educate by default. The small-town comfort and familiarity of Jim Crow Macon was a cocoon, insulating him from the terrible evils in the outside world. Following in the trail carved out for him, Otis Redding's teenage life was now hurrying down streets like the one later renamed Richard Penniman Boulevard, dodging trolley cars under skies clouded by belching smokestacks. His destination was the thicket of "black and tan" blues and jazz clubs.

•

DOORS WERE certainly opening. In 1956, still just fifteen, Otis Jr. found his way to a dive bar in the Bellevue section, on a dirt road at the edge of one of those woods he used to traipse around in. It was called the Hillview Springs Social Club. Otis went there mainly to see a rarity in the clubs, a band led by a woman. Her name was Gladys Williams and she was something of a cult performer around black Macon, a Big Mama Thornton–type blues shouter with a loud, brassy countenance, and in her mid-thirties still attractive in a floozy, boozy way. Gladys's band, booked by Clint Brantley, played all around the state but hit the floor at the Hillview on Sunday nights, drawing full houses.

She had earned a cachet in Macon, able to use leverage with local radio deejays and promoters to further the careers of those she made her protégés—which probably not coincidentally were usually handsome young singers eagerly solicitous of her. Stories were told of Miss Gladys collecting such hunks as trophies and doing more with them than just listening to them sing. Otis was no doubt aware of all that, and was undaunted. He didn't mind doing what it took to move up, and hooking up with older women was a regular exercise. He also had no compunction walking right up to Gladys and asking to be allowed to sing with her band and she, undaunted by his tender age, let him do it. He sang Little Richard's "Long Tall Sally," with its bawdy lyrics of a woman "built sweet" and having "everything that Uncle John needs." He delivered it in his gruffly mellow style and she was tantalized, though aghast at how little the teenager knew about the mechanics of singing. The first thing she told him was, "You ain't got no time!," meaning that his pacing was like a runaway train, not guided by the tempo of the band and with no connection to the audience. In other words, it was all about him.

Yet neither did she have any intention of letting this young singer get away. She had her band tutor him, sat him down front to hear her and other experienced acts. A few weeks later, after spending some private and personal time with him, she put him up on the stage again, much to her satisfaction when the sounds of chatter and tinkering glasses quieted and he seemed to grab hold of the audience. Thereafter, he seemed to be her favorite pupil, and in the dim light and smoky atmosphere of the club the wizened woman and the lean, handsome young man could be seen sharing laughter and some very snug nooks, both with glasses of booze in their hands.

Soon, too, with Gladys pulling the strings, he was entered in the weekly talent show hosted by Hamp "King Bee" Swain, a black disc jockey on WIBB, an early "race music"–oriented radio station which today, on the FM dial, bills itself "#1 for Hip Hop and R&B." At the time, WIBB had only featured this talent-show format for a year or so, after its owner, a visionary man named Tom Maxwell, hired three black DJs—Swain, Charles "Big Saul" Greene, and Ray "Satellite Papa" Brown—and they were important figures in establishing soul music. It was in the WIBB studio, in fact, where James Brown, financed by Greene, cut a demo of "Try Me," his first recording.[5] Swain, a Macon native, had incidentally once blown trumpet in Gladys Williams's band, and owed her a chit or two. His talent show, "The Teenage Party," was held at the Douglass Theatre, built by Charles Douglass, another of Macon's distinguished African-American historic figures, in 1912. With its wide marquee rising over High Street—now Martin Luther King Jr. Boulevard— its boards were tread by everyone from Duke Ellington and Bessie Smith to James Brown, Ma Rainey, and Little Richard.

First prize for winning the Swain show was fifteen dollars, a very nice bit of change for a low-level performer. To prepare, Gladys worked heavily with Otis on James Brown's "Heebie Jeebies," the lyrics of which deflected blame for a bum relationship to "My Bad Luck Baby," a common macho dodge. The preparation not only helped him win in his first try, but also for the following fifteen weeks. As a result Swain's talent show had a lot to do with Redding's first real buzz, something he delighted in recalling. As Otis told it, "I won fifteen Sunday nights straight in a series of talent shows in Macon. I showed up the sixteenth night and they wouldn't let me go on anymore. They wouldn't let me sing no more, wouldn't let me win that fifteen dollars no more."[6]

Not that Swain needed to rig the verdicts. In fact, contrary to the audiences' reaction, he was not as big a believer in Otis as Gladys was. He was more taken with Oscar Mack, another Little Richard acolyte. As for Otis, he had reason to believe that his winning streak would earn some props from the deacon. He was wrong, and one night, after Otis stumbled in far later than he had been instructed to when he went out to sing, the old man was not in a conciliatory mood. Coming to the door of his son's room, standing rigidly in his bathrobe, he heard him excitedly go on about this song or that big shot he met. And when he referred to what he was doing as his "career," the deacon stiffened and hushed him.

"Career?!" he said mockingly, calling it "screamin'" and "teenage foolishness." After they went at it a while longer, the old man ended the argument, telling his son he "wouldn't amount to anything with this singing, this hanging out in nightclubs." His final word was meant to sting the most. "And I'm going to tell you something else," he said. "I'm never going to go and see you in one of those places."[7] It was an exchange Otis liked telling of, not to belittle his father for having such unfortunate judgment, but to indicate the uphill climb he faced and the wonder of it all that he made that climb without support from his father. Still, he no doubt had a little rush in his veins when he recalled those words by Otis Redding Sr., because they echoed inside his head for years to come as he made his way upward.

●

CLEARLY, THE senior and junior Otis Redding had an ambivalent, complicated relationship. Those who remember him tell of the deacon as a tough but fair man, completely dedicated to his family. That was why he was so concerned when Otis got serious about singing. It meant his son would be exposed to a world that Otis Sr. couldn't control and knew very little about. Indeed, given his life as a man of the cloth, it wasn't just a bad career decision, but a direct insult to him. The vow not to go see his son in a nightclub was an easy one to make, since he had never been in one in his whole life. But the deacon didn't turn his back on his son; that he could never have done. All he could do was try to prepare him for the big, bad world and pray that his lessons sunk in. The deacon certainly offered a link between the Good Book and the songbook. And in most every facet of life, Otis the second always channeled Otis the first; the lessons the deacon taught about probity, morality, doing the right thing, living a simple, Godly life, loyalty to family and friends . . . all these were much more than pulpit bromides for him. Otis Jr. intended to live by all the rules in the deacon's book, and to feel deep in his soul every word he sang. He owed the old man at least that much.

Otis Sr., for his part, kept hoping the boy would find the straight and narrow, go to college, and become the first Redding man to earn a degree—the girls, in keeping with the Southern male ethos, one that united blacks and whites, would have no reason to follow such a path, their role being to serve their future husbands as wives and baby-makers. The deacon's younger boy, Rodgers, presented no deviations from the norm, and served as a kind of blessed contrast when Otis Sr. often complained to his friends about his older son's preoccupation. But as adamant as he was, he knew he could never wash the blues out of his namesake's mouth nor the influence of the Delta bluesmen out of his blood. Not by himself. The boy would have to wash it all out alone. At the same time, the deacon had to prepare for the realization that such a thing might never happen; and that if his boy was going to sing for his supper, the Lord would want him to give it all he had, to ride the dream, hard, all the way.

That was the loophole Otis Ray Redding Jr. needed to ease the guilt about crossing the deacon, and how to appease him. He would work. And then work harder.

3

Rockin' Redding

With providential timing, Otis Redding matured into a viable act just as the transition of soul music from pure rhythm and blues to mainstream pop music was taking hold, not with entirely positive consequences for African-Americans. If the rise of Little Richard seemed to portend a grand awakening of "race music" for teenagers, white record industry power brokers, seeing its raw power, quickly moved in. The first time it happened was when the Ivy League–looking Crew-Cuts covered a song from the soul group the Chords, taking the minor top 10 1954 hit "Sh-Boom," and turning it into a number 1 for nine weeks and singing it on *The Ed Sullivan Show*. More egregious was a clueless, squeaky clean 1956 cover of "Tutti Frutti" by the vanilla crooner Pat Boone, which went to number 12, five notches higher than Richard's, who had a theory why. "They didn't want me to be in the white guys' way . . . They needed a rock star to block me out of white homes because I was a hero to white kids," he once said. "The white kids would have

Pat Boone up on the dresser and me in the drawer 'cause they liked my version better, but the families didn't want me because of the image that I was projecting."[1]

By the mid-1950s the white co-option of the form was near total when Elvis Presley broke big. He was another son of the Deep South lower class, his way up charted by a guitar and the blues. He began his career as a novice picker and warbler in Sam Phillips's Sun Studio in Memphis in 1954. But Presley's abiding respect for country's blues roots led him to pivot from rockabilly to smooth, superbly crafted rhythm and blues–style rock and roll that even began easing parents' early vapors about his elastic-legged pelvic swiveling.

Still, the original blues rockers cut deeply into the culture. Little Richard appeared in movies, just like Elvis Presley, alongside hot rock and roll acts like Bill Haley and His Comets—who when they were chosen to sing "Rock Around the Clock" for the opening credits of *The Blackboard Jungle* in 1955, were believed by many to be black. Little Richard was followed onto the silver screen in rock and roll movies by acts such as the Platters, Chuck Berry, the Cadillacs, the Flamingos, and Frankie Lymon, with much credit for this going to the New York DJ Alan Freed, unarguably the biggest and most sincere champion of black music among the white establishment, even if payola was part of the equation. His role was subsequently taken by the slicker and more superficial Dick Clark, who did not shy from presenting black rock and rollers on *American Bandstand*, especially acts he profited from as a partner in the Philadelphia record company Cameo Parkway. The lessons were becoming clear: White brokers could be allies of black rock and roll, as long as they were the ones making the biggest profits. That was the price of civil rights in the vinyl world, and it was worth it if black performers could actually perform as black performers.

•

THAT OTIS Redding had to sing, not by choice but necessity, became a fact in 1958 when the deacon contracted tuberculosis and was confined to a hospital in Rome, Georgia. Because Fannie's income from her work as a domestic wasn't nearly enough to keep food on the table and make the fifty-dollar mortgage payment, Otis had to be the breadwinner. He dropped out of high school—where his presence had become sporadic to nonexistent after late nights at the clubs. While he was able to find a little work on an oil rig out in the flatlands, some roofing and construction work, as well as some hours as a delivery boy for a market, the irony was that the family was eating mainly because he was doing what Otis Sr. despised, under spotlights on a stage in smoky dens of the devil. A few times the deacon, believing his end was near, sent farewell letters to friends. Almost always, he would make a request to help Fannie with his oldest son. "Keep him out of those nightclubs," he wrote.[2]

That wouldn't happen. Indeed, by the age of seventeen, Otis Jr. not only practically lived at the clubs but was already something of a bad influence on others. Because he didn't have a car, he befriended a neighborhood guy, Bubba Sailor, who did. Otis, who now hated going back to his room and the deacon's glare, would talk Bubba out of going to see his girlfriend and instead go hunting greater prizes. "All this pussy out here?" he would tell him. "Come get me. Me and you goin' out." Said Sailor, "It was like Little Richard sang, you don't get no pussy unless you had a car. So we had a combination. I had the car and Otis could sing. So we rolled around pretty good, you know what I'm saying?"[3]

Otis, his reputation preceding him, seemed to have gained immunity from the normal protocols of keeping to your own 'hood. If he wandered across the borderline, the gangs cut him a pass, both because they knew him by name and because he could take care of himself, having proven it with his fists—though he would sooner rely on his charm and coolness, or to comply with a directive from some hood to sing a few bars right there on the corner. He always had a cool about him. Recalling the Rolling Stones' line about not being a man without smoking the right cigarette, his friend Sailor said, "I smoked Kents and he got me smoking Salems."

"Kents?" Otis would say, dripping cool. "That's your momma's cigarette."

He even had his own retinue of sorts, a revolving cast of teen-age singers, some of them neighborhood guys, old schoolmates and co-workers, among them Sailor, Eddie Ross, and Benny Davis. They were a rather ragged clique, none able to afford snazzy suits of the kind the Fabulous Flames wore. But one listen and you'd know who was the leader of the band. At one of his last gigs at the Douglass, in 1958, Otis was so compelling that the leader of another, much bigger R&B band was willing to make room for him knowing that would shift the attention onto the new kid.

Johnny Jenkins, a hunky, loose-limbed, light-skinned, left-handed guitar player, who had a striking resemblance in looks and style to Little Richard, was two years older than Otis and had worked at least as hard building a buzz around the clubs. His band, Pat T. Cake and the Mighty Panthers, formed by drummer Charles Abrams, who was known as "Cake," included Sonny "Hip" Goss, who'd played sax in Little Richard's road band the Upsetters, and lead singer Bill Jones, who called himself Little Willie Jones, after Little Willie John, the teenage R&B singer who was the first to record "Fever." But Jenkins was the clear star, as his eye-catching antics onstage, such as full splits, Chuck Berry–style duck-strutting across the stage, and playing on his knees, gained the group a following.

In other words, Jenkins was the coolest guy in Macon. He spoke in rhyme, never looked scruffy, and had star appeal. He was also nicer to other talent than he should have been—including one singer he helped make better. Jenkins had first seen Otis Redding performing at the Hemp Swain shows and asked if he wanted Pat T. Cake to back him up on his last few appearances. When that gig ended, Jenkins, seeing the visceral reaction to Redding when he sang, made him an offer to join the band, for twenty-five cents a show. It was a pittance, but Pat T. Cake played a wide range of clubs, with a steady gig at Club 15, a popular music and dance club in Macon.

As it happened, Otis was tight with Little Willie Jones, too; in a music community remarkably free of jealousy and cutthroat instincts, Otis seemed to ingratiate himself to everybody. Incredibly, Willie didn't begrudge him when Jenkins brought him in, knowing that the kid had the kind of voice any band would be thrilled to have. And so Willie moved on, remaining friends with the man who replaced him as they both traversed the circuit. Jenkins was electrified with his new find—in his opinion, one expressed frequently through the coming years, he had "discovered" Otis Redding, a claim also made by many others—but impressed on him the necessity to bring more to the table than a voice. Jenkins, a ball of fire onstage, saw Redding as stiff and even a little withdrawn and worked with him on some basic hip-swaying moves and facial expressions. The real difference however was that Jenkins's guitar licks gave Otis's singing a broader emotional pull and context, the right sonic synergy. As Jenkins was always eager to note, "He sounded *great* with me playing behind him."[4]

Otis couldn't disagree. It was the first time he realized the importance of the right accompaniment, though it took some time for him to get used to singing with a showy guitar player. Not stepping on Johnny's toes, all he could do was stand awkwardly clutching a microphone, to the rear next to Pat T. Cake, respectfully out of Jenkins's way at the front of the stage. A publicity still of the group is indeed an awkward sight. While Jenkins, with his pencil mustache and slicked pompadour, does a semi-split, and his bass and sax men play on bended knee, Otis is partially obscured by Jenkins, left hand holding the microphone over much of his face, all but unidentifiable.

Nevertheless, Redding was increasingly the one the audiences came to hear. He got better still at Club 15, where Pat T. Cake's regular Sunday night slot began at 12:01 A.M., when the Sunday blue law prohibiting the sale of booze expired. As his profile grew, he couldn't abide any lulls in performing, and sometimes on his band's off nights he moonlighted with other acts, including one from Memphis called Jazzbo Brown and the House Rockers—yet another case of a soul singer borrowing the name of a more famous singer, in this case Jazbo Brown, the turn of the century Delta blues musician who appeared in *Porgy and Bess* on Broadway. It was also one of numerous bands that affixed the phrase "house rockers" to their name.

Even though Jenkins was the main man of Pat T. Cake, it eventually got to a point where club promoters would run ads for upcoming shows in the *Telegraph* touting not Johnny or the band but "'Rockin' Otis Redding" or "Otis 'Rocking Robin' Redding."

•

TO A mega-star like Little Richard, young climbers such as Otis Redding and Johnny Jenkins were merely two in a long line of imitators. As is always the case in music, Richard himself was derivative of precedents such as Jackie Brenston, the Drifters, and Hank Ballard. Richard generally was cold and distant to other performers whether in his mold or not, and the young Redding was barely on his screen. But Redding picked up something more from Richard than the screechy aspects of R&B. He also learned that the normal rules of God that the deacon always taught him simply did not apply to a man who reached a certain stratum of fame. Little Richard's sexual conquests and appetites were the stuff of legend, not least of all because Richard would brag about them: "What kind of sexual am I?" he once asked. "I am omnisexual! Sex to me is like a smorgasbord. Whatever I feel like, I go for."[5]

If there were any conflicts with God's biblical teachings, Richard had the answer. "When I had all these orgies going on, I would get up and go and pick up my Bible. Sometimes I had my Bible right by me." Despite the pitfalls of living a life of sin and the devil's music—which was particularly parlous to black men on the road, as Chuck Berry found out in 1962 when he was sent to prison for a year and a half on a dubious charge of violating the Mann Act, for taking an underage girl across state lines[6]—Otis had caught the bug. He had begun to enjoy a "smorgasbord" of his own, filling his plate with a variety of women, both teenaged and some many years older, who would wait for him backstage after his shows.

He had also filled out into, a big, chiseled man by 1959. While he essentially was a Little Richard clone, he performed from the opposite angle, as a man's man with a range of emotions, from brash and brusque to vulnerable and hurting. In this way he was less Little Richard than James Brown, who a decade later would put into words and music the ethos that defined both himself and Otis Redding—"It's a Man's Man's Man's World," a song called "biblically chauvinistic" in the irony of its underlying truth that all the material possessions in the world "mean nothing without a woman or a girl." Of the Macon triumvirate, Redding would be the least overt at primping and leering and spouting outright sexual jargon; no references to intercourse, no self-serving ego games, and Lord knows, no gender-bending. While Richard would tell the world how "pretty" he was—a shtick soon to be used by a budding boxer from Louisville named Cassius Clay—Otis was a different kind of cat. He had an aversion to bragging on himself or performing any gimmicks. This of course set him apart from Brown, whose trademark was actually one stolen from his forerunner, who had been brought onstage with the intro "Ladies and gentlemen, the hardest working man in show business today, Little Richard!"

Brown surely earned the honor to call himself that, by working himself to exhaustion, the act peaking with the famous cape shtick, when he would drop to his knees clutching the microphone, then when a sideman draped a cape over his shoulders and began leading him offstage, he would break free and launch into his encore. Otis, however, didn't care to tell anyone how hardworking he was; he wanted the audience to know it. He wanted not to be pretty but bold, with a vulnerable soul. It was a kind of primordial funk style, and he was attracting a good deal of attention with it. Pat T. Cake and the Mighty Panthers had never gotten anywhere near the attention they did with Otis as the lead singer. It was only then that things began to happen for Johnny. Late in 1958, when Satellite Poppa got together a troupe of acts on a tour through Georgia, they made the roster, and some nice bread, dividing three or four hundred dollars per show. But Johnny would have to get used to going on without Otis every now and then when a better gig came along for *him*.

One of those times when Otis was called away, he was given the chance to stand literally where Little Richard had, in front of the Upsetters. Richard, in one of his mercurial sabbaticals from the tor-turous grind of rock and roll, had decided he would sing gospel and become an ordained Baptist minister—a sinecure that would always serve as a respite and guilt balm for his deranged lifestyle. The Upset-ters pushed on, booking gigs around the Southeast, and needed a vocalist. The best they had heard, that Redding boy, got the job. It was a one-off, a temporary arrangement, but Otis could hardly pass up the opportunity to feel like Little Richard and get paid twenty-five dollars a gig for it.

As it happened, both Otis and Johnny Jenkins were moving apace, in tandem. Johnny had been having problems with Pat T. Cake, who wanted to keep the songs they played the same rather than adding new material; Johnny, who had written a few songs and wanted to play them, told Cake he was through and formed a new band, the Pinetoppers, after those fragrant treetops out in the flatlands. He recruited Isaiah "Ish" Moseley, an old pro who had played for a time in Little Richard's band, but the others—who included electric bass player Sammy Davis and another Davis, Charles, who was Otis's old buddy Benny Davis's kid brother, on drums—were primarily there not to step on Johnny's star turns.

When they went out on their first gigs, it was under the aegis of a talent booker, though one hardly in Clint Brantley's league. Rather, he was an eighteen-year-old white Macon native, Phil Walden, a lantern-jawed, heavy drawling freshman at Mercer who thought hanging on the black side of town was cool and representing and booking black R&B acts even cooler.

•

PHILIP MICHAEL WALDEN was a very strange bird, easy for some to pass off as an impressionable white kid trying to fit into black culture. While he looked like a vanilla wafer, skinny enough to break in half in a good wind, there was something compelling about him. He didn't try to speak the lingo of the street or come off like a music expert. He could neither sing a note nor play an instrument. He didn't greet black men with jive or the '50s equivalent of a high five. Instead, he talked like a businessman, with a rush of overheated enthusiasm, telling black entertainers that if they were ever going to make money they would need a manager, that he could guarantee they'd thrive if they went with him.

Many of the black performers came from broken families and had no paternal influence. Even if Walden was a kid, younger than many of the people he ingratiated himself to, he seemed to care about them as people and his fast-talking spiels were focused more on how they would all make money together, as a family, all for one, etc. To many, he seemed much older than he was, and it was surely impressive that he could rattle off the names of obscure R&B songs, promoters, and club owners. On the Mercer campus, where he seemed to hone his skills as a social operator, he was a top student and president of his fraternity. Although he was not from a wealthy family, people thought he was loaded because he made friends with the rich kids. All in all, Phil Walden could talk the talk, and make bullshit walk proud.

He had caught the R&B/rock bug by listening to Little Richard records on WIBB, and a great epiphany for him was actually running into Richard on the street one day and greeting him with the first line of "Tutti-Frutti," whereupon Richard engaged in a brief duet with him. There was a certain daftness to his impetuosity about sidling up to black performers. Much of his time was spent in an *Animal House*–like surreality, entering hardcore black clubs, blissfully, as the only white face in the joint. Rather than being run out the door, he would have patrons schmoozing with him as if they'd known him forever. The first booking he did was a one-shot deal, bringing in Percy Welch and His House Rockers, who had just released the record "Back Door Man" backed with "Nursery Rhyme Rock" on the small Fran label out of Louisville, to play at his college frat party. The first group he made a continuing arrangement with was called the Heartbreakers, whom he booked to play frat parties at Mercer then clubs around town. As his clientele grew, he decided to set up shop in his first office, which was the cramped garage apartment behind his parents' home, where he would be found at all hours, phone stuck to his ear, pitching one or another act to some club owner or frat house.

Alex Hodges, who would come to study at Mercer a year later and become the second employee of the fledgling agency, never met anyone more memorable. "The first time I ever met Phil, he was lighting up a cigarette and he had a matchbook with a logo on the cover, a circle with a *P* and *W* on it, his initials. He had ordered these matchbooks to hand out to people, to singers, musicians. He was just so damn cool. That garage, I remember, he had a name for it—the Sin Bin Din, for no other reason than it sounded cool.

"Here was a kid living at home, goin' to school, and his head was in promotion—*self*-promotion. He already had a name for the operation. It was 'Phil Walden Artists and Promotions . . . Presenting Outstanding Entertainment . . . Key to Fit Your Occasion.' It was long, but it had to be because Phil had *big* dreams."[7]

Walden saw Johnny Jenkins as potential star material and latched on to him after Johnny walked away from Pat T. Cake to start his own unit. Walden, filling his head with promises about what he could do for the band, made hundreds of calls to the clubs. After Otis returned home from the Upsetters' tour early in 1959, Johnny filled him in on his new band and Otis too left Pat T. Cake. Thus, by extension, Otis had himself a manager, in the pasty-faced teenager. Walden, of course, had known of him. The Heartbreakers had been among Redding's victims at the Hamp Swain contests. But Walden had not been able to catch up to the peripatetic young man until he was finally able to make the connection at a gig he booked for the Pinetoppers at the Lakeside Amusement Park early in 1959. By now, Otis was even better than he'd been at the Swain shows, and Walden listened, mouth agape.

As Walden later recalled, "He was singing 'There Goes My Baby' and he did a Jackie Wilson song and he did 'Endlessly,' the Brook Benton song, and he did a Little Richard song. And he just sounded fabulous."[8]

Otis, who had modified his "Rockin' Redding" brand during the time he was with Jazbo Brown's House Rockers—ads billed him as "The Boy Who Rocks the House"—struck the slightly older Walden as bright, ambitious, and eager. As such, they were two of a kind. Like Johnny, Otis got the full-on "Phil treatment," and within an hour of meeting was going over lists of clubs, frat houses, and church socials Walden had compiled. Young and raw, they seemed to know even then how much they would mean to each other down the road, that the timing of this connection was something more than chance. Soon after, they made the alliance official, when Walden signed a personal services contract with Otis Redding, independently of the Pinetoppers. "It was all very naive," Walden thought. "Thank God that when you're young that you're naive like that. If we'd have failed so what? I was only eighteen and he was nineteen when I signed him. I wasn't even old enough to sign a contract. My father cosigned it. It was just blind belief in each other."

Actually, this was a fable promoted by Walden in later years. He did not technically sign Redding then. The relationship was based on a handshake, man-to-man, Southern trust. It is also telling that Walden apparently didn't know that Otis was a year *younger* than him. But then, to many who fell under the spell of the man with a voice that could make time stand still, he seemed older than he was, possessed of talent and savvy always just a bit better than anyone else.

4

"It's Something Called Soul"

By the dawn of JFK's New Frontier, not only was Little Richard becoming passé, but so was Elvis. At the same time, strides in social justice created new challenges. The Supreme Court's 1954 *Brown v. Board of Education* ruling struck down segregation in public schools "with all deliberate speed," but across the Jim Crow South that phrase was taken literally; moving as deliberately as possible, boards of education erected ways to stall a civil right now being as sullied as voting and housing opportunities. De facto segregation marched on, scarred but unbowed. Cast as a relief from these stomach-turning realities of life, the loud, untamed, and egalitarian properties of the new R&B idiom had grown far beyond what anyone would have seen coming in the previous decades when African-Americans were far more docile and accepting of servile stereotypes. Not that anyone was daring enough to write or sing a song specifically addressing this, the most egregious aspect of American life. But the urgency of such causes seemed reflected by a new tenacity in black singers to make their mark. The vehicle of that dynamic was doo-wop, a form of controlled madness, with tight harmonies backed by a riveting bass line and scat-form lyrics, which had arguably begun with the Five Satins' "In the Still of the Night" in 1956, a sensuous love ballad with a hook that went "Sha-doop-n-sho-be-doo."

Of course, it did not take long before co-option hit again, when records by mainly Italian-American vocal groups, the bulk of them from New York—such as the Harptones' "Sunday Kind of Love" and Dion DiMucci and the Belmonts' "I Wonder Why"—hit the market. But the deep bench of soul music was evident in black artists expanding doo-wop to buttery ballads like the Flamingos' cover of the evergreen "I Only Have Eyes for You" and Jerry Butler's emotive lead on the Impressions' first hit, "For Your Precious Love." When Butler left the Chicago-based group, the profoundly important Curtis Mayfield took the Impressions into a gospel-seeded, socially conscious niche, which owed a great debt to the gospel roots of Sam Cooke with the Soul Stirrers. The handsome, impeccably dressed, and unctuously confident Cooke had now moved into smooth, tony soul as the dominant singer of the era, not with themes of godly benediction but carnal conquest, something Cooke practiced, hard, in his private life, with many women. And he wasn't alone in scripting the soul of the late 1950s to the sound and beat of raging hormones. The brazenly sexual, electrifying Jackie Wilson, who after he had replaced the golden-throated Clyde McPhatter in Billy Ward's Dominoes left in 1957 to go solo in his native Detroit, kept pace with Cooke as the hottest draw of the sweet soul pack. In so doing, the lithe, spit-curled Wilson, a live wire of a man, also provided the first real outlet other than pimping and numbers running for a sawed-off, big-talking Detroit hustler and onetime prizefighter named Berry Gordy Jr. Gordy, even with the pedigree of being a member of one of Detroit's most prominent and wealthy black families, seemed incapable of holding down a job. But his persistence paid off when, after failing as a record store proprietor, he was able to sell to Jackie Wilson's manager, who ran one of the speakeasies Gordy frequented, many of what would become Wilson's finest testosterone-soaked anthems, including "Reet Petite," "Lonely Teardrops," and "That's Why."

These black men of high distinction laid critical groundwork and made the music that drove the era. But who made the bread? In the pecking order of the rock establishment, publishers and various power brokers were the CEOs. No better example existed than Dick Clark, who in the mid-1950s had begun hosting an after-school dance party on Philadelphia TV that, carried by rock's rising power, became the baby boomer pipeline for music that had a beat. Soon the show was shown on local stations across the country, setting trends in dance and song, as well as bobby-sox chic and duck's-ass haircuts—leather jackets, however, were taboo. Clark, whose affinity for black talent was noble and unquestioned, also realized the profit potential of soul. He was financially tied to the Cameo Parkway label, which shuttled acts onto his show. Yet unlike the DJ Alan Freed, Clark had the influence to fend off payola charges and moved ever upward, in 1960 breaking out a chicken-plucker named Ernest Evans. As the renamed Chubby Checker, he recorded a cover of Hank Ballard's "The Twist," which became a national craze after Checker performed it on *Bandstand*. The only thing that could change the racial status quo would be the rise of a new class of black autonomy and power. And even then, there would be catches to it.

•

DOWN IN Macon, Phil Walden spent the last year of the decade that changed the way America heard music working the phones hard, but for all the strides he had made, he was so broke that he was close to no longer being able to afford school. Walden years later told of the crisis this way: "It was like January. I was registering for the winter quarter at Mercer. And during Christmas I was particularly generous with everybody, including myself, and spent all the money I'd earned. So I went to see my father and said I needed some money for tuition, and my father was not receptive to what I was doing. He said, 'You know, if you're gonna continue to hang out with those 'Negras'—that was a nice way of saying it; it was a big concession for a Southerner at that time not to say 'nigger'—you're gonna have to depend on those folks.'

"I was president of the fraternity and I thought, socially this is gonna destroy me, 'cause I gotta go over and tell them I gotta drop out. It was so embarrassing. So Otis came into the office and said, 'What's wrong with you? You got the blues today.'"

"I explained the situation to him and he said, 'Well I gotta do some errands, you gonna be here later?'"

A few hours later, Otis returned with a bulging manila envelope tucked under his arm. Reaching Walden's desk, he plopped it down on the desk, spilling out quarters, dimes, nickels, half-dollars, and crumpled bills—sixty-three dollars and twelve cents in all—all over the desk and floor. "I think there's enough there," he said, meaning Phil's tuition money, a stash he said he had accrued by having "borrowed from everybody [he knew]."[1]

In truth, he should have been starting to save those nickels and dimes for his own purposes, having fallen head over shiny heels for a girl, the first one he'd met that wasn't a hussy, a hooker, or a user.

•

ON A lazy, hazy Saturday afternoon in the late summer of 1959, Zelma Atwood, who was just fifteen, went with her friends to see a soul music show at the Douglass Theatre. Petite and almost scrawny looking, she was not classically pretty, but her small frame, quick wit, and fetching smile made her a popular catch for the schoolboys. But she was not easy. Indeed, she never took crap from anyone—not even eighteen-year-old Otis Redding. Though she lived across the back alley from the Redding flat, on Jackson Street, the two of them never met until she caught his eye while he was onstage during a Pinetoppers Saturday matinee. Spying her in the audience, he made a mental note to seek her out after the show—a common rite of manhood for any magnetic hunk who sang onstage was to identify a conquest and cash in after the show. Indeed, as a student of Jackie Wilson and Sam Cooke, Otis had come to see a show as a prelude to some recreation afterward. Usually, he would need to look no further than the women waiting for him at the stage door.

This time was different, however. Zelma was no groupie. Nor was she waiting at the stage door. When the show ended, he found her in the exiting crowd. As Zelma has remembered the moment, he strode over to her like he owned the world and said, "How's it going, baby?"

"I ain't your baby," she told him.[2]

Thrown back on his heels, he persisted. She took offense. Soon they were sniping at each other, which only seemed to stoke a fire between them. Neither walked away, and when the yelling stopped, they began a normal conversation, which continued as they walked down the street. She laughed at his humor, as he did at hers. She found herself more and more under his spell, and he under hers. She was flattered that the man she had just been so captivated by was so taken with her, especially when he could have any floozy he wanted. Under the bold surface, he was just a teenager with uncertainties and pain. And it didn't hurt that he was easy on the eyes. They made a date to see each other again, and before long it was a steady thing. Otis would have Bubba Sailor take them around town in his car, and they would steal intimate moments at either Bubba's or some other buddy's house.

What Otis saw in Zelma was something his friends couldn't quite figure out, but the mystery unraveled whenever he had one of his spats with the deacon, or spoke ruefully of his cleaved home life. When Alex Hodges met them, they were already interlocked, all but inseparable. The chemistry flowed. "It really was a balancing act, the two of them. Otis was a wonderful, big-hearted guy, but he had a little ego and Zelma wasn't enamored of it. She would make it clear to him that his ego was bigger than it had a right to be. She brought him down to earth, and he would then be just Otis. And he liked that she could shoot straight with him, not play him. She was honest. She wasn't a giddy little drugstore-lovin' girl. And she really became a strong woman who could keep him under control, keep his career, the finances, all of it, under control, and shield him. Hell, she's still shielding him today."[3]

In truth, the meek-looking teen seemed even then to realize the power she had over him. A word or two could stop him in his tracks and cause him to heel like an obedient beagle. A common such verbal brake was when he'd start bragging on himself and she'd say, barely above a whisper, "You better learn a little humility." Indeed, having all but lost the family bond with the deacon and Fannie Mae, it was as if Otis counted on her to establish a bond with *her*. Adds Hodges, "Otis never got crazy in his life, for the most part. He didn't live self-destructively. And a lot of that was due to Zelma. She had an important impact on his life. She was an amazing woman, still is, and he really loved and respected her. But most of all he *needed* her."

•

IN KEEPING with the complexities of his lingering relationship with his father, and grudging respect they had for each other, the deacon's patience with him became frayed, but never severed. Once, when he and Johnny Jenkins needed wheels to get to a gig out of town, Otis thought nothing of hot-wiring his father's Mercury—just one of his talents besides singing—and driving off without a word to the deacon, who called the police and said his car was stolen. Not long after, a cop saw the vehicle out on the interstate and pulled it over, ordering Otis and Johnny to get out and lie facedown in the road. Because Otis's ID showed he was the owner's son, no charges were filed—though he and Jenkins missed their gig, costing them some money. To Jenkins, the misadventure seemed only to bolster his feeling that Otis "didn't have much respect for his daddy," something that he thought contributed to his singer's recklessness. About a lot of things, he said, "We didn't know no better. But he was more dangerous than I because I had the sense to back off. . . . He never did back off anything [and] didn't know the word *dangerous*."

In truth, Otis's recklessness had a kind of blithe, spontaneous quality, as if knowing he was wrong and making a bad decision was a kick, and cars seemed to only ignite this facet of his thought process. When he was seventeen, he got himself into trouble again when he sold a car, a '55 Buick Roadmaster he had bought from a garage for sixty-five dollars, either forgetting or ignoring that he was still paying it off. He was arrested for disposing of mortgaged property, pleaded guilty, and paid a thirty-five dollar fine.[4] Such episodes only underlined his increasing boredom in Macon, and the clashes with his father that would inevitably arise when he had to explain himself. The best solution, he came to believe, was getting away for a while, maybe a long while.

Accordingly, in the late autumn of 1960, he had made plans to take a road trip to Los Angeles with his sister Debra and stay with his uncle, Otis Sr.'s brother, who lived there. Debra, who had been the first to graduate high school and had been working as a secretary, had herself become progressively bored with the mundane routines of her life in Macon, and saved up enough money to buy a used car, with the purpose being to spend her summer vacation that year driving cross-country. The deacon, who adamantly refused to allow her to go alone, was actually pleased when Otis's own plans dovetailed with hers. In fact, the timing was perfect. For Otis, of course, music played a part in the equation. Otis figured he had done enough in Macon, a town that now seemed to him too small, and small-minded, to be worth wasting any more time in. Almost nineteen now, he had survived seething vibes but was convinced that a black man could never go far in the business unless, like Little Richard, he went where the vibes spoke to a more liberal-minded America. Having achieved a modicum of notoriety, he was now worried about running afoul of some redneck with a rifle or noose. Once, when Phil's kid brother Alan drove him somewhere, he went through a white area. For that part of the ride, Otis remained slumped down in the passenger seat.[5] Phil Walden couldn't disagree with Otis that far too many folks in Macon were "stupid motherfuckers."

Phil Walden, who people suspected (and he confirmed years later) had higher hopes for Johnny Jenkins than Otis at the beginning, encouraged Otis to go. Phil was still laboring at Mercer and couldn't give his all to any of his acts. And when Otis surveyed his existence as a singer in a band with limited potential, he saw no downside to making the move. As it was, the Pinetoppers had become an afterthought to his more urgent ambitions and Jenkins now had to live with the real possibility that Otis might walk on him at any time.

It was during this interval that Zelma Atwood had begun to have morning sickness. She went to her doctor and was told she was pregnant. When she sat Otis down, he was just as stunned as she. But, seeing how set he was on going to L.A., she did not try to get him to stay. He told her what she needed to hear—he would be coming home to see her give birth. He never, however, mentioned the word *marriage*. Not seriously, at least. As Zelma would later recount, in the liner notes to the posthumous alum *The Definitive Otis Redding*, "When Otis went to California to record I was three months pregnant. . . . He said he was going to California, and he was going to be a star and going to come back [with] all this money, and we going to get married, and I'm like, 'Sure you is.'"[6] But she felt she had no right to blunt his dreams, and so just after Thanksgiving of 1960, Otis followed Little Richard out of Macon all the way to L.A.—

another turn that, literally now, put more distance between him and the deacon, the mounting tension between them also having contributed to his decision to go. Before leaving, however, Otis Jr. blithely told Zelma that, pending the birth, she should finish school. She nodded her head, wanting to believe he'd be there when the time came. But she didn't kid herself and knew there was every chance she might never see him again.

•

OTIS AND Debra Redding headed west, sharing the driving in her used car, and when he arrived, he quickly immersed himself in the L.A. soul music community. He began to hang with a young singer-songwriter named Jackie Avery, who seemed to know everybody who was anybody. Avery took him to a freelance producer, James McEachin, a man who would gain far more notice a decade later as a character actor on TV and in movies, with roles such as DJ Sweet Al Monte in the movie *Play Misty for Me*. A Purple Heart and Silver Star recipient in the Korean War, McEachin knocked around L.A. as a cop and fireman before doing studio work under the name "Jimmy Mack." When he heard Redding sing, he recalls now, "I dropped everything else I was working on. He could draw on something from deep in his soul and it just flooded out."[7]

Soon enough Otis moved into McEachin's apartment on Manhattan Boulevard, where he not only lived but also rehearsed songs, preparatory to a recording date. While there, the producer got to know the young man, like everyone else, thinking he was years older than he actually was. "I had no idea he was only eighteen at the time. He was so good and so confident. He had that swagger. He knew he had talent and he was right. There were some other very accomplished singers living in the complex there, guys from the Olympics, who did 'Western Movies' and '(Baby) Hully Gully.' We'd hang out in my living room and sing, and Otis just took over, he'd be the center of attention. He was a big, personable kid. My wife loved him. Everyone did."

Sparing little expense, McEachin hired arranger Rene Hall, who had worked with Sam Cooke, and paid for a session at Gold Star Studios, a famous shop in Santa Monica where Cooke, Eddie Cochran, and Ritchie Valens had also recorded. Gold Star's acoustics were one of a kind, its glutinous echoes leading Phil Spector to soon make his "Wall of Sound" records there. Otis would cut four songs, the main aim being to make him sound as much like Jackie Wilson as possible. "Jackie Wilson was Otis's favorite singer, he thought Jackie was God. So I let him stay in that direction, the beat, the intro, the whole nine yards."

On the first of two songs written by McEachin as Jimmy Mack, "She's All Right," he even appropriated Wilson's familiar "ah-ha-ha" background vocals and flute accents, with Otis singing in an unnaturally high key that strained his voice. The second, "Tuff Enuff," with its notable early use of "ghetto" misspelling in the title, was less an imitation and a good groove even if it was buried in a jumble of echoed noise. When McEachin had asked Otis for two songs he had written himself, Otis suggested one called "These Arms of Mine," a plaintive, pleasing ballad. McEachin turned thumbs-down. "I thought he was selling himself short with that song," McEachin says ruefully. "I wanted to keep in that Jackie Wilson mold." Instead, the last two tracks were raucous blues rockers, "Gamma Lama" a cop on the Edsels' 1958 "Rama Lama Ding Dong," and "Gettin' Hip," which cribbed from both Little Richard and Jackie Wilson.

According to McEachin, Otis was "easy to work with, very determined," but it was clear he had his own methods. "He didn't just sing lyrics, he made them his own, according to how he felt. He improvised, changed words, sang all around, not up and down. He was like a jazz man, not playing the same note twice." Before finishing that day, Otis left McEachin with serviceable records. "I was happy with them so I took "She's All Right" to KUDU, a radio station in Oxnard.

And the guy there started playing it, played it like twenty times that night. But the problem was, I didn't have the money to properly distribute it in L.A. I needed a label to do that." He pitched the song to several, but the only one that was receptive was a Denver-based label called Trans World, run by Al Kavelin, a Russian-born bandleader who was quite popular in the 1930s when his band included pianist Carmen Cavallaro. Kavelin gave the Redding record to his partner Morey Bernstein. When McEachin played it for him, Bernstein liked what he heard but had a problem.

"I couldn't understand a word he sang," he said.

Replied McEachin, "It's something called soul."

Bernstein had released mostly white pop records by groups like the Hollywood Argyles and Doug and Freddy and the Pyramids, but also a Chicago doo-wop group, the Fabulous Enchanters, whose "Why Are You Crying" is a wonderful relic of the era, with sound effects of a girl sobbing all through it. Another employee there, the magnificently eccentric Kim Fowley, a cape-wearing L.A. industry moth who later worked with Frank Zappa and founded the punk-rocking girl group the Runaways, recalls that "Otis Redding was the first black artist" on the label, and that he "showed up and knocked on the door of the building [with] a tape of 'Gamma Lama' [which he had] recorded in Muscle Shoals."[8]

As is the case with Redding's early career, even people who were there got it wrong. "Gamma Lama" was neither recorded at Muscle Shoals nor bought by Trans World. Indeed, while Bernstein would be yet another on a list of thousands who would later claim to have "discovered" Otis Redding, he seemed not overly interested in him. "She's All Right" and "Tuff Enuff" went out on Trans World just before the new decade of 1960—not under Otis Redding's imprimatur; rather, it was billed as performed by the Shooters, another act McEachin was working with who had played on the Redding session. If Otis Redding's voice was compelling, clearly his name was not.

•

IN L.A., the main conduit for R&B was Johnny Otis, white and the son of Greek parents, who grew up in a black section of Oakland and did most everything a man could do in music. A singer, big band leader, and arranger, he had co-written and produced Big Mama Thornton's "Hound Dog" and played drums on the session (though he was later revealed to have forced the underage, soon-to-be-famous writer/producers Jerry Leiber and Mike Stoller to cede him a writer's credit of the song they had written and a publishing cut, which were later stripped from him by court order when Elvis cut his version).[9] Otis's 1958 big band hit "Willie and the Hand Jive" went number 1 R&B and top 10 pop, taking back the "hand jive" beat that Bo Diddley had appropriated from Johnny Otis, who had written songs with that beat a decade before. A label owner as well, Johnny Otis had become a kind of West Coast kingmaker. His radio gig on KFOX in Long Beach, California, was a soul landmark, playing hardcore R&B. He also hosted legendary Friday and Saturday night shows at El Monte Legion Stadium. There, one could see the likes of the Penguins, Shirley and Lee, Brenton Wood, and Johnny "Guitar" Watson on the same stage. The Beatles even played there in March of 1965.

However, Otis never really got a footing on the L.A. turf, as Debra so enjoyed the new scenery that she took an extended leave from her job in Macon and both she and her brother remained with their uncle into the summer of 1961. But, much as he tried to plant new roots, he simply never got the break he needed. While Morey Bernstein did begin to value the man he "discovered," changing the name on a new batch of records to "Otis Redding and the Shooters" (it only became solely "Otis Redding" much later when the songs would appear on various packages after Redding's death, most cleanly on the Rhino Records' massive 1993 box set, *The Definitive*

Otis Redding), he was in no hurry to release "Gamma Lama" and "Gettin' Hip." "The problem was," says McEachin, "Morey Bernstein didn't know the R&B market. He and Al Kavelin had money, but they had no clue where to put it for a record like that." Feeling adrift, McEachin sold the two songs to Alshire Records, a budget album label, which put out a few promotional copies but nothing more. By then, in mid-summer 1961, Otis was itchy again, wanting his feet to take him back home, not coincidentally, just as Zelma was nearing her due date. As blithe as he was about leaving her in the condition she was in, he wanted now to fulfill his promise to be there when she gave birth. What's more, Debra, too, was homesick and ready to hit the road and resume her life in Georgia. The eight months of living dangerously in L.A. was, for both, done.

As McEachin recalls, "He thought he wasn't getting anywhere fast. He had stopped coming around and I hadn't heard from him. Then someone said he was gone, went back to Macon. He just blew away like a leaf." A laugh. "He owed me some money, maybe that's why he went." Another laugh. "Or maybe it was some of those girls who ran him out of town. Whatever it was, I felt I was remiss in not paying him the attention he deserved, and if he'd stuck around longer we could have gotten it right. But Otis was like that. If he made his mind up about something, he'd do it. I never saw him again. I hear when he was in L.A. five years later or so, he wanted to see me but I was gone, too, to Liberty Records, scouting talent down in New Orleans. We were the two ships, we passed in the night."

In retrospect, it wasn't that those records were bad; the Redding groove can be felt on them all. But they didn't convey the "pain in my heart" emotional lava that came from a certain environment, one he would never stray far from.

"Otis thought he should be in the big town, but he learned he wasn't cut out for it," says Alex Hodges. "Otis was a country boy. When he sang on 'Dock of the Bay' about being so far from home, that was the perfect word for how he felt about home: *dock*. Macon was the dock."

The L.A. detour turned out to be so unfruitful that even Otis got some facts wrong. Abridging considerably, years later he would tell author Stanley Booth, "In 1960 I went to California to cut a record, 'She's All Right.' It was with Lute Records, the label the Hollywood Argyles were on. It didn't do anything [and] I came back to Macon."[10] As disenchanted as he was, the approaching birth of his first child made the decision to leave easier. The sassy, painted-up women in the clubs had made him long for Zelma, and increasingly jealous of what she might be doing back home, and with whom. At first, when she told him she was pregnant, his mind had run wild with the thought that some other guy had knocked her up. She had to assure him otherwise. Suddenly he felt a proprietary need to own her, and for her to mother not only their child but him as well.

He was no longer Rockhouse Redding; he was simply Otis Redding, a man who needed to somehow face being a man and a father before turning twenty-one.

5

"A Lousy Singer"

Otis got back to Macon in early August 1961, the month Zelma Atwood was due to deliver, and went right to work back at the Macon clubs. His impending fatherhood, however, was yet another reason for the deacon to be irritated. What *else* could his boy do to be a sinner? Otis for his part promised to marry Zelma before the child was born, and made good on it, tying the knot on August 17 at the Tindall Heights church, the ceremony performed by the family pastor, Rev. C. J. Andrews. His son, a boy he named Dexter Redding, was born days later. With no money for a place of their own, the three of them moved in with Zelma's grandmother, who had a larger apartment. When Otis said he found a house, they rented that, but only for a couple of weeks, the place being filthy and nearly falling down. When a local record company owner loaned Otis two hundred dollars to find a suitable place, they finally wound up in a bi-level apartment near the Fort Hawkins section of Macon.

Even with the new digs, however, Otis only rarely saw his boy. Getting home from the clubs in the wee hours, he'd sleep until noon, then get ready to go back out and perform, often for such paltry pay that Otis had to pick up other work on the side. But with all the energy and time needed for his shows, it was impossible to hold a job and Otis had been fired from about every nonmusical job he'd had. While this meant that Zelma had to go out and find work, she was still forbearing about his obsession, and was even more impressed with his continued determination and sense of optimism. "He had his own mind about what he would dream. . . . He didn't complain," she said. "If it was fine, it was fine. If it wasn't, it was, 'It'll work out.' That's what he'd say. 'Oh, it'll work out.' And that's how he kept himself going."[1]

By 1962, he had returned to the Pinetoppers, but was getting impatient with Phil Walden, who was about to graduate from Mercer and was ready to build his one-man agency into a more professional operation, which he now named "Phil Walden Artists and Promotions." Walden however was struggling to get more than the usual low-paying gigs for his top client. Not that Phil was rolling in dough, either. In fact, to make ends meet, he had taken a job as a salesman—his true calling—at the Hayes clothing store owned by his cousin Roy, and he even sold fireworks. That allowed him to hire, for pocket change, two other employees, Alex Hodges and Phil's kid brother Alan, both of whom were also at Mercer. Alan, a beanpole then with shaggy blond hair, cut his teeth on the business, helping get gigs for his brother's acts during his hours as a soda jerk at a local club where, he recalled, "We promoted bands like Doug Clark and the Hot Nuts, the Delacardos, and Maurice Williams and the Zodiacs."[2]

Hodges came aboard, he recalls, "because Phil went around school asking guys who could type to send out promotional material, and I could do that. Phil had it all in his mind how to run this little agency. He would make up a budget for things like spare guitar strings, or gasoline for the car we used to take around the bands." Walden rented a closet-sized office on the twenty-first floor of the

Macon Professional Building on Mulberry Street—the Robert E. Lee Building today—a few floors above where WIBB had their office and Hamp Swain did his show. He had two phone lines installed (Sherwood 6-8810 and Sherwood 3-6555) and obtained phone books from big cities, to cold-call nightclubs and pitch the new agency's talent.[3]

Otis believed he had a personal commitment to advancing the company's success, and, Hodges says, he "had a hands-on presence in the office. Hell, he even painted the walls after we moved in." The Walden parents, C.B. and Carolyn, who had once reeled in horror that their son was working with black nightclub singers, pitched in as well, answering the phone when the company "officers" were in class or working other jobs. It seemed anything but a big-time operation, but, as Hodges says, laughing, "We were too young and naive to know how crazy a dream it was." Otis Redding was anything but big-time, either. Yet even then, the jovial, future big-time promoter tells you, "You knew. Instinctively, you just knew he was something special. I mean, Otis had it going on. He was a big, handsome guy who was comfortable with himself. He walked into a room and it lit up."

•

OTIS AND Johnny Jenkins were now only technically members of the Pinetoppers. Indeed, both regularly went alone or together to local record companies looking to cut a record. Either of them could have been the name on the label, with the other playing or singing on the session, just as long as a deal was made. One of those times, in late 1961, Otis, who was too itchy to rely solely on Walden to make things happen for him, strode across the hall of the Professional Building, where Walden's shop was, to the office of a Macon label called Confederate Records, owned by former car salesman Bobby Smith.

Smith had nearly died in a car wreck a few years earlier, leaving him with one eye that he could barely see out of. But he had as sharp a pair of ears as any in Macon. He managed a Jerry Lee Lewis clone named Wayne Cochran, the first self-avowed white soul singer, whose shtick would soon be an Alp-high silver pompadour, flowing, sequined capes, and Little Richard–type leaping and prancing. Smith also had a stable of musicians at his disposal, including Dennis Wheeler, who was white but a regular performer at black clubs. According to Wheeler, who still performs today in the Georgia and Florida clubs, "Bobby really developed a whole culture in Macon that was color-blind. See, among us musicians, nobody even thought about color." If so, it was mainly because racism was so ingrained it seemed almost part of the woodwork in town. Wheeler matter-of-factly recalls the time when as a young man he boarded a city bus with a black friend and without thinking went to the back of the bus along with him and sat down, prompting the driver to kick *Wheeler* off the bus for violating the sanctity of Jim Crow.[4]

Seeking an audience with Bobby Smith, Otis boldly walked into his office with a proposition. As Smith once related, "Otis said he was a singer and wanted to see if I was interested in him. I asked if he had a tape with original material on it, and he said he didn't but would sing for me. He sang 'Shout Bamalama.' That was all I needed to hear. I signed Otis to a recording contract with Confederate Records [and] obtained studio time at the University of Georgia's channel 8 TV studios in Athens to record [the song]." The tune, a reworking of "Gamma Lama" into a tale about an Alabama chicken thief, was produced by Smith as a thinly veiled copy of Gary "U.S." Bonds's "Quarter to Three," with party-like caviling quieted by his spoken "Okay, hold it, hold it" and "a-one, a-two, a-one-two-three-four" intro. The Pinetoppers were the session musicians, plus Cochran, who played bass, but it was a muddy job, the vocal and honking sax echoed into ghostliness at times. Still, infectious as it was, Smith was pleased to have signed the young man—and was careful to do it in a legal fashion, or so he thought.

"What Bobby told me," says Wheeler, "was that because Otis was underage, he had Otis's momma come in and sign the contract. That was how it was done. I know, because my momma had to sign my contract with Bobby. He was very meticulous about that."

Yet this very subject would become the biggest and most hotly argued circumstance in the career advancement of Otis Redding, and it brought home the fact that Otis looked and seemed older than he was. "I thought he was, too," notes Wheeler. "He was so dang big and commanding. His voice made him older. He didn't try to be what he wasn't. His niche was flat-out soul. It wasn't that he had the greatest singing voice, it was just that it was *him*. He was like Ray Charles. Just him, what was inside him. Nobody could ever copy that. But those early records, they didn't do him justice at all."

Regardless, Smith believed he owned more of Redding than Otis may have realized, not having read the fine print. According to that print, he was now Otis Redding's manager, something that Phil Walden had not codified with regard to his work representing Otis. Not that Walden was prepared to accept any such thing. As far as he was concerned, Smith had a record contract with Otis, nothing more, and nothing to stop him from shopping Redding to bigger honchos.

•

IN THE fall of 1962, "Shout Bamalama" and a more Little Richard-esque tune, "Fat Gal," were released, credited to "Otis Redding and the Pinetoppers," on Confederate Records—a circumstance that would quickly become a problem for Smith, who designed a logo that displayed the stars and bars of the Confederate flag. This was a decade before the Southern rock band Lynyrd Skynyrd made this imprint of slavery synonymous with "redneck chic," though with regular explanations that the flag wasn't an endorsement of ante-bellum slavery but Southern "heritage." The flag may have been an innocuous regional relic to Smith, who obviously was no racist, but to those outside the South—and to many within it who proudly flew or pinned it to a car window, pickup truck, or living room wall—it was anything but innocuous.

Smith seemed oblivious to the politically incorrect implications. "He needed a name for the label and came up with Confederate," says Wheeler, "because it was regional. And you know what? I don't recall Otis or any other black person I knew object to it." Indeed, such was the power of a century of conditioning. Yet Smith was not only facing static from politically sensitive quarters, but, like Phil Walden, was running against the white Southern grain by taking black entertainers under his wing. "If Bobby thought about it at all," Wheeler adds, "it was that he was putting black guys on a label named Confederate, he was saying, 'Hey, this is a new Confederacy now down here.'"

Good intentions aside, Smith was given a firsthand lesson in modern civics. He once recalled, "Otis and I went on the road promoting 'Shout Bamalama.' We stopped at an Augusta radio station, WTHB, and we were told by the DJ it would be played if it were taken off the Confederate-flagged record label. I promised to do so. We went on to Columbia, South Carolina, and met with a program director, a guy named Big Saul, at WOIC, who also promised heavy play, but only if the label [name] was changed. Otis and I hit it off very well with Big Saul. As we drove and listened to legendary DJ John R. on Nashville's WLAC, Otis said, 'Bobby, if that man played my record I would think I had made it.'

"When we returned to Macon, I wasted no time creating the Orbit label and putting 'Shout Bamalama' on it. The following week I went to Nashville and talked to John R. and I explained the situation with Confederate and Orbit. John R. was impressed with the record and promised me he would give it heavy duty air play."

It might however have been too late for the record. As Wheeler can recall, letters and calls came pouring into the office from the NAACP about the issue regarding the label name, further muddying the waters for its advancement. For Redding, inured as he was to Jim Crow, there had been no objection to the Confederate label. In fact, Redding's lack of any discernible racial worldview, or much of a sense of what was going on in the news, would never really change much. The Bay of Pigs disaster in '61, the Cuban Missile Crisis the following year, and the March on Washington in '63 would not be on his personal radar. While some early discontent was arising about Vietnam after John F. Kennedy dispatched the first "advisers" there, Otis had no reason to fret. He had registered for the draft, as all young men were required to when they reached age eighteen, but unlike both Walden brothers and Alex Hodges—and Elvis and even Willie Mays—he was safe, given III-A deferment status, as a married man with children—a "Kennedy husband," as such lucky men were dubbed.[5] But he was a family man who rarely saw his family. Confederate, Orbit, whatever the signposts, his attention was almost completely confined to music.

●

OTIS HUNG around every day at the Confederate office, digging the vibes of a record company he thought he might help build. Smith, seeing that Otis was itching to write songs, put him to work on one, for a group called Buddy Leach and the Playboys, who Smith had signed in Atlanta. That was when he unveiled the song James McEachin had rejected in L.A., which Smith thought was brand new and under his aegis.

"We needed a B-side for Buddy Leach," said Smith, "and Otis wrote 'These Arms of Mine' for me. He came to my office to play the song for me. . . . Otis had his guitar and played the song for Wayne Pierce, who played organ for Wayne Cochran's band. Wayne and I both thought it was a terrific song. Otis went with me to the session to record Buddy Leach and afterward I told Otis that 'These Arms of Mine' would be his next recording."[6] The lead singer of the Playboys was actually not Buddy Leach but Dennis Wheeler, who also played keyboards. "We gave it a good ride, but our version was an appetizer," he says. "Otis's was gonna be the main course."

Johnny Jenkins by now had cut his first record, as well, for a label that, like Smith's, had been geared more to white guys in pickup trucks than to the soul crowd. Tifco Records, located in Tifton, down near the Florida border, was owned by Jim Newton, a Dixieland bandleader whose roster was mainly hillbilly acts. In February 1962, after Phil Walden agreed to finance the session—though he needed a bank loan to do it—Jenkins recorded two songs for the label in an Atlanta studio, both guitar-driven blues in the style of the '50s instrumental hits "Raunchy" by Bill Justis, a horn man at Sam Phillips's Sun Records, and Chuck Berry's "Guitar Boogie." One was called "Pinetop." The other, playing off the success of Chubby Checker's now-fading dance craze, was "Love Twist."

The session included Ish Moseley, Sammy Davis, and Pat T. Cake, and the record was credited to Johnny Jenkins and the Pinetoppers, though one important Pinetopper was left out, there being no vocals. But Otis Redding's career would, coincidentally, still be advanced by this record, which was released in May 1962. "Pinetop" was the original A side, but only until DJs began flipping it to play "Love Twist." When that song generated a buzz on the local soul stations, it attracted the attention of a man who would have an enormous impact on the course of American music, even if almost no one knew of him at the time. This was a Runyonesque character named Joey Galkin, a short, garrulous, thirty-six-year-old Russian-born New York expatriate. He had actually grown up in Macon and tried a singing career before turning to booking acts and doing promotion for Atlantic Records in New York. On a whim, he quit, opened a failed bar in Queens, then moved back to Macon on a loose leash for Atlantic, his job to get records played on local radio. At first, Jerry Wexler, the Atlantic vice president, told him, "You're crazy. That's all they need down there is an obnoxious Jew like you coming into the radio stations." But then Galkin called one day and said, "I got a hit," after creating wide airplay for soul bandleader Solomon Burke's "Just Out of Reach (of My Two Open Arms)."[7]

Galkin was originally paid fifty dollars a week, but given a fairly loose expense account, to make hits keep on coming, and he was a minor legend in Macon and Atlanta, often seen holding court in clubs and restaurants, regaling and keeping station directors sloshed, a fat cigar stuck to his mouth, thick horn-rimmed glasses on his nose. Wexler once said that "nobody had ever promoted records the way he did it. . . . He'd be in his car, and whenever he saw a radio tower transmitter, he'd stop, get out of his car, and go hustle his records. [He was] a hustler with good hunches."[8] Galkin also formed a label called Gerald Records to acquire new talent, keeping them in his pocket until he could shunt them to Atlantic, with the requisite 10 percent finder's fee and a 10 percent cut of royalties.

When he heard "Love Twist" on the radio, that became his plan for Johnny Jenkins. While Jim Newton was pleased with the regional reaction to the song, like all small label owners he lived for a chance to partner up with a national network to make it into a big hit. And while Gerald was hardly RCA or Mercury, Galkin's link with Atlantic, combined with his big talk and free-flowing booze, led to a deal. Newton sold Jenkins's two sides to Galkin in exchange for a commission of the sales, and within days "Love Twist" was pressed on vinyl discs reading "Gerald Records." Not only that, by signing Jenkins to Gerald, Galkin technically became Jenkins's manager, and of all the Pinetoppers, even the one who hadn't been on their two recordings.

At this point, Phil Walden, who still focused as much on Jenkins as Redding, had no particular plans for the latter. "I thought my entire world rotated around Johnny Jenkins' guitar," he said years later. "I was convinced he could have been the greatest thing in rock 'n' roll."[9] However, Jenkins and "Love Twist" were only a lever for Galkin. He never did take the record to Atlantic, believing it was not up to the company's standards, but it still sold around twenty-five thousand copies, not at all bad for a first record and far more than any of Otis's previous recordings. Galkin and Walden thought they had a tiger by the tail, and even though Phil, as with Otis, had not signed Johnny to a contract to manage him, he bartered with Galkin as if he had. Before long they were carving up Jenkins's royalty and publishing splits like a duck on a plate, with not a word of input from Johnny himself, and they came to an agreement to split publishing rights. Johnny would get the normal three and a half cents per record, and zero cents of the publishing royalties for his own song.

It was a tangled web of deceit, but the only way both white men could ensure that they would profit from another black talent. And it was the precedent for another private deal between the same two men soon to come, regarding the ownership of Otis Redding.

●

JOE GALKIN had not heard of Redding and only became aware of him when he attended some gigs by the Pinetoppers around Macon. Like everyone else with ears, Galkin was knocked out by him, and immediately broadened his plans. With Otis in the same fold as Jenkins, spoken for by Phil Walden (Galkin probably never knew of Bobby Smith's claim on Redding, or if he did, never took it seriously) the two of them discussed how to get both artists to Atlantic. For now, the priority was still Jenkins. The first step was having him record again, this time in a studio where the New York label had a foothold in the South. Galkin, a man who kept his ear to the ground, was well aware that Atlantic had recently entered into an alliance with the Stax Records label in Memphis.

There, in that old converted movie theater on East McLemore Avenue, the company's co-founders, Jim Stewart and his sister Estelle Stewart Axton, had reaped some national hits. Two of the bigger hits were Carla Thomas's "Gee Whiz (Look at His Eyes)" in 1960 (when the label was still called Satellite Records), which went top 10 pop, number 5 R&B, and became the first of the great smooth-groove soul records; and "Last Night," by the Mar-Keys, the Stax house band, which made it to number 3 pop, number 2 R&B, in 1961. Another, the coolly metronomic, almost dark-hearted "Green Onions," by Booker T. and the MG's, was climbing the charts as Stax's first big hit in the fall of 1962, when Joey Galkin had a good reason to call Jerry Wexler.

"Wexler," Galkin barked, "I want you to finance a session."

"Who?" Wexler inquired.

"Johnny Jenkins and the Pinetoppers. I'm managing them and I want to record them at Stax. Give me two thousand dollars."

"Never heard of 'em."

"You will. Johnny's a great guitarist and one of his sidemen can sing. It'll take two thousand dollars."[10]

Coyly dropping Redding into the conversation was no accident. Indeed, once Wexler agreed to send the bread to him, Galkin scheduled a session for mid-February, as he knew he wasn't going to leave Memphis without somehow getting Otis a witness.

Not knowing any of this, it was now *Otis* who was stagnating. Zelma was pregnant again, necessitating that he had to hustle for a few more bucks. Johnny Jenkins, however, seemed to be playing the game much better. He was able to buy a car, a big red Chevy, even though he had never learned to drive, believing he should be taken around by a driver, which became Otis much of the time. While Johnny would sit in the back basking, Otis would wonder what he was doing wrong. Not that he wasn't happy for Johnny, but he still had no doubt he ranked higher on the showbiz ladder, despite getting nowhere. Worse, Phil Walden had gotten his military notice and would be going into the Army when he graduated from Mercer that year, commissioned as a second lieutenant and stationed in

Germany. As a result, he'd be forced to leave the agency in the hands of his family and Alex Hodges.

The timing seemed less than providential for Otis, who had no other fallback and fewer chits in the industry to cash in. But he still *acted* like he owned the clubs. "I never saw Otis change, not one whit," says Dennis Wheeler. "He was always confident. He believed in himself. If his daddy didn't deter him, nothin' was gonna."

With as little success as Otis had reaped by late 1961, the blandishments of the deacon seemed well-founded. But Walden still believed in him and, in his absence, Bobby Smith lined him up on gigs around town with Wayne Cochran. Wayne and Otis made for a wildly odd couple, but the trade-off of vocals between the two was so irresistibly fun that it always sold out the house. Otis also made several appearances with Eddie Kirkland, an aging blues singer and guitarist who was managing John Lee Hooker. Any paying gig helped, but they weren't getting him far enough, nor was living on the road any easier. Otis, whose loneliness wouldn't leave him alone, even back then, began to bring along Oscar Mack, the man who had displaced him as the regular winner at Hamp Swain's talent shows. Otis made Mack his driver, if for nothing more than bragging rights, and albeit in cars borrowed from friends. If he only knew where the road was going.

●

PHIL WALDEN and Joe Galkin had tiptoed around each other in the weeks leading up to the Stax session. Galkin, playing it cool about Redding, acted as if he cared little about him. Otis, he told Walden, unconvincingly, was "a lousy singer."[11] He also brought up Redding's string of failed records. Walden also played it equally cool. "Phil may have been young, but he had smarts up the yin-yang," says Alex Hodges. "Do you seriously think he would have let Otis get away from him because he was conned by a big-talking guy like Joey Galkin? Phil could see right through him. He didn't believe a word Galkin said. He never let him forget who managed Otis. Not that Galkin would have let that stop him. The main thing for Phil was, 'Hey, let's get this thing done, let's get Otis on tape for Jim Stewart, then we'll cross the next bridge.'"

Bobby Smith was that bridge. With no idea what was happening behind his back, Smith kept his word to Otis, by having him cut a demo of "These Arms of Mine." Smith again took him to the studio, where Dennis Wheeler was hanging out. "He came in and started humming this song, and me and a bunch of other guys just jumped in and started playing behind him. That's something I'll never forget, being with Otis's very first recording of 'These Arms of Mine.' And you know what? It sounded just as good as when he recorded it for Stax. When Otis sang, he didn't hold anything back, demo or not. He sang for the love of singing, not according to where he was. The thing to remember is that Otis loved Bobby, they were very, very good friends, like family." A pause. "But even family don't tell each other *everything*."

How much Otis was keeping from Smith only he knew, though he could hardly have believed he was destined to land at Stax, and he was no doubt being kept in the dark about what was bubbling all about him. All he knew was that he had been slogging away in the clubs and amusement parks, and on nights with no gigs, he took jobs as a parking lot attendant and a hospital orderly. His first daughter Karla's birth was a month away, meaning even bigger bills staring him in the face.

When February came along and it was time for Jenkins's audition at Stax, all he knew about it was that Johnny would need a lift to Memphis. That, of course, was a perfect coincidence for Galkin, whose job it was to get both Jenkins and Redding to Memphis. The other Pinetoppers would not be going, since Stewart had made it clear he was taking a flyer only on Johnny, not his group.

That's all that Smith knew, as well. Always trying to be of help, Bobby helped write his own death warrant when he kicked in a car for the trio to use on the 467-mile drive to Memphis. The car turned out to be owned by Wayne Pierce, whose station wagon was usually parked outside Smith's house. Pierce agreed to give Otis the key. What's more, although Smith had no inkling that Otis might sing for Stewart in Memphis, Wheeler ventures that Bobby would have been all for it, as such an audition might redound to *his* benefit, if Stax and Atlantic became involved with Confederate Records. Phil Walden had indeed told Otis to be ready to sing, and not some Little Richard impression but real soul. But Phil would not be able to go himself. He was preparing for his Army induction, leaving Galkin all the room he needed to present himself as Redding's sole manager.

And so it was, with all this intrigue and clandestine thievery in the air, Fate and an old station wagon took Jenkins, Galkin, and Otis Redding up to Memphis on a midnight ride.

6

"Wait, We Got Time for Another Kid"

The home of the Memphis blues had been another lure for African-Americans migrating from the Deep South. Sam Phillips's work with Howlin' Wolf, B. B. King, and Ike Turner carried over from the blues and jazz clubs along Beale Street in the inner-city west side, where W. C. Handy's band had once played music he said came from "Negro roustabouts, honky-tonk piano players, wanderers and others of the underprivileged but undaunted class."[1] Memphis was bigger but not much different than Macon, under the yoke of Jim Crow. As early as 1866 there had been race riots in the city, and a century later, emotions were still simmering. In the early 1960s, the city closed the public swimming pool rather than obey a court order to integrate it.[2]

But it was white men who provided the connection between past and present, first the bombastic Sam Phillips, then the mild-mannered Union Planters Bank clerk Jim Stewart. Born in 1930, Stewart was a fiddler in a band called the Canyon Cowboys before founding Satellite Records in his garage in Middleton, Tennessee.

He convinced his older sister, Estelle, to loan him $2,500 for an empty storefront in nearby Brunswick, and they became co-owners, welding rockabilly to rock and roll with bands like Fred Byler and the Tunetts, Donna Rae and the Sunbeams, and Don Willis and the Orbits. Making a few bucks, the Stewarts moved to the big town in 1961, converting the old Capitol Theater into an office/studio, and changing the company to Stax Records. The adjoining Satellite record store was operated by Estelle, one of two influential Tennessee women coincidentally named Axton at the time, the other Nashville's Mae Boren Axton, who co-wrote "Heartbreak Hotel" for Elvis Presley.

Estelle's son, Charles "Packy" Axton," formed the label's house band, originally called, of all things, the Royal Spades. Packy played sax, his guitarist was a tall, gangly guy named Steve Cropper, and his bassist was a squat fireplug with curly hair, Donald "Duck" Dunn. Stewart's first house producer, Chips Moman, who had produced the first hits on Satellite, buffed his spare arrangements with the blazing horn section of Axton, Wayne Jackson, and Don Nix. Then, when Moman fell out with Stewart and quit, Cropper became de facto producer for almost all the songs recorded at Stax, with the same small, tight coterie of musicians.

The great Rufus Thomas was an important adjunct. Thomas *was* black radio in Memphis, as a member of one of the country's first all-black DJ lineups, on WDIA. He also already had success at Sun Records and had hosted talent shows that broke out B. B. King, Ike Turner, and Bobby "Blue" Bland. In 1960, he did a duet on Satellite with his fifteen-year-old daughter Carla, called "'Cause I Love You," and then produced her on "Gee Whiz." Father and daughter became fixtures on the renamed Stax label, as Stewart chartered it on a parallel course with Berry Gordy's black-owned Motown label, though Stewart lacked Gordy's autocratic, vise-like grip on all matters in and out of the studio. For example, Motown artists were not even permitted to do, or see, their own tax returns; the company accountants did it for them.[3] Nor did Gordy pay any mind to the inherent conflict of interest in managing the acts whose records he released—the same conflict that Bobby Smith had with Otis.

The beacon-like STAX sign quickly became a magnet for what was the core of a new, collegial Memphis music scene. "Being treated like an equal human being . . . was really a phenomenon," says Al Bell, who came to the company in 1965 and later became executive vice president, then president. "The spirit that came from Jim and Estelle allowed all of us, black and white, to . . . come into the doors of Stax, where you had freedom, you had harmony, you had people working together."[4] Where Gordy built a strict producer-centric caste system in order to distill the blacker edges of blues-based music to expressly appeal to the white market, Stewart just let fly whatever came from the studio, where anyone could have a say in the production.

As a result, the sound coming from the studio was blacker than the famed, heavily formulaic "Motown sound," and Stewart would pointedly append the "Soulsville" emblem to the Stax name. Still, Wayne Jackson notes that Stax "was *not* formed as a 'black music' label. That's a fallacy. Jim wanted the best talent he could find in Memphis. We had all played in the clubs, where there were no racial barriers. I was sometimes the only white guy onstage, and sometimes Andrew Love, a great tenor sax player who came in after Packy Axton left, was the only black guy. The singers were black because they were the best, too, but the musicians were mainly white. The Royal Spades were all white.[5]

Not everyone in Memphis was as sure that Stewart had the interests of the underclass at heart. Years later, Stewart would recall that the city's chapter of the NAACP "wanted to know who I was and what I was all about . . . what my intentions were and if black people would be treated as they should in the company [and] would they ever be in a capacity of management and have real power in the company."[6] Wexler, to be sure, saw how advantageous Stax could be as a talent feeder.

By 1962, with many of the original R&B-oriented labels in decline or gone, Atlantic faced a crossroads. Ahmet and Nesuhi Ertegun, the co-founding brothers of the company, had written one of the unlikeliest but most impressive success stories in popular music. Once they were literally "young Turks" in the business. Born in Istanbul, they had emigrated as teenagers in 1935 when their father was named Turkey's ambassador to the U.S. In 1947 they founded Atlantic, primarily as a jazz label, having become smitten with black musical idioms while living in Washington, D.C. However, as vital as they were to the transition of rhythm and blues to rock and roll, the toothy siblings—the bald, jive-talking Ahmet a pure-bred attention-getter with hip pronouncements basted in a nearly indecipherable accent, while the shaggy-haired Nesuhi remained in the shadows—their traditional tastes relied greatly on heavy-weights like Ray Charles and Bobby Darin. In danger, however, of being curators instead of creators, it fell to the grizzled Jerry Wexler to reinvent the company as a funnel of new voices. A former *Billboard* reporter, Wexler had coined the term "rhythm and blues" for the new genus of blues in the 1950s. But now that term was passé, and the era of LaVern Baker's "Tweedle Dee" and Big Joe Turner's "Shake, Rattle and Roll," which had helped build Atlantic into a player, was long since over.

As in the changing tide of politics, it was obvious that the future of music belonged to a new generation. Indeed, when a new president, the first born in the twentieth century, took office in 1960 speaking of an incipient "New Frontier," he meant a metaphoric landscape of ideas, open to those previously ignored. JFK's prescience could have, of course, also been applied to the culture of young black singers who, having seen the successes and exploitations of the previous generation of black talent, were about to take over, with newer, more

meaningful modes of expression. They had to come from somewhere. Like, say, Macon, Georgia.

•

THE THREE-MAN party from Macon arrived in Memphis on February 9. Instead of checking in at a hotel they went straight to the
Stax office on East McLemore Street. Parking outside, Otis carried all the luggage into the old theater, leading everyone into the
drafty studio, believing he was only there as a drudge, not a performer. After Galkin was taken to see Jim Stewart, and introduced
him to Johnny, Otis, with nothing to do, leaned his back against a
studio wall, crossed his arms, and waited as the musicians began
to set up. These were the men who played on nearly every single
Stax session, an updated Mar-Keys that included Booker T. Jones
on the organ and drummer Al Jackson Jr., Jones being a child
prodigy who was still only eighteen at the time and not yet out of
high school. Now, with Cropper's writing and production skills
evidenced by the breakout success of "Green Onions," even with
Stewart's communal-minded directive that had all members of
the band share the writing credit for the song, the elongated guitar
player was the de facto leader of nearly all sessions, though it was
Booker T. whose name defined the MG's.

A common memory among them through the years was that the
first time they set eyes on Otis Redding, he was a dominating figure but only because of his size. Cropper, who was standing on the
curb when the car pulled up, believed he was "like six foot six," as
he watched Otis unfold from the station wagon and go around to the
trunk and begin removing musical equipment. He had taken out
Jenkins's guitar and a couple of microphones when the elongated
Cropper walked over.

"Hey, man," he said. "You know, we're not gonna need these
microphones. We got our own microphones."

"Well, I'm gonna bring our stuff in anyway," Redding told him.

Shrugging, Cropper continued watching him lug the gear into the building, convinced the overgrown young man was only there as Jenkins's driver—or, as Cropper says with a laugh, "A *val-et*," drawing out the word playfully. "In those days, that's what they called a driver."[7]

Floyd Newman, the sax man and longtime habitué on the Memphis club scene, has particularly vivid memories of Otis that day. Newman, who had provided the indelible spoken intro on "Last Night," cooing seductively "Ooh-ooooh, last night," did not play on the session, but pulls from his memory an image of Redding clad in "a white suit, a hospital suit. I believe he was working in a hospital in Macon and went right from that job and came up here."[8] Newman also swears that Phil Walden was there with him that day, which only proves how unreliable the mind can be when reaching back in time. To be sure, Walden was nowhere to be seen as the band was given sheet music by Jenkins, and then played two songs behind his lead guitar, instrumentals named "Spunky" and "Bashful Guitar." Wexler's two thousand dollars had bought a full three hours of studio time, as Galkin wanted a big enough window for both Jenkins and Redding to sing. But Galkin began to get a little nervous when Jenkins's discomfort recording with strangers drew out the time and prompted numerous retakes.

As the clock ticked, the musicians went through continual adjustments and meetings in the control room, where Stewart sat at the mixing board, getting frustrated. Galkin was, too, and kept checking his watch. Otis, as well, was getting antsy. Having been coached by Phil Walden to get himself some time, he took to bugging Al Jackson between takes. As Otis remembered the scene years after, "I asked if I could record ['These Arms of Mine']. The musicians had been working with Johnny all day, and they didn't have but twenty minutes before they went home."[9] According to Jackson, it finally happened because he had been asked so many times by

Otis that he just wanted to shut him up. "Hey, there's a guy here with Johnny, and he's been after me all day long about wanting to hear him sing," Jackson said to Cropper. "Could you take five minutes to listen to this guy sing?"[10]

•

IT WASN'T Cropper's call, of course, and at around six o'clock, with forty minutes left to the session, much to Galkin's relief, Stewart, more in frustration than anything, decreed, "Okay, it's good," meaning, wrap it up.[11] Jenkins had his two songs in the can. The band started to scatter. According to Jenkins, he should have gotten credit for getting Otis in front of the microphone. He swore he went over to Stewart and said, "Hey, why not let Otis use the rest of my time?" Fanciful as that tale is, it was Galkin, sitting behind Stewart behind the glass, who got it done.

"Wait," he said, "we got time for another kid."

"What kid?"

"The other kid out there. He's a singer."

Galkin, a man Jerry Wexler called "an irresistible pain in the ass," pointed out, in his cloying way, that he had paid for the time and fibbed that Jerry Wexler had only fronted the dough if both kids got to sing."

"Nobody told me," Stewart repeated.

"I thought Jerry told you."

"Jerry doesn't tell me anything."

"Look, are we gonna sit here or are we gonna get this kid in front of a microphone?"

"What's the song?"

Joey had no idea. "Otis," he called to Redding, who was starting to pack up Jenkins's gear, "the big man wants to hear you sing. What you got?"

Newman's version was that the man he believed to be Phil

Walden, who was actually most likely Galkin, turned to Redding as the room was emptying and said, "Otis, you wanna try one song?"

Redding, perhaps not completely surprised, indeed had a song, though not, as Redding would later recall, "These Arms of Mine," but one he had written in Bobby Smith's office, a blues rocker called "Hey Hey Baby." Stewart had him hum a few bars, then called through the intercom, "One more, guys."

By then, Duck Dunn had split; hearing Otis vamp the song, he was unimpressed, as were the other session men. Booker T. and some of the others were outside the door. Lewie Steinberg was on the premises and was asked to play bass. Whoever else was still around sat down—and if you talk to Booker T. today, he will say he was one of them. However, in Steve Cropper's memory, "Booker had already left for the day, so I sat down at the piano, which I play only a little for writing."

"What key?" Cropper asked.

"It don't matter," Otis replied.[12]

When recording "Hey Hey Baby," he tried to sing in a more mature, slightly lower register, though once again his voice became strained on the fadeout. Johnny would recall that "his timing was bad. So I stayed there with him, got it right down pat, enough for them to record something."[13] Indeed, the most compelling element of the tune was a hot-lick solo by Jenkins.

Stewart was not overly impressed. "The world's not waiting for another Little Richard," he said. Stewart, however, was impressed by the *voice* he had heard. "You got another one?" he asked Redding. He did, though he might have been a little sheepish about singing it, as "These Arms of Mine" was not only on the market, performed by Buddy Leach and the Playboys, but also on Otis's demo record sitting in Smith's office. Knowing it was his strongest song, he would sing it again, for Stewart, and when he did, the Stax president was stunned by the unabashed rawness and measured nuance of his voice, little of which had been heard during the first song. As Cropper recalls, "Man, my hair stood on end. Jim came running out and said, 'That's it! That's it! Where is everybody? We gotta get this on tape!' So I grabbed all the musicians who hadn't left already for their night gigs, and we recorded it right there."

Redding had only one directive for the band. "Just gimme those church things," Cropper remembers Otis telling him, meaning quick three-note repetitions on the piano, or triplets, which Cropper would play throughout. The song was, in musician-speak, a 6/8 time signature, a slow, romantic groove caressed by the drum beat. Eschewing any instrumental intro, Stewart had him sing the first few bars sonically naked, accompanied only by silent air and a thick echo. And that vocal stirred some heavy gravy as he began, chucking Little Richard for something deep, something that seemed to make the words quake. "*These arms of-a mine, they are lonely. Lonely and feeling blue*," he began, letting them roll out of his mouth slowly, sinuously. The song's simple lyrics needed no real embellishment other than the remarkably mature nuances he gave them, with a quiver and colloquial accents—high-emotion words drawn out as "yearning-ah" or "wanting-ah."

At the dramatic peak, he sang so softly that it sounded more like he was purring, or even speaking, not quite a prototypical rap. The band came in with a basic rock arrangement, Cropper's triplets stamped by Jackson's metronomic snare and cymbal, and Jenkins added neat little twiddle flourishes. It was by no means a new sound. Clearly derivative of the 1959 Brook Benton R&B ballad "It's Just a Matter of Time," it was the voice that carried every inch of it. Stewart would recall that no one there "jumped up and down and said we've discovered a superstar." He did think the song was "different" but that "we were all tired and bummed out." He announced, "Okay, it's good" and that was that.[14]

Cropper however tells it differently, indicating that Stewart was putting on his diffidence so as not to tip his hand. "When you hear something that's better than anything you ever heard, you know it, and it was unanimous. We almost wore out the tape playing it afterward." Cropper himself says, "I'd never heard anything like that before." Booker T., possibly from imagination, adds, "It didn't seem like an audition at all. It was a performance. It wasn't the size of his voice, we knew lots of people with vocal powers like that. It was the intent with which he sang. He was all emotion." He can even recall that Redding had sung the song in B-flat.

Stewart then took Galkin aside to talk shop. Twenty minutes later, they emerged, with papers for both Johnny Jenkins and Otis Redding to sign. They both scribbled their names, and the lights of the studio were turned out. It had been an eventful three hours, even if neither Otis nor Johnny knew the half of it.

●

BOTH CAME away from Memphis believing that neither of them should hold their breath. They talked about upcoming Pinetopper gigs. Joey Galkin turned his attention to other young talent he made notes to go see perform in the clubs. Both Galkin and Phil Walden, who had been apprised of the double session, took a wait and see approach. And Bobby Smith, with Otis back home, made plans to take him into the studio to record "These Arms of Mine," blissfully unaware that Otis had sung the song at Stax. In fact, nothing much happened for several weeks. Then Smith got a call from his friend John R., the Nashville DJ, who told him he'd been to an industry convention in St. Louis and seen Joe Galkin making the rounds playing a tape of Redding's "These Arms of Mine" for radio station people. The song, he said, was about to be released by Stax, and Galkin was already plugging it. John R., who knew the song from the Buddy Leach version, wondered if Smith knew about it. Smith was dumbfounded. John had some advice. "Better check your contract," he said, meaning the one Smith had with Otis Redding.[15]

Actually, he needed to check the contracts Otis and Joe Galkin had already signed with Jim Stewart in Memphis, which had opened the way for him to release "These Arms of Mine" as a single. Stewart, hedging his bet on Redding a bit, put out the song, backed with "Hey Hey Baby," on his sub-label, Volt, which had been created as a way to get around the policy that radio stations had begun to implement of not playing too many songs from any one label, as a way to avoid payola allegations. Otis had been told only days before, when Phil Walden broke the news to him, that he had signed a Stax recording contract, which would run for three years with two two-year options, at the standard royalty of three and a half cents per record sold. Since he had just turned twenty-one when he signed, it was legal and binding.

It was all too obvious why Galkin had not told Smith: It was pure larceny. Apparently Joe hoped that, once it was all out in the open, Smith would simply hand over Otis to the big boys at Stax and Atlantic, groveling for a chance to get future Orbit records into the Atlantic distribution line. Smith, however, wasn't quite so easily shoved aside. When he recovered from the shock, the first thing he did was to call Otis and ask him how it had happened. Otis, as naive as a man could be, stammered that he thought Stewart had merely wanted to get him on tape and was never told a record was coming out of it.

That was true enough, and of course Smith had not been averse to Otis going to Memphis—quite the contrary. He may have even been okay with "These Arms of Mine" being a one-off record for Stax, to get Otis some well-connected exposure. However, it had all been done in secret, and not only did he believe Stewart had breached Otis's contract with Smith, he also believed that he had undercut a record Smith had out on the market. Nor did Smith know something else, even more insidious, about Joe Galkin posing as Otis's manager in Memphis. Indeed, that little flim-flam prompted Phil Walden, home on furlough, to suddenly hop to it and officially sign Otis to a three-year personal management contract. Walden stuck a paper in front of Otis—yet another page in what was now an endless stream of them—who again signed, and again legally.

Walden wasted no time taking a meeting with Galkin, to whom he was appreciative and who still had a lot of leverage. The two men, again, with not a word of input from the subject of their business, agreed on a fifty-fifty split of publishing royalties on all present and future Redding songs—actually, a fifty-fifty split of the half-ownership of those rights Galkin already owned. That worked out to a quarter cut each of the publishing for Galkin and Walden, half for Jim Stewart. Nothing for Otis Redding. Galkin, a sort of shadow co-manager, would also receive 30 percent of Redding's record sales, in perpetuity.

Smith, still figuring he was Otis's manager and employer, called Stewart, who was curt, saying that Redding was underage and Smith had no case. Feeling like he'd been kicked in the groin, and certain that Otis's contract was legal, Smith next rang up Galkin, who felt no need for soft soap. "Yeah," he told Smith, "I went ahead and recorded him. He wasn't twenty-one when he signed your contract."[16] The only way Galkin could have known that was if he had actually seen the contract; but if he did, he might have seen Fannie Mae Redding's signature on it, obviating the underage claim. Instead, it seemed he had merely asked Otis when he had signed the contract, and merely assumed he had signed it alone, when he was underage. Either way, Smith figured he very much had a case. He told Galkin, "You won't get away with this." Then he hired a lawyer, who immediately bore in on Galkin, getting him to admit he had been after Otis from the start.[17] But Jim Stewart's lawyers—big-time New York attorneys who represented Atlantic—would be able to drag any lawsuit on and bleed Smith dry before the case was ever adjudicated. Reluctantly, Smith's lawyer advised him to come to a settlement. The most Stewart would ante was seven hundred dollars, for the retroactive mechanical rights to "These Arms of Mine." Smith, already tired of wrangling, took it, but under a false impression.

"Bobby thought he was only selling 'These Arms of Mine,' that Otis would still be on Orbit, and Bobby was still his manager," says Wheeler, with a sad shake of the head. "Listen, I loved Bobby Smith. He was a good old boy and here he was up against Atlantic Records. Bobby had one eye and had to put a paper right up to his head to read it, but small print he couldn't read. And what happened was, he got hoodwinked, real bad. He thought he was makin' a deal and wound up signing over *everything*. And Bobby never got over it. He didn't blame Otis and not even Galkin. He blamed Phil Walden, who he thought had planned to screw him over. They were good friends, Phil did booking for Confederate, but it was like Cain and Abel. Bobby Smith, he held a grudge against Phil Walden until the day he died."[18]

Jerry Wexler was also cheesed off. His two-thousand-dollar seed money had gotten him a minor hit to distribute but, more importantly, a talent to be reckoned with. But, now, he wished he had Redding directly on the label. "If things had gone according to Hoyle," he said years later in his authorized biography, *Rhythm & Blues: A Life in American Music*, "Otis would have been signed to Atlantic; we had, after all, financed his first session. But Jim Stewart wanted him on Stax, and our arrangement was working so well that I let it pass.... Had I stuck to business-only principles, he would have been Atlantic's first international star of the sixties."[19]

If anyone had told that to Otis Redding at the time, he would have been the one who laughed loudest.

1

Chops like a Wolf

" "These Arms of Mine" had a belated trip to the charts. Aimed by the Atlantic song pluggers exclusively at the R&B market, it earned a very rare distinction for such a record by somehow showing up in the November 21, 1962, issue of *Variety* as a "record review top pick of the week." It began selling slowly, sporadically, not enough to make a wave. Alan Walden and Alex Hodges found no great rise in temperature on the club circuit over Otis Redding getting a tour up and going, so a caravan was created with Otis and two soul veterans, Percy Welch and Joe Tex, one of King Records' stable of '50s R&B acts. Tex was a ridiculously exciting showman, building a following by opening for, and damn near stealing the show from, Little Richard, Jackie Wilson, and James Brown, with his nimble, even acrobatic moves, in which he used the microphone as a prop, either as a phallic symbol or to be tossed high in the air and caught with perfect timing.

The tour around Georgia and the Carolinas barely broke even, and by the new year of 1963, Otis was once more back in the Macon clubs. Then, during this lull, John R., the Nashville DJ who had first heard "These Arms of Mine" on record, couldn't keep from playing it, even if it was "stolen" from his friend Bobby Smith. He even told Jim Stewart he thought it was a potential smash. Stewart, who had come to hear the song as a black country record for its slow-drawling lyrics, got a laugh out of that, but the jock kept on playing it, night after night. By March 1963, four months after its release, it finally made the R&B chart, peaking at number 85 pop, number 20 R&B, and selling a quite healthy 800,000 copies. In gratitude, Stewart gifted John R. his share of the publishing royalties that had been lifted from Otis.[1] If this was blatant payola, no one ever knew it, or considered it worth looking into. But then, the Stewarts seemed to be bulletproof in matters like these. Estelle Axton, for another example, not only operated the Satellite record store next door, she was somehow able to have it designated by *Billboard* as a "reporting store" in the mid-1960s, one of a number of selective music emporiums around the country from which the magazine could extrapolate its chart rankings, according to the records that moved the most vinyl. And Estelle, an enormously respected figure, did not hesitate to pump up the sales of Stax/Volt product. She also, it was said, sold records that disc jockeys had gotten for free and funneled to her.[2]

At this juncture, money was almost a secondary concern for Otis, who shared the same lineage and predicament of countless other young black singers for whom a signed contract with a reputable record company offered only vague promises of future profit, and hardly ever immediate reward. Alan Walden, handling royalty disbursement in place of his lieutenant brother, basically paid Otis out of his own pocket, as generously as he could, which wasn't very much, given that Walden Artists and Promotions was very much in the red. As Walden says, "Phil had trained me to be a booking agent and the manger of Otis Redding. Twelve hours to run a company singlehanded for the next two years! The first year it was very rough.

Phil told me he left five thousand dollars in the bank—but failed to mention ten thousand dollars worth of debts."[3]

As it was, Otis was probably better off than many other artists who were tenured longer and had bigger hits under their belts. That was glaringly evident at Atlantic, where the backbone of the roster was the Drifters, a band managed by George Treadwell, the former big band horn man who was married to blues singer Sarah Vaughan. This would be the longest-running, and most exploited, franchise in the rock and roll era. Treadwell's penury was what led the Drifters' lead singer Clyde McPhatter to go solo, opening a revolving door operated by Treadwell until his death in 1967, with around sixty members of the Drifters cycling through without ever getting a fair share of royalties. "We were just boys from the ghetto," says Charlie Thomas, a Harlem native who toured with the group well into his seventies. "We were getting screwed all our lives."[4] Another example: Louisiana blues singer Phil Phillips notched a number 1 R&B and number 2 pop hit in 1959 with the haunting "Sea of Love." While it sold over a million copies, Atlantic paid Phillips all of $6,800 and no future royalties. Phillips, who is eighty-seven, says he never went back in the studio because "I never received justice and to this day have not received justice."[5]

But if Otis wasn't much heavier in the pocket for "These Arms of Mine," at least he had a record to sell, and a tour in support of it. With new avenues opening up, Alan Walden and Alex Hodges could book him without making a single call; the promoters were calling *them*. "That little record got around," says Hodges, "especially in the urban demographic. And we were getting sometimes three hundred to four hundred dollars a gig. You could tell things were happening out there. You could feel it. The world was ready for Otis Redding."[6]

•

OTIS TRAVELED mainly solo and rehearsed with local bands, before a backup band was hired to sojourn with him. As Walden describes them, they were "this great band from Newport News, Virginia, that had a great horn section, full rhythm section, and a male singer, Roy Hines, and a female singer named Gloria Stevenson." Looking sharp, they rented a 1949 Flexie tour bus draped with signs reading THE OTIS REDDING SHOW AND REVUE. At times they would play seven nights a week, all in different towns. In fact, about the only thing that broke up these endless travels were recording sessions, something that now were of utmost importance. "These Arms of Mine" certainly earned Otis a return trip to Memphis, and when he went back for a session on June 24, 1963, he was no longer the driver and valet, he was a man Jim Stewart was banking on. Whether he had become more arrogant or simply more comfortable with the musicians, Otis came in completely in charge.

"I mean, we had a lot of strong-willed guys, but this was his *second* time in the building and he was ready to give orders," says Wayne Jackson.[7]

The musicians in the room—Studio B, Stewart was calling it, though there was no studio A, perhaps because Motown's landmark studio was called Studio A—consisted of not only the Mar-Keys/ Booker T. nucleus (Steve Cropper, Lewie Steinberg, Al Jackson) but a horn section for the first time: Wayne Jackson on trumpet, Packy Axton on tenor sax, and Floyd Newman on baritone sax. Newman, who may or may not have been there when "These Arms of Mine" was cut, was bowled over by the young man arriving armed with a full horn arrangement, all in his head. "He had his songs down one hundred percent. He'd worked it all out. He knew exactly when he wanted the horns to come in. He would hum what he wanted us to play. It was a lot like James Brown. He wanted the horns to fill the gap between lines, a basic call and response thing. It wasn't like he was feeling around for something. It was gonna go down only one way."[8]

Otis had also brought along Johnny Jenkins, whose guitar work had so affected the texture of "These Arms of Mine" that Cropper was once again forced to the piano on the first of two songs cut that day. The first tune, a soul-stropped version Cropper had written of an old children's song he retitled "Mary's Little Lamb," was an idea first broached by Chuck Berry's guitar on "Guitar Boogie" and Stevie Wonder on the harmonica in "Fingertips (Part 2)," a song that was shooting up the charts at the time. In Cropper's concept, the song came out with a cheeky urban skew about the little lamb who, in this take, had "bleeks" as white as snow—ghetto slang for dark-skinned white people. Of note too was that the song had backup vocals by the Veltones—a white band that in 1959 had been the first ever recorded at Stax. It was to be one of the few times anyone would ever sing behind Otis.

The other track, without Jenkins and with Cropper on guitar, was "That's What My Heart Needs," a jilted man's plea, with some hip Redding street vernacular: "I'm calling you out loud and clear, baby." Like "These Arms of Mine," it began with Otis kicking right into the lyrics, to be joined by the horns, Cropper's country-style pickin' (Otis's idea), and climaxed with Otis's wailing, gospel-flecked fadeout.

There were flaws in the song but the voice burned hot, and as it hit the market Stewart wanted to keep the momentum and stockpile enough material for a Redding album. By September 26, only three months after recording "That's What My Heart Needs," and "Mary's Little Lamb," Stewart had him back in the studio again, despite Otis having run dry on original material. Instead, Otis brought two songs he and Phil Walden had allegedly co-written before Walden left for Germany, "Pain in My Heart" and "Something Is Worrying Me." If anything, what *should* have been worrisome was that "Pain in My Heart" was actually taken from a song earlier that year by Irma Thomas, the "soul queen of New Orleans," called "Ruler of My Heart," written by the wonderful Allen Toussaint under the pseudonym Naomi Neville. Otis and Walden reworked the title and lyrics, and Otis gave it a muscular, heart-palpitating ride, escorted by the horns of Wayne Jackson, Packy Axton, and Floyd Newman—one variation of what Jerry Wexler would by early 1965 come to semi-officially call "the Memphis Horns."

The song, which the Rolling Stones would also eventually cover, was likewise credited to Redding-Walden when released in October, but it quickly stalled on the charts. Part of the problem was that the performance of harder-core soul records like this could not be accurately gauged because *Billboard*, that same fall, had suspended its R&B singles and albums charts that had been around since 1949, on grounds that the genre had succeeded in crossing over into the broader pop category. This unfortunate decision ignored the still-extant ethnic appeal of black-rooted music, and would last until the magazine wised up and reinstated the R&B chart in 1965 (and endure until 1969 when the "Hot Rhythm & Blues Singles" chart was renamed "Best Selling Soul Singles").

While the "blackout" was in effect, it was as if all but the most popular crossover soul music (Motown, even though a fixture on the R&B list, had no problem coping) was in exile, and the marketing value of a high chart ranking stripped from just about every Stax release. The company, and Otis, had to make do with the *Cash Box* version of the R&B chart, which like the trade paper's other charts were generally less respected, and ranked "What My Heart Needs" at number 27 R&B, and "Pain in My Heart" at number 61 pop, number 11 R&B. Nonetheless, when Jerry Wexler surveyed his rich roster of soul acts and came up with an ambitious project for them, Otis was to be a major part of it.

●

THE PROJECT was a live recording to be made at Harlem's famed Apollo Theater on November 15. The idea, called the Atlantic Caravan of Stars, was hatched by Jerry Wexler and meant to unite Stax and Atlantic acts in a weeklong extravaganza, the second night of which, the traditional Apollo Saturday midnight show, would be recorded and released as a live album showcasing the biggest talent in soul music. It would be one of the top concert events ever arranged up until then, a major leap for soul, and among the assembled acts—Ben E. King, the Coasters, Rufus Thomas, Doris Troy, and the Falcons—Otis was something like a rookie in the big leagues. Hyped heavily in the press, it drew headlines in the black papers, such as ATLANTIC TO RECORD STARS ON APOLLO STAGE SATURDAY in the *New York Amsterdam News*.[9]

Otis, as a "star," would take a step up, singing with the house band for the engagement, one culled from the cream of Atlantic's New York studio session players and headed by sax legend King Curtis and his band, which included a monster brass section, with Curtis, Jimmy Powell, Alva McCain, and Noble Watts on sax; Elmon and Lammar Wright Sr. on trumpet; George Matthews on trombone; as well as Jimmy Lewis on bass and Ray Lucas on drums. The Redding literature features differing versions of how he got to New York. In one account, he drove up from Macon in a Ford XL convertible with his brother, Rodgers, whom he often traveled with, and an ex-boxer, Sylvester Huckaby, as his bodyguard, and that the trio had so little money they had to stay at what Huckaby called "a big old raggedy hotel called the Theresa."[10] Another has it that Redding came all the way alone, on a bus, and had tried in vain to convince passengers he was going to sing at the Apollo.[11]

Jerry Wexler, for his part, recounted that he picked Otis up at LaGuardia Airport, having paid the fare for what was Redding's first ride in an airplane. Expecting an entourage of Macon peeps around him, he was surprised, he would recall, "to see him standing there alone—no valet, no roadie, no manager." Wexler thought there was "something pure about his personality, calm, dignified, vibrant. . . . The Otis I saw that night was essentially the same Otis I would always see. Stardom never changed him. He had a strong inner life. He was emotionally centered. His manners were impeccable. His humor was sly and roguish." Wexler would be especially amused when, after Redding met Ahmet Ertegun, he would call him "Omelet," with a straight face, not giving away if he did so intentionally.[12]

Wexler said he drove Redding to the Apollo, introduced him to the theater's owner, Bob Schiffman, then took him to dinner before dropping him at the Theresa. Rather than a "raggedy" flophouse, this storied old hotel was actually an oasis of elite black culture and society. Its thirteen-story, terra-cotta architecture and triangular steeples high above Seventh Avenue marked a familiar destination for swells who lived in its spacious rooms, including March on Washington organizer A. Philip Randolph, Louis Armstrong, Duke Ellington, and Malcolm X, who fifteen months later, after renouncing the Nation of Islam, was gunned down a few blocks away at the Audubon Ballroom. Fidel Castro had also stayed there in 1960. While Otis was there, a young boxer named Cassius Clay was renting the entire seventh floor for his entourage while he did promotional work for his upcoming challenge to Sonny Liston's heavyweight title that February.

Redding would be second in line at the Apollo shows, coming out after the Falcons and before Doris Troy. He, like many first-time arrivals at the old theater, was a bit let down by what he anticipated as a majestic mecca of black entertainment. The place was cramped, the stench of urine escaped from the bathrooms, the walls and floors were dingy, and as a newbie in the business he was given a dressing room on the top floor, up a long flight of stairs from the lobby. Yet, as with the Theresa, those walls practically breathed with history and tradition, and, rarely for him, Otis was extremely nervous on the opening night of the engagement. He had heard all about the Apollo, how the crowds were demanding and rabid, freely booing and catcalling performers, who, on Amateur Night, would be shooed off the stage by the "Executioner," a guy in a clown costume with a broomstick or a hook.

During these shows, and during rehearsals the week before, Otis was given advice by old pros Rufus Thomas and Ben E. King, yet it was still a daunting experience to go out onto that fabled stage. Said King, "Otis told me he was up from home and he was terrified. [He] said to me, 'You think they're gonna go for what I do, what we do down home?'" What's more, King believed, that fear became something of a permanent trait. "As long as I knew him, Otis never did get over that little bit of stage fright." King recalled that as Redding began, he kept looking to where Thomas was standing offstage.[13]

Rufus agreed, saying that Otis was so nervous and unsure of his stage presence, that not only he but the Apollo MC, King Coleman, had impressed on him that he should go out and focus very narrowly. "I trained him up in the moves, and showed Otis how to catch the eye of one girl, just one girl, and sing to her, so that her enthusiasm spread through the crowd. Coleman introduced him with the line, "He can sing baby, he can sing!" Otis, Thomas said, seemed in a trance. "He kept on repeating how he would miss his band, how his clothes were all wrong." Coleman once described Redding as a "big, bearlike man, sweating and trembling worrying about his suit, his voice, the band, everything."[14]

If so, then, he used the fear to play the part, withdrawing every ounce of passion he had. There was only enough time for him to sing two songs, "Pain in My Heart" and "These Arms of Mine," and he launched into a pair of remarkable exhibitions of both. As Thomas had tutored, he swayed and sometimes caressed the microphone as he would a woman's arm, but he rode solely on his voice. At first, seeming a little kinetic, the teeming audience was noisy, even rude during the early moments of his set, but began to pay closer attention as he emoted with ever more emotional power, drawing a few audible gasps and moans from the young women.

Watching from the audience, Wexler fell in love with Redding's voice, saying later that "Otis was magic," despite what he called the physical "inertia." As he noted, Redding "didn't know how to *move* in those days," a similarity he had with the young Marvin Gaye at Motown. "He just stood still, and he'd bend from the waist." But Wexler marveled at how the voice cut like a vector through aural space. "You could feel this plea coming from him."[15] Another time, Wexler said, "The women at the Apollo loved him, not only for his looks—he was tall, strapping, and handsome—but for his voice and vulnerability . . . Otis had chops like a wolf; his voice was big and gorgeous and filled with feeling. He also had a warmth that tempered the aggressive side of his soul, a porous strain of generous emotion that covered every song he sang."[16]

The last show of the Atlantic Caravan of Stars was, as it happened, on one of the darkest days in history, November 22, 1963. At around noon, Otis and Rufus Thomas were lounging around at the Theresa when people began screaming in horror at something, which, it became clear, was the shooting of the president while in arguably the most hate-filled city in the country, Dallas. Redding sat watching the TV in his room in glaze-eyed disbelief as reports confirmed the worst news imaginable an hour later. Some of the Apollo acts, including Otis, did not want to go on that night, but too much money had been made in ticket sales and the Atlantic honchos recast the show as a sort of gospel funeral, a laying on of hands for a man who openly courted black voters and had met with Dr. Martin Luther King Jr. in the White House after the March on Washington.

The delirium and mighty joy always stoked in the venerable theater was greatly tempered, even shrouded. The audience was muted, and each act dedicated their set to the slain president. When Redding came out, his fear had turned to genuine sadness and worry, allowing his performance to draw upon an even deeper well that night; he left with tears in his eyes. The live album of the gig, *Apollo Saturday Night*, released on the Atco label with a bright yellow and black jacket, had to contend with post-assassination ennui across all music corridors and, like all other music product, suffered for it. (The tracks would also be reissued on *Otis! The Definitive Otis Redding*.)

The spell would be broken in February when the Beatles came to America and immediately transformed the nature of music and the industry. While this was also crucial to recovering from the trauma of Dallas, it would pose a fresh set of challenges for American music, which would need to find a whole new center of gravity of its own in order to survive.

8

Turning the Knife

O tis Redding had been so richly entertaining at the Apollo yet left New York poor, so drained in the pocket that he had to bum a hundred bucks off Ben E. King after the final show (typically, he repaid the loan out of the blue, with King opening a piece of mail one day and finding a check from Otis)—and virtually on the same level playing field as the other acts, even though without a top 40 hit. But he had gained enough of a reputation that Stax and Atlantic were eager to record a Redding album. Such compilations at the time were normally perfunctory exercises meant to wring a few dollars more out of an artist's one or two hits by surrounding them with filler, mainly songs that had been rejected for release.

This formula was applied again; his three modestly successful singles, "These Arms of Mine," "That's What My Heart Needs," and "Pain in My Heart," were padded by covers of Rufus Thomas's "The Dog," Ben E. King's "Stand By Me," Sam Cooke's "You Send Me," the Kingsmen's "Louie Louie," Little Richard's "Lucille," and a real curve, R&B drummer/singer Don Gardner's 1962 duet with Dee Dee

Ford, "I Need Your Lovin' (Part 2)" (not the Four Tops' "Baby I Need Your Lovin'"), on which he repeated the song's gospel-style stop and start mid-song. The supplemental songs were recorded on January 16, some sounding hurried even with Redding's gushing abundance of sincerity on each track, and released two weeks later, not on the Volt label but, as with all the sub-label's albums, on Atco, per the Atlantic arrangement with Stewart. Not that it mattered much; by April, it peaked at number 103 on the album chart (again, there was no R&B album chart).

However, Jim Stewart had to deal with Redding's attempt to pull a fast one with "Pain in My Heart," which was also used as the title of the album. Though Otis no doubt believed he had sufficiently altered Allen Toussaint's tune, when the New Orleans producer got wind of it, he had his lawyer call Stewart, begging to differ. Dead to rights, Stewart agreed to redirect the writing royalties and replace Redding and Walden with Toussaint, as Naomi Neville, on all future pressings. However, in another sleight of hand, when the album was issued in England, where Redding's records were released by Atlantic on the London label, the credits still read "Redding, Walden," and would remain so, out of Toussaint's reach. Since the album hit number 28 on the British album chart, that ploy was profitable.

When it came to the fraternity of the business, sometimes it was more like fratricide. Still, Otis had merged easily into it and despite the slow sales of the album, Stewart hastened to release two more singles in quick succession, "Come to Me," which was cut at the sessions but saved for the next album, and "Security," the latter, co-written by Margaret Wesson, a perhaps too-conscious insistence that his purview was *not* monetary comfort—"Don't want no money, right," he sang, "I don't want no fame." It was the security of "sweet tender lips" that was his reward. If this was a call for deliverance from *insecurity*, it seemed only apropos that the melody, horns and all, seemed lifted from the Impressions' inspirational song whose title could have been intoned at the end of "Come to Me"—"Amen."

•

THOSE WHO actually knew Otis Redding were able to glimpse insights into his personality that ran deeper than the affable, seemingly carefree surface. Dennis Wheeler, for one, got a front-row seat for such revelations. "Otis was the type of guy who had a million acquaintances and few real friends," Wheeler says. "That's why if he really liked you, he'd hang on to your friendship. And he'd want you to experience his life." Once, when the pair exited the Peppermint Lounge, Otis suddenly said, "Come on," and they were rolling up Emory Highway in Dennis's car, with Otis giving him directions to a funeral parlor. A few days earlier, Redding's uncle had died and Otis thought it would be instructive to Wheeler to see how black people held a wake, which was, Wheeler says, "more like a family reunion, a party. His uncle was all dressed up in his casket and people came over and were talkin' to him, makin' jokes, like he was still alive. They'd leave a glass of booze on the casket and dance away." Wheeler, the only white person in the crowd, found himself toasting and dancing with everyone else. Otis, watching him enjoy the proceedings, at one point told him, "Dennis, I want to go out the same way. I wouldn't want no one just droppin' me into the ground. Have a party for me.'"[1]

That he remained close to Bobby Smith and his boys at Orbit, was another "tell," especially considering what had been done to him in the Stax shuffle. Being a favored artist in Memphis was plenty good for the ego, but Redding needed to know he had a sanctuary in Macon, where he spent a decreasing amount of time. When he was home, however, he always hung with the old crowd and even tried to do them favors. Not only were Speedo Sims and Oscar Mack on his payroll, but he also employed both in the backup band he had on standby when he played what would be one very big show a year at home, at the Macon City Auditorium. So eagerly awaited was this event that it earned Otis his first of what would be only a handful of articles in his hometown paper, the *Telegraph*, which on July 11, 1965, headlined a story about the show, MACON'S OWN OTIS REDDING RETURNS HOME, polishing the apple by writing, "With 1965 already half gone, music people have already established this year as THE Otis Redding year."[2]

He also got Oscar, who could sound uncannily like Redding, a shot at the big time, lining up a recording session for him at Stax in May 1964. There, Mack cut two songs, both of which he had written—"You'll Never Know How Much I Love You" and "Dream Girl"—with the latter being a tasty pop-soul confection that Otis unofficially produced, sang harmony on, and intoned a spoken intro paean to "the girl of my dreams." Though the ensuing record did little, Otis, too, would cut "Dream Girl," which would go unreleased until 1990.

Otis also brought in Jackie Avery, who had left L.A. to record in New Orleans. Avery would write for Otis's later protégé Arthur Conley, then in the 1970s he would be hired by Phil Walden's Capricorn Records label, composing "Blind Bats and Swamp Rats" for Johnny Jenkins and recording with the Allman Brothers and on his own, cutting "Our Love Has Brought Me (A Mighty Long Way)." "Otis would have produced all of us if he could have," laughs Wheeler. "He wanted to build his own studio and make us all stars."

This apparently included Johnny Jenkins, who swore until his last breath that Otis never stopped trying to ease the guilt he had over what had happened in Memphis. In 1963, Otis asked Jenkins to join his road band, something Jenkins said he had no interest in doing, one of the most ironic reasons being that he hated flying. Moreover, Jenkins quietly nursed a grudge and later in his life, after Redding had been deified in death, unleashed some harsh words that clashed with the man's saintly public image, telling author Peter Guralnick, "I knew [about] the prostitutes, the whores, but nobody wants to hear none of that . . . Well, you can put him up on a pedestal, call him an idol, but he wasn't no damn idol. He was a human being, that's what."[3]

Even as Otis kept moving up the ladder at Stax, he would make demos at Bobby Smith's new studio at the Georgian Hotel on Mulberry Street, which would be followed by barbecues, hunting and fishing forays, and bull sessions at the barbershop. These routines of life were his buffer zone, a way of keeping his feet planted in the Georgia soil, and refusing to rise too far above it. Once, he and Wheeler decided to have a barbecue at the latter's house, near the woods. Needing some meat, they picked up hunting rifles and waded into the brush. Seeing something move, and thinking it was a calf, Otis took a shot. When the moving stopped, the two men checked the kill and saw that the animal lying dead was in fact a bull, a huge one, so big they couldn't get it across the field, so they left it there. Before the shoot ended, they had bagged some chickens, not concerned that they happened to be in the yard of a farmer who lived in the woods. "We'd shoot and the lights in the house would go on so we'd stop, then when they went off we'd shoot again and go rustle up more chickens," Wheeler laughs. "We went on like that for hours and at the end Otis said, 'Lord have mercy, how many chickens have I stolen?'" Seeing Otis immensely enjoy himself in this country environment, Wheeler couldn't imagine him ever leaving. "Otis could have moved, anywhere, but logically to Memphis so he would be there whenever he wanted to record. All those Stax acts lived in Memphis. But that wasn't home to Otis. That was his place of business. Home was right here."

•

NEITHER "COME TO ME" nor "Security," both released in mid-1963, had lit any fires on the charts. Each rose no higher than number 69, though they found the mid-20s on the *Cash Box* R&B chart. But Jim Stewart was satisfied and further convinced that Redding was only one good song from a breakout. The search for one led to endless commuting to Memphis. On September 9, 1964, Otis cut "Chained and Bound" and "Your One and Only Man," which, if taken as a

Rorschach of where his head was at, perhaps indicated some seriously schizoid divergence about the nature of a man and woman "chained" in love and marriage and the decree that he had better be the only one. On the other hand, no such requirement needed to be said that she be the only one for *him*. As if trying to merge the two abstractions, he clarified in the hip-grinding ballad that he was *proud* of such bondage. The up-tempo "Your One and Only Man" seemed, conversely, to hold back some joyous emotion, possibly a subconscious struggle to give everything to the notion of being a one-woman man. Both were essential Redding bridges to becoming a more nuanced and more mature man, and writer, but "Chained and Bound," released as his next single, failed to catch crossover lightning and stalled at number 70 on the pop chart, though he did plant his flag deeper in the soul turf when it zoomed to number 6 on the R&B, his highest ranking there yet.

On December 28, 1964, he recorded two more, "That's How Strong My Love Is" and "Mr. Pitiful." The former was a cover of a ballad written by Memphis songwriter Roosevelt Jamison, who had sung it as an audition for Stewart. When nothing came of it, Stewart presented it to the ill-fated gospel soul singer O. V. Wright—victim of an early death at age forty-one after years of heavy drug use—who recorded it on another Memphis label. Only days after, Steve Cropper pitched it to Otis, who cut it, the intention being to release it as his next single. The session was beefed up by an already robust horn section, originally featuring Sammy Coleman on trumpet and Packy Axton and Floyd Newman on sax. When Cropper held a dub session, he brought in Wayne Jackson on trumpet, Ed Logan, Andrew Love, and Jimmy Mitchell on sax. All that brass, along with Cropper's stabbing guitar and by turns a thundering and whimpering rhythm section seemed to further brand Otis's gritty, barely tempered pleadings.

However, when the session was done, "Mr. Pitiful" got the play. Written by Redding and Cropper, their first collaboration, it cheekily adopted a moniker that A. C. "Moohah" Williams, an influential DJ at KDIA in Memphis, had recently hung on Otis for the torture he'd put himself through on songs like that. It had been cut as a demo before, and Cropper produced it in a more funky vein, its up-tempo brass accents different from any used before in a Redding song. With the trademark Booker T. piano swirls in the background, Otis seemed completely free and at ease, ad-libbing a falsetto "I want *youuu*, I want *youuu*" over and over on the fadeout, pleading and joyous at once—the prototypical Stax/Volt aural milieu. Cropper's influence on the songs he co-wrote with Redding has often been noted for giving them tighter structure. But Floyd Newman, a cynical old bird if ever there was one, had an alternate, if distinctly minority, view.

"Listen, here's the truth," he says. "Steve was just one of the musicians. A good guy, but he was part of a system set up by Jim Stewart. He owned the publishing and he wanted more, he wanted it all. So when Otis would come in with a song one hundred percent finished, Jim didn't want him to think it was a hundred percent finished. Jim had a setup where Steve would go with the artists somewhere, like a hotel, to work out songs and the next thing you knew, he'd be one of the writers of the song. And Jim had a piece of any song Steve had a writer's credit on. You can't fault Steve for that. He did what the boss told him. That's just how it worked."[4]

Cropper doesn't see it that way. To the guitar man, Redding "had the softness of Sam Cooke and the harshness of Little Richard, and he was his own man. When I wrote with Otis, my job was to help him finish his songs. He had so many ideas that I'd just pick one and say, 'Let's do this,' and we'd write all night long." Clearly, Redding was eager to accept Cropper's aid, as he wanted to grow as an artist and writer. Still, any modifications in lyrics or arrangements were secondary to what Redding brought to the studio. On a technical level, there was not much tinkering required.

"With Otis," Cropper noted, "it was all about feeling and expression. Most of his songs had just two or three chord changes, so there wasn't a lot of music there. The dynamics, the energy, the way we attacked it—that's hard to teach. So many things now are computer-generated. They start at one level and they stop at the same level, so there isn't much dynamic, even if there are a lot of different sounds."

He does agree with Newman about one thing—Redding never changed his own personal dynamic. He was a ball of movement, a blur in the dim studio. And he needed little help to mature as a singer or songwriter. As Booker T. Jones points out, "Range was not a factor in his singing. His range was somewhat limited. He had no really low notes and no really high notes. But Otis would do anything that implied emotion, and that's where his physicality came in, because he was such a strong, powerful man. Backstage, he would be like a prizefighter waiting to get out there."[5]

Lyrically, "Mr. Pitiful" was more nuanced, not just a simple plea/demand for sexual satisfaction. It seems to upbraid a shallow, materialistic friend until the emotion builds to where it becomes clear that he is the voice of his own conscience; *he* is the pitiful one, a beggar for love. What's more, the tonal signature of the song was more pungent. As Newman says, "Otis's songs from then on had a lot of sharp keys, which raise the notes a little, project more, let him sing in a wider range. He didn't even know about keys or theory or nothin' like that. He just knew what sound he wanted, every time."

•

ZELMA REDDING had always been understanding and then some about the realities of the road, never fooling herself into believing he was keeping his fly up. This was anything but unusual; Ray Charles, for example, had twelve children by ten different women, and married twice.[6] Otis was more responsible (or just lucky) and he had no intention of ever having another wife. Indeed, as tough and no-nonsense as Zelma was, like all music wives she had to readjust the traditional meters of fidelity. The reality was that Otis loved her and just passed time with whomever else wound up in his bed. And more than a few "whomevers" wound up there. Alan Walden, who often traveled with Otis on his seamless tours, enjoyed the spillover.

Walden once said that "there were always flocks of ladies backstage waiting just to touch his hand or whatever. Being single, I thoroughly enjoyed traveling with a guy who had such appeal. I stayed in his room one time and had more sexual conquests in one week than I had had maybe in a year before—and all I was doing was answering the phone. It was outrageous." There was a toll to pay, though. Zelma and Otis began butting heads about his endless time on the road and her place in his burgeoning career. As Zelma herself once recalled, "I just felt like I wasn't going to fit with him 'cause he was outgrowing me." Soon, this rumbling stretched long distance. The Temptations' Otis Williams recalls a telling interlude when he ran into Redding while the latter was performing in Detroit at the Phelps Lounge, a popular blues club. Chatting in the dressing room, they were competitive and territorial, but respected each other's style and respective domains. And Otis, who sometimes found it easy to unburden when in the company of those on the same uncertain climb up the industry backstairs, revealed more of himself to the Temptation than he may have realized. "I said, 'Otis, is your show over?' And he said, 'No, man, I came all the way down here to have a phone conversation with my wife, and she done hung up on me.' He was angry. He said, 'I don't play that shit.' Evidently they had an argument and he was turned off by it. But then he said he was gonna fly back to Macon. He was gonna do what he had to do with his life and then turn around and fly right back to Detroit. I stood there and thought, 'I don't believe he's gonna go all the way back there just to get in his wife's face and come on back. I never heard of such a thing. I mean, he was really upset by this argument they had."[7]

It was unclear whether Otis flew home to lay down the law to his woman—or to grovel at her feet for forgiveness. Given his split personality about fidelity and opportunity, and what constituted manliness and weakness, either would have been plausible. Regardless, the next day he would be right back in the same old maw of confusion and inner conflict. Perhaps the result of his flight to Macon became tangible nine months later when, early in 1965, another son, Otis Redding III, was born, which not only smoothed things out a bit with Zelma but honored the name handed down by Otis Ray Redding Sr.

"Mr. Pitiful" b/w "Strong," meanwhile, had a nice run up the charts in the winter of '65. "Pitiful" went to number 41 pop, twenty notches higher than "Pain in My Heart" had and Top 10 R&B (on the *Cash Box* chart). "That's How Strong My Love Is" then broke out on its own, reaching 74 and 18 on that chart. Clearly, the clever and visceral "Mr. Pitiful" had put Redding on a higher level and set the tone for virtually all of his ensuing recordings. In its wake, a second album was pieced together which would include what was now four certifiable R&B hits.

With this success, Redding sessions at Stax had become events. Not only would every employee of the company crowd into the control room to watch, but Stewart, who booked every recording date in his studio himself, needed only to tell his musicians "Otis is coming in" for them to drop whatever they were doing and head for East McLemore.

One song earmarked for the new album had already been recorded, and prospered when released over the summer, "I've Been Loving You Too Long (To Stop Now)," another gushing, wrenching ballad that Otis had written with the mellow, veteran Chicago soul singer Jerry "Iceman" Butler in a Buffalo hotel room when their paths coincided. Hearing Butler sing the unfinished song, Otis said, "Hey, man, that's a smash. Let me go mess around with it. Maybe I'll come up with something."[8]

Butler heard nothing more about it, but Otis turned the ballad into a groaning, fragile plea. As he envisioned the arrangement, and as how it was recorded, it slowly built from quaint piano triplets to, with a sudden shift of key, a horn swell. But the lyrics, again, go deep, as an accusation that, in the relationship he sings of, only his love was real and true, growing ever stronger even as his woman's love grew "tired" and "cold."

Otis pointedly referred to this love scenario as an "affair" and even a "habit." For Redding, it seemed, loving was unconditional, even if it could seem more like a chore. That clearly was baggage he still carried from the deacon's church sermons he absorbed as a child, leaving an unbreakable "habit" that salvaged the morality and sanctity of any breakable relationship. Furthermore, it was apparent that he believed it was his job to save any such union, even beg if he had to. But if he also believed he had earned no demerits for a lack of fealty when he was on the road, he was conning himself. When it came to blame for his selective adultery, he could pin that on no one else.

●

RELEASED ON April 19, 1965, "I've Been Loving You Too Long," backed with "Just One More Day," got off strong. Atlantic distributors shipped one hundred thousand orders in one day and it ultimately had a very nice showing on the charts, *both* charts, going to number 2 R&B and, even better, number 21 pop. As soon as it hit the streets, Otis had called Jerry Butler, excitedly telling him, "Hey, man, it's a hit! I told you it was a hit." Butler couldn't imagine what he was talking about. When Otis said it was the song Butler had come up with, he couldn't believe it. Otis had not told him he had finished the song, much less that he had recorded it. In fact, Jerry was going to cut it himself, as is. He had Otis play it over the phone, and though he still felt somewhat betrayed, the majesty of the record was obvious. No one else could have recorded it as had Otis, he would say that "it was intended for him." Butler told author Scott Freeman, "He sang 'I've been . . .' and then he just paused and let you think about it: *I've been what?* . . . then 'too long.' And he made 'long' a ten-syllable word! . . . Like when Ray Charles says 'Georgia.' It was a statement. It was a paragraph. It was just beautiful."[9]

He told the same thing to Al Bell, an influential black DJ in Washington, D.C., at this point, who was stunned. "Jerry said there was no use in him even recording it, wouldn't even try. And this is Jerry Butler, one of the greatest singers of all time!"[10]

After "I've Been Loving You Too Long," lost steam, "One More Day" broke off on its own run, hitting numbers 15 and 85 (*Cash Box*), respectively. That breakthrough hastened the compilation of his third album, one that Atlantic decreed should be released in stereo, the first time a Stax album was cut in two channels. For this they sent Tom Dowd, the famed Atlantic engineer who had overseen sessions for Ray Charles, Ruth Brown, Bobby Darin's "Mack the Knife," John Coltrane, Charlie Parker, and Thelonious Monk, and whose wizardry on the mixing board had earned him the moniker of "Soundman God."

Dowd installed in the studio Stax's first two-track machine, guaranteeing that if Atlantic acts were barred from Stax, there would be no such injunction for the wizard of the control board, who would be a regular from then on. Even though most studios had four- or eight-track recorders by that time, even two-track recording was a grudging concession by Stewart, who was so worried that a stereo mix might distill the usual Stax sound that he demanded that Dowd engineer a separate mono track. It was a skill that seemingly Dowd alone had. Stewart, though, would only accede to full Stax albums going out in stereo; his crown jewels, the singles, continued in mono.

The bulk of material on the album was culled from several sessions from the past year: "Come to Me" in February; Redding's "I Want to Thank You" (not the Sam and Dave "I Thank You") in April; his "Your One and Only Man" and "Chained and Bound" in

September; "That's How Strong My Love Is" in December, featuring the biggest brass blast on a Redding song yet. He cut six more highly emotive tracks in January 1965: Otis Blackwell's "Home in Your Heart" and Obie McClinton's "Keep Your Arms Around Me"; a cover of Butler's "For Your Precious Love"; Chuck Willis's "It's Too Late"; Sam Cooke's "Nothing Can Change This Love"; and, perhaps most trenchant, cover of Jackie Wilson's "A Woman, A Lover, A Friend." As eclectic and soul-savvy as the list was, many of these titles were deeply founded in Otis's own angst, hopes, and letdowns.

Often given as a fact is that this album marked the debut at Stax of Isaac Hayes, who indeed was listed on the sleeve as one of the session players, on piano. Hayes, an orphan who lived with his grandmother, boasted a shaved head even before it was a style. He had been hired by Stewart at the age of twenty-three after a brief career as a meat-packer and a stint in the clubs around Memphis singing and playing piano with various bands, including one headed by Floyd Newman. When Jim Stewart brought him into the Stax fold early in 1965, Hayes worked with low-level act the Mad Lads, a group of teens in Booker T. Washington High School. The first song he wrote for them, "The Sidewalk Surf," flopped but the next, "Don't Have to Shop Around," an answer to Smokey Robinson and the Miracles' "Shop Around," surprisingly made it to number 11 R&B and 93 pop late that year.

Hayes would branch out, teamed with yet another Booker T. Washington student, Dave Porter, who had hung around Stewart's office bugging him for work and eventually landed a job as a staff writer. Hayes in time would become one of the most identifiable and distinctive of all soul men, sanctifying that very phrase, but in July of 1965, he was making his studio debut on a Redding session, which he would recall, saying, "I was frightened. Here I am in this place I've always wanted to be and all these giants have been through here."[11]

While the album was originally titled *That's How Strong My Love*

Is, Stewart felt the title needed to showcase something stronger than a love song that did only so-so. That something was Redding himself. Atlantic Records was ahead of Motown in one way. As far-fetched as it seems today, the first black-owned record company did not put the images of its own talent on their record jackets, Berry Gordy believing that black faces could only dampen sales, a preposterous notion that endured until 1965. Atlantic, however, had put a large photo of Redding on *Pain in My Heart* and would now array a grid of twenty-four identical images of him on this album. Thus, the next logical step was to use his growing brand to sell the record, the title of which became *The Great Otis Redding Sings Soul Ballads*.

That was surely presumptuous, but a core part of the PR campaign being waged was to convince the industry that Redding was indeed a star. He surely was not, based on sales and crossover appeal, quantifiably "great," not like Ray Charles or Nat King Cole, much less Little Richard or in the hard-earned sense, like Rufus Thomas. But the underground word of mouth about his electrifying concerts was the best selling point Jim Stewart and the Walden agency had. As a cult figure with a sense of anticipation and curiosity about him, the press releases churned out by Alan Walden and Alex Hodges— all routed through Atlantic's promotions department and put out on Atco letterhead, just as Atlantic had to sign off on every Redding song—shamelessly pumped up an identity that Redding himself might not have recognized.

"It was cold in November 1962 but a young man with a lot of soul warmed it up," read a release from late in 1963. "Across the nation people were asking who is this soul master of the blues ballad? The answer was OTIS REDDING . . . In the day of gimmick sounds and long hair, OTIS REDDING had a message! This message was heard by millions as each recording effort continued to prove the REDDING sound was here to stay. . . . 'Mr. Pitiful' is 'Mr. Consistent.'" Another, from 1964, burbled, "OTIS has established himself as one of the nation's top recording artists. 'THE OTIS REDDING SHOW' is constantly in demand throughout the country. The show includes OTIS' dynamic nine-piece show band . . . one of the top road shows in the nation traveling over 150,000 miles in 1964 playing for thousands of fans. 1965 is even bigger as OTIS works from coast to coast. . . . OTIS REDDING is proving he is quite deserving of the title: THE KING OF SOUL!"[12]

9

The King of Soul

Even the Atlantic honchos weren't altogether comfortable with turning a still fairly unknown talent, as prodigious as he was, into a soul sultan. When Phil Walden's release got to New York for perusal, the "King of Soul" title was crossed out by cautious Atlantic editors as being too presumptuous. Walden, however, had also titled the press release with that phrase so when it was sent out to disc jockeys, record stores, and music journalists, the title was simply "Otis Redding." And yet the "King of Soul" emblem was catching on among the soul music crowd, as Walden continued using it in phone calls to music folks. And why not? Redding seemed primed to carry some sort of soul mantle.

Of course, James Brown was far more kingly in the realm of soul, but was already its presumed "godfather," and Sam Cooke, who had in '63 released his *Mr. Soul* album, was in his grave. With Redding the new soul flavor, a sixties kind of hip gold dust was being sprinkled on him and the bookings showed it. "We were up to around two thousand dollars a gig," says Alex Hodges. "We were even *turn-*

ing down offers that everyone else would kill for, because we were so booked up. Black clubs, white clubs, didn't matter. Full houses every night. The sense that this guy had to be seen to be believed was building every day, it was almost mythical in nature. And that was the key. Unlike the Motown acts who had to sell records to go on the road, Otis was an inverted reality. All he needed was to be there, in the flesh. Otis was a live act in every sense of the word. Hearing him on record made you want to see him, you *had* to."[1]

Redding fan clubs were also created, not by actual fans but by the Walden office, which beckoned participation on the back of Redding record jackets and press releases, a ploy commonly used by record artists of the era. "Persons interested in joining Otis's fan club may contact The Otis Redding National Fan Club, Suite 302, Robert E. Lee Building, Macon, Georgia"—the address as well of Phil Walden Artists and Promotions.[2] It was all very audacious, to be sure, but Otis was certainly doing his part, pouring every drop he had into each record, and the DJs were lining up to be recognized as the one who broke him out. He was not a household name quite yet, and nowhere near James Brown's level of recognition to white record buyers, but Stewart was all but laying his company's future on the campaign succeeding.

Otis Redding Sings Soul Ballads, released in March 1965 with a grid of twenty-four identical images of Redding on the cover, was a solid performer, running to number 3 on the reinstated *Billboard* R&B album chart, though once again Redding loitered in the top 100—only peaking at number 75. Meanwhile, at Stax, the old order was fading out, with Booker T. and the MG's and the Mar-Keys having taken a back seat to Redding, mainly employed as his backup band. Other musicians and acts were now breaking the seal at the company, recording in the Redding style. In March, the first session was held for Sam Moore and Dave Prater, otherwise known as Sam and Dave, who had been performing gospel soul since the mid-1950s, and as an explosive, elastic-limbed duo since 1961, their stage show frantic and manic.

They had released a number of records for, among other labels, Roulette Records, until Jerry Wexler signed them in '64 and sent them to record at Stax. This had only recently been possible since Jim Stewart's edict prohibiting non-Stax artists from the studio was overridden by a sweet deal from Wexler: Stewart would be given the usual Stax royalty rate from the sales from Sam and Dave records, and half the publishing royalties on songs composed by Stax song-writers. He could also promote the band as if they were in fact Stax artists, a common assumption in the years to come.[3] Not that Moore and Prater were flattered; expecting to record in New York, when Wexler sent them south they took it as a slur. "We cried about it," Moore once said. "It was like, how could you do this to us?"[4]

While Sam and Dave, along with Eddie Floyd, William Bell, and Carla Thomas were all in Stewart's plans, Redding sessions were given priority. It mattering not a whit that the single release of Redding's rendition of "Stand By Me" late in 1964 failed to chart, even on the R&B list. Another round of sessions had been slated for July 9, and out of them would come the song that took Redding to another new level of respect.

•

TO JIM STEWART, this new album would mark a step up for the new writing/production duo of Isaac Hayes and Dave Porter, who Stewart hoped would become a Stax version of Motown's extraordi-nary hit-makers Holland-Dozier-Holland. After being teamed, the pair was assigned to Sam and Dave, with little success at first. But at the same time they also began to buttress Stewart on producing sessions for other artists, such as Redding, and seemingly imbued whatever they touched with a teeming soul sensibility.

While "I've Been Loving You Too Long" would be the album's centerpiece, Otis wrote two more original songs for it, "Ole Man Trouble" and "Respect." Scion of the royalty of soul that he was, he chose three of Sam Cooke's best-known songs, "Shake," "A Change Is Gonna Come," and "Wonderful World," as well as a number of hallowed tunes from other music gods, including B.B. King's "Rock Me Baby," the Smokey Robinson–written Temptations smash "My Girl," Solomon Burke's "Down in the Valley," and—in the curveball of the playlist—the Rolling Stones' "Satisfaction."

There are clues all over these entries that can help us understand Redding's state of mind at the time. He was, first of all, seeking a song that would heavily dent the pop charts—"My Girl" and "Satisfaction" had both went to number 1, "My Girl" both pop and R&B—and, in fact, had never even heard "Satisfaction" when Steve Cropper and Booker T. sold him on the idea. But the three Cooke tunes quantified the change that had come over him when that original soul stirrer breathed his last on December 11, 1964, only months before Redding was slated to go back into the studio. Like many who went before and after him, Cooke's death was anything but glorious. Inebriated, half-naked, and crazed, he was shot to death by the manager of a fleabag motel in L.A. after checking into a room with a hooker, the mysterious circumstances of which are still in dispute.[5]

Ironically, Cooke had just released an album called *Ain't That Good News*, and while he was still a top-shelf star, with twenty-nine top 40 hits, his inner struggle to remain hopeful despite enduring "times that I thought I couldn't last for long" seemed to Otis the essence of soul going back to the Delta blues men. Indeed, Cooke had written "A Change Is Gonna Come" out of pure despair, shortly after both the accidental drowning death of his eighteen-month-old son and being arrested for disturbing the peace when he and his band tried in vain to register in a Shreveport, Louisiana hotel, prompting an AP headline run in many papers including the *New York Times* that read: NEGRO BANDLEADER HELD IN SHREVEPORT.[6]

Otis had only fleetingly met Sam, when their paths crossed at the Washington, D.C., airport early in the decade. Cooke told him, trenchantly, "Be natural, be you," which became a Zen-like mantra for Otis. To him, it seemed unimaginable Cooke could come to such an end. "The day that Otis heard that Sam Cooke got killed," Zelma Redding has said, "when I looked into his eyes it was just devastating because Sam Cooke was one of his idols. He loved Sam Cooke."[7] The lesson was clear, bleakly so. Even though he was starting to achieve financial security, Redding in his writing seemed to be expressing a kind of hopelessness about breaking free of hurt that was lurking everywhere, especially in matters of the heart. When his cover of "A Change Is Gonna Come" was cut, his mask of pain was as convincing as Cooke's. It was done every bit as a dirge, a funereal horn overture prefacing perhaps the most dour and quietly intense performance he ever gave, one that was hard to hear as a don't-give-up rubric.

The Stax echo effect that washed over the words made them seem ghostly, each searing and streaming from somewhere deep in the soul. At the fadeout, the ghost trailed away, in a shroud of lonely isolation. If Cooke's hushed, ministerial rendition and lush string arrangement was sadly moving in an elegant way, like so many other songs Redding covered, his version conveyed how Sam must have originally heard it in his head, unadorned and with a world of hurt. Clearly, Otis lived in that world, as well, if for reasons that were not obvious at first glance, nor could likely be explained by Otis himself. To all observers, he had no right to brood or wallow in the dark, depressing shadows of the blues. He had not been victim to personal tragedy nor did he bear overly searing scars of Jim Crow. He had found a wife, fathered children, lived as comfortably as a young black entertainer could be expected to, in a hometown that often eased his fears about the outside world, hard by woods and streams and horse trails that could reliably clear his head. However, his comfort with the pain-streaked confessions of the blues was far too genuine to be mere affectation.

Something deep inside him could only be expressed in the many hues of pain and despondence. Clinically, much of this seemed clearly to have swelled as the result of his difficult relationship with Otis Sr., and the grudging acceptance of his career by the man he needed to fully please. It had been his obsession to justify his career to the deacon that had taken him from childhood to manhood without the requisite stopping-off points of teenage angst and exploration. He had surely become a man too soon, trailing confusion and uncertainty as he met and conquered artistic and sexual plateaus. Looking back, he felt he had missed something on the way, something too late to claim. He was too comfortable with the blues, and while that was good for business, even the big, blustery, carefree front he could easily unfurl and use to dominate any environment he was in could not make his diffused burdens go away for long. Certainly, the unwaveringly consistent, and ever more convincing, surfeit of pain in his songs reflected anything but carefree amusement.

•

INDEED, THE sometimes wobbly, trying nature of his marriage was a flaw in his life that he could not easily live with. Trying hard to assure Zelma, but more so himself, that all was well on that front, he reached some sort of détente with her, which Otis had come to believe would be essential to keeping his head together and his career on track. However, as they dealt with his serial philandering on the road, Zelma once related that her fears of being left behind as he shot to stardom had been eased, saying, "It turned out just the opposite, really." In the end, she said, his straying made him appreciate her more. "I think it pulled us together. Oh, he was still a little wild, but after 1965 he changed completely."[8]

That was certainly debatable, as was whether Otis's habitual jealousies had some foundation, although there is no evidence that they did. If the latter, Otis was not prone to talk about them, or to boost his own morality by having to tear down Zelma's. As Dennis Wheeler says, "Otis was very private about those kind of personal things. All I know is that they had their bumps in the road but never stopped loving each other. And for Otis, he had to know his kids would be there. He was terrified that if he lost Zelma, he'd lose the kids, too. He wasn't gonna let that happen. He felt guilty enough about not being there for long periods of time. Everything he did he wanted to be for the kids, the money, the security, everything. I don't know how much he changed, but let's say he changed *enough* to keep the marriage going."[9]

He also wanted to be more in command of his own dealings. Said Alan Walden, "He was always ready to do whatever was necessary and willing to match everything you did. He answered most of the fan mail personally, spoke with disc jockeys on a daily basis and even helped me set up office policies. One time when the company's funds ran low, he offered to put his own road show money into the company to keep it going."[10] Often, Walden would get to the office bright and early, to find that Otis and Speedo Sims had already been there reviewing the receipts and ticket box funds from the night before; sometimes, they came straight from a gig to count the proceeds.

What Walden leaves unsaid is that, as trusting as Otis was, a part of him could trust no one. On matters of money, particularly, there was too much at stake to let the beans be counted in private by promoters, managers, and record company suits. Otis needed to have an accounting, but the accountant in the last analysis was his own, each dollar bill counted and recounted, and all in his own hands. Being in command meant that Otis Redding ran his own show. Never, ever, was he going to put his money, or his life, in someone else's hands.

EVEN CONSIDERING his dedication to family, the fulcrum of Otis's life was the next trip to Memphis. There, among the drafty studios and sloped floors, he would record not only as a singer but as something of a missionary. Indeed, Stax was no more of a mecca to anyone than it was to Redding, whose vocal impact was stroked by the environment he found there. As Jerry Wexler knew, "Stax was the perfect studio setting for Otis," swathed as he was by the right kind of instrumental texture and session men who could virtually read his mind. Jim Stewart's original instinct was right; by keeping the instrumentation spare, the air between notes gave Redding command of a song with just a telltale breath or tremble trailing from a last syllable.

While the loud passages of horn-blaring, brain-scrambling madness in Redding stompers left an audience breathless and damp, his essence was the beat of his soul and a cleaved heart. The tone of what escaped from his throat could be jarring, but purposeful. The *New York Times*' music critic Jon Pareles would write years later that "what makes [milestone songs] resonant, memorable—even great—is the way they irritate the ear . . . an Otis Redding rasp, a Gato Barbieri saxophone yowl, a Buddy Holly hiccup . . . Most music implies that a set of rules is in effect, governing where notes can be placed in pitch and time, and what the acceptable timbres might be; irritants seize the foreground by defying those rules."

Redding surely didn't follow rules, or even know them intimately. In this, he was a product of soul music's roots. The great jazz and blues pioneers unearthed what were called "blue notes"—thus the overall term that stemmed from it—from European instruments, such as the guitar and saxophone, that had never played those kind of notes before by blending them with what Pareles called "the moans and buzzes of African music. Ensuing generations extended the brass snorts and saxophone squeals . . . courting anarchy with increasingly open structures and far-reaching improvisations."[11] Another *Times* music scribe, Robert Shelton, believed Redding was transforming his idiom, song by song. "Soul, capable of so many definitions," he wrote, "might be called a deep-dish Negro concept of involvement and sincerity. In his own writing or performing, soul became a method of performing for Redding rather than a type of material. One always believes that he was centrally involved in the emotions of his song."[12]

Redding did all this with his amazing instrument—not so much with perfect pitch and vocal mechanics, singing as he did from the throat and not deep in his gut, but the prospect of going with it where few had dared go. Of course, rock is mottled with songs more than a little *too* irritating; that, however, was never a Redding consequence. His sense of when to peel back the rawness for a swab of melodic cotton was innate. So it was the job of people like Stewart, Cropper, and Tom Dowd to transfer indelible yet ineffable qualities like this to tape and then vinyl with no degeneration. Booker T. Jones insists of the musicians that "none of us are extraordinary musicians," a far too modest opinion, to be sure, and that "we concentrate on letting people know how we felt when we were playing . . . to create a mood."[13]

Yet the Stax studio itself was an anomaly that contributed to the sound. Stewart had walled off a 47-by-27-foot studio in a corner of the old theater but the walls still had the long curtains on them, which absorbed some sound and prevented too "live" of a sound that could be uneven and harsh. But because the ceiling was 25 feet high and the floor was sloped, the acoustics were distinct, big, and raw. Only the drums were isolated by partitions surrounding them and most instruments bled into each other. Al Jackson Jr. once noted that Motown "uses echo and we don't. We cut our drums flat. I don't use any muffling or anything, I just play the way I feel." Which was usually like a wrecking ball, the massive concussion he made on his snare drum a simple matter of him slamming down "the butt end of my left stick."[14]

Even the tile floors and walls of the john had an acoustic benefit. By running a speaker from the studio, and a microphone to catch the sound, the natural reverb and echo could be added to the sound in the studio. The Atlantic crowd could hardly believe records were being made this way. Even though Dowd installed a two-track recorder in 1963, so that Stax records could be recorded in crude stereo, Stewart would never accede to the multitrack, piecemeal, ground-up process that overtook almost all studio work around the country, keeping everything as real and sweaty as possible. He did the same when Dowd brought in a four-track machine in '66.[15]

In New York, the musicians' unions were still fighting to enforce hoary regulations, such as producers not being able to overdub unless there was a full quorum of musicians. In Memphis, however, where no such unions existed with any authority, musicians played by their own rules. Producers were generally session players themselves, like Cropper, always open to ideas from the floor. This was a reflection of what Muscle Shoals producer/guitarist Jimmy Johnson liked to call "Southern hospitality."[16] That kind of thing always seemed to matter to Otis, more than any acoustical conditions.

•

THE SESSION for Redding's third album would become the longest Stax session ever. Commencing on the morning of July 9, it ran until around 8:00 P.M., at which point the session men had to leave for club gigs. They picked up again at 2:00 A.M., and would not finish until dawn. According to Atlantic session logs, the first track in the can was "Ole Man Trouble." Then came a song that would send the session into immortality. With lyrics that leapt from Otis's pen to manifold avenues of interpretation, the result was not so much a soul classic as a marker of the times. While, for Redding himself, the "respect" he wrote about was a stamp earned by an individual among his peers and within his family, this was a word loaded with social significance. Jackie Robinson had once said of being chosen to break the color line in baseball, "I'm not concerned with your liking or disliking me. All I ask is that you respect me as a human being."[17]

Redding could not have been unmindful of the broader meaning of the word when, according to Dennis Wheeler, Otis wrote the song in Bobby Smith's studio on Mulberry Street, and may have even made a demo there. Another claim on it was made by Al Jackson Jr., who said he commiserated with Otis's bitching about a long road tour he was on, telling him, "All you can look for is a little respect when you come home."[18] Yet another claim, from Speedo Sims, was *he* had written the song, which he said Otis was going to produce for him, but then took for himself.[19] At the time, Redding was in the middle of getting the parameters of his marriage straightened out, and the lines he came up with veered from adamancy—being entitled to get what he wanted, by way of giving his partner what she *needed*—to remarkable toleration—handing her a license to "do me wrong" when he wasn't at home.

He even vowed to give his woman all his money to earn that respect, which in the end was no longer a request but a demand, something he could signify with his now trademark cyclic repetition of "got-ta, got-ta," in this case, having it. This was incredible stuff, cutting right to the bone of his inner feelings and confusion about how to be a man. And he was that; Al Jackson Jr. had no trouble finding the right words to describe Redding: "That son of a bitch was all man."[20] But he was no cartoon. He could be as big and macho as he wanted, but when he sang these words, he was showing unapologetic vulnerability in fighting for his pride *and* his marriage. He was registering fear of being left by a woman, being abandoned, a prospect that scared him to death, as a proof of personal, moral failure and the inability to control his personal life as easily as he could a song lyric or command a room. Of course, the part about doing him wrong may have been a sly accusation that *he* had been the one wronged. However he meant it, though, in two and a half minutes he had fitted his personal life into a commercially marketable song.

When it came time to record "Respect," much thought had been given to amplifying all this emotional undertow. Dipping into the Motown bag of tricks for some crossover oomph, the Stax producers—no one was given that credit, as was the label's practice then, but Stewart, Cropper, and perhaps Isaac Hayes all had a hand in it—instructed Al Jackson Jr. to play a Detroit "white-oriented" 4/4 beat on the drum, banging the snare so hard on every beat that it sounded like a series of firecrackers going off. The high-low staccato bursts of the Memphis Horns were like greased lightning. There was also a subtle, and rare, background "hey, hey, hey" harmony part, sung by William Bell. The melody was strong, the best dance record he had yet done, and the lyrics came off, as they only could have with Otis, raw, hubristic, cocky, yet with not a trace of being a dick.

When it was finished, Otis himself could not have been more pleased with the result. "That's one of my favorite songs," he would say in 1967, "because it has a better groove than any of my records. It says something, too. . . . The song lines are great. The band track is beautiful. It took me a whole day to write it and about twenty minutes to arrange it. We cut it once and that was it. Everybody wants respect, you know."[21]

As for the balance of the album, the Cooke covers, "Shake" and "Wonderful World," were a respite from the soul-clenching themes of "Respect" and "A Change Is Gonna Come." The first was an up-tempo soul rocker with Jackson's gleeful drum fills framing Otis's raspy twang and "got-to, got-to" wails and the second adding a sensuous, hip-grinding beat to the perky original. Redding never took any song lightly, pouring all he had into them. On "My Girl," a song seemingly too innocent for a Stax entry, even with the Motown string lines replaced by Memphis horn lines, he accomplished the impossible: With his bleeding soul and cracking voice, Otis made the brilliant David Ruffin's original paean to love, albeit with a subtle layer of insecurity that it was real, seem less vulnerable and more slick. But after "Respect," the real driver of the album was the least likely—"Satisfaction." Otis claimed that he did not know the song, which of course had gone to number 1 over the summer. Indeed, he knew little of any rock and roll, his car radio always tuned to the soul stations. When it was played for him, the smug lyrics about "how white my shirts can be" and "trying to make some girl" may as well have been in a foreign language. Steve Cropper, looking back, said, "If you ever listened to the record you can hardly understand the lyrics, right? I sat down next to a record player and copied down what I thought the lyrics were and handed Otis a piece of paper and before we got through with the cut, he threw the paper on the floor and that was it."[22]

As the band converted British blues rock into brassy, big-bottomed Memphis blues—certainly one of the first British songs to be covered by an African-American artist—Otis began altering the first verse, then basically ignored the lyrics and simply did *Otis*, vamping exhortations like "We gotta have it, gotta, we gotta have it, gotta, we gotta have it. Keep on grooving, keep on grooving" and "Keep on rocking, rocking, baby yeah. Gotta, gotta have it, you gotta," before finishing with a rolling wave of "got-ta, got-ta, got-ta . . . " No one could quite figure out just what he was singing at times, and, as Otis would later recall, "I used a lot of words different than the Stones' version. That's because I made them up."[23]

Years later, the acerbic *Village Voice* music critic Robert Christgau called it an "anarchic reading" of the song.[24] Yet Redding's design for it, with horns pumping out the melody, was, as it happened, precisely how Keith Richards had originally intended the arrangement, before the horn melody was ultimately played by his famous fuzzy feedback guitar. Around the 1980s, the Stones would perform the tune in the Redding style, though it hardly had a thing to do with the meaning of the song, which Mick Jagger once said "captures a spirit of the times, which is very important in those kinds of songs ... alienation."[25] Otis, who wouldn't be into his alienation mode for another year, just, in the Little Richard vernacular, ripped it up. Where the Stones winked at but never stated the obvious meaning, it now emerged as a proudly horny anthem of getting some, of getting a *lot*. The lack of pretension made it irresistible. Or, as Dr. James Cushing, a Cal Poly San Luis Obispo English and literature professor, and a DJ on the school's radio station, once remarked, Redding's was "more as a song of triumph than a song of frustration. What Otis does with it is that the person might not be satisfied, but at least he has survived enough, whereas Jagger just sounds kind of petulant and pissed off. Petulance and being pissed off is not bad, either, but it's not a noble emotion, and Otis was more noble."[26]

Whatever the real meaning was, a real debate ensued at Atlantic over both whether "Respect" or "Satisfaction" should be the first single off the album and what the title of the album should be. An Atlantic staffer, Taube Garthson, in a note to Tom Dowd, wrote, "When you talk to Jim Stewart, ask him if he has a title in mind for the LP or should we pick one. A suggestion might be 'I've Been Loving You Too Long.'"[27] However, when the record was sent out in August, it had again been decided that Redding's brand had to be its earmark; the title reached for a lot: *Otis Blue: Otis Redding Sings Soul*. The cover, ironically, went *away* from his well-known physical image for some generic luster that dampened the hardcore soul feel. Clearly going for a crossover market, it had a kittenish blonde bathed in an aqua blue tint, head reclined on a pillow, eyes closed not in sleep but beatitude. This was reminiscent of the chic, cocktails-for-two motif of Frank Sinatra and Ray Charles album covers and signaled that Redding would no longer be positioned as a chitlin' circuit act. His potent sex appeal would now be as obvious for white women as black.

Spawning three of Redding's most memorable renditions, the

album, the first Stax LP in which liner notes had not been done by Atlantic but instead by former Mar-Keys lead singer Ronnie Stoots, a.k.a. Ronnie Angel (who also had designed the Stax spiral "stax of wax" logo), was held for release until after "Respect," the first single, was released on August 15 backed with "Ole Man Trouble." It shot up the charts, to hit number 4 on the R&B chart, and 35 on pop. Then a month later, *Otis Blue* hit the market and blew up the soul list to number 1—the only such ranking he would see while alive—en route to becoming the biggest-selling album of his lifetime, and one that would reach gold status and rightly be hailed as a towering landmark of soul. For what it's worth, it was also ranked number 78 in *Rolling Stone*'s 2012 survey of "The 500 Greatest Albums of All Time," in which the magazine noted that his versions of Sam Cooke's "sound and message helped shape Redding's Southern soul."[28]

Actually, it did more. It was another milestone in the ongoing merger of pop and soul, both of which were now becoming blacker and less constrained by old assumptions about what was "mainstream."

●

IN LATE 1965, Lieutenant Phil Walden returned from the Army. Leaving the day-to-day operation of Walden Artists and Promotions to his kid brother had been a risky move. Alan was all in on the promotion of Otis Redding, but he was even younger than Phil and he had little of his brother's innate, singular skill for pitching Redding and closing the deal on bookings, though a good many of those bookings now just fell into the agency's lap. Alan seemed to be fully satisfied as a trusted member of the Redding inner circle, feeding on the, ahem, *perks*, that fell into his lap as Otis's travel companion. And Alan and Alex kept the office humming, along with sundry Walden family members. But when C. B. Walden became ill and pulled out, the agency looked as if it would go under.[29]

Otis, aghast when Alan informed him of this, blew a gasket. As Walden recalled, "Up until that point, I had never seen an angry side of him." Walden says Redding got "all over my butt," and went straight to C.B., telling him, "Pop, we need you." C.B., ill as he was, went back to work, infused with a fresh stash of cash Otis kicked in from his earnings to keep the agency afloat. Not that Alan would ever agree that he had needed help. He points out, "Our gross figures were high and Otis and I had not done a bad job on our own."[30] But everyone was still counting the minutes until Phil returned.

When Phil marched home, he was ready to go all in again. Rather than being completely shut out from his client, he had actually heard Otis's songs played on the radio in Germany, and when he was off duty and would frequent clubs in Hamburg where the Beatles had cut their teeth a few years before, the hipsters there told him about the soulful new "Negro" singer in America named Otis Redding. Had he told them he happened to manage that singer, they would have laughed him out of the place, so he simply drank in the fact that he had a potential worldwide star waiting for him when he got back home, and a hit album. *Otis Blue*, according to Alan Walden, was recorded as "Phil's welcome home present."

Now, though, the second-string at Walden Artists and Promotions gave way to bigger doings. With his worldview expanded, and his tastes now exposed to a European sense of style, Phil Walden wanted to present his top client as a major star. He began to send Otis out on the road with wardrobe bags stuffed with some mighty nice, and expensive, duds. As Alex Hodges says, "Remember, Phil had sold clothes. And he'd been to the chic London clubs. He had an idea how an international star should look. They would go up to New York and buy clothes from the best clothing stores. Italian sweaters, Moorhouse slacks, cuff links, silk ties, Oleg Cassini suits. And, man, he would sweat through everything. And the funny thing was, he'd be lugging all these expensive clothes in a station wagon with his and the band's clothes, the instruments, food, all kinds of shit. It looked like a slum in there." Walden also began to leverage Otis's status as the workhorse of the Stax/Volt stable to start building a cushion for him, including a vanity label for Otis to cultivate and record talent of his choosing, and a publishing company under which he and Phil would own and co-administer the rights to songs Otis wrote. Now, Phil tied up all the legal details, set the companies in motion, and began looking for artists that Otis could produce. He also established Big O Productions, an umbrella for any projects outside of music, with an eye toward getting Otis into the movies, either to compose music or even to do some acting.

Redding's contract was due to expire late in 1965, and with Jim Stewart intent on expanding the two-year follow-up option to five years, Walden needed to see some big changes in the royalty rate, from three and a half to five points, on singles and albums. Otis would need to deliver eight of the former and one of the latter each year. Stewart, who knew this day would come after three years of Redding's peonage, agreed to these conditions—remarkably, given that Redding had become the face, voice, and attitude of Stax/Volt, all, amazingly, without benefit of a major pop hit.

"What happened was," says Dennis Wheeler, "is that Otis said, 'I want my publishing.' He had grown a lot, learned a lot. He was smart about the business, whereas most performers aren't. He didn't just want to demand something; he wanted to own something, own the Otis Redding franchise. And all that came together when his deal with Stax was expiring. He told me people were coming to him with better deals. That's gonna happen when you hit it big. It gives you a lot of leverage. And Phil just turned the knife."[31] And Stewart, the old fiddler, gave in without a fight on all terms. In many ways, Stewart was a square peg in the round hole of the music business. As sophisticated as he had become in the ways of running a label, he was cautious and sharp-eyed enough to know Stax was anything but a moneymaker, its expenses outrunning its sporadic profits. Indeed, he still retained his job at the bank, part-time, but not walking away. Almost nothing about him suggested the cigar-chomping sharpies who had run record companies since the Tin Pan Alley days. Thus, he was not particularly comfortable driving hard bargains. For example, during the 1950s and early 1960s, record company executives normally wouldn't budge on ceding publishing rights, something that they considered spoils of the game; since their labels were the avenues by which songs were produced and released in the marketplace, the executives could conscript the publishing rights, that was the bargain. Stewart himself had done this with the early Stax releases.

Now, though, he had no intention standing in Otis's way as a rising executive, much as he didn't get in his way in the studio when Redding's songs came to life according to Otis's judgments. Handing Otis complete hegemony over his publishing was an important milestone in the industry, more so given that this wasn't a huge white act like the Beatles or Rolling Stones, but a black man who had not yet bloomed as a major star. For that alone, Stewart's standing among his stable of acts, and beyond, to other black artists in general, elevated him to almost mythical proportions as a record man with a conscience and a commitment to the purity of soul music. Of course, that skew overlooked the spoils he continued to amass from writing credits for Steve Cropper, and sometimes himself. And he would, not by coincidence, be made a partner in the new publishing company.

The company, formed on paper before the end of 1965, was called Redwal Music, conflating Otis and Walden's surnames, and Walden opened an office on Cotton Avenue. Joe Galkin, the gnome-like Atlantic bird dog who had made all this possible with his sly machinations in getting Otis an audition and a contract at Stax, would still get a quarter of Redwal's royalties, Stewart's East Memphis Music a quarter, Walden a quarter, Otis a quarter. When Otis would open his own record label, Galkin, who now had little to do with Redding's career except for counting the money he made from it, was made co-owner. These victories won, Walden could now use the bait of the Redding imprint to go about recruiting more talent. And the list would grow long. For Redding, who had once needed to sing so he and his family could eat, this first windfall represented vindication beyond imagination. Even the deacon could get behind him now, which pleased his son but perhaps not without some cynicism about Otis Sr.'s belated support. As Wheeler attests, "After 'These Arms of Mine' hit, all of a sudden daddy realized, 'Wait a minute, that's my boy!'" And he too would be rewarded for it, handsomely. His life had been made a whole lot easier by the devil's music.

10

Just One More Day

By mid-decade, Stax/Volt was a consistent hit factory, though mainly on the R&B charts. Rufus Thomas's seminally funktastic "Walking the Dog" however went to number 10 pop, number 1 R&B, in 1963 and was covered by the young Rolling Stones in '64. The Mar-Keys, Booker T. and the MG's, and Carla Thomas had lower-ranked hits. But Otis Redding had virtually taken over the place, and his sound drove its "anti-Motown" idiom with unapologetically Southern soul. Jerry Wexler was so enamored of the Stax sound that he craved an Otis Redding of his own. That became Wilson Pickett, the same sort of rasp-voiced wailer who had been promoted from the Falcons and recorded for Atlantic, produced by the wondrous Tom Dowd. But they were missing that certain something and Wexler took Pickett to Stax, where Jim Stewart was beginning to get proprietary about his studio, loath to allow anyone who was not on his roster to use it, even his musicians. Wexler, though, was owed a favor and on May 12, 1965, Pickett recorded the milestone soul hit "In the Midnight Hour," which became a million seller.

Pickett, however, chafed, believing that Steve Cropper had appropriated a writer's credit on the song without due cause. Indeed, it had happened in precisely the same way in which Otis and Cropper had collaborated on "Mr. Pitiful," at the Lorraine Motel. "Wicked Wilson Pickett," a snappish hornet of a man, never thought much of the musicians in Memphis and could get nasty when he drank, which he had to do on the sly given Stewart's house rule against imbibing during daytime sessions—so adamant was he that Cropper once said, "I don't know if there was a joint ever lit up in that place."[1] But Pickett never kept his mouth in check. As Floyd Newman says, "I never heard a man use words like that in my life, and I been around the block a few times."[2]

By year's end, Pickett was so distrustful of Stax that he vowed never again to record in that studio. He needn't have worried though. The musicians so detested him they sent word to Stewart not to bring "that asshole" into the studio again.[3] Stewart, too, had had it with Pickett, and any other non-Stax artist wanting to use the studio. Even with his tap into royalties on Pickett songs (another would be "634-5789 (Soulsville U.S.A.)," released a year later, a number 13 pop, number 1 R&B song, co-written with Cropper and Eddie Floyd), Stewart denied access to outsiders. Wexler, griping about ingratitude, took Pickett to FAME Studios, the first of the two great soul shops in the backwoods of northeast Alabama, in the generally obscure town of Muscle Shoals, where more great soul may have been made, per capita, than in any other studio in the land. (In 1969, another Muscle Shoals shop would spin off, led by the FAME house band guitarist Jimmy Johnson, bassist David Hood, keyboardist Barry Beckett, and drummer Roger Hawkins; though it used the name of the by-then-legendary city, that new studio was not actually in Muscle Shoals but two miles to the north in Sheffield.)

At FAME, Pickett recorded some of his biggest hits, including his covers of "Land of 1,000 Dances," "Mustang Sally," and "Funky

Broadway," all million sellers, none enriching Stewart. Atlantic also set up its own shop in Memphis, American Studios, sending Tom Dowd to build the studio to his specifications, foreshadowing a coming split with Stax. Still, Stewart could be content that, of the two big soul soloists, he had Redding. Because while Pickett was a truly superb singer, and had more crossover hits than did Redding, no one, not even Wexler, could claim that he was cut from the same cloth. Pickett, in fact, can be said to be Redding's hard-rocking, soul-stomping side, while Percy Sledge, who would enter the Atlantic picture in 1966, was Redding's (slightly) softer, (slightly) more sentimental side. Pickett may well have been the most commercially successful, and his records, as Wexler said, "were terrific, and strong examples of the Southern school of recording." Yet, when Wexler had to make a judgment of which singer was the best of that breed, he was clear. "Some argue that distinction belongs to another singer, who, like Ray Charles before him, was himself a producer. I'm talking about Otis Redding."[4]

•

JIM STEWART, a most conservative and peculiar man, was not convinced that the middling earnings on his product would ever grow sufficiently for him to be able to quit his job at the bank. By 1965, though, he finally summoned the nerve to do it and, protecting his hard-won turf, he was almost maniacally inclined. Neither was he above exercising a few double standards. While on the one hand he prohibited Wilson Pickett from using his studio, he had no objection loaning out his peerless musicians to record for Atlantic sessions in Muscle Shoals and New York. In those shops, which had magic of their own in the walls, Wayne Jackson, Andrew Love, and Floyd Newman could earn higher wages with their horns as visiting players. Newman in particular was ecstatic to be able to play with his idol and beau ideal, King Curtis, in New York.

Another step forward for the Stax musicians was when two instrumentals, "Frog Stomp" and "Sassy," were released in 1963 under Floyd Newman's name. While Gordy would do the same for pianist Earl Van Dyke a year later on the instrumental "Soul Stomp," he kept his house band anonymous so as not to give them leverage. Stewart, by contrast, freely printed the names of session musicians on Stax album jackets. Neither did Stewart give a hang about spreading Soulsville to the masses in ways Gordy wasn't with Motown. As such, the competition between Stax and Motown was every bit a contrast. Between Detroit and Memphis; between Otis Redding and Smokey Robinson, the two best soul singers who ever lived. Indeed, Smokey's pipes were as dewy and fluttery as Redding's were scabrous and growling. Not that Otis couldn't make female hearts flutter, as well, biting into a romantic ballad. But Smokey was big-city cool, Redding sweaty, Deep South church pulpit hot. Gordy—who, unlike Stewart, craved publicity and, again unlike Stewart, got a ton of it—decreed that Motown songs had soul, but after the early years of rough-hewn R&B, knowing he had that market in his pocket, he aimed for white audiences with a white-glove approach. His girl groups were sent to charm school, balancing books on their head, and the target venues were big hotels and swank nightclubs like the Copacabana in New York (where James Brown and Sam Cooke also famously headlined). The Motown "4/4," or "four on the floor" tempo, with a drum and at times a guitar hitting on every beat, was known to music men as a "white beat," as white audiences tended to clap on every beat, while black audiences liked to clap on every other beat. Motown sessions were massive, Stax's intimate. Redding once delineated the two soul nerve centers this way: "Motown does a lot of overdubbing. It's mechanically done. At Stax the rule is: whatever you feel, play it. We cut everything together—horns, rhythm, and vocal. We'll do it three or four times, go back and listen to the results and pick the best one."[5] Rufus Thomas, who died at eighty-four in 2011 after a glorious and very well-lived life, once put it in characteristically Rufus terms: "Motown had the sweet, but Stax had the funk."[6]

Actually, Motown had plenty of funk, too, but each camp tended to dismiss the other in some way. Al Bell, the influential DJ, gilds the lily in saying of Stax that "it was the only label in America that had a bottom, a big, fat bottom bass sound. It was like a snake charmer, it mesmerized me, it shook my bones."[7] That unfairly ignores the legendary Motown bottom constructed by the greatest bass player who ever lived, James Jamerson. But Stax people liked to boast of the regional purity in its sound, which was created in multiracial common cause of its musicians. Even though Motown, too, had biracial musicians in its ranks who could play a hell of an R&B groove.

The flip side for Stewart was that, if anything, he was more sexist than the notoriously so Gordy, never believing that women could sing soul as well as men could. Stax would only fleetingly try the girl group thing. In 1964, there were one-off records by acts called Cheryll and Pam, and Barbara and the Browns, as well as several by singers Wendy Rene and Barbara Stephens—but the quota of female artists was pretty much filled by Carla Thomas. Nor were background singers often used, a given at Motown but to Stewart an encroachment on the star's territory—or, as Booker T. Jones believed, Stewart was too cheap to pay for them.[8] He also and actively sought songs written by the artists themselves. While Motown's creative hierarchy was ruled by staff writers/producers, Stewart didn't even identify a producer on any record until 1967, usually leaving the credit to read "Produced by Stax Staff," which could include anyone on the studio floor. Stax writers worked in collaboration with the artists. This was one reason that so few Stax songs were covered by other labels during the decade; as rooted to a given act as any Stax recording was, little room was left for interpretation, as Jerry Butler determined in regard to Otis Redding (although there would be one glaring exception, as Otis would soon learn).

The "other" Otis of sixties soul, Otis Williams, founder of the

Temptations and sole surviving member of the iconic group fronted by David Ruffin and Eddie Kendricks, still has just the slightest trace of geographical chauvinism in his mellow voice when he observes, "Stax definitely had that Southern feel. You hear a Stax record and you immediately think 'the South.' I was born in Texarkana, man, I grew up with those blues. But Motown had a much broader appeal. Not that we didn't get into the horns, too. Motown was trying to copy Stax to an extent. Stax laid it on full force, it was very exciting, but it wasn't geared to a crossover market like us."

Williams has cause to preen; the Temptations had one huge hit after another in the '60s, the lushly soulful "My Girl" in 1965 their first number one hit, both pop and R&B. But he maintains the rivalry between the labels was a friendly one. "Oh yeah, we played dates with Sam and Dave, Eddie Floyd—but not with Otis. He didn't need anyone to help him sell tickets. We would run across Otis from time to time. You couldn't have met a nicer guy. He admired us and we admired him, and when he did 'My Girl' [on *Otis Blue*], we couldn't help but take it as a compliment. He did it in his . . . fashionable way. It was wonderful to hear him do it. But we had no real desire to cover Stax songs. We would cover the Beatles because everybody was covering the Beatles, Otis too. But I guess Stax felt they needed to cover our stuff."[9]

•

TO BE sure, Phil Walden did not care to position Otis Redding as a Vegas lounge act, or need to teach him charm. He clearly was not middle-of-the-road fare, not yet. All soul acts were to some degree sexual but Redding's stage act screamed it. From his mouth, "Respect" was a euphemism—hell, laying down a man's gender-given right—for sex. "I've Been Loving You Too Long" reached its virtual climax with a repetition of "I loved you once, I loved you twice . . . ," all the way up to "ten times," at which point the unbearable delay of the climax reached its end. The overt nature of sex and a man's right to it, even when he was apologizing, in nearly every Stax record kept some doors closed to artists like Redding.

While the Temptations, Supremes, and Four Tops made plenty of TV appearances—regularly on *Ed Sullivan*, the teen-oriented *Shindig!* and *Hullabaloo*, and two Supremes-Temptations network specials—Otis's TV shots were sporadic. Reflective of the Stax "regional" status and the fact that such shows justifiably booked acts with hit mainstream records, Otis mainly performed on local dance-party shows like *Shivaree, Shebang, 9th Street West*, and *The Lloyd Thaxton Show*, the only real national exposure coming on Dick Clark's *American Bandstand*, moved to Saturday mornings, and his after-school show *Where the Action Is*. The *Sullivan* show, like an engagement at the Copa, was still waiting when he died.

Although in 1965 Jim Stewart would reach into the rival camp and hire Al Abrams, a great promotions man who had helped Motown get off the ground, the blacker nature of Stax made its artists a tougher sell when it came to appearances on the tube. For all Redding's years as a soul potentate, American audiences had to make a sincere effort to seek out Stax/Volt records in stores to find him. To make matters even more difficult, only five times would they ever find an album by him—reflecting Stewart's aversion to the marketability of albums, which the company only put out forty-two of until 1968. Motown, meanwhile, obsessively packaged and repackaged its product, releasing hundreds, sometimes three a year by the Supremes or the Temptations. The irony was that Redding's well-thought-out albums had presaged a growing nature of the 33-rpm record as the best way to hear out an act in full context, sampling the range and nuances.

Redding especially stropped the trend, his huge sales numbers almost entirely from slow but steady album purchases, which of course has remained the case since his death. But even his single releases would linger, on both charts, sitting there to be discovered by the next wave of buyers who heard of him through the grapevine, stoking curiosity. Though *Otis Blue* never rose above number 75 on the pop album chart, it remained in the top 100 for 34 weeks, longer than some that had gone top 10. Most of his records accrued sales of around a quarter-million copies, as his fan base kept expanding. In the record business, this is a far more preferable, and profitable, path than a top 10 "rabbit" that burns out and quickly fades away. The work also did something else. In an inversion to the assumed order of things then, it was *he* who legitimized the new rock movement, and one band in particular. As a story in the English music paper *Record Mirror* enthused, "Final R&B acceptance for the STONES? (Yes, Otis has recorded 'Satisfaction.')"[10]

•

WHILE IT would have pleased Stewart and Atlantic to no end if one of those slow and steady records kept on running into the top 10, no one at Stax tried to nudge him to make a consciously compromised crossover record, for fear of ruining a good thing. By '65, when he was certified in his niche by being voted the top R&B male vocalist in a *Cash Box* reader poll, his singles were regarded as tidbits, teasers for his current or next album and show. The following single after "Respect" wasn't the logical choice, "Satisfaction," but rather the product of the next Redding session, on November 5, 1965, when he cut "Can't Turn You Loose" and "Just One More Day," two more titles in the litany of psychiatrist-couch ruminations about his life that he could best say in song—though he himself downplayed the titles and lyrics as mere fodder. When Alan Walden once wondered if he needed more thematic variety, Otis told him, sternly, "You worry about the damn lyrics; *I'm* gonna worry about settin' the groove," his belief being that people who listened to his songs barely heard the lyrics.[11]

This clearly was his way of insulating his gut-level feelings, no doubt allowing him to plumb them even more. "Just One More Day," unwound like a tortured James Brown song with the same sort of searingly vulnerable concession as in "Respect," vowing to do, say, and buy "anything" to be able to "cherish" his woman.

The song, co-written with Steve Cropper and Memphis saxophonist McElvoy Robinson, hit so hard that it was chosen as Redding's next single. But it was "I Can't Turn You Loose" that etched what would be the single most identifiable riff of the sixties' soul idiom, the undulating roller-coaster ride of horn flourishes that escort him through breakneck attestations of . . . *something*, though the words were truly so secondary that they really *were* immaterial. There was also more than a little thievery, something Jim Stewart was clearly not averse to. Cropper, looking for an arrangement with the energy of the vocal, came up with something for his guitar that was very, very close to the opening bars and entire driving bass line of Holland-Dozier-Holland's "I Can't Help Myself (Sugar Pie, Honey Bunch)," which came out in April 1965 and roared to the top of the pop and soul charts.

Cropper described the melody line as "just a riff I'd used on a few songs with the MG's. Otis worked it up with the horns in about 10 minutes as the last thing we did one night in the studio. Just a riff and one verse that he sings over and over. That's all it is." And yet Cropper wasn't so blithe when the record was issued with only one writer's credit—Otis Redding. Given that Wilson Pickett accused *Cropper* of stealing such credits from *him*, and Floyd Newman's contention about Jim Stewart gaming the process so that Cropper would be given credit as a rule, Cropper felt jobbed enough to go to Stewart, who said his name would be added in future pressings but, without explanation, not on *album* cuts of the song, where the bulk of Redding's sales were generated.[12] Indeed, this wouldn't be the half of it; at the time, no one could have prefigured the endless album rereleases and repackaging of Redding material. It was similar to the fast one Stewart had pulled with the reparations to Allen Toussaint for "Pain in My Heart" by neglecting him in England. Nor would it be the last time he would need to make reparations to other writers.

Such was the life of a label owner in charge of doling out lucrative royalty credits. Angles were made to be played, chances taken, rules remade, people screwed. Indeed, Cropper can look all day now for a vintage copy of "Turn You Loose" with his name on it, and not be able to find one. However, because it was common, such matters did not disrupt the personal relationships within the industry. Cropper was about as tight with Stewart and Redding as a man could be, and remained so. And Stewart was always regarded as a man who would do just about anything for his stable, even if just a little bit more for himself.

Still, the fact that Stewart avoided a copyright infringement suit from Motown regarding the song was as impressive as the song itself, though it probably helped that he played it cool, releasing as the A-side "Just One More Day" first. After it got to number 15 R&B and 85 pop, "I Can't Turn You Loose," which the DJs had already been playing, broke out and galloped to number 11 R&B early in 1966, fusing almost at once into the new centerpiece of Redding's stage show, which had been honed to a fine art and was really what animated him. As Booker T. Jones put it, offstage, "Otis was more distracted, not sure of himself. He couldn't make the same movements in the studio when he sang. He was more restricted." That stiffness, though, always melted in time. Onstage, he came on molten, dripping with sexual animalism. "He would do that thing where he stomped the left foot, then the right. And we all played with more intensity around him. He had that magnetism—'I'm a man!'—and he knew it, too."[13]

As if proving that hits seemed to matter less with Redding than perhaps any other soul artist, he was in constant demand, playing around twenty-five shows a month that kept him away from home, apart from the two children who were beginning to get used to him not being there, and further ate at the very relationship with Zelma he was begging in song to maintain. All this was a pretty price to pay for the halting success of his records. Indeed, his next two singles, "My Girl" and "A Change Is Gonna Come," failed to make even the R&B chart. Stax in mid-1966 finally released "Satisfaction," which didn't suffer the same fate, going to number 4 R&B, 31 pop. With the hit, Otis Redding's traveling show became so big that when Stax had put together a caravan of the label's acts late in 1964—taking a page from Motown, it was billed as the "Stax Revue"—and booked a heavily promoted show in L.A., Stewart did not, could not, object that Otis passed up the tour rather than disrupt his own endless touring. The last time he had done so was back in '63, when the Revue came to Macon. With Wilson Pickett, Carla and Rufus Thomas, Booker T. and the MG's, the Mad Lads, and a couple of lesser acts, Stewart had more than enough to sell out and make important headlines. But it was settled law now that Otis Redding, unlike any of the other acts, could do all that and make all the money, all by himself, with high pop chartings superfluous. It ran counter to every rule known to the industry, and the wonder of it was that he was the only one who could pull it off.

•

AS STAX's share of the soul pie was fattening, it was clear that Berry Gordy had some serious competition, but also that Jim Stewart and Gordy were in a kind of symbiotic, mutually beneficial alliance. As an interrelated musical idiom, Stax/Volt and Motown were both after the same thing, which Gordy had codified early on with one of his first Motown hits—"Money (That's What I Want)." Gordy was undoubtedly better at earning it, by miles, building a more self-reliant business model. But in the ether above dollars and cents, together the soul labels did nothing less than prop up American music when, in the wake of the Beatles' great leap forward, came an immediate shakeup. No longer did Broadway's hoary power structure of song publishers and producers—who had actually been responsible for some damn good early-to-mid-'60s soul, such as the Drifters, J. J. Jackson's "It's All Right," the Corsairs' "Smoky Places," Chuck Jackson's "Any Day Now," and Garnett Mimms's magnificent "Cry Baby"—seem to matter.

As the white pop of the early 1960s began to seem increasingly passé, the recasting of the music culture gave black singers and musicians such a loyal and rabid following of their own—and one so different from the British Invasion acts—that it was resistant to skinny, pale English lads in tight suits, pointy-toed boots, and cereal bowl hairdos. According to the *Billboard* pop charts, there had been only two black acts among the top 30 songs in 1963, Stevie Wonder and the Impressions. In '64, that jumped to six (excluding Louis Armstrong's novelty show tune "Hello, Dolly!"): Mary Wells, the Supremes, Martha and the Vandellas, the Raelettes, the Drifters, and the Dixie Cups. In '65, it was eight, and never to fall below five again.[14] This, too, was pungent irony, since groups like the Beatles and Rolling Stones owed their eyeteeth to black artists from Muddy Waters to Motown.

Now, the Motown/Memphis niche, emulated by a number of black-oriented labels, entrenched but new enough to be fresh, was the only real alternative to the Brits. Indeed, soon black artists engaged in a reverse invasion, touring England and other European countries. The Stones revived men like Muddy Waters and John Lee Hooker, the Yardbirds Sonny Boy Williamson and Howlin' Wolf, by not only covering their songs but sharing stages with them so they could enjoy a last ray of sun for their work. But within the new generation of rock, contemporary black singers like James Brown took the old masters to a higher level of truth and hellfire. And Otis Redding seemed to be the apostle of the new gospel called soul.

•

THIS RIVALRY of racial "frenemies" played out against a tableau of hard-fought racial progress, something that was late in coming to Macon. Martin Luther King Jr., who was born in Atlanta, led protests in Albany, Georgia, in the early '60s during a time when twelve hundred blacks were jailed for marching in the street and organizing boycotts against segregated businesses in Savannah, Brunswick, and Rome. In Atlanta, which claimed to be "the city too busy to hate," the Ku Klux Klan flourished. Indeed, at least 103 Southern cities desegregated their lunch counters before Atlanta. Up in Macon, there was unrest, too, including a 1963 bus boycott, but with little impact or notice. Dennis Wheeler found out that racism was alive and well in town. He remembers cops turning a bus of civil rights workers back at the city line. Wheeler himself participated in a sit-in at Woolworth's downtown, when, he says, "Me and a bunch of my friends, black and white, sat down at the lunch counter. We were expecting a big incident, maybe get arrested, but they didn't blink, they just served us. Nobody wanted any trouble. Jim Crow was there but it was like, let's just keep things cool."[15]

Elsewhere, things were far worse, and grim news would be seen and heard on the news in Macon. But for Redding, the closest he came to seeing violent racial unrest was when he became the innocent catalyst in a near-riot. Both times it happened, crazily enough, during the annual homecoming concerts at the Macon City Auditorium in 1966. On July 17, as a sold-out house of seven thousand was watching the show, a white cop named C. C. Dorough, meandered through the hall and found a black man in the basement illegally selling liquor. When he slapped the cuffs on the man, said the cop later, he was "jumped by a gang of Negroes." Dorough said he was thrown to the floor, beaten, and disarmed, and the assailants clambered up the stairs. He called for backup and the exits to the auditorium were sealed, causing panicked spectators to bang on the doors and confront cops, who began to arrest people. The next day, UPI reported on the incident, with the Macon *Telegraph* running a story headlined 50 NEGROES IN MACON, GA., ARE ARRESTED IN MELEE,[16] the exact headline that also ran in the *New York Times* a day later.

A bigger impact on Otis was made by what he saw with his own eyes on the road, when the realities of Jim Crow clashed with the serendipitous vibe of his stage act. "Otis hated the segregation he saw all over the South," Wheeler says. "He'd be told he and his band couldn't stay at a hotel or eat at a restaurant. He'd say, 'Man, this is crazy.' He'd talk to the manager or owner, tell him who he was, and be able to talk them into letting them stay. He wouldn't confront anyone. He said he was stopped on the road in the South quite a bit by highway patrolmen because he and his band were driving along at night on those back roads. That was always a danger. But Otis more or less laughed about it. Hell, he even said he could get along even with the KKK!"

Redding however was neither an idealist about institutional bigotry, nor would he walk around expecting people to touch his hem. If they did, they might have felt the bulge of a .38 pistol he kept tucked in his waistband under his sport jackets. Lover of country-boy comforts that he was, he had no problem keeping a shotgun in the closet and withdrawing any firearm when he felt he needed to. Alan Walden once said: "We all did. If you travel long enough you are going to meet certain people who will try to take advantage of you and we certainly had our share of fistfights, shootouts, and other harassment; like having to go to the back doors, filthy hotels, and bathrooms or no service at all. During these incidents I feared no man, Otis was a street fighter and with Huck along as his bodyguard they both could handle almost any situation."[17]

However, there was at least one situation when they went too far. Days before Redding's homecoming concert in 1964, one of Otis's friends, Herbert Ellis, was beaten up after confronting another man, David McGee, who had been flirting with Ellis's girlfriend. Learning of this, Otis, Sylvester Huckaby, and two others, his childhood running mates George Watson and Bubba Howard, drove in Otis's flashy Cadillac (stealth apparently wasn't an issue to them) to McGee's house on Roy Street, where they got out and began firing through the windows. Otis shot McGee in the thigh and Otis himself was hit by some buckshot fired by McGee or his brother Willie, who was wounded in the stomach by Huckaby. Howard took some buckshot as well, enough to send him to the hospital, before the gang fled in the Cadillac, which was also shot up.

Amazingly, no one was seriously hurt in this Wild West shootout and only Huckaby was charged, with assault with intent to commit murder. More amazingly, nothing seems to have been written about the incident in the local papers and Redding—who was often cut a break by cops in Macon, such as when he was stopped speeding, which he was, a lot—was never detained and, two days later, did the show at the Auditorium, supposedly in cold fear that someone might take a pop at him. Yet in the end, Huckaby was only given two years' probation. The McGee brothers then filed separate civil suits against Redding; David McGee was awarded a mere five hundred dollars, and Otis settled up with Willie McGee for an undisclosed amount.[18]

This jaw-dropping shootout, involving one of the top artists in music history, remained generally unknown for decades. Not a word of it appeared at the time in the Macon papers, nor thereafter, and it was buried in the dusty archives of the Bibb County courthouse until the publication of the 2001 Redding biography by Atlanta writer Scott Freeman, who dug up the court papers. Few of the acquaintances who were around Redding say they ever knew of the surreal incident—Alex Hodges, Alan Walden, and Al Bell among them—and given the serious, and potentially disastrous, nature of it, the question naturally arises of whether there was some kind of cover-up, though the juicy details certainly would have made for some salacious headlines across the nation. Still, even if the McGees could have exaggerated the extent of the shootout in their court filings (a strong possibility in light of the lenient penalties involved), the most striking thing about it is the clue it gives into how astonishingly bad Redding's judgment was. Having come so far, it seems beyond fantasy that on the eve of a major concert, he would have risked everything to uphold the honor of a peep—by perhaps killing someone in a wanton act of violence.

This insane, psychotic episode alone makes a joke out of the oft-chanted hosannas to Otis Redding's saintly character, one being Steve Cropper's absurd insistence that Otis "didn't have any vices, and didn't have any faults."[19] Redding may well have, as Cropper says, "made everybody feel great . . . always wanting to help people out and always paying people compliments," and on some level the incident may have said something about Redding's tenacious loyalty to friends and an old-world sense of eye-for-an-eye street justice. But, given the stakes, and the trivial nature of how the incident began, this was a raw example of abominable judgment, a vivid demonstration that he had not taken to heart anything that the Rev. Otis Redding Sr. had preached on those Sunday mornings.

As a companion postscript, Sylvester Huckaby, after Redding's death, would file in and out of prison as if through a revolving door, convicted at various times of burglary, grand theft, dealing heroin and cocaine, and—not by surprise—illegal firearms possession. In 1990, he was shot in the head, execution style, as he left his house in Macon, a murder never solved.[20]

Few would ever have a clue that Otis was not very far from that lifestyle in his youth. At the least, Redding liked to live fast and clearly had some uncontrollable impulses beneath the endless charm and seemingly cool-headed sensibility. The good news was that he had a way and a means—a voice given from God—to avoid a fate like Huckaby's. That voice, and a lot of money, it must have occurred to him, would be able to make any problem disappear.

•

WHEN IT came to coping with racial change and peril, Redding, like all other black entertainers running the gauntlet in America, could only hope his music and charm might help out in some small way. "You know, it was sixty-five, sixty-six" says Dennis Wheeler. "What could one man do anyway?"[21] Yet perhaps it was not coincidence that, late in 1965, Jim Stewart felt it was time to hire an African-American to an executive job at the company, the only man at Stax who could have been called an activist, and ease the heat.

Enter Al Bell, one of the hippest of industry denizens. Born in Arkansas, Bell had gained notice as a DJ at black radio stations WLOK in Memphis and then WUST in D.C. during the time of the March on Washington, from where he broadcast his show that day. A peripatetic guy, he also owned a soul label, Safice Records, which was likewise being distributed by Atlantic. He was somehow able to walk a tightrope between enterprise and conflict of interest, and promoted soul concerts at the Howard Theater and in Memphis as well, having first run across Otis at one show just after the release of "These Arms of Mine." Knowing that coming to Stax would be a step down in pay grade for Bell, who was making six figures at the time, and would also necessitate divesting Safice, Stewart nonetheless rang him up. Bell had to admire the man's chutzpah.

"Al," he said, "my sister Estelle and I have talked and if you come to Memphis, we'll give you an equity interest in the company."

Bell was intrigued, but needed to know what the Stewarts could pay him. "I can give you a hundred dollars cash," Jim said. "And Jerry Wexler has agreed to give you a hundred dollars."

Bell laughs. "I just said, '*Whaaaat*!? Man, my momma didn't bring up no fool.' He said, 'Al, think about it.' And I did, and it began to make sense. I was breaking so many Stax records, it was a small step to work for them, work with Otis Redding, Carla Thomas, Booker T. and the MG's. I loved what was happening at Stax but no one ever knew if it would be here today, gone tomorrow, because it was always in such dire straits, economically."[22] Looking through the broader lens of one small record company standing as a pivotal lever in the future of black music and black capitalism, Bell soon was packing up his Nash Rambler and driving with his wife to Memphis. Absorbing all he could of the operation, he spent two weeks just listening to freshly pressed Stax records. Then he began putting in his two cents on which ones to release, the first of which was "You Don't Know Like I Know" by Sam and Dave, on Christmas Day.

A man of much intrigue, Bell had also been a confidant of Martin Luther King Jr. After dropping out of Philander Smith College in Little Rock in 1959, he'd worked in Midway, Georgia, for the Southern Christian Leadership Conference (SCLC) and marched with King in several demonstrations. He left the SCLC when he came to believe that the aim of the movement shouldn't be passive resistance but, as he puts is, "economic development, economic empowerment." When he settled into radio, Bell developed something else: a vast pipeline to the black stations across the country. He had done enough favors for Stewart to be repaid with a job at Stax and was hired in 1965 as head of promotions. As a result, it was no coincidence that Stax/Volt product became more in demand and its hits more plentiful. Berry Gordy now had a bigger rival than he could have imagined.

11

Crossing Over

"*Otis Redding became as close to me as a brother. He was a genuine, sincere, transparently honest person. He was in spirit a country boy like me, but he could have been anything he put his mind to. We were natural people, we didn't put on airs. And until the last day I saw him, he never changed who he was. When I came to Stax, I like everyone else would be excited when we knew he was coming in. When he got there, he would go around to all the offices, greet the secretaries, the people in the finance department—that was his favorite—and it was just Otis being Otis. The whole atmosphere changed. It became an Otis Redding environment. His personality was that poignant. It just penetrated you.*"[1]

Al Bell had every intention of continuing Redding's role as the heart and soul of Stax. But he also wanted to get him off what he regarded as a treadmill, Stax's reputation in the industry as a regional label. By 1965, Berry Gordy hadn't found "Hitsville" to be descriptive or specific enough of a crossover factory and adopted "The Sound of Young America" as Motown's motto, pointedly refusing to bow to any regional or racial skew. Bell's response was to label Stax/Volt "The soul label for your swingin' turntable," and "The Sound of Memphis." He applied not traditional marketing to Stax but what he called "social science," or a jive version of it. This meant retracing the travel routes of the black migration, by getting records initial play in the South then up the path of the Mississippi River to the big Midwest cities, then to the biggest markets, New York and Los Angeles. As Bell remembers, by capturing the outer trails, he could induce those two huge markets to play Stax records, not just with sales figures but jive. "When I walked into those markets I would have respect," he said. "I wouldn't have to speak in soprano; I could speak in bass."

Given free reign by Stewart, the horn-rim-glasses-wearing, natural-born pitchman went to work, as he says, and "focused one hundred percent on building Stax." He had already paid Stewart a nice dividend—when he joined the company and divested Safice, a bonus for Stewart was that Bell brought to the label one of his acts, and partner at Safice, Eddie Floyd, a smooth-voiced, elegant man who had gone solo after his tenure with Wilson Pickett in the Falcons, a group founded in Detroit by Floyd with Mack Rice that had a marked influence on Berry Gordy's ensuing label. Although their lead singer on their biggest hit, "You're So Fine," was Joe Stubbs (the brother of Levi Stubbs, who would front the later signal Motown group the Four Tops), Gordy had no use for any of the Falcons, and it would be years before Floyd and Pickett landed at Stax and Atlantic, respectively.

When Bell and Floyd were part of the Stax fold, Bell recalls, "I sat down with each of the musicians, to get a sense of their affinity for soul music." He also met with the singers, looking to carve a niche for each. Otis Redding, of course, already had a niche, but the problem Bell found was, again, the regional identity, which in the broad lens was a barrier for all the artists, keeping more than a few songs from realizing the success of "Green Onions." That reality had left many suffering from a kind of inferiority complex.

To counter that, Bell implemented some motivational tools. An oversized "thermometer" charted record sales, set to burst when it hit a certain level. As for promoting Stax product, he says, "I came at it from a social science standpoint. I studied the history of black music, how it moved up the Mississippi and fanned out to the big cities, and the music preferences of each city. They were all different, so I put out not just one record at a time but dozens, forty, fifty. I got to know all the retailers, all the record store owners, the clerks. I'd send them in-store-only copies to play. If a Temptations record came out, I'd make sure an Otis record, or a Sam and Dave, or a Rufus Thomas, would be playing in the store. People would come in for the Temptations record, hear ours, and walk out with both." Laugh. "I worked for Berry years later and I once told him about this. And he was like, 'You did *what*? I said, 'Berry, I rode your coattails!'"

With Redding, Bell's strategy utilized Otis's own history. "I knew about Otis because John Richbourg in Nashville played 'These Arms of Mine' on WLAC for a solid year, and that WLAC was a fifty-thousand-watt, clear-channel station that was heard in fifteen states. So with Otis I always went into those markets first, they were like his backbone. I'd stock all the retailers and stores in that corridor with his records. When a store can sell five in-store copies of a record, that's pure profit. So they would be tellin' customers about how great Otis Redding was. It all built from there."

Some at Stax were amused by the glib, quirky Bell; around the halls, he was sometimes referred to as "God" for the mountains he seemed to be able to move within the industry to get Stax records heard.[2] On his orders—and he would be on the phone around the clock to the acts out on tour—performers who had had little personal contact with the public were making appearances at record stores. For Otis, Bell's aim was to make sure he got him played outside Southern markets. "Stax product was basically selling [only] in the South. In no time at all I established Otis, Carla, and Rufus in the northeast corridor." The west coast would be next. And, now,

Atlantic Records wanted an even larger part of the action. By hook. Or crook.

•

HIRING BELL was just one auspicious development for Stax in the fall of 1965. Months before, in June, Jerry Wexler had broached Stewart about formalizing Atlantic's distribution alliance, which, incredibly, had never been codified by any written agreement. Atlantic had always just charged Stewart what it wanted for its distribution expenses plus a 10 percent cut of royalties on the records it pushed, slightly more for the albums that were released on Atco. The ruling order at Atlantic—the Ertegun brothers and Wexler—had prospered from the alliance but they, too, were aghast that a company so good at making music was so bad at making money. Stewart, for his part, was equally uneasy about rumors within the industry that Atlantic was looking to improve its own shaky economic health by offering itself for sale in the new wave of corporate mergers and acquisitions.

Thus, both Stewart and Wexler were eager to get a deal done, with Stewart perhaps too eager for his own good. His biggest concern was making sure he had an escape hatch should Atlantic be sold. With that in mind, he asked for, and received, a clause stating that, in case of a sale, Stewart could exercise an option to renegotiate the terms of the distribution deal or terminate the deal outright, or within 180 days should Wexler no longer remain with Atlantic as a stockholder or employee. However, in the manner of Bobby Smith, he pretty much glossed over the rest of the thirteen-page document, not even having lawyers vet it, and what may have been intended as a lowball offer pending negotiations were never negotiated. Atlantic, unwilling to commit any upfront cash, also specified, almost insultingly, that Stax/Volt needed to provide at minimum six master recordings a year—this despite the release of twenty-nine singles alone in 1965. Even though Stax itself manufactured each record at its own cost, it could not release any unless approved by Atlantic on a small scale limited to "your local market" to "test the salability" of the records.[3]

For Atlantic the five-year agreement virtually annexed the little company on East McLemore Street. Stax would earn—on its own records—a royalty of fifteen cents per single sold and 10 percent of each album, at 80 percent of the list price, less whatever Atlantic would charge for additional expenses, taxes, and packaging. Even for the brotherhood of thieves that was the record industry, it was a heist, or a gift, from what the Atlantic lawyers probably figured was a chicken begging to be plucked. Such failures by Stewart to negotiate more than explained why Bell arrived at a company spitting up red ink.

"I had no idea what was in the contracts. I thought the Stax contract was like my contract with Atlantic for Safice Records, which was much fairer. It wasn't my place as an employee to say, 'Let me examine the contract,' but I didn't need to. I came to Stax because it was ninety thousand dollars in the hole and it was about to go under. I knew Jim was upset because in his mind Atlantic wasn't promoting his product as they should, which is why he hired me. He had no choice in renewing with them, he still needed their distribution network. But it was my job to start generating money so we could keep the company alive."

Atlantic could thank its lucky stars for Bell, who came in blazing with confidence and a profusion of bold ideas that salvaged the Stax identity and transformed a bog of worry and imminent doom into a bustling, confident beehive. He also made Atlantic work its behind off, keeping up with the lava flow of releases he authorized, though this was filling Atlantic's coffers more than Stax's, an equation that did not bode well for the future. Most everything Bell did was new for Stax, but one thing he would not do was disturb Otis Redding's creative routine.

"Only a fool would have interfered with him," he says. "I was fascinated watching him. He would come in, sit in a chair with a little acoustic guitar next to Steve Cropper and in front of Al Jackson, play and sing the song and hum the horn parts. He and Steve would work on it, then they'd start recording, bit by bit, the rhythm section first, then the horns. It wouldn't stop until it was done. Sometimes it got so hot in there, Otis would strip off his shirt, but he'd never stop singing."

Bell was most intrigued with the instinctive groove between Redding and Jackson, whom Bell says were "like Siamese twins. When you listen to 'Try a Little Tenderness' is when you really hear that happening. It was Al who brought those rhythm changes into play, while Otis was singing the song."

Whatever songs were sent out, he notes, none of them were based on potential appeal to white buyers. "No, no, no," Bell wails. "We weren't looking for crossover records or obsessing over finding a pop hit for Otis. That didn't matter for any Stax artist. They all had to be authentic, they had to believe in, *live in*, those songs. Nobody ever did that better than Otis. It wasn't about hit records. It was about music that made us feel good and other people feel good."

Bell claims he never paid attention to the trends, what was on the charts, who was hot. He had his own barometer, "from the heart." He had his own feel about what African-Americans wanted to hear, what moved them. As for Redding's records, putting them out was a mere prelude to what became a heavy promotional barrage. However, it pained him that not enough ears in that market were hearing Otis, and thus would not flock to the stores for his records. That could be said as well for all Stax artists, some of whom seemed to ebb and flow, rising to the top on a whim then receding into partial obscurity for months, even years. For Bell, the solution revolved around separating Redding from the rest of the soul crowd, and thereby dragging the Stax stable into wholly new territory.

"I had to find a niche for him. Oh, I loved Motown, broke out all their records as a DJ. But it was a whole different animal from us. Berry was influenced by Detroit, the assembly line, and he figured out a way to produce a sound that would be accepted by white radio, and they would have tracks with that sound before having an act do the vocals on 'em. That isn't organic. It's commercial, but it ain't natural. Our arrangements were designed to reflect each artist. You wanna know why Motown never covered Stax songs? It didn't fit their formula! The problem was, what we were doing was too black! It was up-front and in your face! We wanted the general public to come to us, not us going to them. We had hits but our validation was our black audience. Then when the white audience discovered us, we didn't get whiter—*they* got *blacker*. And that's when we went from being in debt to one million dollars ahead, in one year!"

•

THE BOOKISH, hermetic Jim Stewart could never enjoy the fruits of being both musically and financially in the black, with cause. He had to pay down old debts, with no help from Atlantic, while recording, manufacturing, and promoting records that he'd be making mere pennies on. However, Otis didn't need to mortgage living la dolce vita. Stewart rigorously paid his artists their due royalties—a bond that Berry Gordy was always accused of not keeping by his artists—but this paled beside what was made out on the road. By 1966, Redding's net worth was estimated at over one million dollars.[4]

Now that he was a shooting star, it seemed cool, even necessary, for the soul crowd to aver some sort of propinquity to him. Little Richard, for example, who had barely had the time of day for the young Redding back when Richard was king and his protégé just another imitator, was taking all sorts of credit for the new comet streaking across the sky. "I gave him his start!" he would say, and still say years later when he repeated it to writer Stanley Booth, adding, "I was his idol!"[5] Of course, Richard said pretty much the same thing about everybody who ever sang rock and roll after him, but it was especially urgent now to take proprietary action with respect to the building imprimatur of Otis Redding.

Across the soul landscape, performers were starting to take on Otis's "look." Stax singers had to dress to kill on the road and even Otis's barber in Macon, one Walter Johnson, was a known quantity. Percy Sledge and Sam and Dave came in all the way from Memphis to get their hair styled by Johnson.

Redding still traveled light however, his retinue usually one or the other of the Walden brothers and Speedo Sims as a bodyguard, valet, and road manager. Rodgers Redding, after he was out of the service, resumed going on the road with his big brother. A secretary provided by the Walden agency, Carolyn Spikes, sometimes made the trip, but Sylvester Huckaby, his travel limited as part of his plead-down sentence for the shootout in Macon, seemed to be out of the circle by 1965. Whether or not the riot and the gun incident had anything to do with it, Alan Walden recalled that the agency's strategy for Otis now had him playing only one gig in Macon a year, the homecoming at the City Auditorium early each summer. This event, he said, "became so big I enlisted my father, my mother, and my two cousins Robert and Roy Walden, and my younger brother Clark and his wife to help make the shows' run successful."[6]

The trappings were all there: Cadillacs, newer buses, better hotels. Soon, they were looking around for a private plane, so Otis Redding could ride in style. The high life was his now, the still-limited sales royalties more than balanced out by his touring profits, which Phil Walden, and sometimes Otis himself, collected after each show and carted around in a strongbox until they got back home. Then, it would go into the Redwal account, from which only Redding and Walden could make withdrawals. It would be jointly decided how much Otis needed and the rest would be invested, at the start, in modest real estate deals.

Otis himself was gobbling up real estate. He had moved the brood to their first house, on Commodore Drive in the Shurlington section of East Macon, the most upscale neighborhood open to black residents in the still mostly segregated city. There, as Dennis Wheeler recalls, the driveway "looked like a parking lot,"[7] stacked up as it was with Cadillacs (one of them purple) and the champagne-colored Ford Fairlane he had bought Zelma even though she hadn't learned to drive yet. Also there much of the time was the Fairlane he had bought for the deacon, who seemed now to have few quibbles over his son's career choice. But there would be one more move in his future, to his dream house, way out in the country, where he could breathe fresh air, ride horses, and provide his kids with wide open spaces to romp. He had Walden hire realtors to scour the countryside and approved a three-hundred-acre stretch of rolling green farmland in Round Oak, on which he began construction of what is the shrine and epicenter of the Redding legacy: the Big O Ranch. He sunk $125,000 into the land and construction of a faux log cabin home early in 1966. Intentionally, it wasn't easy to get there, or even find.

To do so, one must head north on Highway 129 and ride until traces of civilization disappear up in Jones County, where the scenery becomes nothing but rolling farmland and open sky. There is some wonderful history here. A brick storefront window of the Round Oak historical center reads "Miss Lillie Gordon's store, circa 1925." Confederate monuments from the Civil War still stand, such as the White graveyard and a field identified as the site of the Stoneman Raid, the 1864 campaign led by General George Stoneman immortalized in the Band's "The Night They Drove Old Dixie Down"—the tracks that "Stoneman's cavalry" tore up being those of the Central Georgia Railroad that still run parallel to Route 11. There is, too, the African Methodist Episcopal Church, one of the first churches founded by freed slaves, one of ten in Jones County.

At Mile Marker 18, a semi-paved road trickles off into the wilderness—OTIS REDDING DRIVE, the sign says. You have to improvise and drive over the tracks to get to it, and after a mile or so the brush clears and several big white ranch homes are visible. A weathered sign on a thick iron gate framed by white stone columns says THE BIG O RANCH, the acreage of which meanders into the woods beyond a lake and around another Civil War cemetery. Once here, Redding was home. But even with this expanse, he almost immediately began to buy up more surrounding land, to build homes for the deacon and Fannie Mae and Rodgers (Debra, along with her three sisters, had by now moved permanently to Los Angeles). He spent much of his time populating the stable out back with horses that he would saddle up and ride through acres of country he now owned. Visitors sometimes would have to wait for him to finish riding, or even plowing some of the fields.

Dennis Wheeler recalls, "He had a few crops, vegetables, stuff like that. He had pigs, cows, and chickens. But he just liked getting out and doing things a country farmer would. I'd see him working on an old tractor he bought. A guy with all those new cars would work for hours repairing a tractor from like 1950." The snazzy wheels, clearly, were a signet of being rich and famous. But it wouldn't have been living in the real world, the world he still embraced, if there was nothing to fix.

•

IT WASN'T exactly the high life, more like *Mayberry R.F.D.* But the land was all his, every inch of it. And when he was at the Big O, he was farmer Otis, tinkering, plowing, getting his hands dirty. The hint that this farmer didn't need to milk cows and was fat in the wallet was the chrome and steel parked in the driveway, which to him were like toys. One time when he was home he came into Bobby Smith's studio and said to Wheeler, "Hey, come on back here, I wanna show you something." He took Wheeler outside, where a Ford Galaxy 500 convertible was parked. Beaming, he went on, "This Ford talks." Whereupon he pulled out of the front seat a gadget that looked something like an oversized telephone and began to showily call up people, each call requiring around ten minutes to get a dial tone. "It was a mobile phone, the first one of those I ever saw," Wheeler says. "I thought, 'Why would anyone need that?' With Otis, cars were made to drive once and discard, then go buy another. He'd give the old ones away as gifts, to friends, sometimes to strangers."

If he was riding high in 1965, so were those whose lives he had materially changed. Up in Memphis, Stax, even as, or maybe because, it battled perpetual debt, was lit up and recording virtually around the clock. The session players were constantly working, not only in that studio but on their own road trips to Muscle Shoals and New York, and playing clubs like Hernando's Hideaway in Memphis. "Oh yeah, we were all doing better," says Floyd Newman. "The rate was the same but we were playing around the clock. I ain't gonna tell you how much I was pulling but I did all right. And I'll tell you something else. Otis was a main cause for that. He made us part of his world, which made *everybody* want us to play on their sessions."[8]

●

THE SOUTHERN soul scene was taking shape in many small ways, and Stax seemed to be the center of whatever good was bubbling up. There was, for example, the breakout of Sam and Dave. Jerry Wexler indeed knew what he was doing with the struggling duo, who by all appearances had no chance to thrive. They were an odd couple, to be sure; not only did they not like each other much, they both sang tenor, Moore slightly higher; according to Wexler, "Sam [was] in the sweet tradition of Sam Cooke or Solomon Burke, while Dave had an ominous Four Tops' Levi Stubbs–sounding voice, the preacher promising hellfire."⁹ After working long hours with Steve Cropper writing songs, and a lean two years being put under the aegis of Isaac Hayes and Dave Porter, Sam Moore, whose reluctance to team with Dave Prater only complicated things, didn't take easily to the formula, saying years later that "fifty percent of what they presented to me at Stax I didn't like."¹⁰ Like Otis, he craved doing Sam Cooke and Jackie Wilson songs. He resisted when told to sing in a high register, which Hayes and Porter knew made his voice come alive. So they would rehearse Moore in a low key, then in the studio have the band play in a higher one. "I would get angry," said Moore, "but that's what I would do."

The result, the giddy, screeching joy that would define the act, was first heard when they recorded the Hayes-Porter "You Don't Know Like I Know," which made the R&B top 10 early in 1966. Then, so the story is told, when Dave Prater had to hit the bathroom during a session and Hayes, or in some versions Porter, called for him to finish, he shouted, "Hold on, man, I'm comin'!" Thus came the title for the song that broke them—although it had to be altered when radio stations were skittish about the unintended sexual innuendo, the inanity of postmodern puritanism confirmed by the forced addition of an "a" before "Comin'," such making it all nice and sanitary. Jim Stewart also needed to recut the song so the vocals could reflect the change, but slyly rereleased the original in its place with the new inner label. The song went number 1 R&B and, importantly, number 21 pop, and Sam and Dave would record twelve more R&B songs. Part of the lure of their songs was the subtle but implied one-upmanship between Sam and Dave, set to amazingly crisp and clever Hayes-Porter arrangements. On "Hold On," for example, Booker T. Jones—who had returned to Memphis after a sabbatical to earn a music degree from Indiana University—played a tuba over Duck Dunn's bass line to further underscore the pounding beat.

For them, Stewart had made an exception to his no-outsiders rule, his cut of Hayes-Porter songs an obvious inducement, but also because, unlike Wilson Pickett, Moore and Prater paid obeisance to him and the musicians. As a reward, Wexler allowed Stewart to release selected Sam and Dave singles and albums concurrently on Atlantic and Stax. As they hit their stride, they reeled off some of soul music's signature nuggets, topped of course by "Soul Man," a song that Hayes would bask in the rest of his life—this despite the fact that nearly everyone who first heard it cringed at the commercialization of black slang used mainly as a sarcastic put-down of other black men acting self-consciously cool.

"It was the current trick phrase," says Wayne Jackson." Everybody was calling each other that, like, 'What's happening, Soul Man?' And I hate that kind of stuff. I was a full-grown man, and that didn't appeal to me. I thought it was embarrassing . . . another real lesson that corn sells."[11] Removing the irony and making the term the ultimate expression of black male pride, Hayes and Porter elicited from the pair an absolutely dead-on performance, immortal right down to Moore's celebrated impromptu cry of "Play it, Steve!" before one of Cropper's ticklish guitar licks. It went number 1 soul and number 2 pop, and when the duo performed it onstage during their uproarious shows it had the effect of placing veteran soul men like Otis Redding at the very least on no higher a rung than the new class of soul men, if only for a while.

Another, Percy Sledge, arrived that year as well, to carve deeper into emotional soul. Signed to Atlantic, the Alabama native hit the jackpot right out of the gate with a song he had co-written, "When a Man Loves a Woman." Recorded in another of those backwoods Alabama studios, in Sheffield, the slow, sensuous balled went right to the top of the R&B and pop charts, gold record status, and an eternal lifetime of cover versions and movie and TV soundtracks.

These new soul classics posed a challenge to Redding, who couldn't hope to compete with Sam and Dave in dance-worthiness, nor should he have cared to. He was certainly no slouch onstage; indeed, what separated him from acts like Sam and Dave and other fireballs was his emotional renderings, which cut deeper, and relied more on melody and hushed intervals that echoed his words and divided the explosive bursts. And if Percy Sledge had bested him in one song—Sledge had three other singles that went top 20 and top 10 soul, none with anywhere near the same impact—Otis had dozens that elicited the same sort of emotional pull, and could touch people in subtly different ways.

"He was supremely confident," Al Bell says. "That was in many ways a front, but he knew he could always trust his own judgment, which is why we left him alone. I always thought Otis Redding could be whatever he would have wanted to be. He had the inner drive of a diesel, and just as much belief in himself. Other artists were looking all around show business to see what was going on, the trends, the fashion, the content of songs. Otis didn't feel he needed to do that yet. And this was something that rubbed off on me. I never cared what was happening in the business. In fact, I always thought Otis was the one setting all the trends."

12

The Whole Damn Body

Otis Redding, to his credit, never seemed to take any of the personae people hung on him, Mr. Pitiful or the King of Soul, even a little seriously. This explained why he had fun parodying that image when he recorded "Love Man" in 1967, a song not released until after his death, when it would be a sly wink from the grave about a man who was "six feet one, two hundred and ten," a prize for every woman who breathed, who could please her around the clock. It was fully intended as a spoof of generic lady killers, not unlike him, and would inevitably define him as a good-natured, harmless, even lovable kind of cad. The very qualities that every successful soul man has always embodied.

His next big step came when Phil Walden had booked him for a three-day Easter weekend engagement in L.A. at the Whisky a Go Go, the then-two-year-old music club/discotheque on the corner of Sunset Boulevard and Clark Street. Named after a similar hot spot in Paris, this rudder of the rock and hippie chic scene was where music's bigwigs hung, watching a passing parade of aspiring acts and snorting cocaine, shielded in VIP sections reserved for them by the main owner Elmer Valentine. It was an intimate place, 250 seats, but the Whisky stage was where the Byrds, the Turtles, and Johnny Rivers had gained traction, and where, not far down from Sunset outside another club, in November, a police "riot" during a confrontation with counterculture types would inspire another new act, Buffalo Springfield, to write "For What It's Worth." In June 1967, Van Morrison's Them would take the stage, their opening act the Doors.

There were two things that conjoined these wide-ranging acts—they were invariably white and sang rock. No major black performers had gotten a booking there, but Walden had no trouble securing three days for Redding, which he and Otis envisioned as a crucial inroad into the rock mainstream. Jim Stewart immediately signed off on plans for a live album to be recorded from the shows and sent Al Jackson Jr. to act as de facto producer. Atlantic's brain trust also thought it would be an exploitable product, and Nesuhi Ertegun flew cross-country to oversee the details of the album. On opening night, Ahmet Ertegun also arrived and watched from the VIP lounge.

Otis had warmed up for the gig with an April 2 appearance at the Hollywood Bowl, the seventeen-thousand-seat band shell nestled under the comely HOLLYWOOD sign in the hills surrounding it. The Bowl, founded in 1922, had been a regular venue for philharmonic and symphony orchestras, operas, and pop and jazz singers such as Al Jolson, Judy Garland, and Ella Fitzgerald, and had hosted the Beatles in 1964 and '65, the latter performance recorded for a live album. Redding, booked for a concert to benefit the Braille Institute of America, was the only soul act among the likes of Donovan, Sonny & Cher, the Righteous Brothers, the Turtles, and the Mamas & the Papas, and was on and off before he could leave much of a mark in the biggest house he had yet played. Still, the crowd was up on its feet as with any Redding performance, and he told Walden if he got another open-air venue, with more time, he would kill.

•

THE WEEK before the Whisky gig, he arrived in L.A. along with his ten-piece Otis Redding Revue. This outfit consisted of three sax men, Robert Holloway, Don Henry, and Robert Pittman; trumpeters Sammy Coleman and John Farris; guitarist James Young; bassist Ralph Stewart; drummer Elbert Woodson; and even a trombone player, Clarence Johnson. Another member, Al "Brisco" Clark, a horn man whose band had often backed up James Brown, would serve as the emcee for the shows. There were also three background vocalists Otis liked to call his "protégés," Katie Webster, Carl Simms, and Kitty Lane. At the Whisky on opening night, the house was sold out and dozens of L.A. blues buffs who worshipped Redding hung around on the street outside trying to hear his voice seeping through the walls.

The crowd inside came mostly out of curiosity and word of mouth, his éclat more known to the Sunset crowd than any of his work. When Brisco introduced Redding by screaming the names of some of his successful R&B songs, there was almost no reaction. Otis then ambled onto the stage, looking like a time traveler from another era. In a simple black tux, he was wedged between gyrating go-go girls in hydraulic cages, wearing spangled green hip-hugger pants and crop-tops. Trying to keep his concentration, he reeled off a two-hour-long set, not saving an ounce of juice. According to Atlantic Records logs, over the three shows, recordings were made of practically every song he knew, no less than *eighty-six* tracks in all, though many of these were multiples of the same songs. He sang around two dozen each night, opening with "Pain in My Heart" or James Brown's "I Feel Good." Liberally sprinkling the set list with covers, he also threw in Brown's "Papa's Got a Brand New Bag," "Satisfaction," "Put On Your Red Dress," "If I Had a Hammer," "Danny Boy," and "A Hard Day's Night." At one point a young black woman shouted out, "Otis, would you please sing 'These Arms of Mine'?" "Yes I will," he said chivalrously, and did.[1]

The audience at first didn't seem knocked out, their applause polite, and his voice began to get hoarse from trying so hard to get them going. "Right now," he said at one point, nearly out of breath, "we're gonna sing a soulful song, ladies and gentlemans [*sic*], for everybody that's unhappy, and this song is something everybody need and everybody wants, and I been trying to get it." That, of course, was "Respect," which perked up the mood considerably. He then had them for good with an exhausting "I Can't Turn You Loose," which only a cadaver could have sat still through. Rising to their feet, martinis in hand, the Hollywood elite in suits and mini-skirts shouted back at him his improvised chants of "got-ta, got-ta" and "hold on, hold on."

"Holler as loud as you wanna—you ain't home!" he commanded.

Watching from the side of the stage were members of the Rising Sons, who had done a brief opening set. Though the band never made it big, two members would, Taj Mahal and Ry Cooder, in blues-folk and as a guitar legend, respectively. Taj Mahal recalled that "at that time, Otis was it. Great band, great songs, great show . . . one of the most amazing performances I'd ever seen, and I've seen some great performances."

It wasn't that Redding had a certain style, it was just that he could articulate the sum and substance of soul so convincingly. After performing, Taj Mahal couldn't wait to get offstage to watch Otis do his thing. By the second night, Cooder had tuned his guitar in the same key in which Otis wrote most of his songs. A bigger thrill for the group was when Otis asked to borrow that guitar to do some noodling around when he had an idea for a new song.[2]

When the tapes of the Whisky gig were played for Stewart, however, he was aghast. Stax had paid good money to hire Wally Heider and his famous mobile recording studio to get a studio level of perfection, yet Stewart thought some of the musicians were off-key and decided to keep the album on the shelf. The L.A. critics, however, ate up the show, seduced like everyone else who ever experienced Redding in the raw. The show, raved *Los Angeles Times*' music writer Pete Johnson, "was the most exciting thing that rock-worn room has ever harbored," calling Otis "a magic singer with an unquenchable store of energy and a great fluttering band." Titling his review OTIS REDDING'S SOUTHERN-STYLE BLUES BAND LETS OFF STEAM, Johnson was not shy about hyperbole: "Drawn by his growing popularity, a fervid audience shoehorned into the club, chorused in on some of his songs, and, at one point, interrupted his introduction of a ballad by clamoring for more of his fast-paced tunes. Redding was assured of an In Group following . . . when, from among his spectators, emerged Bob Dylan, trailed by an entourage of camp followers."[3]

Johnson thus earned the right to pen the liner notes when, in 1968, during the rush to get out posthumous Redding material, the first incarnation of the album was released, *In Person at the Whisky a Go Go*. It was limited to just ten songs, the ones least affected by acoustic clinkers. Yet, opening with "Turn You Loose" and closing with "Respect," the work drew much critical praise, as it does decades on, for its sense of gritty soul undiluted by rock pretenses.[4]

It would be another fourteen years before eight more unreleased tracks were issued, and until 2008 for a far more complete record of the engagement to come out. Then the 2010 *Live on the Sunset Strip*, which contained that *entire* set list of the three shows, bumbles and stumbles and all. One reviewer noted that, in these, "Otis struggles for traction as his startlingly inept road band flails about behind him, out of tune and out of sync . . . Otis has to tell them the key of 'I've Been Loving You Too Long' before he performs the song, and then even he hits a few flat notes along the way."[5] But it was nonetheless clear why at the time the engagement could be filed under "conquest." His voice, unrelentingly sincere and overwhelming present, could likely have saved him from any disastrous stage complications. Few have ever had as deep a reservoir of personal ingratiation. In a 2010 retrospective longtime chronicler of the L.A. rock scene Harvey Kubernik headlined an article for the Goldmine .com website that read: OTIS REDDING WAS KING OF THE SUNSET STRIP IN 1966.[6]

A telling footnote of the L.A. interlude was that Otis thought he might have stumbled onto that elusive crossover hit. Robbie Robertson, the writing juice of the Band, who at the time was backing Bob Dylan, recalls that while recording "Just Like a Woman," Dylan asked him, "'Who do you think would be good to cover this song?' And I said, 'Otis Redding. He's one of the greatest singers that ever walked the earth.' And he said, 'Really?' I said, 'Absolutely. He would just tear it up.'" After catching Redding's show at the Whisky, Dylan's manager Albert Grossman took Dylan and Robertson backstage to meet Otis and Phil Walden. "So we get together and I'm pitching this song. And Otis says, 'That sounds great to me' and we play this song and he says, 'Oh man, what a song—she breaks just like a little girl. Oh, that's fantastic. I'm definitely gonna record this.'" The song clearly did seem compatible with the Redding oeuvre, its lyrics about the fragility and pain of love. Yet when it wasn't on Redding's next album, Robertson asked Walden what happened to "Just Like a Woman."

Walden told him, "We went in and recorded it and Otis couldn't sing the bridge. Otis said, 'I don't know how to sing the bridge,'" referring to oblique lines in that portion of the song that dealt with conjoined bits and pieces such as fog, amphetamines, and pearls. Robertson recalled, "Walden said Otis couldn't get those words to come out of his mouth in a truthful way. The rest of the song, no problem. And I thought, God, I understand that. If you can't sing something with a complete honesty, then you shouldn't be singing that song, and he was just being honest about it."[7]

•

ALEX HODGES, who now was doing his own hitch in the Army and stationed in Europe, was kept in the loop about the business at home. "Phil sent me every new Otis record, and let me tell you, I was a very popular guy because whenever I'd play it, a crowd would grow around me to listen. He had fans everywhere. I was in Turkey for a while, and I was the most popular guy in Ankara." When Hodges told Walden of Redding's foreign constituency, Phil booked his first tour in England later that year. The Otis Redding experience wasn't about one-nighters in the sticks anymore. Indeed, being booked into places like the Whisky a Go Go was part of a master plan to go broad, go big, beyond the ken of the soul circuit. When Phil and Otis had meetings in the office, they would take turns shouting "We're gonna conquer the world!'" It was a joke, but it really wasn't. It was deadly serious.[8]

Wringing every drop out of the California market, Redding would be back in the late summer, headlining an August 21 "Midsummer Dance and Show" in Oakland's Continental Club. Not to be outdone, Bill Graham, the *big* Bay Area promoter at the Fillmore Auditorium, had begun booking soul acts for his place, with the Temptations playing there in late July. A hatchet-faced man who held the future of many rock acts in his hands, Graham was a Jew born in Berlin as Wolodia Grajonca, and as a child had walked with his family hundreds of miles to get out of Nazi Germany. Rarely, however, did he have to venture far to book an act he saw as in the vanguard; usually, managers came to *him*, and his intense ego and volatile temper made him both a respected and loathed figure in rock. But Graham wanted Redding, badly, to do what he had done at the Whisky before an auditorium full of rabid young rock pilgrims, who had made the Fillmore ground zero of the psychedelic-cum-flower-power culture sparked by the Beatles' teasingly lyrical and sonic parables of hallucinogenic reverie.

Graham made his name promoting rock, but loved blues and soul. In fact, the Fillmore itself is located on Fillmore Boulevard and Geary Street, a grid that was called the Bay Area's version of 125th Street and Lenox Avenue, and was originally leased to a black entrepreneur, Charles Sullivan, who booked acts like James Brown and Duke Ellington. Graham, an ex-mambo dance champion and born hustler, began promoting dance troupes in the early '60s and after Sullivan was found murdered in June 1966 took over the lease on the grand ballroom.[9] While rock acts like the Grateful Dead, Jefferson Airplane, and Janis Joplin leaped out of the city's underground scene, Graham spoon-fed young hippie audiences the elixir of soul, booking R&B and soul acts to open shows for the rockers. King Curtis had recorded a live album at the Fillmore, with Billy Preston on keyboards and Curtis's legendary saxophone buttressed by the Memphis Horns.

Memphis was, in fact, Graham's focal point for soul, not Motown. And he was one of the west coast's legion of Redding acolytes, the centerpiece of the idiom for Graham. He had seen him perform in L.A. and was so smitten he told Harvey Kubernik in the August issue of the Brit music fanzine *Melody Maker* that Redding was "the single most extraordinary talent I had ever seen . . . a six-foot-three black Adonis . . . who moved like a serpent. Or a panther stalking his prey."[10] Graham, who died in a 1991 helicopter crash returning from a concert, would recall that "there was an *ultimate* musician everyone wanted to see. Everybody said, '*This* is the guy.' Otis Redding. He was *it*."

That summer, Graham flew all the way to Macon to ask Redding personally to commit to a series of holiday shows in December. Even though Otis would never have come close to the new "acid generation" idiom, or even had any idea what the screaming, adenoidal, long-haired rock bands of the day were singing about, he liked the challenge. Graham recalled, "I could have offered ten thousand dollars, which would have meant I would have been dead. Out of business. Or I could've said that when I talked to artists I respected, Paul Butterfield, Michael Bloomfield, Jerry Garcia, when I asked, 'Who's your guy? Who's number one on your list?' they all tell me it's *you*."[11]

Otis and Phil Walden were a bit leery of the scene. L.A. hippies were one thing, but the Haight-Ashbury kind were something really wavy. They asked, said Graham, about "the kids . . . and the drugs they took. They thought it was like voodoo rites out there. The lights, the paints, the crazy clothes. It was *strange* for them." To Graham, the sale was made because he himself "was a pretty straight guy and I didn't dress fancy." They signed off on the gig and career move. Or, as Walden would later say, another move into territory that other white promoters advised him not to go. Even in 1966, black entertainers, he recalled, were expected to reach only so far. "They're never satisfied," was the refrain.

"Why *should* they be satisfied?" was Walden's response. "Why shouldn't they want the same damn things [as whites]? I never would be satisfied with just the finger. I wanted the hand too. The arm. The whole damn *body*."[12]

•

WHEN HE'D get to the 'Frisco Bay, it would be with some much-needed fresh material on his plate—his newest release, in May, being the emotive, measured ballad "My Lover's Prayer," which, backed with a bright and bouncy "Midnight Hour" sound-alike called "Don't Mess with Cupid," had gone top 10 soul and 61 pop. On August 2, he made it to Memphis for his first session in months, cutting ten songs for the album that would take the place of the aborted live one. The result, *The Soul Album*, was an eclectic brew. Just three tracks were co-written by Redding—the previously recorded "Just One More Day," "Any Ole Day" (with Steve Cropper), and "Good to Me" (with Memphis blues singer Julius Green). The rest were paeans to the four corners of soul, past and present, with covers of Wilson Pickett's "634-5789 (Soulsville, U.S.A.)," the Temptations' socially aware "It's Growing," swamp bluesman Slim Harpo's "Baby Scratch My Back," country soul man Roy Head's "Treat Her Right," the old Bessie Smith wailer "Nobody Knows When You're Down and Out," Jerry Butler's "Cigarettes and Coffee," and Sam Cooke's "Chain Gang."

It was fascinating as an homage to his contemporaries and idols, and to his own near infinite breadth within the soul genre. The cliché that Redding could make any song seem his own was settled law; his renditions were uniquely his, the precedents merely vague outlines for his own emotionally supercharged versions. In "Cigarettes and Coffee," by example, his woebegone plea to save a love gone bad was every bit an update of the classic song of hopelessness, "One for the Road," leaving indelible images of an Otis Redding, unable to sleep, sucking on cigarettes and downing coffee in the wee hours while talking on the phone with "my baby." His granular texture and mood changes, with every little nuance seeming preternaturally anticipated by the sad horns and tinkling honky-tonk piano, cast an almost visual image of a man about to rupture in agony before the sun came up.

While each track created a similar mental picture of despair and hope, the album's potential for spawning even R&B hits was limited. Indeed, though the album was his deepest penetration yet into the white mainstream, peaking at number 54 while holding its soul credentials by going to number 3, no single would come from it. On August 30, only weeks after the album was out, Otis was back in the studio to record two original songs in the *Otis Blue* mold. One of them was the unforgettable "Fa-Fa-Fa-Fa-Fa (Sad Song)," the rhythmic repetition of that musical syllable something that would become a Redding signet. As Dennis Wheeler tells it, "I asked him one day, I said, 'Otis, why'd you put all them 'fa fa's' in there, and he patted his butt where his wallet was bulging in his back pocket and said, 'I put my fa fa in here.' He meant fatbacks, I guess, really greenbacks, but the country boys call 'em fatbacks—not pork but big bills." A laugh. "But maybe that was after the song made him all that 'fa fa.'"[13]

Actually, whatever other meaning the syllabic repetition had for Otis, "fa-fa" was what he would commonly hum in the studio to mark where the horns would play—and, perhaps with a wink, he would say he took the drily melodic horn riffs of the song from the theme of the TV quiz show *The $64,000 Question*, though it had been off the air for years.[14] (Sly Stone would crib those riffs note for note in the 1970 hit with the Family Stone "Everybody Is a Star.") In the tradition of similar nonsensical rock/scat patois like "Doo Wah Diddy Diddy" and "Da Doo Ron Ron," he and Cropper realized that certain gibberish just seemed to work to match lyric to melody. The whole song, in fact, developed, as had "Mr. Pitiful," a good-natured kickback for Otis, or as one retro-review perceived to be "a slight dig at his gloomy image."[15] It was subtly so, since anything he ever sang was like a bleeding wound, and the lyrics brought the usual Redding unburdening, now with the admission that all his life he had been singing sad songs, the only kind he could sing.

The tells were that the opening horn riff was almost satiric in its pomp, and the interplay with the Memphis Horns slyly cuing his rolling cascade of the "fa fa fa fa fa fa fa fa fa" hook beefed up by a harmony vocal by Dave Porter. It was the most fun he ever had during a recording. The song unfolded in a slow, funky groove, the mood so relaxed that it apparently was necessary to note in the title that, yes, it was a sad song, carrying the joke further. "Sad Song" was done too late to make *Soul Album* and, with "My Lover's Prayer," it would go on the next LP, which after a thirteen-song marathon session on September 13 yielded six more tracks. The work came out in mid-October as *Complete & Unbelievable: The Otis Redding Dictionary of Soul*, an affected but accurate recognition that he had indeed rewritten the dictionary definitions of soul. Its cover, returning to the *Otis Blue* formula, was graced by another winsome woman, but this time she was black.

This lava flow of Redding product was enough to satiate any Otis, or soul, aficionado, the work including some of his best blues busters, some real curios, and a good bit of filler. Like "Satisfaction," his newest foray into rockin' soul, a cover of the Beatles' "Day Tripper," was recognizable only by the title and a few phrases from the original about a cheating lover. Riding a steamroller of hard rhythm tempered a little by a church organ, his paroxysms of *something* from start to finish—intermingling lines with more of his trademark "got-ta, got-ta" paroxysms—was deliriously incoherent and just as infectious. And the usual Otis curveball was his keening version of the 1946 ditty "Tennessee Waltz," confirmation that country music often has the same elements of pride and pain as the best soul song.

There were two other Redding-written songs, the ballad "Ton of Joy"—containing the all-time great Otis line about a lover who "sets me on fire but I'm willing to burn, children"—and the finger-popping dance song "She Put the Hurt on Me," featuring a slinky Booker T. organ line. Also featured was another by Otis and Al Bell, under his birth name Alvertis Isbell, "Sweet Lorene," a good, workmanlike soul turn perhaps most notable for the inclusion of the mid-sixties street slang "I'm gonna sock it to ya"—a phrase that would soon be used to give even more juice to another of his songs, turning it immortal.

"That was all Otis," Bell says, "everything was spontaneous. We hadn't planned on writing together. I wasn't a songwriter but I was good with words." Fatefully, Bell happened to be in the studio with Stax piano player Allen Jones. Encountering them, Otis invited Bell and Jones to flesh out the song with him, asking for lines and riffs that might work. The "sock it to me" exhortation was one Otis thought of using, for no other reason than it sounded right. Not sexual, as was the derivation of the phrase, but because it fit into a cranny he needed to fill during the vocal. "It was a way of saying, 'Gimme some soul, gimme some heart, gimme your attention! C'mon—sock it to me!'" says Bell. Even so, *everything* he said or sang sounded like it meant something sexual.[16]

The Hayes-Porter duo was represented on the LP by "Lord Have Mercy" and "I'm Sick Y'all," which they wrote with Cropper and is one of the hardest rocking and "British" sounding of Redding entries. But the killer was another Tin Pan Alley cover, of the kind that simply no one else would have even attempted. This was "Try a Little Tenderness," which more than anything else would become his most enduring personal proverb. That result was a surprise to Redding, inasmuch as he recorded it only because the Stax staff—Stewart, Cropper, Hayes, and Porter—believed the pop tune originally done in 1932 by the Ray Noble Orchestra could be contoured to an anguished Redding treatment. Indeed, it had actually been one of Bing Crosby's most soulful ballads, his crooning coated by lush strings in the 1933 version, and one of the most venerable Tin Pan Alley standards. It had also been covered to death by everyone from Frank Sinatra to Jimmy Durante to Mel Tormé to Aretha Franklin, who gave it its first soul burnishing on her third album for Columbia in 1962 and, in the clincher for Otis, Sam Cooke, as part of a medley on his *At the Copa* album. Estelle Axton's contribution to these selections should not be overlooked; from years of seeing records come in and go out the door at the Satellite, she had an encyclopedic knowledge of pop music and which songs fit the mold of each artist.

For Otis, the fit of "Tenderness" was its lullaby-like first eight hushed bars, which gave any singer free reign to show off his or her soft side, at a deliberate meter that most versions maintained throughout while the orchestration swelled behind them—such a sweet confection that Stanley Kubrick had to use an instrumental version of the song for the opening credits of the darkest comedy of all, *Doctor Strangelove*. Cropper and Hayes/Porter pretty much let it all fly live and congeal according to what Otis felt. After a brief horn intro peeled away into a quiet gospel-style piano, Booker T. organ and sax fugue, he began the prelude, each word drawn out with meticulous phrasing and restrained but heaving emotion. The words he applied to women aging too fast and too lonely, such as "weary" and "shaggy," beckoned him to pull back from his usual demands for satisfaction and, delicately and hushed as he could, transform himself, appeal for a little bit of tenderness as a salve.

He continued at this pace and pitch for two more verses, the rhythm still muted, until, out of nowhere, Al Jackson, sensing Otis was going to detonate before long, quickened the beat, to double-time. "We didn't know he was gonna do that," Duck Dunn would say. "It was amazing."[17] Feeling the fire now, Redding eschewed the lyrics and went all *Otis*. Raising the volume, the pace and the key, horns blaring all around him, he barreled into a near seizure of semi-lyrical Otisisms that went on until the song had gone nearly four minutes, blasting right through Jackson's cheddar-sharp cymbal ruffle designed to tell him he was running too long. Checking the clock, and knowing a four-minute track would never fly on the radio, Stewart faded it out with Otis still in a lather, keeping it at 3:50 on the album and cut down to 3:20 for single release, though it prevented listeners from getting every drop of arguably the best Redding performance ever recorded.

Released probably a few weeks too soon, *Dictionary*'s light-hearted touches were personified by the cover art of a natty, grinning Otis, in a red jacket and vest, white slacks and shoes, and graduation cap, tassel hanging next to his face, standing beside an enormous textbook with the album title and an enigmatic, over-sized "My-My-My" at the bottom. Well-received when put out in mid-October, the album had to fight off *Otis Blue* and reached only as high as 73 on the pop chart, 5 on the R&B. The single of "Fa-Fa-Fa-Fa-Fa," released weeks earlier as a teaser, notched rankings of 29 and 12, followed in November by "Try a Little Tenderness" going to 25 and 4—modest numbers that belie how deeply both songs, and the album, burrowed their way into soul as the idiom of choice in a new cultural mainstream. Indeed, Jon Landau, who had reviewed Redding as a twenty-something Brandeis history major and freelance rock writer before finding his own comet to ride as Bruce Springsteen's producer and manager, would write in the liner notes of the album's 1993 expanded CD rerelease that *Complete & Unbelievable* was "the finest record ever to come out of Memphis and certainly the best example of modern soul ever recorded."[18]

And yet, soon, Otis Redding would want more.

13

Making the White Feel Black

The autumn and early winter of 1966 were a whirlwind for Otis. The first order of business was a trip to England. The timing was auspicious, given that *The Soul Album* was selling briskly in England, as would *Dictionary*, and his singles now were almost always top 40 hits there: "My Girl" and "Day Tripper," both of which failed to chart at home, would run to number 11 and 43. Phil Walden had also been itching to take the Redding brand to the far corners of the global market, one that had been opened for soul artists by Motown. In 1965, Berry Gordy exported his wildly successful Motortown Revue to England, planting soul in the breadbasket of the British Invasion and firing the imagination of British blues rock groups that until then were kept off BBC radio and only heard on stations broadcasting from "pirate" ships out in the English Channel.

Walden, who knew nothing of the turf, partnered with English promoter Harold Davison to arrange a two-week tour in September through midsize ballrooms and music halls of a few hundred to two or three thousand seats, with the intention of keeping it low-key in case England wasn't quite ready to snap up tickets in bunches to see Redding. Indeed, Davison found that local promoters weren't offering the moon; the dates he booked pulled on average around £500 to £600 pounds, or $800, each. When the Orchid Ballroom in Purley offered £300 against a percentage of the gate or £650 pounds outright, Davidson took the latter. Even so, Walden laid down the "Redding Rule": His man had to be top-billed and close every show—a rule no one ever questioned, not even Ray Charles, who at a recent show with Otis in Miami, had been bluntly told he had to go on before Otis or lose the gig, which he needed. Charles was coming off a dreadful year in which he was arrested for the third time on heroin possession, given five years' probation, fined ten thousand dollars, and forced to take a year off while at a rehab clinic. He finally kicked the habit with his own treatment, which, he once said, was "I vomited and vomited and vomited till there was nothing left to vomit. And then I vomited some more. I was heaving up poison."[1]

Even though Charles would soon be back to elite status, winning a Grammy the next year for "Crying Time," such was Redding's prominence, and leverage, that he still could have pulled rank on Brother Ray. And when Otis arrived in London with nine pieces of his touring band, leveled expectations or not, he seemed like a visiting dignitary. He was met at Heathrow Airport by a limousine provided by Brian Epstein, the Beatles' manager, who had earlier in the year visited Stax to get a look at the place and possibly arrange for the Fab Four, who worshipped Redding, to record *Revolver* there. Epstein however backed off when he visited the theater and it became clear mobs would surround the place.[2] In September of 1966, though, it was the mobs around Redding that became a security concern, and mitigated any chance that the Beatles could somehow meet him on their home turf.

As if an attempt to re-create and transfer some of that old Beatles voodoo, Redding was ushered into a room at Heathrow for a press conference with the Brit reporters, then driven in the limo, while the band bundled into a bus to his hotel, where a small cadre of fans milled about on the sidewalk. The tour itinerary was a checkerboard of venues, the Ram Jam Club in Brixton to the Gliderdrome in Lincolnshire to the Farnborough in Hampshire, as well as several London halls. At each stop, Redding's intensity, a trait not often seen onstage by the phlegmatic English rock acts, lit up the room, but, despite the hype, not the box office of the outer areas. Barry Dickens, Davison's assistant then and later the head of England's biggest booking agency, recalled that Redding "went down well but the crowds weren't huge."

The London gigs however were more satisfying, prompting *Soul Music Monthly*—a newspaper not in America but England—to venture, "Otis should receive a mention in the *Financial Times* this year. The attendances on his recent tour, especially in the London area, were quite phenomenal. 6,000 people paid ten shillings to see him at Purley and it was later announced that 8,000 had forked out twenty-five shillings a head to see him at Tiles," the Mod club in London where the Animals and the Who regularly played.[3] Indeed, the Orchid show made Dickens grit his teeth. Had he made the percentage deal, he said, Otis would "have walked out with about 1,500 pounds. That was one of my worst deals ever."[4]

Otis had no problem with the erratic attendance; he was more put off by the British food, which he and his band, who were all used to the soul food on the chitlin' circuit, thought tasted like cellophane. Conversely, the Brits who accompanied him reeled at the cologne and deodorant Otis covered himself in, the strength of which could choke a horse, an example of what Europeans regarded as dainty American vanity. And yet Otis seemed to be lapping up adulation that felt different than the kind at home, never tempered by any racial complication. He must have felt like Josephine Baker, the sublime "Black Pearl" of the 1920s and '30s who, untethered by racism or censorship, giddily danced almost nude in the Paris nightclubs and became a French citizen. If too many white American hipsters seemed like dilettantes, the fans of black music over there actually revered artists like Redding.

This was something that dawned on earlier blues travelers like Little Richard, who took advantage of the fact that British music tastes seemed to be fixated on black artists far more than the American music mainstream, even if the English crowds tended to see the roots of pain and slavery in the music as a quaint notion without real context. "It would be England that made Otis a star, a superstar," says Floyd Newman. "They were not hung up on race there. In the U.S. a musician is just a musician. In Europe, Japan, France—they're artistes! We signed as many autographs as the artists. They knew where you came from, where you were born, your whole life."[5]

By far the highlight of the trip was Otis's September 16 appearance on the ITV network's popular Friday night TV show *Ready Steady Go!* Like the almost full roster of Motown that had been featured on the same show during the '65 Revue tour hosted by Dusty Springfield, Redding was not just a guest; the entire program was built around him, and American soul music. Introduced as "the great, the one and only Otis Redding," he came on with "Satisfaction" and "My Girl," then introduced Eric Burdon for a British blues rendition of "Hold On I'm Coming." He later returned with "Pain in My Heart," "I Can't Turn You Loose," "Shake," and "Land of a Thousand Dances," intermingled with go-go girls and overheated audience members.[6]

The performance came as a revelation to many Brits who had never heard, much less seen, him, but now knew that, as *Melody Maker* noticed, "Otis Redding is unbelievably cool."[7] It was another pivotal soul milestone, such that it was clear—as with his brush with the L.A. in crowd—Redding would need to keep riding this wave, too. Almost immediately, Walden, knowing the next Europe trip was going to be legitimately a big deal, went to work on it, this time making room for the biggest of Otis's Stax labelmates, but still with the proviso that everyone and everything else—and that included

Jim Stewart's interests—would be secondary to Otis and his interests. And if Stewart felt this was undermining his authority, he was hardly in a position to quibble about it. That was how excruciatingly cool Redding was.

●

THE LESSONS of his latest conquest had the usual ripple effect across the soul board. That fall, other acts began crossing the ocean blue to play their own ballroom tours. By Christmas, a headline in the black *Philadelphia Tribune* announced, NEGRO ROCK & ROLL "BIG" IN LONDON.[8] But, as fast as he moved, Otis was back killing American audiences, jumping right into a two-month tour with Sam and Dave. It had been suggested by Al Bell as a way to bump Moore and Prater up into major stars, as sharing space with the Otis Redding Revue would be a publicity boon. But it was something Otis needed for his own purposes, having realized that he needed to be more kinetic onstage, to keep pace with the other Stax acts that had been turning up the heat on him. Thus, according to Moore, Redding was able to eat some of his pride. As Moore tells it, Otis relaxed his usual insistence that he not share the stage with another top-shelf act to make room for the pair on a two-month jaunt that kicked off with a week of shows, commencing with a November 26 Thanksgiving gig, at the Apollo Theater. Remembering how stiff he was the first time he was on those historic boards, Otis actually was taking quite a chance having Moore and Prater go on before him.

"That tour lasted 62 days," Sam Moore once said, "and Otis saw to it that we would co-headline with him, although of course he would close the show. That was quite a generous thing for him to do, but he had an ulterior motive, see. I used to tease him, say, 'You sure you want this? 'Cause when we leave that floor it's gonna be kind of hot.' But he *wanted* that. It made him move. Because Otis could get very lazy, but if you pushed him, shoved him, it would be all over for you. And I always enjoyed seeing how he would react, that I could put pressure on him to top himself each night." Moore also took some credit for pushing Redding, sartorially. Sharp-dressed man that Moore was, he ribbed Otis about his ankle-cut slacks, which to Redding and others reared on soul revues of the 1950s, and James Brown in particular, had a purpose: allowing audiences to better observe the fancy footwork of the performers. And while Otis did primp up his wardrobe, the high pants remained intact. To Moore, he was the quintessential "clean-cut gentleman."[9]

Jerry Wexler also believed Otis took a crucial step up in staying at the top of the pack because of the connection with Sam and Dave. That rivalry, Wexler said, "sharpened him."[10] Sometimes he would bitch about it. Almost as a running gag, he would tell people between shows that "those two motherfuckers" were making him work *too* hard, that "they're killin' me," and coming too close to upstaging him.[11] However, Al Bell knew Otis too well to take that seriously, and says that Redding *needed* that challenge, to keep getting as much out of his tired body as he could.[12] Walden knew it, too, saying that Redding "had to invent something or else he couldn't have gone on after them. He told me, 'Boy, they're makin' me work, baby.' And he started to move onstage . . . Sam and Dave unquestionably put fire under Otis, as Joe Tex put fire under Otis. But Otis also put fire under both of them more so than they did him. The truth is, there were other issues beside this that were involved. And the issues were between them so let's leave it at that."[13]

Otis, who was as irritated by Moore's egocentric manner as Sam's own partner, nonetheless kept his pride at bay dealing with him, albeit with a certain ambivalence. When asked in early 1967 what he thought of Sam and Dave, he admitted that he thought more of the Righteous Brothers. "When I first heard the Righteous Brothers, I thought they were colored. I think they sing better than Sam and Dave"—before, as if catching himself, adding, "But Sam & Dave are much better showmen. Sam & Dave have been together for ten

or twelve years. I think Sam & Dave are my favorites."[14] However, he
indeed began to move more, and appreciated being in a challenge.
He also traded in the sweaters for pastel colored jackets and even
three-piece suits onstage, though the ankle-high cut of his trousers
remained. He would update only as much as he needed to, which
wasn't much. And, in retrospect, hall of famers though they were,
and with all their crossover hits, Sam and Dave could never have
done anything other than open for Otis Redding.

•

THE TOUR was periodically interrupted when other opportunities
called. The biggest was the Fillmore gig, but in the weeks before,
Otis seemed to be everywhere a man could be in L.A. Six years ago,
he couldn't get the time of day in Hollywood, but now there were
gigs constantly, and a TV appearance on *American Bandstand* on
December 3, when he lip-synched "Fa-Fa-Fa-Fa-Fa" though, if one
were to gauge the relative popularity of Stax and Motown, it was
telling that, the very next night, the Supremes would be singing
their hit songs on one of their many spots in prime time, *The Ed
Sullivan Show*. There would be a lot of Redding to hear. "Try a Little Tenderness" stayed on the chart ten weeks, during which fold of
time he got to the Bay Area for the December 20–22 run at the Fillmore, where rock history was being written seemingly by the day. It
was just one of a slew of gigs booked on the coast, but the one with
the most potential reach. Wary of a repeat of the Whisky a Go Go
stumbles, he came with a new edition of his band, which had been
playing previously as the Robert Hathaway band, veteran pros all.
Graham would say of the show, it was "the best gig I ever put on in
my entire life,"[15] suddenly discovering that in the city where rock,
young, and white unite, Redding was like a god to the biggest acts.

"Every artist in the city asked to open for Otis. The first night, it
was the Grateful Dead. Janis Joplin came in at three in the after-

noon the day of the show to make sure she'd be in front . . . no musician ever got *everybody* out to see them the way he did . . . If you liked
R&B or white rock and roll or black rock and roll or jazz, you came to
see Otis."[16] Otis chose the Grateful Dead—who had covered "Pain in
My Heart," Jerry Garcia lowering his voice several octaves to catch
the blues groove, though it sounded as much country as blues—then
Johnny Talbot and De Thangs and Country Joe and the Fish. "Can
you imagine?" says Alex Hodges. "What other soul act in music at
that time could have headlined the Fillmore three straight nights
and have a rock band as his opener? I always have said that when
Otis came on, it was as if nothing like that had preceded him. It was
like it was something brand new."[17]

Fillmore-style psychedelic pop-art posters, the work of artist Wes
Wilson, billed THE OTIS REDDING SHOW, IN DANCE—CONCERT, FROM
9 P.M. UNTIL ?, his image transposed on a smoky green background
beside a blood-red "Otis Redding and his Orchestra." At three bucks
a ticket, it must have seemed like the steal of the century. Otis hit
the stage looking like a one-man new wave, covered tightly in a green
suit, black shirt, and yellow tie, a key chain hanging from his belt—
Graham's black Adonis. Knowing he was the ruler of the universe.
Beautiful and shining, black, sweaty, sensuous, and passionate . . .
[a] sheer animal." He didn't dance but rather strutted, his voice filling the hall, the "got-ta got-ta" syllables stabbing the dank, pungently
sweet air, tearing to bits every musical and social boundary.

He said little by way of banter between songs, and instead grunted
like an elegant caveman, "Yeah . . . whew . . . Hey! . . . party! . . . Oh
yeah!" When a young girl in the front row kept dreamily screaming "Otis! Otis!" he came forward, bent to one knee, and cooed a
breathy, "I'm gonna s-s-sock it to ya, baby," causing squeals and
matching shouts of "yeah!" in the crowd. As always, everyone was
on their feet, clapping in time to songs they were not entirely familiar with. These were mostly young, white teenagers, proto-hippie,
in or on the way to college, from upper- or middle-class families, yet

on this night, and the two to follow, for a fleeting hour of their lives they felt *black*. This was something that probably could not be said when whites were in a James Brown audience, or even a Sam and Dave audience, and it was unlikely any other performer but Redding could carve such a social dynamic. It was that revelation that led Graham to say years later, "By far, Otis Redding was the single most extraordinary talent I had ever seen. There was no comparison. Then or now."[18]

Otis came away from the performance as he had from the Whisky and in London, wondrous that he could put a spell on people so different from him. In the dressing room swathed in towels when Graham came in, he called out, "Bill! I *love* these people!"

Almost speechless (not generally a Graham trait) the promoter stammered, "Otis, I can't tell you, Jesus . . ."

Otis, though, was looking for something other than flattery. Interrupting Graham, he said, "Very nice ladies here. *Very* nice ladies."

Phil Walden, who had made the trip with him, looked back years later with the observation that "Otis was quite fond of the women out there. He was pretty fond of women *everywhere* he went. He left his mark, shall we say."[19]

•

THE TWO remaining shows were equally orgasmic—literally so, apparently, to the esteemed San Francisco music writer and critic Ralph J. Gleason, who was something of a muse of the city's new hippie scene. Gleason, fifty at the time and a habitué in the pages of the *San Francisco Chronicle* and the counterculture *Ramparts*, had interviewed virtually everyone who was anyone in music, including Elvis, Hank Williams, and Bob Dylan, and had written liner notes for Frank Sinatra and Miles Davis albums. His review of Redding was perhaps the most glowing he ever wrote. Otis, he said, "was pure sex," in "everything he did," in "every word he uttered," and "every motion he made," and "the most completely sexual thing" he had ever seen. He would not forget what he'd seen. In 1967, when Gleason would cofound the molto hip biweekly *Rolling Stone* with fellow ex-*Ramparts* editor Jann Wenner, he would also help stage an outdoor concert near his home turf, in Monterey, and didn't intend to leave Redding out.

This obviously would afford Jim Stewart another chance at recording Otis live deep within the world of California mainstream pop. However, Stewart, who had felt burned by the aborted Whisky a Go Go live-album project, had no interest in getting such a performance on tape again, not to mention at a venue so far out of the Stax ballpark, geographically and culturally.

Meanwhile, Otis was back on the road again, this time with a mini-soul revue touring in California, featuring Marvin Gaye, the Five Dimensions (*not* the pop soul Fifth Dimension but a British blues band that played backup on Millie Small's "My Boy Lollipop," and in which a teenage Rod Stewart briefly played harmonica) and Gerald Wilson. The first show was Christmas Eve at the Sports Arena in L.A. and the following day was in San Diego. And, now, after the rush of the Fillmore gig, Otis seemed to have a momentary bout of arrogance. As reported by the black L.A. newspaper *Sentinel*, "Otis Redding, the rock singer, failed to make many friends here the other day when he was slated to appear on the Christmas Eve show. [It] failed to draw well, and Redding reportedly would not go on. But the next night, when the show went to San Diego, a capacity crowd was present. But not Otis Redding."[20]

Beyond having to refund his hefty advance, he had done himself no good ending the year on such a sour note, and was an augury of some acidic times ahead. Indeed, as he was rising almost beyond his own control, the business of Otis Redding seemed to be something that existed in the ether, separate from the "pitiful" fellow he portrayed himself to be in his songs. Redding had seemingly made self-admitted fragility and the gnawing need not to be alone something intrinsic to the otherwise obligatory macho soul man facade, and made the image of a new kind of black man with feelings that not only screamed but hurt into a bankable idiom.

14

"The Only Son-of-a-Gun This Side of the Sun"

O tis was rapidly nearing hallowed ground by the beginning of 1967. In that year, the *New York Times*' Robert Shelton would write in retrospect that Redding was as polished a performer as any in the rock gentry, and was "comparable, perhaps, to the life-is-sad-but-bearable moods of Frank Sinatra . . . what might be described as 'an ecstasy singer,' finding both joy and pain ecstatic and communicable emotions."[1] So, too, was he capable of self-mockery, a component that made his songwriting wonderfully engaging.

On a broad arc, Otis had accomplished more than he could have been aware of at the time. One of the better repercussions of the now fully fledged soul genre was that singers like Otis Redding, Wilson Pickett, Sam and Dave, Marvin Gaye, Stevie Wonder, and the Temptations need not step aside for white acts covering their songs, usually badly but also with more market success. Those days were, mercifully, over. The crossover appeal of these acts was carved on the singularity of their respective niches; simply, their songs could not be attempted without acute embarrassment, excluding when a Stax hand redid a Motown song (witness Redding's cover of "My Girl"). And now, apropos of Redding's "Satisfaction," soul acts could cover rock and roll standards with impunity, with a whole new groove, and were valuable even if few of these works matched the sales level of the original.

White or "blue-eyed" soul acts—the term having been semi-seriously coined by black Philadelphia DJ Georgie Woods in the early '60s, and more cynically adopted by music journalists in the British press apropos acts such as Tom Jones and even the Beatles and Rolling Stones—were of course free to create a similar groove. Some, including the Righteous Brothers, Rascals, the Soul Survivors, and the Box Tops, even did so admirably, frequently aided by producers like Tom Dowd and Muscle Shoals' Rodney Mills and Jimmy Johnson. Then again, by the mid-sixties most rock songs were in some form an inculcation of the soul groove. However, the old rule still applied, only now as stone cold reality: When something new, and salient, was heard in pop music, it came from the soul stew, and if it was appropriated by the white rockers, it was almost always inferior.

Knowing this was a tremendous impetus for men like Otis Redding, who was practically knighted when he crossed the ocean. Otis, to his credit, now had a worldly view, quite more layered and empowering than when he was still in Macon, and an insouciance that other soul singers simply did not have. Alex Hodges attests to the fact that "around sixty-six, sixty-seven Otis really grew. He was still the country boy but he could walk into a chandeliered room filled with guys in Guy Laroche tuxes and women in Yves Saint-Laurent gowns, wearing his cardigan and casual slacks, and regale them, always know what to say. Women who hadn't smiled in years were almost swooning like schoolgirls."[2] Redding was compatible with the paradigm shift in culture from "A Hard Day's Night" to "Norwegian Wood," from beach blanket bingo movies to *What's New Pussycat?* and *A Man and a Woman.* Indeed, this was

the very same distance between "Shout Bamalama" and "Try a Little Tenderness."

Still, no matter how decked out he could be, and despite rising
from the streets of Macon, Redding cultivated the image of a country boy, something that kept him grounded in the soil and manure
of the backwoods he loved. As it would turn out, this would provide
an opening for Jim Stewart to continue keeping pace with Berry
Gordy. Late in 1965, Motown recycled an old niche—the soul duet,
which dated back to the '50s teaming of Brook Benton and Dinah
Washington. First they paired Marvin Gaye with Mary Wells in
1964 on the modestly successful album *Together*, then with Kim
Weston for a smash pop and R&B hit "It Takes Two." Stewart liked
what he heard, and believed there was a natural chemistry in tone,
style, and geography between Otis and Carla Thomas—"his rawness and her sophistication."[3]

When he posed the idea to them, neither Otis nor Carla was
crazy about it. Worse, she was on leave from recording, studying
at Howard University for a master's degree in English. That meant
they would need to lay down their vocals for some tracks at separate sessions, whereupon their vocals would be stitched together.
Carla also fretted about doing harder soul than the sweet ballads
that were her meat. Otis talked her into doing the album, but he too
had limited time and could only compose one song, "Ooh Carla, Ooh
Otis," co-written with Al Bell, again as Alvertis Isbell. The other ten
tracks were all covers, including "It Takes Two."

The Hayes/Porter team would be charged with finding the others, which included their own "When Something Is Wrong with
My Baby" and "Let Me Be Good to You," as well as Eddie Floyd's
"Knock on Wood," and Aaron Neville's "Tell It Like It Is," and the
oft-covered blues song "Lovey Dovey" (co-written by Ahmet Ertegun). But they struck gold by choosing "Tramp," west coast blues
guitar legend Lowell Fulson's pop and R&B hit of the year before.
Hayes and Porter took Fulson's humorous monologue of a coun-

try sod whose possessions pale beside the fact that lovin' "was all
he knew how to do," and made it a sassy point-counterpoint of the
mating game. Perhaps to rub it in on Motown, they took a guitar
lick from the Temptations' "I'm Losing You" to break up the steady
melody of the original. Otis and Carla had a ball with it, sending
up and putting down materialism and superficiality. Carla, playing
the bitchy gold digger to the hilt, surprised herself with her ability
to improvise put-downs about the country bumpkin from the Georgia woods who doesn't wear "continental clothes and Stetson hats."
They gamboled on, going back and forth, jabbing, joshing, strutting, and flirting, clearly attracted to each other's arc despite the
barbed protestations—until Otis dropped the pretense and 'fessed
up that he may have been a bumpkin but a rich one, with a string of
cars in his driveway, something he didn't need to imagine writing
the song—and not only that, but a "lover" too, just like all others in
his lineage.

The trippy beat and the counterpoint dialogue between the two
would still be as cheeky and fresh when it was heard endless times
through the years. The album, *King & Queen*, as in "of soul," was,
as Robert Christgau's retro-review calls it, "enormously vivacious,
catchier and funnier [than] most soul music," adding, "Carla
Thomas was never anything special, but with Redding counterpos-
ing his rhythms, she sounds like she could scat with Satch himself
(well, almost)."[4] Released on March 16, 1967, it had liner notes written by, of all people, Tennessee's Republican Senator Howard Baker,
who in a few years would co-chair the Watergate hearings. Having
Baker participate was Al Bell's idea. "It was a scratch each other's back thing," he says. "He wanted to rub off our success and we
wanted the publicity. So I said, "We'll come to D.C. and present you
with a plaque and take pictures. I went up with Otis, Carla, her dad
Rufus, and Jim, and the pictures ran in the papers. That was a big
deal for us."[5] That Baker knew almost nothing of Stax was reflected
in his notes, which lavished more praise on Tennessee Ernie Ford,

Dinah Shore, Pat Boone, Minnie Pearl, and Elvis, than on Otis or Carla.[6]

King & Queen went to 36 pop, 5 R&B, and made top 20 in England. This, in turn, led Motown to play one-upmanship, creating the heavenly pairing of Gaye and Tammi Terrell later in 1967. Stewart, in return, planned another Redding-Thomas album. The war between the soul shops was getting good and hot now, and for Stax, it was a most satisfying reminder that whatever Motown could do, they could do just as well. Or better.

●

THAT THE Redding avalanche had continued to roll, and make tons of money, despite a paucity of pop hits, was no longer an anomaly but proof of the gathering dominance of albums as the primary means of sales. It was paradigm in the music business that Otis himself helped bring about. Where in the 1950s and early 1960s they were cheaply packaged excuses to wring some more sales out of one or two hits, the albums of the mid and later '60s were thoughtful showcases for well-regarded talent, the better ones stitched a tonal narrative in which songs seemed to follow each other logically, even if there was no real ligature between them. While an album could create a hit when the DJs plucked a popular cut off it, there was no real *need* for one if an album just went on selling and stuck on the LP charts for months, something common for Sinatra, the Beatles, and Redding. This paradigm fit Redding well, given that he was not interested in selling his soul, or selling out soul, for a formulaic hit. What's more, by the late sixties, as Al Bell says, "The general public was moving toward him. They were buying those albums like crazy."

Not that the crossover conundrum didn't increasingly become an issue. Otis, who could look all around him and see the fruits of his success, was still waiting for that big hit with mainstream white audiences. He might have had one in 1966, with a song that

Cropper wrote with Eddie Floyd during a thunderstorm, "Knock on Wood," the repetitive cadence of the first word a conscious effort to replicate the Redding "stutter." Floyd, in fact, says he wrote it for Otis, but Jim Stewart thought it was too much like Wilson Pickett's "In the Midnight Hour." Other accounts have it that Jerry Wexler, wanting to break Floyd out as a singer, told Stewart to send Eddie into the studio; when he did, the result was a song that went to number 1 R&B and 28 pop.[7]

Perhaps tougher for Redding, was the irony that the Memphis sound was virtually being copied all around the soul meridians. Over at Motown, they may not have seen fit to cover Stax songs but its manicured formulas of the mid-'60s soul sound had given way to heavier, funkier horn arrangements, which by the time a now mature Stevie Wonder recorded "Signed, Sealed, Delivered I'm Yours" in 1970, he sounded more Memphis than Motown. Somewhere along the line, it just seemed Redding too would *have* to get the big crossover hit, and while the issue was becoming a bit prickly, no one was really rushing him to do that at Stax given his sales and his almost permanence on the R&B charts. And to be sure, the old fissures between black and white were slowly being bridged as pop was increasingly embraced by soul. In *Billboard* and *Variety*, mentions of Redding and other Stax artists pre-1966 had been scarce and fleeting, their records almost never pitched as a "top single of the week." A breakthrough of sorts came in the October 19, 1966, *Variety* when the trade paper finally had a review of a Redding record, *The Otis Redding Dictionary of Soul*, on page 184 in the Record Reviews column, which also included Simon and Garfunkel's *Parsley, Sage, Rosemary and Thyme*, Peggy Lee's *Guitars a là Lee*, Liberace's *New Sounds*, Chet Atkins's *From Nashville with Love*, and the soundtrack from *A Man and a Woman*. The unsigned review read, "Otis Redding, one of the top current purveyors of the rhythm & blues idiom, belts with terrific force in this set. About half the songs in this set are his own compositions . . . . He also does an unusual version of 'Tennessee Waltz' and an up-tempo slice of 'Day Tripper.'"

These dishwater entries, in an age before record reviews in the trades, were shallow and a joke as actual music critiques. They still could nonetheless move lots of vinyl—one reason why record companies routinely purchased expensive ads in *Variety*, *Billboard*, and *Cash Box*, which often was the price to pay for a review—really a blurb—of a pivotal act, though Al Bell had no budget for such ads and had to pitch Stax acts to the trades with his cheek, not checks. The second time Redding made that same page was an April 26, 1967, review of *King & Queen*, which, it read, "brings together two of the top names to come out of the Memphis school or rhythm & blues" and hailed "a solid string of R&B ballads delivered [with] a powerhouse beat." Again, more than the boilerplate notices, the victory here was that Otis was on the same page as mainstream giants and climbers, in this case albums by Ella Fitzgerald and Duke Ellington, Steve Lawrence and Eydie Gormé, Morton Gould, Herb Alpert and the Tijuana Brass, Cream, the Hollies, the Paul Butterfield Blues Band, and the Who. Still, it was only on the "other" charts where one could gauge what was going on in the black world. Randomly perusing the *Billboard* R&B singles list on October 22, 1966, one would have seen:

1. 634-5789 (Soulsville USA)—Wilson Pickett (Atlantic)
2. Baby Scratch My Back—Slim Harpo (Excello)
3. Love Makes the World Go Round—Deon Jackson (Carla)
4. Get Ready—The Temptations (Gordy-Motown)
5. Shake Me, Wake Me (When It's Over)—Four Tops (Motown)
6. One More Heartache—Marvin Gaye (Tamla-Motown)
7. This Old Heart Of Mine—The Isley Brothers (Tamla)
8. Darling Baby—The Elgins (V.I.P.)
9. Stop Her on Sight (S.O.S.)—Edwin Star (Ric Tic)
10. I Want Someone—The Mad Lads (Volt)[8]

The spawning ground of three soul music giants—Little Richard, James Brown, and Otis Redding—was the streets of Macon, Georgia, seen here looking east down bustling Cotton Avenue in the early 1900s from the corner of Walton Way and Poplar Street. The clamor and smoke-filled skies would remain constant into the 1950s, as would the music scene that tempered Jim Crow segregation.

Among the many who could take credit for discovering Otis was Macon DJ Hamp "King Bee" Swain, whose talent shows made the teenage Redding so popular that he was barred from the competition after winning fifteen times in a row. Swain, still active in the city's music scene, is seen here in 2008 at the Georgia Music Hall of Fame Awards ceremony in Atlanta, where he became the seventh DJ inducted. *(AP Photo/Johnny Clark)*

Perhaps the earliest photo of Otis Redding, taken upon his signing with the then-fledgling Stax/Volt Records, portrays a baby-faced Redding as a kind of updated Cab Calloway, complete with zoot suit. The Otis the world came to know looked quite different, usually in casual slacks and sweaters or snazzy designer suits. But the smile and the hungry look in his eyes would remain constant.

(© Michael Ochs Archives/Corbis)

Redding's career prospered because of two novices whose aim of managing and booking black singers clashed with most whites' prejudices in Macon: Phil Walden and his kid brother Alan, the latter seen here (at right) in 1964 with Otis and his own father , C.B., Walden, in front of a flashy new car that Otis had bought with his early royalties. Phil Walden would become the South's dominant record industry figure for two decades. *(Courtesy of the Middle Georgia Archives, Washing Memorial Library, Macon, Georgia)*

Stax Records were always a collaborative process. Alhough producer's credits were not given until after Redding's death, the de facto producer for nearly all his songs was Steve Cropper, the lanky guitarist in the peerless house band. In this candid shot taken during a studio session, Cropper listens for the proper tone and texture, qualities that were enhanced by the unique acoustics of the converted theater where Stax was based. (© *Michael Ochs Archives/Corbis*)

Performing on the road was particularly critical to soul acts whose records received little play on white radio stations. Equally at home on the black "chitlin' circuit" clubs or venues with integrated audiences, Otis was always backed by rockin' bands such as this brass-heavy unit in 1966 that included drummer Johnny Lee Johnson, later to be called "Jaimoe" when he was an original member of the Allman Brothers Band. (*Courtesy of the Middle Georgia Archives, Washing Memorial Library, Macon, Georgia*)

The classic Otis Redding pose is seen in this 1966 promotional photo—smiling, confident, and handsome, almost bigger than life, reflecting the sizzle and charm of the man and his music, as well as capturing his no-doubt-about-it belief that he was about to become a major crossover star. *(Courtesy of the Middle Georgia Archives, Washing Memorial Library, Macon, Georgia)*

As Redding rose as a top-tier performer and his sold-out shows became legendary, Stax Records—fueled by Redding, Sam and Dave, Carla Thomas, and Eddie Floyd—rose as a challenger for Motown in crossover soul. The marquee on East McLemore Street that once was emblazoned "Soulsville U.S.A." still lights up the Memphis sky, meticulously re-created by the Stax Museum of American Soul Music, which stands on the site where musical and cultural history was made. *(Photograph by Nuria Andres; courtesy Stax Museum of American Soul Music)*

Redding's success was overseen by Atlantic Records' swaggering honchos Ahmet Ertegun (left) and Jerry Wexler (seen here presenting an award to singer LaVern Baker). The venerable New York R&B label made Stax/Volt viable by distributing the latter's records—until, in 1967, it was sold to Warner Brothers along with the Stax catalog, which left Stax in the lurch and nearly caused the struggling Memphis label to fold. (© *Michael Ochs Archives/Corbis*)

Sometimes referred to as "God" in the hallways at Stax, former DJ Al Bell came to Stax in 1965 as promotions director and rose to become co-owner, in the process guiding Redding into the music mainstream and co-writing several songs with him, as well as reviving the label in the 1970s. Bell, seen here in 2014 emceeing an event in Austin, Texas, also led the effort to create the Stax Museum. (© *Jim Bennett/Corbis*)

Aretha Franklin's immortal 1967 cover of Redding's "Respect" made Otis a mint in royalties while enshrining the song as one of the most profoundly significant pieces of music of the turbulent 1960s. Franklin's wailing version foretold that women's rights were tied into the civil rights movement and that a woman, too, could demand that her man give her not only some R-E-S-P-E-C-T but also "sock it to me."

Pure joy and soulful conviction etched on his face, Redding belts out a song during his biggest tour de force: his knockout performance at the Monterey International Pop Music Festival on June 18, 1967. Taking Southern soul to the hippie enclaves of northern California during the "Summer of Love," he wowed the crowd and outshone even Jimi Hendrix and Janis Joplin, a triumph that made him a rock and roll icon. *(Courtesy of the Middle Georgia Archives, Washing Memorial Library, Macon, Georgia)*

Two very lucky men, James Alexander (left) and Carl Simms, gaze forlornly from their Madison, Wisconsin, hotel toward Lake Monona as rescue crews dragged it for survivors of the plane crash that killed Redding and seven others the day before. Alexander and Simms were members of Bar-Kays but, with no room on the plane, had to travel separately. *(AP Photo)*

The saddest of the "sad, sad songs"—which Otis once crooned were the only kind he sang—were the last one he left to the world. Recorded just three days before he died, "(Sittin' On) The Dock of the Bay" would become his biggest-selling record and only number 1 chart hit, even though the song spoke of the loneliness that "won't leave me alone." It has since become one of the most played and covered songs of all time, fulfilling the promise of his amazing talent.

Steve Cropper, who was pivotal in the writing and recording of "(Sittin' On) The Dock of the Bay," has become nearly as legendary as the artists he produced and played guitar for at Stax. In 2012, he caught up with Redding's sons, Otis Redding III (left) and Dexter Redding, who recorded in the 1980s as a duo, at the inaugural induction ceremony for the Memphis Music Hall of Fame. *(AP Photo/The Commercial Appeal, Brandon Dill)*

No one has done more to keep Otis Redding's legacy alive than Zelma Atkins Redding, whom he married when she was fifteen and who devoted her life being the mother of his two sons. A meticulous guardian of his estate, she made a rare appearance at Redding's induction into the Rock and Roll Hall of Fame in New York on January 19, 1989, when Little Richard gave a colorful induction speech for the man who idolized him. *(AP Photo/Susan Ragan)*

Besides his records, Redding fans can remember him by visiting monuments in his hometown of Macon and the memorial for him at the Monona Terrace Convention Center in Madison, Wisconsin, overlooking the lake where his plane went down. Here, a one fan holds a rose to place on the memorial stone, while another stands with his young children, who read about the soul man who died far too young but left a long legacy. *(AP Photo/Wisconsin State Journal, L. Roger Turner)*

That was still the port through which Otis Redding's records sailed onto the market—such as his cover of "Satisfaction," which on this chart was sitting at number 14 with a bullet. Motown had hit the jackpot in crossover appeal, while Redding was waiting for his shot. He was moving along a steady course, racking up royalties but remaining still pretty much a mystery to all but R&B-conscious white buyers, who found Otis records more readily available in the black record stores from which *Billboard* extrapolated its R&B list. Of course, it would have been impossible to determine whether blacks were buying records in white stores, making the two charts highly unreliable indicators to begin with. But the truth was that "slow and steady" could have been the motto of the man himself. Because Redding was so entrenched and seemingly immune to (and removed from) cultural and industry fads, he did not need to be force-fit into trendy Fleet Street "mod" fashions, flowery shirts, flare-bottom pants, headbands, and bandannas, such as were covering the lanky physiques of even black acts at the time. The Temptations had put their tight suits, skinny ties, and ankle-length slacks in the closet. God knows, tattered jeans, bargain basement jackets, and, soon enough, "Sgt. Pepper" psychedelic drum-major duds never found their way to East McLemore Street.

One other divergence between Motown and Stax was that, while both soul labels had maintained their ground during the transformation of rock, the "Redding look"—natty, shiny, sharp-creased, conservative, even if bathed in sweat—remained proudly square albeit eminently cool in its own way. And this could be traced to Redding alone, since, as Floyd Newman notes, "he never changed one iota from the time I first laid eyes on him. I can tell you one thing. Had he lived, you never would have seen the guy in those aluminum space suits like George Clinton and Earth, Wind and Fire, no six-inch heels and scarves around his hair like Jimi Hendrix. Uh-uh."[9] To be sure, the only thing that changed was that his old process was replaced by a modest Afro. It was all the "mod" Otis Redding needed.

•

BY 1967, and with an estate valued at over a million dollars, he had all the money he needed, too.[10] Not that he didn't crave more. Getting into rarefied rock air had almost literal meaning for many solo and group acts, mandating that they step up from endless bus rides on crevice-pocked back roads through the hinterlands to comfortable seats on commercial airplane flights—and then, for those in the elite, on private charter flights and, for a very privileged few, their own private planes. Of course, the history of such private flight in the entertainment industry was an already grievous one. Plane crashes had claimed the lives of notables from bandleader Glenn Miller in 1944 to the tragic troika of Buddy Holly, Ritchie Valens, and "The Big Bopper," J. P. Richardson, in a field in Crystal Lake, Iowa, during a winter Midwest tour in 1959, to country superstars Patsy Cline in 1963 (along with Grand Ole Opry cohorts Cowboy Copas and Hawkshaw Hawkins) and Jim Reeves in 1964, the last two having fallen from the sky over Tennessee. Still, obvious perils aside, for the big-time rockers slumming it on a rickety bus simply wouldn't do, and Otis was no exception. Not only did he believe the Lord would bless and keep him, things like walking away from a shootout with neither a scratch nor punishment may have led him to judge himself invincible from harm. At times, he could act just the opposite, expressing fatalism about life that was bigger than any human had the power to alter.

Thus, beginning in 1965, he had begun taking flying lessons, working toward learning how to fly in a twin-engine Beechcraft H18, the same kind of plane that James Brown had been using before he stepped up even higher in class and bought a sleek, black-painted Lear jet for $713,000—which he proudly boasted about in his 1968 song "America Is My Home," declaring the Lear proof that a soul brother had reached the pinnacle.[11] The H18 wasn't a Lear, but for the younger soul brother on his own flight path upward, it was definitely a status symbol, and Walden gave in and shelled out $125,000 for Otis to buy the plane he was learning to fly in, though it wouldn't be until December that he would hire a pilot and use the plane to ferry him around.

That year, too, *Jet* reported that he had "200 suits and 400 pairs of shoes."[12] Thus, it was good timing that he could now move all he had to where space seemed unlimited. Alan Walden, who had once slept on Otis's couch in his cramped first apartment, having no place of his own, had now stepped up, too, having been given a guest room out in the new house. There, he says, they "could ride horses, go fishing and hunting, and just do anything we wanted to without people staring at this black man and white man doing things together, laughing and having a good time. Otis and I both loved Round Oak and planned to make it one of the largest ranches and farms in our state. We grew vegetables and hay and raised cows and hogs. We even had fresh eggs from our chickens, and an occasional glass of goat's milk from a pet nanny goat. He built a three and a half acre lake for fresh fish and the largest privately owned swimming pool in the state in the shape of a Big O. Plans were drawn and construction was scheduled for an airstrip so he could land his [plane] at the ranch."[13] During the summer of 1966, the BBC sent a film crew to make a documentary on Otis's life for British television and he ended up coming off as an ebony Lil' Abner in overalls. He was seen riding a tractor, chopping down trees, and lugging firewood into the house.

He disliked leaving the place so much that he would build a recording studio with state of the art equipment in the basement, the goal being to make his demos there. At the same time, Phil Walden began construction of a studio in downtown Macon, which he wanted to make the center of Redding's recording, with his own musicians, so he wouldn't need to go up to Memphis. Otis had been renting a house in Nashville for those visits; soon, he hoped, he wouldn't need it, according to plan. Macon, as the blueprint went, was soon going to have a renaissance, be the epicenter of soul, just like in the fifties, only this time built not around Little Richard but Otis Ray Redding Jr. If everything fell into place, Otis would be able to record in a studio in his hometown, and at times in his own studio at the Big O Ranch. And if that happened, he allowed himself to project, no longer would the commute to Memphis be required—a heavy symbolic shift far more significant than having a private jet. This had little to do with any major disagreements with Jim Stewart, at least not yet. Instead, though eminently grateful for all that Stewart had done for him, he saw progress through a cold, business-is-business prism, in which the already storied studio on East McLemore Street that he had carved into the loam of American pop music might recede in importance—to the new musical order that Otis Redding envisioned was about to coalesce right there in his own backyard, hell, within his own four walls.

•

IN FEBRUARY 1967, Jerry Wexler was something like a soul king himself. His early revelations and premonitions about Stax and Southern soul had been right on the money. Now, he turned to finding Atlantic's first female soul singer since Ruth Brown. Early that year, he signed another child of a preacher, Aretha Franklin, who had won early fame singing in the choir for her famous father, Reverend C. L. Franklin, at the New Bethel Baptist Church in Detroit. She quickly became a hot club act and had a few R&B hits with Columbia, before the label, who never fully utilized her gospel roots, let her go. Digging her deep-throated but feminine soul, Wexler took her to Muscle Shoals and recorded her first Atlantic song, "I

Never Loved a Man (The Way I Love You)," which went top 10 pop and R&B in 1967. For the follow-up session, Wexler believed he had a surefire song for her. Tom Dowd, engineering the session, which was moved to Atlantic's New York studio at 1841 Broadway, didn't know what it was until he came in and asked Wexler what song was to be recorded. Told it was "Respect," Dowd thought the melody was familiar.

"I know that song," he said. "I made it with Otis Redding like three years ago."[14]

Not that flipping the gender thrust of the song wasn't a tricky business. In 1967, a woman simply did not demand respect, not openly, and certainly not sex. Yet Wexler, who co-produced the song with Atlantic engineer Arif Mardin, allowed priceless embellishments that were suggested by Aretha and her sisters Erma and Carolyn, two of her backup singers. The result not only preserved the intent of the song but also conveyed an even rawer sexuality. Here, she would demand her man obey her and give her "propers." Of course, there was the epochal "sock it to me" refrain by the background singers, which few listeners would even be able to recall had been used by Mitch Ryder in 1966 on "Sock It to Me Baby" and—unbeknownst to all but the most hardcore Redding fans—by the man himself on "Sweet Lorene." And though Al Bell notes that Otis's exhortation of the phrase was a shout to the world to sit up and listen to him, through Aretha's lips it could not possibly have been mistaken for anything but mandatory sex as the bargain for him coming home.

Neither did the new version discard Otis's highly unconventional lyric about the woman spending his money—with his assent, as long as she delivered the respect, and lots of it. Here, in Aretha's take, she would give the man all *her* money for a little time with him—a very un-feminist notion, especially in the 1960s, and one that might have caused double takes among both sexes. Instead, with Aretha's astonishing range and zeal—not to mention King Curtis's blazing sax solo on the added break, taken note for note from Sam and Dave's "When Something Is Wrong with My Baby," and ballsy beat of several members of the Muscle Shoals rhythm section—it exploded into a license for a woman's right to "get some," without stepping back an inch as a cultural/racial rallying cry. The most enduring embellishment of all—the spelled-out "R-E-S-P-E-C-T," preceded immediately by the still-enigmatic "Take care, TCB"—may be the single most profound writ of common law ever heard in pop music history. It surely paved the way for women to be able to be more than second-string vessels of pain and desire—as did, appropriately enough, Aretha's older sister Erma Franklin that same year with "Piece of My Heart," for Shout Records. That song was built around the proposition that a woman can be tough, a battle cry line seemingly made for Janis Joplin, who immortalized it in her 1968 cover with Big Brother and the Holding Company.

Using two idiomatic phrases—"Sock it to me" and "TCB," the latter a short-lived late-'60s acronym, originally in the black community, for "taking care of business"—might have made the cover a '60s curio. But when the song was released in April 1967 as the first single from Franklin's groundbreaking *I Never Loved a Man the Way I Love You* album, it had a universal appeal, staking ground for both men and women to repeat the strange slang that few knew the meaning of. Streaking to number 1, pop and R&B, and staying there for eight weeks on the latter, it won Franklin two Grammys, elevating her to the role of the "Queen of Soul"—and netting for Otis Redding a bigger royalty windfall than anything else he ever wrote. Still as fresh a piece of music and ontology as has ever been recorded, the redux also turned out to be an unprecedented boost to the visibility of Otis Redding, who was regularly mentioned as the song's composer when it was played on the radio. Even Otis was blown away by how much his song had been stretched and a little hurt and sheepish that Franklin had the big crossover hit he hadn't had with it. Indeed, the song was now so viscerally associated with Aretha that Wexler would decades later insist it was really about *her* life, saying, "If she didn't live it, she couldn't give it" and "Her middle name is Respect,"[15] despite the fact it had come from the pit of Redding's soul and angst. Although Otis had not met Franklin, and would not get to know her well beyond the sound of her incredible voice, he realized at once the full potential and cosmic power she had given his words and music. Even if resentful on some conscious level that she had bettered him, he was gracious enough to indemnify Aretha and praise her for a superior version. Himself humbled by it, when he performed the song now, he too was spelling out "R-E-S-P-E-C-T" and the "take care, TCB" line, a titanic nod to a young singer. What's more, the magnitude of the Aretha version made other strong women try to repeat the formula. Etta James, the soul priestess of the 1950s, tried to make a comeback by also covering and flipping the gender of one of Redding's songs, "Security," without much success.

But now Redding had added pressure, too, to live up to his cemented reputation in the booming American soul market. That meant he could not go much longer without a pop hit and remain inviolate, even if he was still in a nice sinecure. His records were prominent on the black stations, and those stations were increasingly becoming the new top 40 outlets, in a few years to be the most listened-to format in the country. As Alex Hodges says, "I equate what was happening in music in sixty-six, sixty-seven with the rise of hip-hop in the sense that white suburban kids were buying the kind of records that had sold only in the black record market. Otis was wildly popular with the young crowd, the college crowd. He was really a rock act, and began to sell more records in that demographic."

To be sure, Otis's crossover appeal, and potential to change the ground rules of future rock/soul fusion, was palpable. Robert Palmer, the *New York Times*' music writer, ventured in 1968 that "Otis Redding, Booker T. and the M.G.'s, and the Mar-Key horns . . . just may have been the greatest rock-and-roll band of all time [and]

rank with Elvis Presley's Sun recordings as a pinnacle of American vernacular music-making."[16] Then there was Otis's take. With
sharp analytic distinction, he pointed out that the idiomatic lines
were blurred and claimed for himself the most salient term of the
new rock order:

> Everybody thinks that all songs by colored people are rhythm
> and blues but that's not true. [Little] Johnny Taylor, Muddy
> Waters, and B.B. King are blues singers. James Brown is not
> a blues singer. He has a rock and roll beat and he can sing slow
> pop songs. My own songs, "Respect" and "Mr. Pitiful," aren't
> blues songs. I'm speaking in terms of the beat and structure
> of the music. A blues is a song that goes twelve bars all the way
> through. Most of my songs are soul songs.[17]

For many with more than a passing interest in the evolution of popular music, Redding's credentials needed no further burnishing in
1967. A year later, another *Times* music critic, Robert Shelton, would
eulogize him with the grandly sweeping conclusion that, "In his
final year, Redding symbolized the transfer of leadership in Negro
pop music from its long-standing base of popularity in Detroit to
the closer-to-the-roots center of Memphis . . . the essence [of which]
lies in the greater simplicity of elaborate recording techniques in
the Tennessee studios. Redding made a near-fetish of simplicity, yet
his was not a style without its artifices, its subtleties, and its overwhelming impact."[18]

•

UNFORTUNATELY, REDDING'S impact and talent was not transfer-
able to those who were coming up right around him. As successful
as the Redding brand was, his custom label, Jotis Records—the
new shop operating out of Macon—was doomed from the start. The

first to come aboard was Macon soul singer, and Otis sound-alike, Billy Young, whom he took to Memphis in 1965—Redding's contract renewal deal with Stax having given him the right to book Jotis sessions there, with the top session men—to cut two Redding-penned tunes, the ballad "Same Thing All Over Again" and the dance song "The Sloopy," the name applied to a brief dance fad spawned by "Hang on Sloopy," the McCoys' 1965 bubblegum cover of the Vibrations' original soul song a year before. Both songs were produced by Otis in a tight, clean manner, though when the disc came out, they read only "Produced by Big O Productions." Then, late in 1965 when Redding played a show in Baltimore, the local DJ Rufus Mitchell played him a ballad, by the nineteen-year-old Atlanta singer Arthur Conley, called "I'm a Lonely Stranger." Conley's gospel-flecked, high-pitched trill reminded Otis of Sam Cooke. He had Conley rerecord the same song at Stax and when it was released, Otis was magically listed as co-writer. A follow-up single, Conley's own "Who's Fooling Who," would come out in early 1966.

In between Conley's records, Redding and Walden also added the long-limbed and sexy Loretta Williams, whom Otis had heard singing in a club during a Revue trip to Mobile, Alabama, where she lived. He first hired her to be a backup singer in the Revue, with a promise to pay her, she says, a weekly salary of "$450 to $650," which was "more than I ever made."[19] He then signed her to Jotis and during a trip to New York for an Apollo Theater gig, he recorded her at Atlantic's studio singing two songs, his "Baby Cakes," a frantic dance record later covered by Maxine Brown, and a ballad written by Williams, "I'm Missing You," which when the 45 with both songs was released late in '65, the latter bore the writing credit "Redding/Williams."

Redding considered Conley to be a major league talent. However, with Jotis unable to move decent numbers of vinyl, even with Atlantic distributing the records, Otis and Walden folded the label in 1966. This meant that Jim Stewart was no longer under any compunction to allow Conley to record in his studio. Not happy about his protégé being given the Wilson Pickett treatment, Otis began to nurse a grudge against Stewart and spent quality time not on writing new songs but on shopping Conley to other labels. After getting assurance from Atlantic that it would still distribute Conley's records on Atco, Otis obtained a contract for him with the FAME studio's in-house label, then booked an early January session with Conley at the Muscle Shoals shop to record a tune they co-wrote, "Sweet Soul Music." This was a soul hymnal. Appropriating, and baldly so, Sam Cooke's "Yeah Man"—which began by asking rhetorically, "Do you like good music?"—they copied the melody, some lyrics, and the background hook. Conley answered the opening question with the response "Sweet soul music." Otis had replaced the litany of dance fads of the Cooke piece with the names of soul stars and a taste of their signature songs, including Lou Rawls, Sam and Dave, "that Wicked Wilson Pickett," and of course Otis Redding, whose signifier was a string of "fa-fa-fa's." The final shout-out went to "the king of 'em all," James Brown.

Redding, through Phil Walden, began to pump the song even before it was released, with Walden feeding word of it to music writers. The February 4, 1967, *Record World* complied, reporting that "Otis Redding makes his debut as producer with the new Arthur Conley recording of 'Sweet Soul Music' on the Atco label." This placed Otis as far as he had ever been from the Stax brand, and no one in Memphis could fairly object. The question now was *how* far he would get from it.

15

London Calling

By 1967, things began to get tense on the road for Redding. He had come a long way from the days when he was comforted traveling with his bobos, only one of whom, Speedo Sims, remained, because he could be used as a backup singer. Redding's main focus now was on his band, which had grown from just a few players to a twenty-four-piece orchestra, including bandleader Mack Robinson. However, the personnel in the band constantly changed. One of two drummers he employed at once was John Johan Johanson, who as Jai Johanny "Jaimoe" Johanson would be an original member of the Allman Brothers Band. First, though, he played on forty-two dates with Redding. Another player, saxophonist Richard Spencer, was here and gone, a few years later to form the soul group the Winstons with two others who had sojourned with the Redding band, guitarist Quincy Mattison and drummer G. C. Coleman, whose syncopated solo on their 1969 song "Amen Brother," the flip side of the cross-over soul hit "Color Him Father," is now regarded as the genesis of the hip-hop beat, the style once codified by producers as the "Amen Break" and, today, as "jungle" music.[1]

Much of these gigs were a communal experience, basted in the excitement of backing a human firecracker every night. Johanson can recall, with a sense of wonderment, when the bus pulled into Nashville, where they were slated to perform on a TV show. When the host, a WLAC DJ, got drunk and couldn't go on, he says, Otis not only sang but stepped in as the emcee, a moment that would be golden had it been somehow preserved.[2]

However, they could only take the grind of endless travel and inevitable strains for so long. Indeed, contrary to Redding's insistence that the Stax studio cats be paid, he was apparently less inclined to reach into his pocket to take care of these lesser, fleeting musicians, many of whom were hired locally, played a few gigs, then let go.

Clearly, he was not an easy man to be around, especially after the Whisky a Go Go episode. Whereas in the past he would let slide a screw-up or two by the musicians, any such clinker would be punishable by a fine, usually ten bucks, a substantial hit for guys who had to share as little as a hundred dollars between them per show. And the pressure only mounted to put on pitch-perfect performances every single time. Living under the gun, one sour note away from a fine, many turned to drugs for comfort, not that any had been strangers to such chemical comforts given their profession. And, apparently, if Otis was strict about their performance onstage, he looked the other way offstage. Loretta Williams, as "the only girl traveling with about 20 sex-starved, pot smoking, drunken, and sometimes just downright crazy men," recalls her time with the Revue as a treadmill of nonstop verbal abuse. One of them, she says, a black trumpeter she identifies as "Blood," called her "an ignorant nigger girl," prompting a fist-throwing, hair-pulling fight between them on the tour bus.[3]

Neither was Otis apparently so chivalrous. After the dust-up, he let her ride in his Cadillac instead of the bus, sharing the privilege he always had for his own travel, but on a desolate road in Waycross, Georgia, revved up the motor and tore down the road at near a hundred miles an hour, laughing at her screaming for him to stop. Worse, she figures she "was the only sober one in the car. . . . I was almost out of my mind with fear," and after he finally did stop, "Otis had to shake the life into me to get me to calm down." Just as frightening an experience was when she saw him lose his temper, which she says could happen when the musicians pressed him for more money. She recalled a sax player named Skag who she made out to be "a habitual heroin user." After he "had a little too much to drink and used too much heroin," he made such a demand, whereupon "Otis got real nasty about it, started cursing the guy out . . . and told the other guys they weren't getting any more money." Skag told Otis he would either pay up or, he said, "I'm going to take it out on your ass." Recalls Williams, "Otis really beat the guy and kicked him something terrible, right there in the dressing room. I thought that was the most awful thing, for him to take advantage of a man after he was down and drunk. . . . I felt that night he was a cruel man."

The musicians themselves were no bargain. Williams claimed that they "would steal anything that wasn't nailed down, hotel supplies, food, or hotel goods, take innocent young girls off with them, away from their homes, doing ungodly things to them, sometimes six or seven guys on one girl . . . the mothers and fathers would have the highway patrol out looking for us and chasing the bus." Other times, "hotel bills were not taken care of, guys would skip out on the bills because Otis wouldn't pay us on time."[4]

•

FOR LORETTA WILLIAMS, being given the chance to be a protégé of Otis Redding was a high in itself. When the lights would come up and she was only feet behind him, the experience was almost beatific. She remembers the swirl of noise, flashing lights, horns rising in a crescendo, and seeing "women going crazy" when he would appear "in an electric blue shining suit, with all his fine jewelry sparkling, those great big glassy eyes, great white teeth, thick shapely lips, not a hair out of place, his legs sliding and shaking to the music . . . Women would give their life just to get near him, want to undress for him. After the show they would run down the hallways trying to kiss him or get an autograph." But this spell only went so far, especially after her record came out and neither Otis nor Walden, who became her manager when she signed with Jotis, paid her anything; all the writing royalties went into the deep pockets of Redding and Phil Walden. Despite this, when she says Motown wanted to buy her contract, Otis refused, assuring her that he would make her "a big star."

After weeks in close quarters with Otis, she came to see him as a common thug and sexist abuser. She says he would "talk about the women he slept with and degrade them. . . . He said he hated the white women and would use them, do them real bad, because of the times he remembered, how the white man had dogged him and his people back down in Macon [and] so he wanted to take it out on their daughters . . . I would feel so sorry for some of those poor girls, and when he would finish with them, he would kick them out, sometimes with no clothes on, and make everybody laugh about it."[5]

Williams, too, wasn't immune to the temptations of life on the road. When she first started with the Revue, she had a boyfriend back in Mobile looking after her two children, and Otis let her be. But that changed when she took up with Mack Robinson, becoming involved, according to her, in a wonderfully sordid web of sex and money. It seemed that Otis became convinced that Robinson was, she says, "stealing some of the payroll [the proceeds of several shows], holding it back or giving it to me [and] one time he even accused me of being an accomplice to it. Mack got furious and cursed him and threatened him. . . . Mack was known to go for bad, when it came to fighting he was crazy. I was afraid they would wind up in a fight or a killing."

Soon after, her story goes, Robinson "managed to take Otis's briefcase loaded with cash [and] skipped out with it. None of us knew where he went. Otis pitched a hellbound fit but to no avail. Mack was too smooth for him." Discovering the theft, Otis "had the law trying to track him down. . . . I thought if Mack called me or tried to see me, Otis would kill him, if he caught him." Williams says she did meet up secretly with Robinson, who gave her some of the money, and that with Robinson gone Otis became abusive. "I wouldn't agree to sleep with him or indulge in his fantasies. [He said] I had been Mack's old lady and I was gonna do what he said or else. I said no way." When she says she turned to Speedo Sims for comfort and wound up in his bed, Otis trashed his old friend.

"You mean you would rather be with this guy who don't have nothing to give you and you wouldn't give me none?" she quotes him.[6]

The end for her came when, during a stop in Roanoke in February, she became ill and Otis ordered her to sing or else not be paid. Says Williams, "I told him I didn't have to stay and be treated like this. We exchanged a few more ugly words and he finally told Speedo, 'Give the bitch her money and send her home.'" At that, she says, "[I felt] as though I had been freed from a terrible bondage." Though she walked away, because her contract was still in force she was unable to sign with any label. Never has she collected any royalties on the two Jotis records. "I was," she avers, "point blank cheated out of all my royalties and pay." Her postscript is that, a few months later, all the musicians in the Revue during her time in it "had left him because of the way he had treated them."

Taken together with the shootout on Roy Street, Loretta Williams presents Redding as a man with a full plate of twisted, near psychotic impulses masked by a carefully constructed image. Still, it must be noted that nothing she alleges has ever been corroborated by anyone else, either by the now-deceased Mack Robinson or any other band member. Alex Hodges, hearing the lurid accusations, agrees with only one thing. "Singers often find they have to reorganize their bands. You want to put a little twist on something. It's not about being friends. A band needs a leader. Otis was a leader." As for the portrayal of Redding as a petty tyrant, thief, and abusive cad, he laughs and says, "Maybe she meant Wilson Pickett or Ike Turner."[7]

Al Bell adds, "I'll say this, none of us is perfect. I know Otis wasn't, and he never would have claimed otherwise. But all that crap, I don't believe a word of it. That's not the guy I knew."[8]

•

ONLY FIVE years removed from booking Otis into frat houses and dive bars, the Walden brothers were living a drunkard's dream. Another by-product of Redding's influence, Walden Artists and Promotions by mid-1967 was a virtual cartel, representing over forty-five artists, the cream of Southern soul, including Redding, Sam and Dave, Arthur Conley, Percy Sledge, Clarence Carter, Johnnie Taylor, Eddie Floyd, Rufus and Carla Thomas, Joe Tex, Booker T. and the MG's, Albert King, the Willie Mitchell Orchestra, James and Bobby Purify, James Carr, Alvin Cash and the Crawlers, Albert Collins, Clarence "Gatemouth" Brown, the Meters, Roscoe Shelton, Big John Hamilton, and Bobby Womack. A Willie Mitchell protégé, Al Green, was signed that year, as was Tyrone Davis. Almost forgotten soul pioneers like Etta James and Mable John also came aboard. Alan Walden recalls, "All the success had generated wealth for all three of us, a company airplane, El Dorados, Continentals, Thunderbirds, nice homes. We truly seemed on top of the world. Business was booming. Each new recording by Otis sold better than the ones before."[9]

It was, of course, Redding who had made it all possible, and still occupied most of the Waldens' time. And the most ambitious, and necessary, studio bookings were still to come. The biggest of them would take Otis back to England, where he had unfinished business. Phil Walden began putting the details together of another trip there, as did Jerry Wexler, who had an eye for a big-impact production. He and Atlantic had already made a deal with EMI, its European distributor, to release Stax/Volt product under the Stax imprint for the first time. Now, he urged Jim Stewart to gather up a Stax/Volt revue, which had not performed save for one appearance in 1966 in L.A., expressly for a tour of the UK and the continent. Once there, the plan had it, recordings would be made of some of the performances for a live album. Tom Dowd would man the control board during the shows, armed with two four-track recorders that he would scrounge up in a London studio. To grease the way, three Stax/Volt records were released in England in March, Redding's "Day Tripper" cover, Sam and Dave's "Soothe Me," and Eddie Floyd's "Raise Your Hand."

Stewart not only agreed but said he too would go along, a real rarity since he seemed surgically implanted to his seat in the studio control room. If he seemed more carefree than usual at the time, it may have been because Walden, who by 1966 had most Stax acts churning up commissions for him, would arrange the financing himself, from large advances forwarded by promoters at each venue. This was not as altruistic as it seemed, of course. Walden intended the journey to be another Redding conquest, not part of Stax as much as *above* it, and sold the tour as that of the Otis Redding Show. Billboards and posters advertising it as such were printed. Thus the optics had to be that of Otis taking his friends along for the ride. Walden required that all the details be his to make. Atlantic, even with its long tentacles in Europe, had no say, either. Walden partnered up with promoter Arthur Howes, who had booked the Beatles' first shows as a supporting act around London. Working the Atlantic connection, he hired EMI publicist John Abbott.

Al Bell would not only come but, with his jive-talkin' skills, act as emcee, though he would quickly give way to DJ Emperor Rosko, an American-born disc jockey who had worked on pirate radio and would soon join the BBC's new Radio One. Otis, for a change, wanted Zelma to go with him, something she never did, but she demurred in order to stay with the kids on the ranch, reasoning that it was hard enough on Karla and Dexter to almost never see their father without both of their parents being absent for a long period. Indeed, the tour would be a six-week slate of near-daily bookings in England, France, and Scandinavia. When the plans were made, however, and the Otis Redding Show theme got around, causing grumbling by the other Stax acts, Walden had to keep the peace by changing the theme to the Hit the Road, Stax tour—which may have had an inside-joke quality, given that Otis may have longed to say just that. In fact, it seemed more than just a nice gesture that Redding demanded that Arthur Conley, whom Stewart had passed on, be given a place right alongside—and billed *above*—Sam and Dave, Booker T. and the MG's, the Mar-Keys, and Eddie Floyd.

Putting Conley on the bill at all, says, Al Bell, was a case of Otis "sticking it to Jim" and his proprietary injunction against non-Stax artists using his studio. Attesting to Otis's authority, a non-Stax artist—an Atlantic artist, who benefited Wexler but not Stewart— was going to be a star of the Stax/Volt Revue, though Stewart was able to keep Conley off the recordings that were made. Nor would this be the only price Stewart would have to pay for Otis's relation- ship with Conley, as he would find out. The grumbling about it was constant, more so than it was about Percy Sledge, another Atlantic artist scheduled to be on the tour, his leverage and drawing power proven by the certification of "When a Man Loves a Woman" as Atlantic's first gold record, though he, too, heard some flak. Con- ley's addition meant that a rather unknown, unproven non-Stax act would displace a deserving, and better known Stax act, which turned out to be Rufus Thomas, who'd given years and hits to the company, and William Bell. The whole thing was thrown together so fast that the musicians were told barely days before they would be taking off for London to buy new suits, one green, one blue, and to inform the clubs where they moonlighted that they wouldn't be around for a couple of months—which for Wayne Jackson, cost him his regular gig. "I didn't really dig the suits," he says, "so I just packed a sweater and some turtlenecks. We were gonna go to Norway for a show, and I thought I'd need them. I basically wore them the whole time."[10]

As much as Otis bitched about having to follow Sam and Dave, that's exactly what he'd be doing again on the tour, needing that same kick in the behind when it would be his turn to close each show, something specified by Walden. Taking no chances that a pickup band might ruin a performance, Stewart insisted that the combined might of the Mar-Keys, Booker and the MG's, and the Memphis Horns back up all the acts, requiring them to have to relearn the rhythm lines of songs they hadn't played, in some cases for years, and learn a number of rudimentary dance steps taught to them by Isaac Hayes. All in all, the tour would be a heavy lift, and everyone knew on whose shoulders the weight would be.

•

ON MARCH 14, 1967, the day before the troupe departed, Otis went into the studio to cut two sides, "I Love You More Than Words Can Say" and "Let Me Come on Home." The former—written by Otis, Eddie Floyd, and Booker T. Jones—was as sensuous and delicate a ballad as Otis had ever sung. Cropper, Hayes, and Porter believed it merited some aristocratic unction, and talked Jim Stewart into doing something he always resisted, hiring a coterie of violin players. The strings smoothed the usual Redding grain, echoing the luxurious classical R&B slow jams of the past, and the opening word—a drawn-out *"Pleeeease"*—was a perfect channeling of James Brown. The latter, too, broke the mold, as a play to the rock crowd: Cropper's high-frequency metallic guitar line and tambourine accents followed his more structured cadence, even when he was running the song out in form, chanting "got-ta, got-ta, got-ta get home."

These were two highly instructive songs, presaging a new direction, and the course of "More Than Words Can Say" would be watched intently when released in mid-April. For now, though, the only priority was to "Hit the Road." On March 15, the troupe landed at Heathrow and was taken to a reception at the Speakeasy club. As they had done for Otis before, the Beatles sent limos for all the acts, all of whom would have only one rehearsal day in London. In addition, the tour had already hit some early bumps. Percy Sledge, perhaps because of the Stax/non-Stax static, had dropped out and Carla Thomas returned home after a few days. (One account says she had a commitment to appear at a civil rights benefit in Chicago,[11] but Bell says she left after taking ill.) The killer schedule made for a whirlwind, leaving no time for sightseeing, only seamless shows and rides to and from. Whenever they were spotted on the street outside the hotels, Jackson could barely believe it. "The European people went crazy, they just went crazy. We felt like the Beatles did when they came to America." Bell recalls that "even the bellhops treated us like stars, and I mean me, too, a nobody. It was like if you had a black face and looked somewhat cool, you were special. We'd never experienced that before." But that also applied to the white Stax delegates, the sight of whom produced actual gasps among some in the audiences who hadn't realized there *were* whites who played music like that. "Before we went to London," observed Steve Cropper, "we hadn't been thinking outside the block we lived on. Now, we were *worldly*."[12]

Of course, Otis had already tasted this kind of adulation, and only received more. When the Stax tour was announced, *Hit Parader* had reported it as OTIS REDDING IN LONDON,[13] the dates were freely sprinkled with attendees like Mick Jagger, Keith Richards, Brian Jones, John Mayall, Ray Davies, and Pete Townsend. The Beatles, in the midst of recording *Sgt. Pepper*, made it to a branch-off concert by Carla Thomas at the Bag O' Nails club—where in May Paul McCartney would meet Linda Eastman. Thomas was backed by Booker T. and the MG's, and after playing a cover of "Yesterday," she nearly flipped out when Paul McCartney came backstage, and trailed after him like a lovesick schoolgirl trying to prolong the meeting.

The first show of the Otis tour was on March 17 at Finsbury Park's Astoria Club, the city's largest music hall, where two weeks later Jimi Hendrix would set his guitar on fire for the first time, burning his fingers in the process and sending him to the hospital. A year later, the same venue would also play host for the Beach Boys, who would record their live album *Live in London* (reissued in 1969 as *Beach Boys '69*) at the same venue.[14] With its barrel-vaulted ceilings, the Astoria Club's acoustics were ideal for recording, as can be heard on the ensuing *Otis Redding: Live in London* album. Mounting the stage to close the show, Otis told the crowd, "It's good to be home." He did essentially the same set each night, and at two shows that first night at the Astoria: "Respect," "My Girl," "Shake," "Day Tripper," "Fa-Fa-Fa-Fa-Fa," "Satisfaction," "Try a Little Tenderness," though when the second tapes were made, at the Olympia in Paris four days later, he added "I Can't Turn You Loose," "I've Been Loving You Too Long," and "These Arms of Mine."

The reception the troupe got was like vespers, and they earned it. The order for the first half of the show was Booker T. and the MG's first, then the Mar-Keys, Conley, and Thomas (when she was there), followed after intermission by Floyd, Sam and Dave, and finally Otis. Practically the entire time, the Mar-Keys and the Memphis Horns would be onstage, where it got so hot that Dave Prater actually fainted a few times, whereupon, in a James Brown–like riff, but for real, attendants would come out and begin to drag him off stage. Prater would come to, pump a fist, break free, and race back to midstage to continue the song.

As for Otis, he was wired. Rosko would bring him on by inciting the crowd to spell his name, rising to a crescendo. Then, Bell recalls, "He went from one end of the stage to the other, he just couldn't keep still. He had energy that I'd never seen before." It carried him through the whole gamut of the Otis poses: on his knees and pleading to up on his feet with thighs vibrating to strutting across the stage stomping to the beat. The reaction from the sold-out houses was almost hysterical and the British music press was hyperbolic. STAX—THE RAVE SHOW TO END THEM ALL, frothed *Melody Maker*, though some sniffed that he was too concerned with winning over the crowds with "all grins and smiles on what ought to be the most soulful of numbers."[15] Crowd banter and affability, however, had been something Redding had been working on in his general broadening, and only a twit could have confused this with a lack of voltage. "I can truly say that Otis didn't have a bad show on that tour," says Jackson. "You have to remember, we'd never backed him up in a live show so we were like the audience, it was almost shocking to see how he worked a room. The audiences would be chanting 'Otis! Otis!' when other people were performing.

"I think we knew probably half the songs, we couldn't rehearse them all, so we just did what he always did in the studio, follow what he was doing, go with his flow. I'm sure we messed up a lot of things but you couldn't tell because of the noise and Otis would just plow through a song." It hardly seemed to matter that sometimes his numbers were performed at a faster pace and with the lyrics altered on the spot from the recorded versions. With Redding, a song had a three-minute life of its own each time he sang it, and, as such, different in many ways. Often he would instruct the musicians to play the slow songs slower and the fast ones faster, believing audiences reacted more viscerally. This was only common sense, the feel of a live crowd radically different than that of an insulated studio in which technical perfection was expected. In front of a full house of screaming people, energy and emotion ran higher, and to everyone's amazement, particularly so in Europe. Adds Jackson, "And so he turned it *way* up over there. I mean, those people would get so carried away, women would be crying, others would rush the stage and cops would drag them out. It could get ugly, and I was scared seeing it. Nothing happened like that in America."

Except, as Otis could have rejoined, coolly, from his vantage point, "Oh yes it did. Happened all the time."

•

THERE WOULD be no live performance on British TV this time, but the BBC's famous *Top of the Pops* show produced a video during a tour break of Otis lip-synching "Fa-Fa-Fa-Fa-Fa," which would run on March 23. These pre–MTV era films were common in Britain but almost never produced in the U.S. This explains why, apart from the Monterey Pop reels, there is so little performance video of Redding other than what was taken from a BBC film made of the Revue on their stop in Norway on April 7—itself a truly remarkable document. A similar reel of an early 1965 Motown Revue show on the BBC's *Ready Steady Go* program, a hoedown with the Supremes, Smokey Robinson and the Miracles, the Temptations, Martha and the Vandellas, and Stevie Wonder, also displays this near-hysteria, but no one in the Detroit stable pulled people out of their seat, and nearly out of their minds, as did Redding. And because Motown's top acts were all over American TV and were even the subject of several prime-time documentaries, this lone European tour serves as a microcosmic time capsule of Stax in real time. The "Fa-Fa" video, too, is a one of a kind Redding amulet. In it, he lounges in a chair, loose as a goose, the Memphis Horns behind him—Jackson in his V-neck sweater, Andrew Love, and the newest Horn, Joe Arnold. Rolling through the song, when he reaches each, "Your turn!" he swivels to either nod at or gently poke Jackson, who grins while fake-playing his trumpet.

"You know something," he says now, "that's the only video Otis ever did and I don't even remember it, when or where we did it, anything. We may have been out late the night before, had a few too many. It was a good thing we didn't have to play it live."

When they did play it live, they were studio tight. Indeed, there was every reason that after the first tapes were played, the album project had grown to cutting separate live LPs, two by the troupe and one each by Redding, Sam and Dave, and Booker T. and the MG's. What this also meant was that Redding's material had to be stretched thin over several of the albums. Thus, on the troupe's London LP there would be only one Otis song, "Shake," and on the Paris volume, just "Try a Little Tenderness." Both would be teasers for the ten-track *Otis Redding: Live in Europe* album that came out in July with liner notes that began, "You should've been there, but since you weren't, you'll have the opportunity to hear, literally see and definitely feel this one man band of soul."

Outside the windows of the tour caravan the signs morphed from London to Paris to Cardiff to Leicester to Leeds to Wales to Glasgow to Bristol to Manchester to Burnley to Birmingham, then to the Scandinavia leg, first stop Stockholm for a show at the Grand Halle Theater. This was real culture clash, some in the audience having never seen a black person outside of the movies and album covers. Almost no one spoke English—though what they heard in London was just as undecipherable—and without those Beatles-donated limos, they didn't know if the cabdrivers would get them to the hall. The troupe would make sport of it by hurling obscene American slang at the drivers. While the locals here might not have understood a word of it, they had heard of Stax. And at concerts, the crowds were dressed in formal wear. By now, Otis was telling people in the troupe how much he missed America. In fact, according to Zelma, "He would call four, five times a day, not paying any attention to the time difference. He'd be all excited and say, 'I blew them away.' And I'd say, 'Okay . . . but it's four in the morning.'"[16] Still, he was up, sky-high for each show along the route.

He would come out in his cardigan and leisure slacks, looking sheepish, but by the end of his two wild encores, the whitest people on earth, in their tuxedos and gowns, were among the phalanx of humanity around him, all prancing and grinding.

This was repeated in Oslo and Copenhagen, the former being

where that historic film captured the only celluloid record of the Camelot that was Stax/Volt, and of a Redding never more animated, the last quarter-hour of the concert a blinding haze of sight and sound. Aptly, in the city's sports arena, Redding, again casual but with a sport jacket over an open-necked shirt, was like an athlete, all muscular and lithe. Doffing the jacket and sweating through his shirt, after two encores he waved goodbye to the suit-and-tie-clad audience and bounded behind Al Jackson, who had a towel around his shoulders, toward the curtain, where he played peek-a-boo with the audience then came back out for a *third* encore, with "Try a Little Tenderness," seeming to wring the very last drop out of himself—but, after the Norwegian host began to wrap up, here he came again with another round of "got-ta got-ta hold her hold her . . ." the last syllable in front of the curtain he *finally* disappeared behind. Jackson, extending the horn riff, says, "I was playing but I couldn't take my eyes off him. At that point, I was a fan, not a musician."

However, Jim Stewart may not have been as much of a fan of Redding's in-person style as the audiences. According to one account, Stewart began to fret when he watched the first few shows from the audience when Otis altered the pace of songs that Stewart had produced so meticulously in the studio, believing that the ballads were too languid and thus altered their essence. He then pressed the issue with Otis, telling him in the dressing room before one show, "You have to drop those tempos, and drop them right now."

Reacting territorially, he drew a line between their respective domains, saying, "Jim, you run the record company but *I* perform live. That's *my* business. These people don't know shit about this record, they just wanna be entertained." Stewart, who rarely raised his voice, communicating any ire he had with cutting sarcasm, was said to have peered through his specs and mocked, "Oh right, you're a fucking *star*." Whereupon, Otis allegedly walked away muttering, "Fuck him."[17]

Wayne Jackson says he witnessed this heated colloquy. On the other hand, Al Bell dismisses it entirely. "I do not recall anything like that," he says. "Jim's focus was *not* on the live album, it was on the performance. We wanted to firmly establish Stax and our artists in Europe. A live album is just that. And Jim Stewart was/ is not stupid. When the artist performed onstage, it was natural to increase or decrease the tempos, by the feel, the vibe of the audi- ence. Jim knew this and he would work with them to settle down in the studio."

Whatever went on, or didn't, Stewart never said another word about the tempo issue, which ceased being one when the tapes con- firmed Otis knew what he was talking about: The stage *was* his office, where he knew how to provoke maximum excitement. But he *didn't* know the business, and may have been a little too open to people with a good line but not the best of intentions. Jackson recalls another instance of Redding pique in London one day at the Mayfair Hotel, when he said "two big black cars" pulled up and Otis ducked into one. A while later, they returned and when Otis got out, he "slammed the heavy door behind him, not looking back. 'Damn!' was all I heard him say as he [went] through the lobby door and stomped to the elevators." He goes on, "Rumors flew, and I don't know what to believe. But . . . it was easy to imagine that the Euro- pean Mafia was pushing him to be exclusively handled by them. I thought it might be true. And I knew Otis wouldn't have liked it one bit if anyone had tried to corral him like that. . . . To this day, I don't know what happened."

●

AFTER THE tour and when Redding returned stateside, rumors con- tinued to fly around him, centering on whether he would defect to another record company, with Atlantic the obvious choice, possibly even trying to legally get out of his Stax contract before it was up in

1970. Lending credence to the notion, Phil Walden was practically joined at the hip with Wexler, confiding in him far more than with Stewart, to whom he all but stopped talking. At least one person, the garrulous Wayne Cochran, who in 1967 was living in Miami, fronting a band and making biker movies, later claimed when Otis played in that city and visited him that "he had just agreed to sign—him and the artists he managed—with Atlantic" for six million dollars up front. "He was about to transfer it all to Atlantic, and Stax would basically exist no more because Otis [and Phil] managed all their artists."[18]

There was no doubt that Redding had outgrown Stax. The live albums from the European tour were unmistakable proof. The Redding live set far outpaced the two by the troupe, going to number 32 pop, 8 soul, and 14 in the UK, though all these albums would have enduring residual value. In 1991, Stax would rerelease the two-volume CD set, and in 1993, yet another, with *Hit the Road Stax*. In 2008 would come the sixteen-track *Live! In London and Paris*. However, for soul historians, the ultimate spine-shiver was the BBC film of the Norway date, which would not be marketed until Atlantic's corporate overlord Universal Music Group released the seventy-five-minute *Stax/Volt Revue Live in Norway 1967 (Reelin' in the Years)* DVD in 2007, with the only known concert footage of "Fa-Fa-Fa-Fa-Fa," which with Otis's renditions of "My Girl," "Shake," "Satisfaction," and "Try a Little Tenderness" can leave one breathless.

Thus, in light of his growing bigger and further apart from the company, it seemed the only question was not if he'd jump to Atlantic but *when*. Wexler all but admitted he was pulling on Otis's strings to do so. And, says Al Bell, such a turn "wouldn't have surprised me, given what we learned later about what Jerry was up to. I know a lot of things he was doing, things I don't want to get into right now but they were . . . well, I won't get into it. I'll just say that by 1967 Wexler didn't want to be a partner with us, he wanted to take everything away from us. The fact is, Atlantic could provide Otis with advantages he didn't have with us. Stax was not a record label, it was a production company, with limited resources."

To be sure, honor among thieves being what it is, Wexler was already engaged in a sub-rosa screwing of Jim Stewart, the cruel impact of which would be made clear some months later. But the other side of the coin was that Otis was very sensitive to the fact that he had a stake in Stax Records. Added Bell, "In every way, Otis *was* Stax." Dennis Wheeler, who was still in Macon, also noted that he never heard any such threat from Otis, who while he had done something similar to Bobby Smith in the lean days, "was loyal to a fault, and a sentimental guy. He knew how dirty this business can be, but he wasn't going to let Stax go down the drain."[19]

Nonetheless, Otis's relationship with Stax was deteriorating. While it was true that he was, in effect, the scope of Stax/Volt, his stamping of an entire sound endemic to Southern blues/soul meant that, by extension, he wasn't only Stax—he was also Muscle Shoals, where producers like Rick Hall and Jimmy Johnson swaddled their horns and rhythm section arrangements in the Redding template, by turns blaring and bleeding, the meters and cadences now familiar and comfortable in nearly every song to come out of a Southern soul shop. Wilson Pickett, Sam and Dave, Eddie Floyd . . . they all played in the Redding ballpark. Otis was, indeed, all that had evolved in the sonic resonance of his voice, his range, his persona of bigness, rawness, and emotional explosiveness. He was the tail that now wagged Atlantic Records and no one had to tell him that, with as much of the music topsoil that he owned, he deserved more than Stax could now give him.

On a personal level, everyone at the label still had immense affection for him. To create a semblance of the old solidarity, that summer of 1967 he hosted a massive barbecue out at the Big O Ranch, inviting everyone, and most of them came, in awe of the Ponderosa he had built himself, stuffing themselves with prime rib from Otis's own black Angus cattle. But the Arthur Conley power play made them see a different side of him, one they ascribed to something they thought they'd never see, an arrogant one. Where in the past he used to make light of the Big O anonym as a joke, a PR prop, he had come to freely and seriously apply it to himself in normal conversation, answering the phone in character and, to end a debate about something, "That's what the Big O wants." Once, when a promoter balked at his price to perform and asked if he thought he was James Brown, he replied, "No, baby—I'm the Big O."[20] And every time he said it, he was poking fun less at himself and lording it over someone else.

However, vanity was a quality shared by the rank and file at Stax. The European conquest was such a high for everyone that, Duck Dunn once said, when the troupe "found out how big we were, everyone kind of got up in the air about it . . . every day they were saying, 'You've got to cut a hit record.'"[21] The problem was, no one seemed overly eager to actually put in the work to do that. As Bell puts it, "We came back feeling we were as big in England as the Beatles were in America, that we had it made. But when we saw and felt the same old roadblocks in America, it was like, 'What's the use? Let's just rest on our laurels for a while.' I was so excited because we had reached a high point, but then that old hunger was gone and we started sinking."

Stewart wasted no time putting out the live Europe albums, to great success, but rather than get right back to studio work, he sent the Revue out to another show, in Atlanta, for an industry convention, punctuated by the barbecue at the Big O Ranch. If this was an escape from the pressure of having to keep spiraling higher, and actually work at it, someone would have to keep Stax moving not forward but upward, putting its weight on his back. That someone was Otis Redding, even if, as Wayne Jackson says, "We were really worried that the label might lose him."

But turning to Otis was no sure thing. Indeed, having won over

Europe, he could take no victory lap back home—"I Love You More Than Words Can Say," strings and all, was a flat-out bomb, getting no higher than number 70 pop and just 30 R&B; the flip, "Let Me Come On Home," given a run of its own, charted only in England. After all of his success, rather than being regaled for what he had already recorded, he still needed to conquer the American rock cognoscenti, on its own turf, on opposite coasts.

He did notch a new personal highpoint when Arthur Conley's "Sweet Soul Music" screamed up to number 2 on both the pop and R&B (soon to be called "soul") charts, an enormous royalty payoff for Otis but one Jim Stewart had missed the boat on. Still, said Bell, there was nothing to regret. "We didn't begrudge Otis. He wanted to produce, but who could he produce at Stax? So we were happy for him. That song became the national anthem of soul, and our big acts were mentioned all through it! Not Atlantic's. Ours. How was *that* for free publicity? That record sold a million copies, and every time it was played it was an advertisement for Stax Records."

Actually it was more an ad for Otis Redding, so much so that he could avoid real trouble for having pilfered Sam Cooke's song with no credit for his hero. While he may have believed his open reverence for Sam and tribute versions of his songs on every one of his albums earned him a waiver from copyright infringement, the publisher of the song, J. W. Alexander, did not oblige. Alexander, a gospel singer and producer who discovered Cooke and owned all of his songs, sued Redding and Atco, though without acrimony as Alexander and Redding admired each other. Otis settled quickly, giving Alexander's publishing house, Kags Music, a small, undisclosed sum and the publishing credit on the song in place of Redwal. While Alexander did not ask for a writer's credit for Cooke, he did have one more demand, that Otis keep on covering songs from the Cooke catalog, no small wonder given how much he had made for Alexander already doing so, and Redding easily granted this.[22]

Stax, of course, was not a party to this latest song-credit tussle.

But when Conley's first album was released, titled after the hit song and including five others written or co-written by Otis, it seemed something like an Otis Redding declaration of independence. Redding even wrote the liner notes, saying, "I think Arthur Conley is one of the most fantastic singers in the entertainment business today" and ended with a bit of precocious posturing: "Being an A&R man is still a new thing for me. Arthur makes the job exciting through his great artistry." Not once did he mention Stax Records. And, most pointedly, was a notation on the album jacket. It read, "Produced by Otis Redding."

16

Peace, Love, and Otis Redding

As the summer of 1967—the one that wore the patent of the Summer of Love—began to unwind to the accompaniment of *Sgt. Pepper*, "Light My Fire," "Incense and Peppermints," "Groovin'," "White Rabbit," and "A Whiter Shade of Pale," one hundred thousand human gypsy moths with dilated eyeballs converged on Haight-Ashbury wearing flowers in their hair, or so the song said of those going on the pilgrimage to San Francisco. Otis Redding would come, too, or at least close enough, but not with any flowers in his Afro, or weed or acid in his pockets. He would come because another of those portentous turns in the road lie 112 miles to the South of the Haight, in a place on the edge of Monterey Bay, close enough to feel the surf.

Several months earlier, plans were formulated for an annual rock event there, one in the manner of the Monterey Jazz Festival, which had been held each September since 1958 on the rustic twenty acres of the Monterey County Fairgrounds, with the performers—including the likes of Billie Holliday, Louis Armstrong, Duke Ellington, Dizzy Gillespie, Count Basie, and Dave Brubeck—going unpaid and profits from ticket sales donated to music education. The festival's promoter, Ben Shapiro, watching the formation of a rock culture just up the coastline, had been broadening his purview; in 1966, one of the acts was the Jefferson Airplane, and this year Janis Joplin's Big Brother and the Holding Company would play. Shapiro's idea was to consolidate the separate three-day festival, not on five stages spread through the grounds but one, attracting perhaps one hundred thousand people, five times that of the jazz venue.

To do that, he'd need to attract some pretty big rock names, and the first person he approached was the Mama and the Papas' John Phillips and the band's producer Lou Adler, in L.A. They thought it sounded cool enough to put the word out to Paul McCartney, Mick Jagger, Paul Simon, and Brian Wilson, and soon seemingly everyone with a claim to rock royalty was involved in some way, including the Beatles' publicity man Derek Taylor. A board of governors convened that included Jagger, McCartney, and the Stones' manager Andrew Loog Oldham, and sponsors began lining up to kick in funds for performers' travel expenses, stage construction, lighting, and security, the latter of which would be under the watch of the Hell's Angels, an iffy prospect to be sure. Bill Graham contributed $100,000.

The Monterey city council hemmed and hawed but approved when money was put aside for local charities. The weekend of June 16–18 was chosen, with ticket prices ranging from $3 to $6.50, though it would be impossible to stem a tide of gate-crashers. A documentary film would be made of the proceedings by D. A. Pennebaker, who had made a similar visual record of Bob Dylan touring England. It all added up to a major event, and not surprisingly, Otis Redding was invited to the party, with Andrew Oldham telling Phil Walden it would be the defining moment of Otis's career. The problem was the no-pay part. Otis's first reaction was to say forget it. But when Graham made a pitch, Otis could not say no, out of gratitude. Al Bell also had a promotions man in the Bay Area, Freddie Mancuso, a "hippie type guy," he says, who explained how big a deal it was, and that it was his chance to show he really *was* the top act in the world. Bell agreed. "Oh, God, yes, I wanted him to go. Man, he *had* to go."[1]

The hedge was that, besides the hippies, many attendees would be holdovers from the folk and jazz scene, purists that once booed Bob Dylan off the stage at the Newport Folk Festival for playing an electric guitar. How would they react to Southern soul? It wasn't booing that might erupt, but, worse, blasé diffidence. As well, Otis needed a backup band, having fired his last one after returning from Europe. Fortunately, Jim Stewart—with much convincing from Jerry Wexler—agreed that for an engagement packed with so much significance, he would do his part, sending out Booker T. and the MG's and two Memphis Horns, Wayne Jackson and Andrew Love. They wouldn't need to buy new suits this time; they took the same lime green ones they'd worn in Europe, as would Otis.

BY THE summer of 1967, soul in the deepest sense seemed an afterthought. Even though Smokey Robinson was on the festival's board of directors, Berry Gordy had forbidden his stable from performing at a rock venue; and the Impressions dropped out, leaving only Redding and Lou Rawls, who after years on the R&B circuit had finally found an audience for his high-toned soul, with a gold album and a number 1 R&B hit, "Love Is a Hurtin' Thing," in 1966 and a Grammy in 1967, though he was all but overlooked at the festival. Some major white acts, not sold on the compensation or the benefit of being merely one among a pack of acts that might dilute the impact of each, backed out, too: the Beach Boys, the Kinks, and Cream. The Doors were snubbed and Donovan was refused a visa because of a drug bust.

The Monterey International Pop Music Festival would commence on Friday, June 16, with Simon and Garfunkel, Eric Burdon, Johnny Rivers, Rawls, and the Association; the Saturday show, Joplin, the

Byrds, the Jefferson Airplane, and Redding; Sunday, the Grateful
Dead, the Who, Buffalo Springfield, Ravi Shankar, Jimi Hendrix,
and the Mamas and the Papas. Adjunct acts like Country Joe and
the Fish, Quicksilver Messenger Service, the Blues Project, the
Paul Butterfield Blues Band, Moby Grape, Canned Heat, the Electric Flag, Laura Nyro, and Hugh Masekela would be sprinkled in.
As unfamiliar as Otis was with most of these acts, to many of them
he was the most eagerly awaited. Janis Joplin, for one, kept touting
him to anyone who would listen, saying, "Wait'll you see him. You
gotta see him. Otis is God, man." At one point, Grateful Dead pianist Pigpen wanted to know, "So does God have a big dick?" "Only if
you believe in him," she replied.[2]

In recognition that the hordes might not have come to see him,
but would leave with a tingle when they did, Otis was given the cov-
eted closing slot on the middle night. Another young black musician
causing the same kind of stir was of course James Marshall Hen-
dricks, but not as a soul man, those days gone since he had played in
Little Richard's backing band in the mid-1960s. Hendrix soon was
moving down the same fateful, albeit opposite road that took Otis
Redding to Monterey. His mission, he said, was "to do with my guitar what Little Richard does with his voice."[3] With his guitar seemingly able to evoke any ungodly sound he wanted it to, even when
played with his teeth, he had risen by circumventing soul and American audiences. Just twelve days before, the Experience had been on
a bill with Cream and Procol Harum at London's Saville Theatre.
Paul McCartney himself had urged the promoters to book him,
and Hendrix would be introduced onstage by an acid-blitzed Brian
Jones. Jimi Hendrix's time had come. But so had Otis Redding's.

•

AROUND TWO hundred thousand people, many actually with flowers in their hair, attended the three idyllic shows, close to one hun-

dred thousand alone on the second night, not a one of which seemed able to focus their eyeballs. Wayne Jackson still seems a bit fazed by the sight of hordes "openly smoking pot and dropping acid. There were cops roaming around but it looked like nobody cared. Cops, hippies, and marijuana all mixed up together." To him, it seemed not only crazy but "scary."[4] Sweet, pungent aromas wafted across the grounds, carried by the cool sea breeze. With some performers bedecked in pastoral robes and with druggy montages projected onto blinding screens behind the stage, these were tribal rites of an era unfolding by the minute, but not quite metaphysical enough for competition to recede. The Who—tipped off that Hendrix would climax his set by copping Pete Townsend's signature shtick of smashing his guitar to bits, accompanied by smoke bombs—refused to go on after Hendrix and took an earlier slot.

Otis had no such competition, but worried endlessly that he had made a mistake. Zelma, who made the trip with him, recalled him being more nervous than she'd ever seen him, not eager to have to conquer an event with so little soul in order to ensure his place in the newest rock reformation. On the 17th, as the night went on, similar fears grew among those who encouraged him to play Monterey. Phil Walden later said that Jerry Wexler told him that night, "I think this is a mistake," something that occurred to him after watching the Jefferson Airplane "with all the psychedelic stuff and the light show and everything." Wexler barked, "You don't have all that!" whereupon, Walden said, "My heart just jumped, like what have we gotten ourselves into?" At that moment, however, he spotted Otis waiting to go on, looking like "he wasn't concerned about anything."[5]

Indeed, contrary to what Zelma remembered, Otis seemed a little *too* unconcerned. It was obvious to Walden that Otis was on an unnatural high, trying to relax by taking some hits from a joint someone had slipped him. To be sure, Otis was hardly a virgin when it came to drugs, having been around much of it on the mean streets of Macon and on the chitlin' circuit. Indeed, the hippies and their dope hijinks may have seemed quaint by comparison to what he'd seen in his own bands; one account even had him sending someone all the way to New York to "score a bag" of heroin for one of his players after he ran out of the stuff in Texas and was desperate for a fix—one of those typical wild tales that somehow come from *somewhere*. Yet never had Walden seen him take a toke before going onstage. "Man, don't smoke that shit now," he told him. "Not before we go on."

Clearly less than nervous, Otis said, "Aw, fuck, don't worry about it, man."[6]

Worse, Otis had put so little preparation or thought into the gig that, when Walden asked what he was going to sing, Otis couldn't tell him. He was going to do it on pure feel. Walden suggested he start with "Shake." The rest, it would be, well, potluck.

•

WHEN OTIS was set to go on, it was around 1:00 A.M. and getting cold. Rain had also begun to fall, prompting concerns that if it became heavier, the show might have to be halted as a precaution that someone holding an electric guitar might be fried. But while John Phillips cursed the rain, Otis, with just enough cannabis in him to be *Otis*, was ready to roll. Brought out with a perfunctory introduction by the drily subversive comedian and TV star Tommy Smothers, Otis bounced on stage in his incandescent turquoise suit, the Memphis Horns blowing as entrance music, looking, as the Grateful Dead's Bob Weir said, "twelve or fourteen feet tall,"[7] and broke into "Shake," volleying the title with the audience, who, after each line would enter with a more fervid cry of "Shake!" His feet twiddling like James Brown's, he blew through the song, to a rich reception. As Robert Christgau noted in *Esquire*, all he'd needed to do was "trot his big self onto the stage and rock into [the song] and he had made it, wham bam thank-you-ma'am. The rest of his act—

the dancing, the chuckling, the running around, the whole image of masculine ease on which [his] career is based—was icing."[8]

"He knew from the get-go he had 'em," a relieved Walden said. "When he got that kind of reaction, he was better than great. He'd notch it up."[9]

It was after "Shake" that he uttered, famously, slurring his words slightly, "This is a song that a girl took away from me," chirpily but with some grit, before adding with a half-laugh that the girl was "a good friend of mine. . . . This girl took this song, but we're gonna do it anyway." A snare burst from Al Jackson set in motion an especially pleading, high-fever rendition of "Respect," into which he dropped a convincing "ooh Lord" into the off-the-cuff riffs, which moved at a tempo at least twice as fast as that on the record Jim Stewart had produced, and, fortunately, was not there to see. Finally hitting a last note, he was exhausted, and the crowd was, in the vernacular of the day, out of its tree, flat-out crazy. Having been so revved up, people were standing on fragile chairs, girls riding piggyback on men's shoulders, half-naked, through the rain.

Prodded by the cops, Phillips, when the song ended, motioned him to the side of the stage and told him, "We've got to get everybody in their chairs again." Otis sardonically told him, "I thought that was the whole idea, to get 'em *up*."[10]

Still, he promised he'd calm everything down, at least until he tanked everyone up another time. Stage center again, he said in a soothing voice, "We'd like to slow it down this time, and do a soulful number." Then, "This is the Love Crowd, right?"—in a fey voice, "Half ironic, half-intimidating," thought *New York Times* critic Renata Adler,[11] and which might have come off as a put-down if not for the entirely ingenuous attempt to grasp something he didn't really understand. And they began to wake up—"Yeah!" they shouted back.

"We all love each other, right?" he went on, bringing another raucous reply.

Sensing an opening, he was yelling now, smile streaming across his face: "AM I RIGHT?"

An even louder "YEAH!"

"LET ME HEAR YOU SAY YEAH!"

"YEAH!"

Now bringing it back down, to smooth and mellow, he grinned and said, "All righhht."

Then, wrote Christgau, in a kind of play-by-play, "on some unheard but nevertheless precise beat, Redding began to . . . well, emote, part-singing, part-talking, part-moaning: 'I've been [Steve Cropper lightly on guitar] loving you [pause] too long [lone shout from press section] to stop now,' and the Mar-Keys started to blow, and the arena was in an uproar once again. Superspade was flying high."

"Good God almighty I love ya!" Otis blessed the crowd. Then, "Jump again—let's go!" Now he was into another smoking benediction, with an equally explosive "Satisfaction," after which, feeling no pain, he dedicated "Try a Little Tenderness" to "the miniskirts, I dig 'em." This, his closer, was a number he always transformed into a raw, throbbing nerve. Now, sweat glistening on his brow, an overurgent passion in his voice, he launched into the raging manifesto of deep love and mournful regret. When he got to the signature "got-ta got-ta-got-ta" and "ta-ta-ta-ta" rapid-fire machine-gun bursts, couples hugged and pawed each other as they danced in the cool night air. "I got-ta go now, I got-ta go," he rasped, but after a quick exit, he quickly reappeared for the encore that was an extended ending of "Tenderness," a roiling, rolling tide. "Let me have some . . . let me have some," he repeated endlessly, to the vamping of the band, as his name was flashing on the screen behind him in strobe-lit blobs, helping blast everyone into a climactic frenzy. Brian Jones, watching with Mick Jagger and Jimi Hendrix offstage, was even seen crying as he watched this great paroxysm onstage.

And then, like the clouds of pot smoke around the fairgrounds, he was finally gone, his presence needed on a radio show, but the vibrations of the performance were still consuming voltage. People stood, calling for more, the buzz in the air around them almost audible. The set had lasted about a half hour, far too brief, but plenty sufficient for him to claim victory, again, having received what Christgau reviewed as "the most tumultuous reception of the Festival" he and the Mar-Keys "all conservatively dressed and groomed, succeeding with nothing more than musicianship and a sincere feeling for the roots of the blues." This, of course, was an obvious counterpoint to the molten performance given by Hendrix the following night, when he literally left jaws agape. He fell to his knees during "Wild Thing," "humped" an amp, and "made love" to his guitar by squirting lighter fluid on it, setting it afire, then smashing it, indeed doing what Townsend feared he would, soldering generational nihilism with undefined sexual rage, which made the Who almost forgettable that night. Not that it was very compatible with the gentle sexual "freedom" ethos of the "love crowd," and Hendrix still would not be fully accepted by American audiences and critics.

Christgau contrasted the two performances with no mercy for Hendrix's—"a psychedelic Uncle Tom," he wrote, a stunningly boorish phrase not lessened by its intended irony (as was his subsequent defense that "'psychedelic Uncle Tom' is more accurate than 'just another Uncle Tom'")—whose act was "a consistently vulgar parody of rock theatrics." In reviewing the D. A. Pennebaker's brilliant documentary *Monterey Pop*—an aural and visual feast if ever there was one—which came out over a year after Redding's death and a year into Hendrix's hard upward thrust, Christgau called the pair "two radically different black artists showboating at the nativity of the new white rock audience. . . . I admired Redding and was appalled by Hendrix," though "in retrospect they seem equally audacious and equally wonderful."[12]

•

OTIS CAME away from Monterey even cockier than before. Giddily, he and Walden culled newspaper reviews, all of which hailed him. Beyond the personal victory, however, the indelible impact of Monterey was palpable. Early in 1967, some in the industry had begun to sour on an increasingly glitzy incarnation of soul, typified by Motown ditching almost all of its formerly top-shelf acts to showcase, and enjoy untold riches from, an ultra-glamorous Diana Ross. By the end of summer, with Otis slaying diverse pop music venues at home and abroad, his glittering moment at Monterey seemed to relight the soul spark, as if Redding's performance had officially solidified soul as a component in the white rock and roll mainstream. The avatar of the newest soul assimilation had not changed his style or sensibilities; as Al Bell had predicted, the rest of the world had. And now, reassuringly, the soul man whose pyrotechnics came all from within his own soul was a massively significant icon, whose future turns demanded to be observed, and heard, as he further assimilated.

That Redding had initially captured the cream of the white rock cognoscenti was a key element in all this, allowing *them* to bask not only in his glow but their own prescience. One of those was Jon Landau, who had been touting Redding in the underground rock press for two years. Now, seeing him on his biggest stage yet, Landau would say his Monterey performance was the "highest level of expression rock 'n' roll has yet attained" and that "Otis Redding *is* rock 'n' roll . . . past, present, and future."[13] Or at least until Landau latched on to Bruce Springsteen and transferred that very same honorific on *him*.

In August, *Hit Parader*, asked, "Who will be the big soul singer, the one to last and last? We have James Brown, Joe Tex, Wilson Pickett [or] Otis Redding." In a semi-answer, the magazine noted that "Otis believes Wilson Pickett should get the crown as the best and he isn't just being modest."[14] As it turned out, he had already transcended soul. A month later, when *Melody Maker* released its annual reader poll, Redding, who had been seventh in the previous year's vote for "world's top male vocalist," ended Elvis Presley's decade-long, seemingly permanent hold on the accolade. And Phil Walden sure got a lot of mileage out of *that* one.

To be sure, not all in the white literati were ready to swoon over Redding, not even in England. Nik Cohn, the acidic Brit music journalist, who was all of twenty-one when Redding died, dismissively insisted in his then-important 1970 epistle of the rock evolution, *Awopbopaloobop Alopbamboom*, that the typical Redding performance was "instant grunt and groan" and the Stax template a "sweat-and-Tom syndrome [that] has much to answer for." Monterey, he sniffed, had *even* made room for Redding and Ravi Shankar, as if he was an appurtenance.[15] In this light, Otis was fortunate that his time didn't cross the threshold of an era when white critics felt empowered, impudent, and immune enough from bad taste and limited scope to freely call black performers "Toms," without figuring in that an entire race, and most of another, saw it quite differently. Still, this may not have been personal. Indeed, it was significant on some level that, as far as soul had come, it could be insulted as freely and dimly as white rock was.

●

IN SEEKING the middle of the road after Monterey, the rub for Redding was that white rock and black soul were running in opposite directions—acid rock toward soul, black rock toward the area vacated by white acts. Motown, for example, would soon be recording metaphoric pseudo-drug anthems like "Psychedelic Shack" and "Cloud Nine," and Otis took seriously his new mission to assimilate somehow into the rock terrain. During a trip to New York early in January 1967, he was invited by Buffalo Springfield's drummer Dewey Martin to catch the band's East Coast debut after signing with Atlantic, at the ritzy disco Ondine's on Fifty-Ninth Street. Otis saw the chance to further see what this L.A. rock thing was about, and Martin excitedly told everyone he met, "I called Otis and he's coming to see us tonight," though Springfield's producer Brian Stone recalled, "Everybody thought Dewey was full of shit."[16] But Otis indeed blew in, causing his usual ruckus, and was more than enjoying the evening when the band called him up on the stage, whereupon, as Atlantic promotion man Mario Medious said, "Otis was so drunk that when he took a bow, he fell over. But then he sang with them and he was fantastic."[17]

Apparently adopting Springfield as a sort of accessory during his stay in New York, he also was at the session during which they cut Neil Young's "Mr. Soul," a session that, legendarily, saw Stone's co-producer Charlie Greene punch Stephen Stills in the mouth. Otis was taken with Young's curiously soulful nasal delivery and clever, earthy, and surprisingly bluesy lyrics that hit home with him far more than Bob Dylan's. In Young, he again thought he'd found his key to the rock door. As Stone remembered, "He said, 'Holy shit, I love that song, man. I want to record it. I'm gonna cut that song, man.'"

Like many such ideas that streamed in and out of Otis's head, however, this one was soon forgotten as he tried to find his own path to American chart success. In his meticulous process of deciding what to do, pandering to alien rock territory just never felt right to him. Neither was Monterey going to catapult him to the promised land. "It wasn't gonna be a performance that put Otis over the top," Phil Walden once recalled, "it was gonna be a song."[18] Al Bell, though, believed that since Otis was winning over white audiences, there was one idiom that could fit his style. "We'd had discussions about this, and I told him we needed to get a folk-sounding song from him. That was the only time I ever got involved with telling him what he should write. Because I felt we could get the black stations and some of the middle-of-the-road stations, the top forties. I could even see an album. I had a title for it, *Otis Redding: Soul Folks*."

This was not such a radical idea. Just for one example, the Four Tops had scored big with a cover of the Left Banke's British-influenced folk-rock hit "Walk Away Renee," which was easily molded into a soul and pop chart hit. But this kind of tinkering posed some vexing inner unease for Otis, who never before had to think about how to balance going deeper into rock while holding on to his native soul roots. The *New York Times*' Robert Shelton wrote that year of the artificial barriers still being invoked, "The white rock 'n' roll craze, British and American, helped build an audience for Negro blues performers. [But] if the blues is truly a language, and an international language at that, why must it be spoken exactly the same way by all and spoken in the same terms? On their own level, Joe Tex, Otis Redding, and Percy Sledge are folk-derived performers as much as Bukka White and Mance Lipscomb. . . . Compatibility, not irreconcilable differences, is the message."[19]

Otis clearly took Bell's advice under advisement, perhaps more than Bell would have thought.

●

REDDING HAD scant downtime after Monterey. Walden had booked a tour of California for him, which would conclude with a weeklong gig at San Francisco's Basin Street West nightclub. As the Mar-Keys had gone back to Memphis, and having fired his band for an umpteenth time, this one after the mess with Loretta Williams, a new backup band from Memphis flew out to meet up with him. This group was a six-piece unit that had been serving as the backup house band at Stax. Known as the Bar-Kays—a name not coincidentally similar to the Mar-Keys though its genesis was a Memphis dance blues band—the group was named after a Bacardi street billboard near the studio.[20] They were, in Stax-style, integrated, with keyboard player Ronnie Caldwell the sole white, playing with guitarist Jimmie King, sax man Phalon Jones, trumpeter Ben Cauley, drummer Carl Cunningham, and bassist James Alexander. None of them were even twenty, yet they already had a hit under the belt, one they had collectively written, the instrumental "Soulfinger," the title coined by Hayes and Porter. Driven by fluttery horns, the song featured raucous street kids who were paid with Cokes to make noise and chant the title.[21] (It also recycled Otis's old "Mary Had a Little Lamb" riff.) The result went to number 3 R&B and 17 pop in early summer. The flip side, "Knucklehead," written by Cropper and Jones, also charted briefly.

Otis had rarely used a band so small over the previous four years, so they rehearsed with him before Monterey, and he was pleasantly surprised that they could re-create big band arrangements with only two horns. They joined him when he was back on the road early the morning after Monterey, headed for L.A. What he could have used was a few days rest, for his body and his punished vocal cords, which had been giving him trouble ever since Europe and even gave out for fleeting moments during some overheated performances, such as during "Satisfaction" at Monterey, after which his throat was inflamed and he could speak only in a whisper, sounding like Edgar Buchanan. Sipping hot tea all the way down the Pacific Coast Highway, he ignored the pain and held back nothing on the tour, with the only chance to rest coming between shows.

During the Basin gig, one account has it, he was staying at a hotel with the band, when Speedo Sims, again working as road manager, witnessed Otis being hectored by so many female fans that he had to move hotels, renting Bill Graham's houseboat in Sausalito, north across the Golden Gate Bridge.[22] The boat was moored on the main dock of Waldo Point Harbor, a poetically serene setting that even during a cold snap and under gloomy gray skies, with the incessant din of choppers taking off and landing at a nearby heliport, was isolated enough to cushion his bones and make him both reflective and melancholic. The dock itself, however, was hardly serene, with hard-rock bands rehearsing loudly at the other end and the battered hull of a semi-sunken ship called the *South Shore* being used by squatters.

Still, Otis freely mingled with these "dock people" and he and Sims would literally sit each day on the dock of the bay, watching ships roll in and then away, prompting Otis to begin jotting down rudimentary song lyrics of just that peaceful vision, playing an unhurried melody on a guitar, perhaps mindful of Al Bell's advice about trying a little folk along with tenderness. But Speedo, having been around him when he had written songs before, was baffled. "I couldn't quite follow it," he once said. "We must have been out there three or four days before . . . I could get any concept where he was going with the song . . . He was changing with the times is what was happening."[23]

Otis as much as confirmed this to Zelma after getting back to the Big O Ranch, where he strummed and sang the unfinished song for her, as he did with most every tune he wrote. Her reaction, as she once recalled, was that "I really couldn't get into it."

"Oh, God, you're changing," she told him.

"Yeah," he said, "I think it's time for me to change my music. People might be tired of me."[24]

•

ZELMA'S LUKEWARM reaction to the song made him turn away from it temporarily, leaving it unfinished, not even recorded in demo form at his home studio. In the meantime, there was much else on his plate. In August, he was in New York to play in the first of what would be an annual outdoor concert series in the humid summer air in Central Park. Called the Rheingold Central Park Music Festival, its promoters, Hilly Kristal and Ron Delsener, usually booked three or four acts per show—Duke Ellington and his orchestra, Muddy Waters, John Lee Hooker, and Thelonious Monk shared the stage. But Phil Walden laid down the ground rule that Otis had to play alone. OTIS REDDING STARS IN 2 PARK CONCERTS read a headline in the *New York Times*.[25] Both shows sold out the seven thousand seats, leading the promoters to add a 10:30 P.M. show. At a buck a seat, the demand could not have been anything less than a stampede.

Indeed, the Otis Redding operation had gotten so big that Walden could not possibly book all of Otis's appearances himself anymore and also have time for his other properties. To arrange most of the tour dates, back in 1964, Walden had hired, for a 10 percent cut, a major New York agency, Shaw Artists Corporation (SAC), which booked top R&B talent like the Platters, Dinah Washington, and the Drifters. An early SAC contract for a March 1964 Redding gig at Baltimore's Royal Theater shows that he made six hundred dollars, a typical high-level fee at the time for him. Three years later, a SAC tally sheet of a one-week period in July 1967 looked like this:

7/21 Columbus, Ga., $2,000; 7/22 Macon, Ga., $2,000; 7/23 Greensboro, N.C., $2,000; 7/24 Chattanooga, Tenn., $2,000; 7/25 Atlanta, Ga., $2,000; 7/26 Birmingham, Ala., $2,000; 7/27, Little Rock, Ark., $2,000; 7/28 Mobile, Ala., $2,000.

Furthermore, these figures, which were on the low end of his scale, were *advances*; often, he would clear thousands more when all the tickets bought were added in. For another Atlanta date, at the city's Municipal Auditorium on July 17, when all the cash was counted for 5,500 tickets, he walked away with $16,247.50, after taxes of $502.50.[26] Otis himself would often pack this kind of cash into an attaché case, not willing to have promoters send SAC or Walden a check. By the end of some tours, he would be walking around with over a hundred grand in that case, which he would dump on Phil's desk the way he had the chump change that kept Walden in school. Phil would then bank or invest it for him.

What's more, the doings of the Redding corporation, Otis Redding Enterprises, Inc., were lucrative enough to draw the attention of the IRS. That year, when another booking agency sent Walden a proposal for future shows, it somehow got into an audit of the company's finances, leading the IRS to wonder why earnings from the proposed gigs had not been declared. "As you can imagine, that caused us a lot of agitation," recalled Alex Hodges.[27]

But the IRS did not find anything amiss, and once the IRS was out of the way, Redding looked down the long road and all he could see were bookings, stretching far into 1968. His retinue had grown after Monterey into a fourteen-piece band, valets, bodyguards, and assorted roadies who seemed to appear from out of the blue. One of those was a former Navy veteran Walden took under his wing, Twiggs Lyndon—his actual name—whom he made Redding's road manager, working with Speedo. A bearded, tattooed guy with an eye for detail, Lyndon had worked in that capacity for Little Richard. Unfortunately, he also had his own share of demons to deal with and in 1970, as road manager for the Allman Brothers, he would stab a club manager to death, claim temporary insanity created by the rock and roll lifestyle, serve eighteen months in jail and six months in a psych ward, and go right back to managing. In 1979, he died while skydiving.[28]

The crowd around Redding was the freight paid for a figure who was traveling at the speed of sound now. But there was a price for Otis, too.

17

Hard to Handle

Otis Ray Redding Jr. wore his crown uneasily, not least of all because he came away from the Summer of Love with his vocal cords having paid the price for nonstop gigs and never learning the mechanics of singing from the gut instead of the throat. In late summer 1967, he had kept a solo engagement in England, but by the fall he was just beat, his throat scorched, unable to hit the highs. When he was in New York, he had gone to a throat specialist and been told he had developed polyps in his larynx, some over a year old and in a real danger of becoming cancerous. The doctor said he needed surgery, then not to sing a note for a two-month recuperation. It was a diagnosis he tried to ignore, thinking that if he could only rest for a while, time would heal those delicate cords. But, as itchy as he always was to keep on the move, he wouldn't have been able to keep off the road for the two months, anyway. The last hurdle was the fear that surgery would alter the tone and power of his voice, that he might not ever be able to sing again. He hedged, then listened to Phil Walden and others and decided he had no choice. He would have the surgery at New York's Mt. Sinai Hospital.

"He really was worried, we all were," says Al Bell. "You're talking about a gold mine in that throat, that voice. Believe me, we were on eggshells every day. Our future was in that throat."[1]

Because it was the first time in his life he would be under anesthesia, and unsure if he'd wake up, he grew melancholic and fatalistic as the surgery date approached. Making Otis Redding Sr.'s future more secure, he drew up papers cutting the deacon in for a 60 percent interest in Otis Redding Enterprises, the corporate umbrella of his financial holdings. To the father who now only had words of encouragement for his son's musical obsessions, this was only a first step, telling whoever would listen that he soon was going to displace Walden and be his son's business manager.[2]

Days before Redding was to leave for New York for the operation, he threw another bash at the ranch, for three hundred invited guests who once more gorged on what came out of the barbecue pit: five hogs and two cows, medium rare and covered with hot sauce. It was, Zelma once said, "our own Woodstock."[3] But rather than enjoying the affair and the company, Otis was sullen and angry, mainly because he hadn't been able to finish filling the ninety-thousand-gallon swimming pool. Zelma begged him to relax, saying not everybody wanted to go for a dip. But relax he couldn't. Neither was he anywhere near himself physically. He had planned to sing in a jam session with Sam and Dave and Arthur Conley but was so physically spent he couldn't even raise himself from his chair, which he took to for greeting guests, like the Pope on Sunday in Vatican City.

Nevertheless, the surgery went without a hitch, performed by a Mt. Sinai throat specialist who was so starstruck that he said he would waive his fee, but only under one condition: that Otis, with whom he talked endlessly about hunting before the operation, would send him a rifle with a scope.

Because he had gone to the operation alone, Otis spent his twenty-sixth birthday, September 9, mostly by himself, crammed into his narrow hospital bed. The good thing was that he finally, enforced or not, was able to let his body heal and recharge. Within a couple of days, he would return to the ranch for the two-month convalescence, under orders not to speak beyond one or two words, or sing at all. For Otis Redding, that was about the hardest injunction he could exist under. But worse was that the Summer of Love turned into the autumn of opportunity, with him nowhere in sight.

•

AS OTIS arrived back at the Big O Ranch, the maddening crosscurrents of the late sixties caused Al Bell as much anxiety as Otis's layoff. Even as Redding had begun annexing white audiences, suddenly, incredulously, it became the *black* stations—the ones making the biggest noise in radio—that he sometimes had to work the hardest to get Redding played the way he used to be. "It was unbelievable," Bell remembered. "In Atlanta, the major black station never played Otis Redding. He was played on the pop station. I would ask them why and they talked about his speech impediment, the way when he spoke he might mix up the syntax or get a word wrong. I'm serious. The black jocks had a problem with that, and it's part of our culture going back to the blues era, because for some blacks that kind of music reminded them of something they wanted to forget about. And now with black artists starting to get into protest and 'serious' music, guys like Otis were thought of as illiterate, which was not the case. Otis had limited education, he wasn't book smart, but he could think on his feet. You don't write songs like that being empty in the head."

Bell likes to quote the Martin Luther King Jr. proverb that "attitude, not aptitude, gets you altitude" in recalling Redding, and still bristles about the irony of Otis's leap into the music mainstream— that, as African-American pride fused into black nationalism in the

late 1960s, the support he'd had in the black community was fray-
ing. This was not because of any feeling that he was selling out, or
betraying his natural constituency. Rather, it was that black pride
had begun to require a certain level of sophistication that precluded
even black performers of recent vintage who couldn't quite live up
to a standard of intellectuality. Even a brilliant songwriter like Otis
Redding, to some of the newer, younger black cultural maw, seemed
to be just too backwater for comfort, as the black migrations north-
ward over the decades formed a strong urban sensibility and embarrassment about the rural culture many had left behind. And that
made Bell's neck burn. "You'd think all black people would have
treasured Otis," he goes on. "But this was the sixties, they were yelling 'Uncle Tom' at other brothers. You had to think a certain way,
talk a certain way. That made me sick. There has never been a man
who lived a more exemplary life than Otis. But you can't make an
idiot see what he don't wanna see."

Indeed, African-Americans of note were not only being encouraged to be black as loudly and proudly as possible, but to also financially support the movement. So were corporate entities who made
their profits from black artists. Among the latter, Atlantic Records
was the prime donor, contributing money to Jesse Jackson's Operation PUSH, often after Jackson would drop in unannounced at
the company office looking for a check, which Jerry Wexler later
described as a kind of shakedown. If Wexler didn't pay, Jackson
would try "to subvert our artists and turn Wilson Pickett and Otis
Redding against me so he could set up a picket line and get more
money from me."[4]

These "shakedowns," if that's what they were, seemed to be
common knowledge within the industry. In 1969, for example,
when Jann Wenner interviewed Phil Spector for *Rolling Stone*, his
first question was about "black militancy" and "black resentment
against whites" in the record business, his example being Stax.
The reclusive producer, never noted for being politically correct,

answered: "Oh yeah, man, [certain blacks were saying] 'We bought your home, goddamn, and don't you forget it, boy. You livin' in the house we paid for, you drivin' a Cadillac we got, man. It's ours. You stole it from us.'" . . . This is why you have the music business dominated in the black area by just two companies. Because there is just really no place for them to go. They've just sort of disbanded. Other than Motown you don't see any groups, colored groups."[5]

Jackson would surely disagree with the inference that his "black militancy" was actually depressing black entrepreneurship, and that he was shaking down Jerry Wexler, but Bell had a similar anecdote. "There was a guy in New York. I don't even know his name, but he was putting pressure on Atlantic and I protected Jerry from this guy. In Memphis, we never had anything like that until Martin Luther King was killed. We were a white company with a mostly white staff in a black neighborhood, and I was the liaison to that community. If anyone had a problem they'd come to see me and we'd talk it out."

Apparently, though, someone did try to put the heat on Otis. Wexler, in his 1994 memoirs, wrote that Redding "had a positive sense of racial identity but resisted the blandishments of militants who tried to turn him against us and his manager, Phil Walden . . . despite stories to the contrary he was anything *but* the cliché of the backwoods country boy come to the big city. Otis knew what was happening."[6] In fact, it may not have been coincidental that, around that time, Otis had come up with the notion of creating an alliance of sorts. Quietly, he spoke with Solomon Burke about it, and then James Brown, who wrote in his memoirs that Otis called him when he was performing in Cincinnati, using his nickname for James. "Bossman," he said, "I've got an idea I want you to help me with. I want us to form a union of all-black entertainers. We can start with the singers and musicians we know, and then we can get actors and dancers and the rest later on."

"What do you want to do that for?" Brown asked.

"It would give us all more leverage in the business. No more getting messed over by the white promoters and managers and people in the record business."

Brown begged off, noting that when there had been white and black musicians' unions, "we just wound up second-class citizens."

"It wouldn't be like that, Bossman. If the big stars stuck together, they could see to it that a lot more black entertainers got work and got treated fair."

"I can't do it, Otis. I don't believe in separatism. I think that's going backwards, and I don't want to be part of that."[7]

The conversation clearly showed that Redding and Brown were moving in opposite directions, politically. Yet Otis had a strange system of political values, based less on issues than a gut feeling. During the 1967 mayor's race in Macon, when Democratic incumbent B. F. Merritt was challenged by a onetime proud segregationist and country singer, Republican Ronnie Thompson, it was the latter whom Otis took a liking to. They were an odd couple indeed, especially since Otis's lawyer of record was black Georgia senator Leroy Johnson, a political ally of Merritt. But when Thompson needed a campaign office, Otis had Phil Walden clear space in the latter's office for him. On election night, Otis and the candidate watched the returns come in, electing Thompson and helping usher in Georgia's new Confederacy of Republican bigots. Otis didn't live to see Thompson do his job, which included issuing "shoot-to-kill" orders to police to stop possible looting in 1970 and driving a National Guard tank onto a Macon elementary school campus to intimidate would-be criminals.[8]

Whether or not Otis would have ever followed James Brown into full-fledged Republicanism is impossible to say. But it is clear that he revered the man, and Brown always was fond of him. Once, when Redding and Brown were giving shows in Houston at the same time, Brown at a bigger hall, James ended his show by telling his audience, "I'll see you at Otis Redding's show," guaranteeing Redding a sell-out crowd, and the two men did an impromptu duet onstage. Soon after, Otis took Brown's advice seriously, and gave up on his union. However, there would be one piece of urgent advice from Brown that Otis would not heed—which, as would become tragically clear soon enough, would be the biggest mistake he ever made.

•

OTIS WAS certainly smart enough to know how perilous it would be for a black entertainer to be a political lightning rod. While a white folksinger like Barry McGuire could have a hit with a song like "Eve of Destruction," a black soul singer would have been committing professional suicide. Still, on the other side of the spectrum, there was equal pressure from an impatient black press for performers to demonstrate their patriotism and their empathy for black soldiers fighting a jungle war that made no sense, against an enemy that posed no existential threat to them. This frustration was evident in October 1967 when the *Amsterdam News* demanded to know why the top black music acts weren't doing as white artists did by going to Vietnam to entertain troops—an imbalanced proportion of whom were black. Indeed, during the height of the war, from 1965 to '69, African-Americans, who constituted 11 percent of the American population, made up 12.6 percent of the fighting force, and 14.9 percent of combat fatalities.[9] This outsized representation may in part explain why soul music was increasingly being heard on Armed Forces Radio, though the integration of soul into mainstream might be the definitive reason.[10]

Otis would take care of *that* omission in due time. But, for now, politically meaningful enough for Redding was that he had taken soul into the marrow of rock, white rock, a phase that seems, in hindsight, almost a blurring of the racial divide, even if it did prove illusory. Phil Walden once put it this way, "It's simplistic, but it was awfully difficult for people to hate when they loved the music so much."[11] Thus Otis was no doubt pleased when he gave an interview for the August *Hit Parader* which ran with the headline "HELLO MR. SOUL." He blew a kiss to the odd generation he was seducing: "I like what these rock and roll kids are doing. Sometimes they take things from us, but I take things from them, too. The things that are beautiful, and they do a lot of beautiful things." But he also had some stern advice for his recent forebears.

> I'd like to say something to the R&B singers who were around ten years ago. They've got to get out of the old bag. Listen to the beat of today and use it on records. Don't say we're gonna go back ten years and use this old swing shuffle. That's not it. I know what the kids want today and I aim all my stuff at them. I'd like to see all those singers make it again. I'd like to take Fats Domino, Little Richard, Big Joe Turner, Clyde McPhatter and bring them into the bag of today. They'd have hits all over again.

Openly now, with no prompting, he aired the thoughts he'd had about following Hendrix's lead, notwithstanding the discomfort he had experienced in the UK during his long tour.

> I love England from head to toe. I love the weather, the people . . . the people are so groovy. They treated me like I was somebody. They took me wherever I wanted to go. I loved Paris too. They sang along with almost all the songs. But England is beautiful country. If I were to leave the U.S., I'd live in England. But I'd never leave the U.S.

For now, his devotion to country was as political as he needed it to be, as Stax moved from underground to mainstream recognition. The fruits of not offending whites were rewarding. The *Melody Maker* poll that ranked Redding the top male singer in the world was an important step, and the Stax imprimatur was such that

Steve Cropper, riding on his shout-out by Sam and Dave, came in fifth among all the world's musicians. In the U.S., *Billboard* had a survey that named Booker T. and the MG's the top instrumental group of 1967, their song "Hip Hug-Her," which Cropper wrote with Al Bell, the best instrumental recording. Carla Thomas won the National Academy of Recording Arts Sciences (NARAS) award for most promising female artist of the year—*six years* after she had her first hit.

Otis was politically savvy enough to understand that there were issues he could, and could not, safely come out for. In the early fall of 1967, when Secretary of Labor Willard Wirtz asked Stewart to produce, as a public service, an album of Stax/Volt artists aimed at inner-city black kids called *Stay in School*, Otis off the cuff sang the title track, beginning, "Hi, this is the Big O, Otis Redding . . . take a listen," and warning that "without an education you can only be a tramp. Grow your iron shoes, no haircut, just plain ole country." Notable for its proto rap—most of the album was spoken word—and as the only recording on which he accompanied himself on guitar, it was distributed to DJs across the country, and for a time was being requested by listeners.

But now Black Panthers were showing up at the door, a memory that still makes Wayne Jackson shudder. Yet Bell had no such queasiness. "I had no problem with the Black Panthers. They were from our neighborhood, they wanted to protect us, support us. They were big fans of our artists and never threatened us. They were pressuring record companies to play more black artists, fighting segregation and racism. We didn't have problems with the blacks—we had problems with the *whites*, the police out on the road, the rednecks."

●

OTIS, MEANWHILE, had larger concerns than the Black Panthers. Not only was there the matter of his vocal cords following surgery, but, provided they healed with no problem, what sort of songs he would test them with. Before he left the hospital in New York, Jerry Wexler dropped by his bedside and the two discussed how Otis could expand his repertoire to meet a new cultural paradigm. As he once recalled, Redding never could stand pat. "He was always re-evaluating and reassessing himself and he was always concerned about his material and his sound. He always wanted to know if it was contemporaneous, whether it was changing fast enough, whether it was a happening sound." Contrary to the facile latter-day bromides about everyone's lack of urgency about it, Wexler said that Redding's maddening failure to close the deal on a top 40 hit was something he was "always concerned" with. "I think it tended to sadden him, chasten him a great deal, the fact that he couldn't get the kind of hit that James Brown and Wilson Pickett were getting."[12]

For Wexler, one tell was at Monterey when Otis prefaced "Respect" with his throwaway line about "a girl" who took his song. While most sensed no great umbrage, Wexler believed there was hurt in his voice, that Otis was "troubled" that Franklin all but owned the song now. And although this became another means of motivation for him—a "goad," as Wexler put it, to "make him work harder"— Redding was never overly secure about his writing, or a new song. Often, he would play a demo of a song for Wexler and warily ask, "What do you think?"[13]

Now, at the ranch with strict instructions to rest his voice, Redding cast his mind on that new direction, one not fully formed in his mind or throat. But he had thought about it enough to know that his entire body of work, his entire persona, was built foursquare on his honesty, being who he was. He would not be able to sing, even obliquely, of drugs. However, he *could* write of "day in the life" recitations. In fact, he already had, with the song about sitting on the dock and dreaming of being left alone, which he was on the ranch, though rather than feeling mellow, wasting time did nothing but make him prowl like a caged lion, unable to sing, driving Zelma nuts. She once said, "That was the most time we ever spent together. And I wasn't used to him being around every day. . . . He sat around and moped and worried about whether his voice was going to be all right." When he started ordering her to do menial things like getting him Kool-Aid, she says she thought, in jest, "Oh God, when are you going to get well and leave?"[14]

Bravado aside, Redding seemed less self-assured, even scared to—as Aretha Franklin sang in "(You Make Me Feel Like) A Natural Woman," her new chart-topper—"face another day." Years later, his brother Rodgers would speak of him as being "confused" for much of his life, even as he rose hard as a star, a conclusion underlined by his periodic lapses of judgment or ego-driven confrontation such as the bizarre shootout, the blowout with Jim Stewart in London, and, if true, the frightfully out of character, mean-spirited episodes related by Loretta Williams. Alan Walden, not going quite as far, but not sugarcoating his friend, speaks of Redding as "naive" and never fully formed as an artist or adult.[15] Certainly, his behavior sometimes reflected a conflict with his traditional, church-based notions of love and marital fidelity that he never completely resolved. As naive as he was, he needed every bit of the direction and management given him by Phil Walden.

Walden, though, was of little help in the area of song development, and the first time Otis felt his pipes were strong enough for him to record, on September 29, he made a quick trip to Memphis to cut just one track, another chestnut cover, "The Huckle-Buck"—a dance fad recorded by Kay Starr in 1955. The song's origin, however, was a 1949 R&B tune released under the Savoy label and performed by its co-writer, Paul Williams, who, by the time Otis covered it, was James Brown and Lloyd Price's musical director and did session work for Atlantic. Otis took it back to its blues roots with another hoarse, horn-festooned improvisation, using almost no original lyrics as he threw in shout-outs to the Mar-Keys and vowed "We're gonna do it!" in Detroit, D.C., Chicago, and other soul centers. It was naturally catchy, but also a barometer that he wasn't ready to get back to serious recording yet. What's more, he seemed constantly irritable and became convinced that the rights holder of the song he wrote with Jerry Butler, Richard Shelton of Chicago's Curtom Publishing Company, founded by Curtis Mayfield in 1963, had not been square with him. On November 7, he wrote on Redwal stationery, with his image in the right-hand corner.

> Dear Mr. Shelton:
> Please submit an itemized statement for the royalty earnings
> on "I've Been Loving You Too Long."
> Thanking you, I remain,
> Sincerely, Otis Redding

Shelton replied, stiffly:

> The only money accruing to your account was paid to you
> recently with an itemization on the check stub. If you care to
> audit our books they will be made available to you on reason-
> able notice.[16]

•

AS OUT of focus as he was, he was adamant that Walden set up bookings for the late fall and into 1968. He also had decided to go where no black entertainer had gone, to Vietnam. When he did a publicity photo shoot with Vice President Hubert Humphrey in D.C., in November, Humphrey made a request that he visit Vietnam with the USO. He agreed, committing to what the *Amsterdam News* and others had been so adamant that black performers do. The following month, his vocal cords were fully healed, and he had broken through the mental block and written some two dozen new songs. Bundling them all up, he packed and headed for Memphis, booking session time at Stax for December 9. In the meantime, keeping the Redding fire burning, Stax had issued a best-of compilation album, *History of Otis Redding*, a nifty, trenchant sampler—and the only "greatest hits" package released during his life—that included "Respect," "Try a Little Tenderness," "Mr. Pitiful," "I've Been Loving You Too Long," "Fa-Fa-Fa-Fa-Fa," "These Arms of Mine," "Shake," "Security," "My Lover's Prayer," "Satisfaction," and "I Can't Turn You Loose." Released in November, it had a very odd cover illustration of him, eyes closed, grimacing, seeming as if he was weeping.

The winter season was now closing in, and fortunately, Stax had Redding product on hand. He had months before cut his first Christmas records, one the old 1947 seasonal standard "Merry Christmas Baby," as well as a duet with Carla Thomas, "New Year's Resolution," written by Stax staffer Deannie Parker. Nearly every big-name singer had a Christmas album, including Jackie Wilson and Sam Cooke, with Stax releasing its first entry, Thomas's "Gee Whiz It's Christmas," in 1963. The concept was nothing new for Stax, however, which held an annual Christmas concert in Memphis, but only now did it get Otis on vinyl, a fortuitous decision to be sure. The following year, Atlantic would release the *Soul Christmas* album, which would also carry Otis's cover of "White Christmas" and "Merry Christmas Baby," along with amazing Southern soul–dipped gems like Clarence Carter's "Backdoor Santa," Solomon Burke's "Presents for Christmas," and King Curtis's "What Are You Doing New Year's Eve," with a guitar solo by Duane Allman.

With building momentum in the studio, the business of Otis Redding was rolling again. As Alan Walden looked back, "We had conquered the black market and Otis was voted the number one soul singer in the world—*Billboard* had a vote where he came in second only to James Brown. We'd had the tours of Europe, Monterey, the Fillmore. His records were now all over the pop and R&B stations and charts. Otis was breaking big on TV as well."

Feeling good enough to tour again, even if only a mini-tour, with dates in Nashville, Cleveland, and Madison, Wisconsin, the second week of December 1967 had been booked as a tune-up for a resuming of the kind of schedule he was used to. Further exciting him to no end was the fact that he would be riding in his beloved Beechcraft H18 on the tour. Walden had also signed him to play a Christmas concert at the Fillmore, with Bill Graham agreeing to shell out fourteen thousand dollars, an astounding amount at the time for only one concert. On top of this, Al Bell had booked him to play in a February concert Bell was promoting in Little Rock.

The Bar-Kays had just finished recording their first album when Otis summoned them for the mini-tour, which would begin immediately after Otis's first earnest recording session in months.

•

ON TUESDAY, December 6, he burst back into Studio B for what would be an unbelievable series of marathon sessions. He eased into it by cutting an obligatory follow-up to "Fa-Fa-Fa-Fa-Fa (Sad Song)" called "The Happy Song (Dum-Dum)," using the same beat and call and response horn lines, flipping the mood from mirthful sadness to morose gladness, and the fa-fa's to "dum dum baby de dum dum." So many songs were recorded during this trip to Memphis that some of the sessions are undated in the Atlantic logs, and cuts like "You Left the Water Running," "Open the Door," "Wholesale Love," and "I Got to Go Back (and Watch That Little Girl Dance)" given Stax catalog numbers but seemingly left dangling in space.

He came in with a sheaf of songs, either complete or in nuggets, with all manner of ideas floating around in his head. Much of this was the result of his endless playing of Beatles songs that had him hearing some strange things. Encountering journalist Stanley Booth in the studio, he told him, "Last night I played *Revolver*, and on 'Yellow Submarine,' you know what one of 'em says? I think it's

Ringo, he says, 'Paul is a queer.' He really does, man. 'Paul-is-a-queer,' bigger'n shit."[17]

HE SURELY was ahead of his time—two years later masses of people would swear a close listening of Beatles songs revealed that Paul wasn't queer but *dead*. In either case, Otis came in with several Beatles-style songs, which with the rest would eventually help fill three posthumous Redding albums. One of them carried Zelma's name as a co-writer, which came about when she composed a poem during his time on the European tour, when her loneliness was eased by the fact that she had "dreams to remember," which sounded like a projection of a time when she wouldn't have him at all. When he came home and she read the poem to him as a potential song, he joshed that she had no business writing songs—which she later said was endemic of his provincial ethic that "he wanted me to be the housewife and the mother"[18]—but, without her knowledge, he expanded it into a tale about seeing her being held by another man and walking away in tears, instilling a heavy gospel feel using a choir of female backup singers, a first for a Redding record.

Al Bell also claimed another credit on arguably the best song of the batch, "Hard to Handle," which certainly did stray onto new ground. As he recalls, "It was the same as with 'Sweet Lorene' and 'Ooh Carla, Ooh Otis.' No one was around in the studio but Allen Jones and I came in and we started bandying around lyrics. Otis said he wanted to send up guys who are real cool—*baaadass* cool—and lines just flew out, like 'Here I am, I'm the man on the scene.' He got rollin', really havin' a ball." The song, in fact, was Otis unshrugged, completely unapologetic about including some backwater parlance such as "drugstore lovin'" and an intonation of "yes I am" that came out "yessiram."

The Beatle-flavored songs, meanwhile, "You Made a Man Out of Me" and "Nobody's Fault But Mine," were driven not by horns but by Steve Cropper's slight-fingered guitar riffs, which allowed Otis to sing in a mid-range and keep his wailing to a minimum, such as on "Thousand Miles Away," which once would have had him braying at the moon. This was a necessary adjustment now, as his thin voice on most of these tracks is at least a thousand miles away from what it was on, say, "Respect." Almost none of the arrangements were played either loud or fast, and none of his vocals concluded with the usual "got-ta got-ta, got-ta" frenzy. "Think About It" sounded like a semi-spoken demo vocal.

Other tracks included unvarnished throwback soul ballads such as "A Waste of Time"—with one of the most sinewy guitar/bass lines ever heard—"Champagne and Wine," and "A Fool for You," and some tricked-out up-tempo soul like "Demonstration" and "Direct Me," featuring classic melodic Cropper chords. There were also two covers: a splendid, minimalist, bouncy redo of the Impressions' socially conscious soul anthem "Amen," which Otis had darn near copied on "Come to Me"; and a jazzy take on Clyde McPhatter's "A Lover's Question"; and what *sounded* like a cover of James Brown, "Out of Sight," closely tracking "Papa's Got a Brand New Bag." Rounding it out was the funky, almost bossa nova beat of "Johnny's Heartbreak."

Otis had to be satisfied that he could get through as many songs as he had and still have a voice, but, if he was honest with himself, he would have known his days tearing up a song and leaving audiences damp were likely over. If he was to continue prospering, it would *have* to be with a different genus of song, one relying on restraint and quiet emotion. Perhaps this epiphany hit him the next morning, Wednesday December 7, when he headed to the airport. Something nagged at him—the song that he couldn't put out of his mind, but also couldn't seem to finish. He had left the tentatively named "Dock of the Bay" out of the sessions, but now he had to record it. At the airport, he told the driver to wait, and got out and called Cropper.

"Crop," he said, "I got a hit."[19]

18

"So I Guess I'll Remain the Same"

Back at East McLemore Street on December 7, 1967, most of the session players had dispersed for the day. After Cropper told Jim Stewart that Otis was headed over to cut another song he was sure was "a hit," Stewart rang up most of the usual core of sidemen. To his everlasting regret, Floyd Newman wasn't called. "That was the only Otis session that I didn't play on. Jim didn't book me for it, and I'll never forgive him for that. Nobody knew it would be Otis's last session, of course. But I should have been there."[1]

There is a disagreement in the Redding literature about the date of the session; some have it as happening on December 6 or 7, or both, and Rob Bowman in *Soulsville U.S.A.* somehow places it on November 22.[2] But the ultimate source, the massive archive of Atlantic session logs, confirms the December 7 date, and that the working quorum for the session was Cropper, Duck Dunn, Booker T. Washington, Al Jackson, Wayne Jackson, and Joe Arnold, all of whom were perplexed about the song Otis came in with. It was simple, spare, just a couple of lines, and, unlike most of his other works, had no horn line. Indeed, it was in no way near complete. As Cropper would recall, "When Otis walked in, he said, 'Crop, get your guttar.' I always kept a Gibson B-29 around. . . . Otis played and sang a verse he had written." That, of course, was the woebegone yarn of him lounging in the morning sun, and not moving from that spot until the evening came, the hours consumed watching the ships in the bay come and go.[3]

Cropper, as always, induced him to think of similar thoughts, in this case ones he'd had on that dock, where he landed after roaming two thousand miles from home, which became another line, as did the not wanting to do what ten people advised him to do. The backing track was done totally off-the-cuff, shrouded in melancholy tones and tempo that matched the mood of what Otis was singing, and Cropper suggested a bridge sung at a higher key and slightly faster pace, taken from the Association's "Windy"—an R&B/pop group Cropper thought was a gold mine of riffs and hooks. Booker T. called the song "beautifully simplistic—all major chords. Otis's lyrics touched me—about leaving home and watching the bay, trying to figure things out as everyone's pulling at you. My notes on the piano fed into that. I wanted to capture a maritime feel—the sound of a boat on the Mississippi River, and the sounds of gospel and New Orleans. I put those flourishes around Otis's voice."[4] Dave Porter also made a key contribution. When Otis thought there should be a better first verse than the one that had him bathed in the morning sun, Porter thought otherwise, and the immortal opening stayed where it should have.[5]

Wayne Jackson called the song "simple and funky—like a call and response in church." There was also something no one had done, with the possible exception of Guy Mitchell on his fifties hit "Singing the Blues"—whistling as a riff. That's how Otis ran out this song, with a surprisingly mellow warble fused with Cropper's guitar and Dunn's bass. "Otis always liked to ad-lib at the end of songs," said Cropper, "so I added in about ten measures of instrumental background for him to do so. But when the time came, Otis couldn't think of anything and started whistling."[6] The consensus has always been that he did this only as a placeholder, to be replaced later either by horns or some kind of lyrical stream. As Cropper once told it, the song itself was an example of a Redding who was now "much more conscious of the importance of lyrics," and that "we had worked out this little fadeout rap he was gonna do, an ad-lib thing. He forgot what it was so he started whistling."[7] But Al Bell insisted it was no accident. "Without a question, Otis had it in his head before recording. The whistle was intentional."

Indeed, he would do it on each of the three takes of the song that day, which makes the Cropper story hard to believe. And, in retrospect, it was a perfect instinct, exactly what a daydreamer would do while wasting time. So perfect that it too was melancholic, not carefree. Nothing else about the session was remarkable or eventful. As always, the rehearsal started out as chaos, then scattershot chords gradually fell into a cohesive arrangement, at which time the tape was turned on and Al Jackson banged his sticks together and gave the "one-two-a-one-two-three" downbeat. However, on the first two takes—which can be heard on the 1992 *Remember Me* album of Redding outtakes and alternate versions—his voice is scabrous and the whistling part so terrible that engineer Ron Capone said through the intercom, "Well, he won't make it as a whistler." He got it right on take three, but it was still an anomaly, a whole different side of Redding, the general tone a bit too dark and against the grain for most, including Bell.

"I happened to hear the song being completed and I stopped in my tracks because I didn't know if it was Otis in there. It sure didn't *sound* like him. The song definitely had the folk thing, but as far as being a potential hit song, with Otis a record would always come out screaming, like the song says, 'please release me!' This one, we didn't really know what it was."[8]

What it was, as it happened, was a sonata of loneliness and regret, two elements previously not alloyed in a Redding oeuvre, in which even the self-denoted "sad songs" had the cool breeze or hot lick of uplift and optimism that everything was going to be all right. One could construe "Dock of the Bay" as a breeze of liberation, of striking out on one's own according to deep convictions of belief. But any way one can look at the lyrics, there is foreboding and resignation. The loneliness that "won't leave [him] alone" merges on the same long, long road to nowhere, all the way to a splintery dock on a bay, where the realization blowing on the wind is that it "looks like nothing's gonna change" and "everything remains the same." In other words, even if he knows he can't do what ten people are telling him to do, what *is* he to do? In his voice, it sounded like the hardest dilemma a man could have.

Bell put it this way: "The brother was hurting. And when we hear it, we hurt."

At Stax, however, the early soundings were not encouraging. Bell wondered about its practicality. When he had broached with Otis combining folk with soul, he didn't intend for the soul element to disappear, as Duck Dunn believed it had. "It had no R&B whatsoever,"[9] was his initial reaction. Certainly, anything Redding sang was by nature soulful. But this was the first song he'd ever written expressly for the studio and not the stage, perhaps a sign that when he looked at his future, live performing would take a back seat to production—again, a Beatles precedent. But how in the world would he sing the song in front of a hyped-up audience, with no run-out, no tied-in-knots, "got-ta got-ta" convulsions, just . . . whistling?

Stewart, Dunn said, "thought it was too far over the border," and Duck himself admitted, "It didn't impress me. I thought it might even be detrimental." Cropper begged to differ. He had become not only the song's co-writer but its biggest defender. Obsessively, he kept the musicians' overtime, making up more horn parts, dubbing different parts, playing tape over and over at ear-splitting levels.

Still, Otis didn't know if it was quite right. Capone kept saying notes were clashing. Booker T., for his part, *was* sure it was right.

"That's a mother," he said.[10]

●

OTIS HUNG around in Memphis until the next morning. He was hoping he could work on the song more, or at the very least decide what the heck he would do to run out the song in place of the whistling. As for the opinion that he needed to "soul" it up, there was the possibility that background singers, maybe the Staple Singers, who had been signed to Stax to do gospel harmonies, could step in. Nothing was resolved, however, and he headed out again for the airport, saying he'd be back on Friday morning—crowing that he would be arriving in his private plane—to pick up the Bar-Kays and go to Nashville.

Cropper didn't wait. Otis, also by instinct, had on the first take thrown in some seagull-like *caw* noises, which some took as a joke. But Cropper didn't. "I went over to a local jingle company there, Pepper-Tanner, and got into their sound library and come up with some sea gulls and some waves and I made the tape loop of that, brought them in and out of the holes, you know. Whenever the song took a little breather, I just kind of filled it with a sea gull or a wave."[11] But he also had to stop, since he, Booker, Dunn, Al Jackson, and Dave Porter had to prepare for a Saturday gig at Indiana State University.

Even without the embellishments, Otis was sure he nailed it. "This is my first million seller, right here," he told Alan Walden when he got back on Wednesday night to the Big O Ranch, where Walden was living in a log cabin.[12] Phil Walden had left for an industry convention in Las Vegas, but the plans for the weekend Midwest swing were set. He tiptoed out the door the next morning, met his pilot Richard Fraser at the airport, and all but skipped into the plane for its maiden flight. Fraser, a twenty-six year-old former Air Force pilot, had also become a close friend, and Otis sat in the co-pilot's seat as the plane flew to Memphis.

Once there, he spent a little more time in the studio listening to the tapes of the "Dock of the Bay," and schmoozed with William Bell and Dave Porter in the latter's office over fried chicken and Cherry Kijofa wine. Then, intending to finish his hit song, he said he'd see them after the weekend gigs. He walked out the door in his impeccable shirt and slacks, exiting the theater that he'd first walked into wearing hospital scrubs. It was, of course, for the last time, but that might have been the case anyway. According to Wexler, two weeks before, Otis had called him and asked if he would produce his next record, perhaps in New York with Tom Dowd.

"He wanted to move from the Stax sound to the more polished and bigger sonorities of, let's say, Ray Charles," Wexler said in his memoirs. "I was flattered out of my mind—but worried about the political implications with Jim Stewart."

"No sweat, Jerry," he said Otis assured him, "I'll take care of that part of it."[13]

●

THERE WAS a kind of Russian roulette aspect to Redding's prized Beechcraft. The plane had eight seats in the cabin, and because there were two other members of the troupe on this journey to Nashville—Carl Simms, the Bar-Kays' vocalist who would sing harmonies, and seventeen-year-old Matthew Kelly, who was their valet—it was agreed that, among the band and Kelly, two of them would have to fly commercial on each flight, according to a rotation.

To Otis's relief, the Nashville gig, at Vanderbilt University, betrayed no trace of vocal fatigue after the intense sessions. The troupe landed in Cleveland early the next morning, and Otis and the Bar-Kays appeared on a dance party show called *Upbeat,* on which, clad in a leisure top and slacks, he performed one of his songs—"Respect"—before singing a closing-credit duet with Mitch Ryder. That night, they played two sold-out shows at Leo's Casino, a venerable soul club on Euclid Avenue, where a reviewer called him and the band "a well-oiled machine."[14] Two more shows remained, at the Factory, a club on West Gorham Street in Madison, on Sunday night.

Otis knew he was hot again. Appearances had been scheduled on *Ed Sullivan, American Bandstand, Johnny Carson, Joey Bishop,* another *Where the Action Is.* A duet album with Aretha Franklin was in the works and a sequel album with Carla Thomas. Phil Walden had been sent two movie scripts for Otis to read, the producers not wanting him to merely compose a score or sing in the movies, but to act in them. Walden put them on the desk Otis used when he came into the office, for Monday. Otis *had* to be hot. As he told people, hardly believing anyone could be worth that much, Walden had just taken out an insurance policy on him for a million dollars.[15]

Still, Otis must have wondered that weekend why, if he was all that, he needed to slog through a hard Midwest winter, which did not make an exception for his visit. The weather was atrocious and the skies looked anything but friendly that entire weekend in Cleveland. When he looked skyward, all he could see was dense fog and thick gray clouds. It was cold and raining in sheets and the forecast called for more of the same. On Sunday afternoon, Richard Fraser arrived at Hopkins Airport and was told by controllers that all commercial flights had been grounded and strongly recommended that he not fly. As well, when Fraser inventoried the plane with a mechanic, the battery power was low, enough for Fraser to be concerned. Otis asked him if he thought he could get the plane up and down safely. Fraser, who had logged 1,290 flight hours, 118 of them flying Beechcraft planes, said he could. "Then let's go," Otis said. He simply refused to believe his pride and joy, despite some mechanical problems on previous flights, was not invincible. Only weeks before, he had posed for a now-iconic PR photo striding in front of the plane, guitar in hand, looking as proud as a man could.

Yet, when James Brown had heard that Otis was learning to fly the same kind of plane Brown had gotten rid of, he warned him he was gambling with his life. "On the last morning we talked," Brown recalled, "I said, 'That plane is not big enough to be doing what you're doing. It can't carry all those people and all that equipment. You shouldn't be messing around with it like that.'"

"Aw, it's all right Bossman," he said Otis told him. "We've had a few problems, but it's doing okay."

Years later Brown wrote in his memoirs, "Somebody was fooling Otis. They tried to do the same thing with his twin-engine that I did with a Lear jet, and they couldn't do it. That plane was an old plane, with a bad battery and a lot of service problems, and it had no business flying in that kind of weather."[16]

What's more, after the Nashville gig, as Bar-Kays sax man Ben Cauley would later recall, "One of the guys said the cabin was cold and asked a hangar employee to start the electrical heating system to warm it up. But the employee said no, the battery was low and we'd better wait until the pilot revved up the plane."[17] Both Otis and Fraser were confident the battery was sufficient enough to fly. A credit card receipt from early that afternoon from a Sohio fueling station at the airport shows that 146 gallons of gasoline and oil were pumped into the tank, at a cost of $62.65, signed for by Fraser on Otis's credit card.[18] And, recalls Alan Walden: "Otis always took pride in not missing an engagement. He was advised not to fly to Madison but he didn't want to disappoint his fans and took off anyway, leaving with the words, 'Gotta make that dollar.'"[19]

As it happened, not far away, the Mar-Keys were already victims of the Midwest winter as they tried getting to Indiana State. "We flew on a puddle jumper to Indianapolis to catch our connecting flight," Cropper said. "The whole north was icy, and we arrived in

Indianapolis late, missing our connection."[20] At Hopkins Field, each member of the Redding troupe boarded. As for James Alexander and Carl Simms, who were the odd men out, as much of a hassle as it was to catch a separate flight to Madison, they would soon know this was the luckiest day of their lives.

19

Amen

Early on the morning of December 10, 1967, three years to the day after Sam Cooke died, Otis Redding called home. Zelma told him he sounded depressed. He said he was just tired. He wanted to speak to the kids, but only Otis III was awake and he said a few words to the boy. He then said goodbye to Zelma, jauntily telling her to be "real sweet and real good," but not an obligatory "I love you," words that did not trickle from his lips easily.[1]

The Redding Revue filed onto the H18 at 12:30 P.M. and the little plane, with OTIS REDDING ENT. painted in scripted letters on the top and the registration number N390R on its underside, lifted off into the turgid air. When the plane reached cruising altitude, Otis got up and moved to the cockpit, sitting in the co-pilot's seat. But did he actually *fly* the plane at any point in such ominous weather? He was not licensed yet, only permitted to fly with a pilot, with no passengers, and it would seem preposterous that he was actually doing anything at those controls. Yet this was a question that would cause a great deal of speculation, and agitation, because of what happened next.

At 3:25, after nearly three hours in the air, the plane, flying northwest, was around ten miles south of Truax Field, when Fraser radioed Dane County Regional Airport and received clearance to land. The plane then began to descend through the heavy clouds on its landing path, which took it over Lake Monona, the middle of three lakes nearly surrounding Madison, between Lake Waubesa and Lake Mendota. To get to the airport, the plane would have to clear the lake and make it four more miles over land. Hearing nothing more from Fraser, the tower kept trying to communicate with him, but his radio had died en route, part of a fatal power failure in the plane. On the radar screen, the plane was a blip four miles from the runway. Then the blip disappeared.

•

NO ONE will ever know exactly what went wrong that day, only that something made the engine suddenly sputter and quit. Apparently Fraser, unable to see anything through the low fog, was attempting an instrument landing, that is, if any of the instruments were even working. Simply, he was flying blind. An eyewitness on the shore of the lake would say he saw the plane, its left wing lower than the right before it banked sharply and hit the lake. The plane did not break up, however; instead, rested atop the freezing water for several minutes, bobbing up and down, before beginning to sink about a half mile from land.

Controllers had alerted rescue crews, and additional crews were sent to the scene by emergency phone calls from area residents. The first responders were there within minutes, though the choppy, frigid waters made it difficult to maneuver to the wreckage. By the time they reached the area, the plane was underwater but, miraculously, one person was out of the plane and in the lake, clutching a seat cushion for dear life. This was Ben Cauley, the trumpet player, who had been asleep until the crash jolted him awake and threw him from the cabin and into the frigid water, still strapped into his seat, which was also a flotation device. Not knowing how to swim, he gripped the cushion tightly in his hands and bobbed in the water. He was close to losing consciousness when a police launch came into the area and cops saw him, not far from where the dead bodies of two other men were floating, later identified as Richard Fraser and Jimmie King.

Cauley, his limbs numb from frostbite, was pulled onto the boat. He was taken to a hospital and treated for exposure but was remarkably free of injury and able to tell the rescuers, and the press, that he had heard the screams of the two men near him before their cries went silent and they drowned. He had no idea what had happened to the others. After a while a cop came over and told him he was a lucky man. He asked why. "Because everybody else is dead," the cop bluntly said.[2]

That was the only conclusion the rescue teams could have reached. The plane had sunk to the bottom of the forty-foot lake at a 45-degree angle, its nose buried deep into the silt, its fuselage twisted and torn open, its left wing and engine missing. Other than the two bodies discovered with Cauley, there were no signs of the remaining passengers and pilot. Divers were in the water for hours, with great difficulty in treacherous conditions. But while it would be days before the plane could be lifted to the surface, missing its left engine and propeller, it was obvious no one could have survived. Cauley, meanwhile, would offer the only explanation of the crash there would ever be: "I was sitting behind Otis on the plane—back to back, next to the door. I fell asleep and the next thing I knew the pilot was telling us he was having trouble."

Cauley would paint a picture of chaos and confusion in the plane. "I couldn't breathe. The engines sounded real loud and I had a funny spinning sensation of falling through space. I thought the plane had hit an air pocket." Redding, he said, stayed calm. "I didn't hear him say a word. Didn't see him do a thing." The next thing he knew, the plane hit the water and "I managed to get out and hold on to a seat cushion. I didn't know how to swim and one of my shoes had come off. It was so cold. About twenty minutes later a boat came and pulled me out. I was in shock. Everyone else was gone."[3] At other times he spoke of awakening just before the plane hit and seeing Phalon Jones looking out a window and saying, "Oh, no!" and, in the water, Cunningham and King calling for help before going under.

This was basically the scenario that began to spread in evening editions of newspapers and radio and TV bulletins all across the country, even with all but two victims not identified or extricated from the plane. Redding, in these early reports, was presumed dead in the crash, and all through the night authorities worked to confirm his identity. When the crash was reported, Al Bell was in Las Vegas with Jim Stewart, attending the same industry convention as Phil Walden. Both Bell and Stewart found out about the crash when they were paged in the hotel ballroom and heard the news from people back at Stax.

"We were in a state of shock," Bell remembered. "I couldn't even move. We made immediate plans to go back to Memphis. We didn't know what to do, who to talk to. We were just walking around in a daze, hoping against hope that it was a mistake, that Otis would be found alive somewhere."[4]

That was Zelma's hope, too. At around 5 P.M., she got a call from the Madison coroner who recounted the string of events and told her that one of the bodies recovered was that of a black man who was "tall and dark and has on a black undershirt," apparently describing the still-unidentified King. Trying to stay calm and fighting back a wave of fear, she barked at him, "That's not Otis!" For one thing, she said, he didn't wear underwear. He was also an expert swimmer. He was out there, alive, they just hadn't found him yet. "Go find him!" she ordered. She then dialed Richard Fraser's wife, Diane, who, because her husband was identified, had already been notified by the coroner's office.

Picking up the phone and hearing Zelma on the other end, she cried, "Dick is gone. Otis, too."[5]

•

RESIGNED TO the truth, Zelma broke the worst of all possible news to Otis Sr. and Fannie Mae. For the proud, forceful preacher who had prayed to the Lord every day nearly all his life, an initial stoicism dissolved into something most people around him never saw—a man of mere flesh and blood, breaking down and sobbing uncontrollably in the strong arms of his wife. As would soon be evident, the deacon surely died a little himself that day, and as he was unable to pull himself together, it fell to Fannie Mae, the normally quiet matron of the family, to hold the family together. It was she who took the burden off Zelma by telling the children that their father was now in the hands of God, and tried to ease the pain by taking care of them as Zelma and Otis Sr. prepared to travel to Wisconsin to claim the body.

One by one, people in the extended Redding family began to learn that Otis Redding was indeed dead. Alex Hodges, in the Walden office back in Macon, answered a call from someone in the Madison police department, matter-of-factly asking for verification of the city Otis was supposed to be in, before being given a brief explanation of the crash. Dave Porter, still in Indianapolis with the Mar-Keys, called his wife. "When he came back," Steve Cropper recalled, "he looked like a ghost. His wife had told him that Otis had died in a plane crash. We couldn't believe it." Jerry Wexler was, as it happened, at Kennedy Airport picking up a delivery of master tapes sent by Stax, including Redding's song about sitting on the dock of

a bay, when someone told him Otis had been killed. Ahmet Ertegun, when he found out, came home and "sat down on the sofa and
cried."[6]

Floyd Newman heard about it on the radio, as did many of the
Bar-Kays' families.

"One of their mothers," Newman says, "lived right down the
block from me. She heard it and ran out into the street, crying hys-
terically."[7] Dennis Wheeler, hearing the same bulletins, hoped he'd
heard wrong. "I called the station and said, 'What did you just put on
the radio?' They hadn't found Otis's body yet and I was saying over
and over, 'Otis, I know you're alive. They'll find you.' But when it hit
home, I just broke down and cried. I felt like I'd lost my brother."[8]
Wayne Jackson said, "Andrew Love called and told me. It hit me like
a punch in the stomach, still does today."[9]

Only a few miles away from where the plane was under the lake,
at the Factory, people had lined up for hours to see Otis's show that
night. When they got inside, Rick Nielsen, one of the members of
the band that was going to open for him, the prophetically named
Grim Reapers (later to become famous as Cheap Trick), told the
stunned audience of the tragedy and played a dirge of Redding
songs as people wept. Today, the few original posters from that
show fetch around seven thousand dollars.[10] In Miami, Wayne
Cochran closed his nightclub and told everyone to go home and
pray for Redding's soul.

Early Monday morning, crews were back in the lake when the sun
came up, and were able to remove Otis's body from the plane. He was
still strapped into his seat, wearing a dark suit and collarless shirt,
his ankles primly crossed as if in repose, looking almost serene, not
a tear or wrinkle on his clothes. As the body came out of the water,
photographers, not kept away by cops, snapped pictures. The other
victims entombed in the plane were also recovered, and like Otis,
taken to the morgue. The night before, Cauley had told investiga-
tors that two other members of the band had taken a commercial

flight to Milwaukee, and cops went to the airport there and found Alexander and Simms. As Alexander recalled, "They scooped us up and drove us to Madison. And I identified the bodies."[11]

Although it would be reported that Otis's face appeared to be unscathed, those photos would clearly show cuts and blood on his forehead. A columnist for the Madison *Capital Times*, Doug Moe, saw one of the rescue cops' report reading, "There was a head wound on Redding, right between his eyes, plus several other cuts around his face and neck. The right leg was also broken."[12] But no autopsy would be performed, and it would never be officially determined if the head wound, likely the result of his body pitching forward and throwing his head into the instrument panel, had killed him or if he had drowned. Nor did it really matter. Either way, it was an untimely and unacceptable way for a man, any man, to die.

ON MONDAY, a glazed-eyed Zelma flew with a grim-looking Otis Redding Sr. and Twiggs Lyndon, to bring Otis home to Macon. Zelma and Phil Walden also began making arrangements for the funeral at Macon's City Auditorium and burial at the Big O Ranch, on December 18. Relatives of the Bar-Kays also came to take the remains of their lost sons home to bury in Memphis, though it would take until Tuesday for all the bodies to be salvaged.

That same Monday, much of the nation awakened to news of the tragedy, with more complete information. In Memphis, a headline read MEMPHIS IN TEARS! In Macon, REDDING FEARED DEAD IN CRASH. In Madison, SINGER OTIS REDDING, BAND DIED IN LAKE MONONA CRASH. The *New York Times*, perhaps less impressed with his identity, went with SINGER IS FEARED DEAD IN AIR CRASH.

By Tuesday, photos of the plane, grotesquely upside down on a raft and dripping water, appeared in papers across the country. The tributes streamed in from all around the world. The Beatles issued a statement mourning his "tragic death." The nascent *Rolling Stone*, the birth of which occurred just as Redding died, had to print its first of a very long list of rock and roll eulogies to come; in it, the magazine's young publisher/editor Jann Wenner averred that Redding's material "was not only suited to himself but to the entire medium. His voice was rough, but it carried with it a style and a grace and an originality that was rare in the field of rhythm and blues, rock and roll, rock and soul or whatever it's called. Otis was a man of music. The Memphis sound was going to take over soul in 1968. Everyone knew it, and Otis was the front man at Stax. In 1968, he was going to become 'the King of them all, y'all.'" The last line went, "Otis was the Crown Prince of Soul, and now the Crown Prince is dead."[13]

For one of the few times in history, the impossibly tragic and horribly unfair death of Otis Redding meant that hyperbole wasn't only excusable; it was absolutely *necessary*.

•

THE STAX family mourned his death particularly hard. Otis Redding wasn't their prince, he was their sun king, their prized possession, their model of black enterprise and consummate professionalism. Literally minutes after the funerals of the Bar-Kays in Memphis almost everyone on the roster—from Jim Stewart and Estelle Axton, down to the secretaries and janitors—made the sad trip to Macon. Zelma and Phil Walden pieced together all the details of a service that would be fitting enough, in a place big enough to accommodate visitors from all over the world. That turned out to be none other than Macon's City Auditorium, where Otis had played his annual homecoming concerts and where the riot had broken out after his show in 1966. No funeral had been held in the building since that for a city politician in 1947. The logistics of staging such an event on short notice were difficult, and many whites in the city still didn't know who Redding was. But Mayor Ronnie Thompson repaid Otis's personal friendship by cutting through the red tape and quickly getting permits for the family, and invitations were sent out to hundreds of Otis's friends and associates who requested seats.

At around 6:00 A.M. on the morning of December 18, a copper casket bearing Otis's body was taken from Hutchins Funeral Home to the arena, where the casket—kept closed, unlike Sam Cooke's glass-covered coffin at his funeral three years before—was draped with flowers and a long single line of mourners came through and filed past, the first a stooped woman with a cane named Mary Durham. By noon, every seat of the 4,500 in the hall was taken, and thousands more people who could not get in lined the streets outside. As with most final rites of the famous, the somber mood conflicted with the hysteria of gawkers who came mainly to check out the stars in attendance and called out to them. They were not disappointed either, as one star after another emerged from long limos, including James Brown, Jackie Wilson, Aretha Franklin, Stevie Wonder, Sam and Dave, Wilson Pickett, Joe Tex, Johnnie Taylor, Carla and Rufus Thomas, Percy Sledge, William Bell, Solomon Burke, Clarence Carter, as well as the lesser known Stax musicians—although, in the crush, Floyd Newman couldn't get in, which still angers him.

Hamp Swain was there, too, as were Bobby Smith and Dennis Wheeler, who, remembering Otis's wish for when he'd be sent to his grave, says, "I didn't party—but I did raise a glass to him that day." Joe Galkin was in attendance. Ronnie Thompson and Leroy Johnson as well, with the mayor reading a proclamation calling Otis "the Ambassador of Goodwill." One person who stayed away was Johnny Jenkins, who—no matter his feeling about being used as a stepstool for Otis—was so crushed by Otis's death that he couldn't bear to see the box holding his body. Another person not there wasn't quite so broken up. Loretta Williams said later, "I didn't feel no sorrow or pain for his death, at that time, because I had been hurt by him and felt he died owing me."[14] Eerily, on the day of the funeral, Eddie Floyd was in England and his plane had engine trouble and aborted its takeoff, careening down the runway before safely coming to a stop.[15]

Presiding at the funeral was Rev. C. J. Andrews, who had married Otis and Zelma, and prayers were offered by him and two other ministers. As the hourlong service in the dense arena wore on, gasps of crying filled the hall, the emotion swelling during gospel blues renditions sung by Joe Tex, Johnnie Taylor, and Joe Simon, with Taylor having to stop and gather himself before continuing on "I'll Be Standing By." During Simon's "Jesus, Keep Me Near the Cross," Zelma, who had maintained a stoic grace, suddenly began wailing loudly and stamped her shoes against the floor, until two among a group of white-clad nurses stationed in the crowd in case of emergency, hurried over and calmed her.[16]

Booker T., constantly dabbing at his eyes, played the organ for the ceremony, with "Come Ye Disconsolate" as the processional and Otis's "These Arms of Mine" as the recessional. Several of Otis's close allies rose to deliver a few words, with Alan Walden saying, "Before Otis I had never loved a man outside of my immediate family and relatives. He was the first." Arthur Conley recalled that he was so shook up that when he arrived, he began displacing people in the front row. "I didn't give a shit who was there, I was going straight to the coffin. I stood there and gave him all my feelings."[17] He tried to speak but broke down. Jerry Wexler gave the eulogy, in a voice choked with grief, saying, "Otis was a natural prince" who "communicated love and tremendous faith in human possibilities, a promise that great and happy events were coming." He credited him with staying on his own turf rather than following fame to where the rich play, a signal for other black performers to stay in the South. Wexler concluded, "Otis sang, 'Respect when I come home.' And Otis has come home."[18]

The pallbearers were C. L. Walden, Swain, Arthur Conley, Speedo Sims, Sylvester Huckaby, and the trio of soul men, Tex, Taylor, and Simon. When they carried the casket down the church steps and into a hearse for the ride to the Big O Ranch, Zelma, in a dark suit and veil, again seemed to snap, screaming in anguish as she was led to the hearse, the children taken separately by nurses. A frail Fannie Mae Redding, no longer able to be strong, also had to be helped as she exited, while Rev. Redding—his own heart to give out within a few months—wore the same grim, pain-contorted face he had when he claimed his son's remains.

Things had been mostly dignified and respectful until James Brown emerged from the auditorium, sparking a near riot as mostly teenagers began to mob him, forcing security and his bodyguards to surround him and clear the path to his limo. Then began a long, slow procession of headlight-shining limos to Round Oak, where Zelma said Otis had wanted to be buried. There, the casket was entombed in a white marble mausoleum only a few feet from the driveway, the crypt visible to Zelma whenever she passed the windows of the kitchen, forever home. Conley was still nearly catatonic; years later, his career never again on track, he said of that grim day, "It's like a blank, but I felt that I was being suffocated watching them lower the coffin into the ground." Of the loss of his mentor, he lamented, "I missed Otis terribly. When he died I was still the frightened little boy who had to survive in a tough business world. I didn't have the guts to speak up for myself and did as I was told."[19]

Steve Cropper, like Conley, was unable to say anything at the funeral and burial lest he fall apart. He later told *Hit Parader* what he intended to say, that "in spite of the hard-driving quality of many of [Otis's] songs it was the fundamental gentleness that he shared with Sam Cooke that distinguished him from most urban soul singers. My original feeling for Otis wound up to be my final feeling, he was a pure man. His love for people showed in his songs. He was always trying to get back to his baby—or he missed her, she was the greatest thing in the world. His approach was always *positive*."[20]

NOT SO positive was the license taken by some in the media—mainly the black media—when it came to those photos of Redding taken at the crash site. While mainstream newspapers mostly refrained from printing them, two black-oriented publications did not. On December 14, the weekly *Milwaukee Courier* ran one of the lifeless Redding being pulled from the water, strapped into his seat, the coroner standing above him. The same shot made the *Philadelphia Tribune* two days later, and, with another showing a crumpled Redding, the right side of his face lumpen and hooks being attached to him from a crane, in the December 28 *Jet* along with two more photos of Bar-Kays members in body bags. The photos, taken by photographer Denny Connors, were a ghastly sight that upset Zelma terribly and would subject the publications to enormous criticism from their readers.

The *Jet* article, built around an interview with Ben Cauley, who still had no feeling in his hands, contained some fresh information, including a tip-off that Redding had recorded a song Cauley called "Sitting On the Dock."[21] But the disturbing photos were part of a general cheapening of Redding's death for the sake of sensationalism. Because he was so curiously in the co-pilot seat, even though the small Beechcraft had no cockpit and the pilots' seats were immediately in front of the passengers, this itself became the angle of some of the coverage—again, mainly in the black press. The *Tribune* page-one story was headlined REDDING DIED IN CO-PILOT'S SEAT and subtitled "Otis Helpless When Plane Hit Water; His Body Didn't Have Single Scratch," which was grossly incorrect. A snap judgment reached by some was that Otis had been flying the plane, a conclusion that gained traction when writer Robert Sam Anson stated it as fact in *Esquire*.[22] Even now, the Temptations' Otis Williams recalls Redding's death this way: "I saw the pictures of him sitting in the pilot's seat like he was trying to fly the plane. And I said, 'Come on, Otis. Why'd you do that?'"[23]

There were, to be sure, some juicy tidbits that would dribble out. The most tantalizing had to do with a certain attaché case. A police report by officer Ralin Phillips indicated that Redding when found was wearing a Bulova watch and carrying a black leather billfold with $302 in cash, as well as what "appeared" to be a package of marijuana. But when Zelma was apprised of this, she asked about whether something else had been recovered—the "large amounts of cash" that Otis would have been carrying, as he normally did on the road, in an attaché case. As it happened, another police report by a sergeant named Ted Mell said of the rescue team, "They located no other survivors; however, they did pick up a small dark gray attaché case." Yet it, and whatever stash of money Otis may have had in it, had apparently vanished. After several years, so did Mell's memory of it. Asked by writer Doug Moe about it in 1983, he answered, "To be frank with you, I don't even remember any attaché case." Another officer who had been in the rescue party, William Diebold, added acidly, "You want something for the record on that attaché case? You won't get it."

Indeed, the investigation was so shoddy that it was unable to verify *any* small details, which through the years became fodder for probing reporters. In 1981, an article popped up in, of all things, an obscure paper called the *Madison Music Guide* which said cocaine and opium were discovered at the scene, as well as marijuana in the plane, something no one had ever confirmed.[24] There were of course recriminations about the plane being fit for flight—Johnny Jenkins would claim he had seen the Beechcraft during one of Otis's layovers in Macon, and when Otis again asked him to come out on the road with him, Jenkins said, "I'm not going up in that"[25]—and about Phil Walden for buying it. The National Transportation Safety Board (NTSB) meanwhile, having completed its first celebrity aviation accident,[26] didn't quiet the rumors or quell the imaginations of conspiracy theorists when it issued the report of its investigation—or rather, merely a one-page summary with basic information of the plane and perhaps the most unsatisfying conclusions to any such report in history:

TYPE OF ACCIDENT—UNDETERMINED
PROBABLE CAUSE(S)— MISCELLANEOUS —UNDETER-
MINED FACTOR(S)[27]

The unabridged report, if in fact there was one ever delivered, was never made public, and likely does not exist anymore, given that the NTSB purges its files every twenty-five years. Neither were the missing propeller and engine ever located. However, it's clear Fraser was far too confident in his battery and had an insufficient backup generator, which proved to be a fatal mistake. The spare synopsis, assessing no cause or blame, is the only record for the crash, and, since the plane was recovered almost intact, the only possible explanations for it is that there was no flight data recorder on board—such equipment not being required in private planes—or that the agency simply took the easiest route. If so, the entire investigation into the matter of Otis Redding's death was a mortal insult to the man.

EPILOGUE

"Wouldn't That Have Been Somethin'?"

If he be not fellow with the best king, thou shalt find the
best king of good fellows.

—William Shakespeare, *Henry V*, Act 5, Scene 2

Otis Redding's death, an event that was cruel by any ratio-
nale, touched a great many, including those who had never
met him. WE MISS OTIS REDDING, read the sign outside the Forest
Park Church of Christ, situated just south of Atlanta, days after the
funeral in Macon. Such a sign at a conservative Christian church,
one which forbade musical instruments in its worship services and
had a largely white middle-class congregation, was most peculiar,
unless one knows that the blood of Southern soul runs through the
veins of the region's residents.[1] Otis Redding played a large role in
injecting it there, and his death was mourned even by those who
knew him least; in the March 1968 issue of *16*, the editor of the
teen-girl magazine, Gloria Stavers, reserved a page for a simple,

black-bordered box that read: IN MEMORIAM, OTIS REDDING, DEC. 10, 1967, NEVER TO BE FORGOTTEN.

At Stax/Volt Records, however, and in the offices of its Northern overlords, mourning had to share space with cold business, and Jim Stewart was tasked with figuring out what to do with the catalog of Otis's unreleased songs. He couldn't begin with something upbeat like "Hard to Handle," in his view the best Redding song he had, nor even "Dreams to Remember," which would have been an appropriate epitaph. As a result, "Dock of the Bay" became the default choice, even though it ran into hurdles. Because Stax was only a pro forma label and more of a supplier of product to Atlantic, according to their agreement, Atlantic had to approve its release. Jerry Wexler, after hearing the tape, hated the song, not for a lack of soul as much as what he heard as technical flaws, such as Otis's vocal being overwhelmed by the instruments, a complaint he had about most Stax records. He was refusing to put it out unless changes were made. The tape and notes came back to Cropper, who said he simply could not bear to work on the song with Otis gone. He swears he changed exactly nothing and sent the tape in.[2] If so, he must have had a good laugh when reading about Wexler in future years taking bows for having "stood up" for his demand, although in his later memoirs Wexler acknowledged he didn't know at the time that Cropper had submitted the same tape.[3]

For Cropper, the sad irony was that "Otis never heard the waves, he never heard the sea gulls, and he didn't hear the guitar fills that I did."[4]

When Zelma had first heard the finished song, she felt something unfamiliar, something discomfiting, as if an alarm was sounding. As she would say years later, "It seems as though the song was letting you know, 'I won't be here a long, long time.'"[5]

Indeed, the absolute gut-center of the song was something that could only be heard in a voice, not a twist of a knob—a man's vulnerability, which came in doses large and small. Al Bell, who was unconvinced about "Dock" when he heard it in the studio, soon was able to give full credit to Wexler as the deciding vote to release the song. "He was right, and we were all wrong."[6]

Stax put "(Sittin' On) The Dock of the Bay" on the market December 28, 1967, whereupon it clambered upward. When it reached number 1—pop and R&B—the week of March 11, 1968, the song finally gave Otis the gold record status that had been so elusive in life. Zelma, who had not been off the ranch since he was buried, traveled to Memphis to receive a symbolic record commemorating the song's gold status. Few picked any quibbles with the song, though Nik Cohn issued a left-handed compliment, saying it was "his least fake work in ages."[7] It was a fitting, fatalistic coda for Redding that the last song he ever recorded, and one that nobody outside of the studio would ever get to hear him sing live, was the one that would wind up on the most turntables—enough for the song to be rated as the sixth most played song of the twentieth century, over six million times on the radio,[8] and loads more since. It also won him his only Grammy (in 1968 for Best Rhythm & Blues Performance, and another for writing, with Cropper, for Best Rhythm & Blues Song). Even so, the fact that he had died submerged was a final irony, and a sadder song than it would have normally been, a plea for simple reclamation that drowned with him, leaving an eternal image of a weary man finding comfort in watching the ships roll in and away again as a final interlude of peace before dying.

In fact, the premonitory aspect sensed by Zelma was what touched many who were perhaps only fleetingly aware of Redding. For Bell, it actualized his suggestions of a folk-style soul idiom in ways he could never have imagined. Decades later, *Rolling Stone* would be dissecting the song as "a folk melody of indelible, simple force," noting that Otis's "lyrics have all the immediacy of conversation, but he sings the line with an undertone of yearning that makes the record unmistakable soul music, and the final triumph of his deep, swift career."[9] But it wasn't just the alienation of the lyrics, it was the entire mood set by its sad chords. Indeed, in 1968 King Curtis covered the song in tribute as a minimalist, jazz-oriented instrumental on his *Sweet Soul* album, and it was almost as sobering, in retrospect something of a preface to his own demise, in 1971, when he was murdered by drug dealers on the steps of his apartment building, another nail in the coffin of soul.[10] This sort of undressed emotion can be felt if one listens to the two imperfect, wound-scraping Redding outtakes of "Dock of the Bay" on the *Remember Me* album.

Although Otis never would get to Vietnam, his song did and in a way he would have appreciated. Decades later, it would be noted that the loneliness of men caught on killing fields in other people's war games perfectly dovetailed with the lyrics and mood of that song, and that some veterans still choke up hearing it. The enduring popularity of the tune among Vietnam vets was, it would be written nearly a half-century after its release, its power "to transport, to connect, and to heal . . . What saved those soldiers in Vietnam, and continues to save them today, are songs like '(Sittin' On) The Dock of the Bay.'"[11] Bitterly ironic is that whenever Wexler would hear the song in later years, *his* visceral reaction was anything but sentimental. While recognizing it as "spiritually nourishing" to project Redding "seated in some heavenly rapture on some big dock-of-the-bay in the sky," and that music fans were "taken with the mystical coincidence of the song and Otis's death," he wrote, it "did nothing to ease the pain of his passing. There has never been the slightest solace in it. Even now, when I hear [it], I feel a rush of resentment and anger."[12]

•

WHEN IT was released a month before his death, *History of Otis Redding* caught the same bracing wind and became his highest-charting album yet, going to number 9 pop and number 1 soul, and number 2 in England—its éclat being that, according to a belated review in

Variety, "It will serve as a memorial album."[13] Atlantic also hurried back onto the market *Otis Blue* until it could cobble together a series of posthumous Redding albums, and it hit number 6 on the pop chart. In February, the posthumous *The Dock of the Bay* album was ready, filled out by tracks as old as 1965, and it sailed to number 4 pop and number 1 soul, and number 1 in England. Then, only four months later, *The Immortal Otis Redding*, stocked with the tracks from the December 1966 session, hit the market, apparently a bit too soon, as it stalled at number 58 pop and 3 soul, though four singles from it—"The Happy Song (Dum Dum)," "I've Got Dreams to Remember," "Amen," and "Hard to Handle"—got moderate rides up the charts. Ensuing albums did less well, as they were stocked with, in some cases, years-old tracks of historic but little other value.

There would be an even sadder aftermath to his death, as well. On April 29, 1968, just as "Dock of the Bay" was falling on the charts and a new spring and summer of rock was boiling up, Rev. Otis Ray Redding Sr., who had become pastor of Lundy's Chapel Baptist Church, felt pain stabbing his chest as he lay in bed in the cabin Otis had built for him and Fannie Mae at the Big O Ranch. He had been heartsick and almost catatonic most days since the crash, spending his time on the front porch staring into the woods, lost in his own private thoughts, and not feeling kindly disposed to the God he had preached for all these years but who still took his son. Helpless when his heart began to give out, he was taken to a hospital but died on the way, at age fifty-six. He was buried next to Otis in the family mausoleum, knowing, as his son had, that father and son had made peace, and the son had indeed made the old deacon proud, after all.

But Otis Ray Redding Jr., who had conquered the music landscape at Monterey, was virtually forgotten only a year after his death, his songs and sound quickly becoming dated. While singles would be periodically, and decreasingly, released from the vaults through 1971, none seemed to be a must-hear. He still had a legion of fans and students, of his music and Southern soul, who would grab up anything that was released, but there was less of an urgency about it—the rock world moved fast, waiting for no one and was always regenerating and recasting. Otis Redding, important as he'd always be, quickly became past tense. And as if on cue, as soon as the Redding era ended, things quickly began to happen that beclouded the future of Stax.

•

JUST FOUR months after Otis Redding died, on April 4, 1968, a single shot fired by a drifter named James Earl Ray killed Dr. Martin Luther King as he stepped onto the balcony of his room at the Lorraine Motel, the place where so many of Stax's soul classics were written. King was in Memphis to support striking sanitation workers, a festering boil of the town's animus toward mostly black union workers. That night, as several American cities burned, Memphis seemed too stunned to do anything but mourn. At Stax, the black musicians shielded Steve Cropper and Duck Dunn as they left the building. Jim Stewart and Estelle Axton, fearing the building might be set on fire, bundled up the master tapes from the studio and locked them in their car trunks. Isaac Hayes, who was living at the Lorraine, couldn't write for a year after.

In 1969, Memphis had its own offshoot of the Black Panthers, the Black Invaders, and one of its enlistees was the Mad Lads' lead singer John Gary Williams, who that year would be convicted and imprisoned with three others for planning to ambush a white cop in retribution for the arrest of another Invader. Weeks later, a battalion of fifty policemen stormed the Invaders' headquarters and shut it down.[14] Yet Al Bell, who dealt with the Panthers' "little thugs," in his words for the younger Invaders, by extending them his hand, "with a hundred dollar bill in it" recalls, "We stayed calm, and while Atlantic was moving away from soul, we were about to give it a whole new life." Indeed, even with tension in the air, the first order of business for the company was to rebuild the catalog after Redding's death. But since all of the other Stax/Volt acts had been fading fast, not having him around made it seem all the more impossible.

●

WHAT REDDING would have done and where his evolution would have taken him and soul music is pure conjecture, but the same cannot be said of the change he wrought in the industry at Monterey, when soul was shown to be so powerful and far-reaching that it indeed was the sound of mainstream music. Not only was Joplin on this byway now, but Jim Morrison by decade's end was singing not with organ piping but horns and harmonicas blaring on "Touch Me," and Robbie Krieger's B.B King–style R&B guitar licks on "Roadside Blues."

This transition cut both ways: The Chambers Brothers may have foretold what Redding would have gravitated to when the veteran gospel soul group switched sonic gears and started going to hard funk when they covered "I Can't Turn You Loose" in 1968, which rode to number 37 on the pop chart and eased their route into funk rock with the stunning primordial "psychedelicized" classic "Time Has Come Today," which they plucked off an album they had released a month before Redding's death. This was the formula that broke out Jimi Hendrix. Redding may not have been a rock and roller but "Dock" proved he knew that soul in the I-wanna-testify, torch-song Stax fold had withered. And while lush, romantic soul would have another rising in the mid-seventies disco fad, which unleashed the infectious "Philly Sound" perfected by the producing team of Kenny Gamble and Leon Huff, a more serious form of introspective soul was the highly personal, socially relevant works of Stevie Wonder and Marvin Gaye. That idiom would have offered Redding much room to work within. In any case, he would not likely have stayed in the middle of the road for long before getting antsy, and the borders would have been broader. As Floyd Newman said, "He woulda been there. He was built for the long run because he did it all, singing, writing, producing, owning a label. He would have adapted, probably better than Hendrix would have had he lived. But both of them woulda been there. And wouldn't that have been somethin'?"[15]

Cal Poly's James Cushing views Redding in the light of something even more allegorical, his premature death falling from the sky as "a re-kindling of the great myth of Greek god Dionysus, who is the young man who dies young. Or Orpheus. The dying youth is one of the great classic and romantic figures."[16] In rock and roll, that field is crowded, but circumstances make some deaths more painful and more chimerical, at once. Those circumstances had, in retrospect, been surrounding Otis Redding all his life.

•

JIM STEWART, who had been so trusting when he signed papers shoved in front of his nose by Atlantic Records, found himself looted in 1968. Stax had been slowly losing money for years, its share of profits from the partnership with Atlantic too little to keep pace with expenses—something the Jerry Wexler and the Erteguns made no easier by kicking in a total, according to Stewart, of five thousand dollars, not a dime more. "If it wasn't indentured servitude," Al Bell muses, "then I don't know what else to call it." Then, with the shock of Redding's death still reverberating, Wexler casually informed Stewart that Atlantic had been sold to Warner Brothers–Seven Arts for $17.5 million. That figure was a lowball offer that "Omelet" Ertegun was dead set against but was outvoted by Nesuhi Ertegun and Wexler; Ahmet blew it, big time—the deal would be called "one of the worst financial decisions in the history of the record business."[17]

This lamentable decision was motivated by both Atlantic losing Ray Charles and rumors that the venerable company would be fingered in a curiously underreported payola scandal the FCC had been investigating "mainly regarding the black acts," which might damage the label's future standing, though no details about how this alleged scandal worked, or who was involved, were provided.[18] Ertegun also believed that Motown had "superseded" the Atlantic— and Stax—sound.

Coincidentally, Atlantic had heard the call of rock and pop, making tons from the blue-eyed soul group the Young Rascals. Ahmet Ertegun, livid that Atlantic's English distributor, Decca, had refused him American distribution rights to the Beatles' early records, made a new licensing deal with another Brit giant, Poly-dor Records, which allowed Atlantic to distribute in the States the power trio Cream, who began recording with Tom Dowd. That led to similar work with Led Zeppelin, Yes, the Byrds, and Buffalo Spring-field. Soon would come the Rolling Stones.

By the terms of its distribution deal with Atlantic, Stax now had the right to renegotiate. However, Stewart, believing he had lever-age in Stax's argosy of soul, was stunned when he was informed that the priceless Stax/Volt song catalog was now Warner's property, since the agreement that Stewart never really read gave Atlantic sole authority to sell it to any new buyer. This was an insidious but perfectly legal backstabbing. Had Stewart read the clause and run it past any dime-store lawyer, he would have seen that his lifeblood had been legally drained from him. Nothing he could do now by way of a lawsuit could wash away the ink that, in effect, gave away the store to the Atlantic slickers from New York.

The deal confirmed every long-held suspicion about the corpo-rate thieves who ran music since the Tin Pan Alley days and, to men like Stewart, that the brotherhood was more than one of thieves but Lucifer incarnate. Still, while Stewart would forever live with that unforced error, he had been wise and wary enough to have added the renegotiation/termination clause. Negotiations proceeded, but all Warner would give him was the same distribution deal and wouldn't budge on the catalog. In practical terms, that meant Stax would gain not a cent from the deal. Indeed, when Al Bell went over the books, he discovered that the Stax royalty rate had been paid not at 15 percent but at 12 percent, a difference that in itself amounted to millions in the long run. Moreover, he could find in the books direct cash outlays from Atlantic to Stax that totaled all of five thousand dollars, which seemed like what the Erteguns might have spent on a sumptuous dinner at Smith and Wollensky Steak House.

In May, Stewart and Axton exercised the excruciating but principled option to walk away from their legacy, which they were now prohibited from claiming as their own or profiting from. Even Wexler, who turned out to be not a key man as much as a backstabber, had no compunction saying that the terms that made this heist possible were "unfair" to Stewart, but that he didn't grasp the import of the deal, that the lawyers and not he or the Erteguns were the bad guys. Once Wexler did grasp it, he had even wanted to "give them back their catalog, but I couldn't because the lawyers had put it over." But he wasn't contrite enough to keep from adding a final insult to Stewart by taking back Sam and Dave, nor to fully admitting to Peter Guralnick, with pride that "the name of the game was whatever the traffic would bear."[19]

"Oh, Wexler knew exactly what he was doing," said Al Bell. "Again, I know all the dirty laundry, what he was doing. Atlantic wanted to take over Stax, run it out of New York. But then after Otis was gone and we weren't as relevant, they wanted to be rid of us. They wanted Jim to sever from them. Their offer was a poison pill. That's what that was all about."

Choosing some most unfortunate words, Cropper added, "When we turned them down, they just looked at us with their big Jewish eyes and said, 'Okay, we'll take Sam and Dave back.' It was real high school. Then they went ahead and killed their career."[20]

Stax would never again see a dime from the brick, mortar, and blood of its own history; only in concerts could their performers profit from singing their own songs. For the release of any Stax/Volt song recorded before the alliance was severed, and on any repackaged album or single, the label would read Atlantic Records or Atco, and, starting in the nineties, the Stax label would be the domain of the specialty nostalgia company Rhino Records.

Stax was out from under Atlantic's thumb, at the price of losing that precious music catalog, but a week later it was back under another thumb. In what was the new industry model, with entertainment conglomerates devouring the smaller independent labels, Stewart had little choice but to sell the company to Paramount Pictures, which itself was also owned by a corporate overlord, Gulf and Western.

Even so, with the Atlantic distribution network gone, with Redding gone, with the ennui that set in after Martin Luther King was killed, with Memphis as a whole deeply wounded and stigmatized, Stax/Volt was now in free fall itself, a loss leader in a game of corporate pickup sticks. Without its priceless catalog, its future was vague at best. Had Redding lived, one can imagine a totally different result. The Erteguns and Wexler, still needing him to remain viable, surely would have sweetened the deal for Stewart. Even if Otis came aboard at Atlantic in 1970, Stax would have been working on a better percentage, and it's not likely Redding would have been happy about it if Atlantic wanted to screw his fellow Southern soul men. Thus, for various reasons and considerations, the seeming denouement of Stax looked like less the natural course of events than something like cause and effect; that for all purposes, the heart of Southern soul ceased beating on December 10, 1967.

•

WITH REDDING's soul-crushing demise, Phil Walden had lost not just his friend but his anchor and his lever. As Alan Walden proudly boasts, "Next to Motown we were the largest management company in the world. The first sixteen gold records came very fast for us and continued to grow to over fifty."[21] Then, all that was gone, left on a frozen lake in Wisconsin. Though Phil Walden maintained his personal management roster of soul acts, most of whom quickly faded out, he renewed himself by taking a sharp detour into another new branch of regional music—rock music. This was a smart detour. While Otis might have had a place at Woodstock, given how he lit up Monterey, only two black acts performed on Max Yasgur's farm, Richie Havens and Sly and the Family Stone, before half-a-million post-hippie wayfarers in August 1969—*not* including the by-then even more white-oriented Jimi Hendrix, who was now the unquestioned, and ephemeral, "king" of a generation that would prematurely lose nearly all of its musical high priests and priestesses.

The seventies were beckoning as yet another new era in pop music, but one that remained in flux, seeking the same clues and answers that Otis had been looking for. The counterculture of the '60s was fading and Walden saw an opening. He used his spanking new studio to make records for a new label, Capricorn Records, which spawned another branch of soul, *white* and Southern. His first act, the Allman Brothers Band, owed a large debt to the '60s soul men—their song "Soulshine," for example, was a note-for-note copy of James Carr's "A Man Needs a Woman." Soon the legendary Southern studios that had unfurled the best African-American music ever created were perfecting soulful redneck blues, many bands managed either by Phil or Alan Walden. Alan seemed cursed though, seeing three of rock's most compelling shooting stars—all of whom were at one time or another under his watch—die: Redding, Duane Allman, and Lynyrd Skynyrd, whose lead singer Ronnie Van Zant also went down in a doomed airplane, killing him and three others.

Within a few years, the Waldens were no longer players in the industry, with Phil unable to continue Capricorn Records after being sued for millions in unpaid royalties by the Allman Brothers. Walden's old partner, the Shaw booking agency, sued him, too, as did his wife, for divorce. Going the same route as had Jim Stewart, Walden sold off his label, leaving himself no leverage in a new era. The elder Walden brother went into a personal tailspin of cocaine addiction, which he came out of in the 1990s with a short-lived revival of Capricorn. Then he quickly lost it again, before passing away in 2006 of cancer, at age sixty-six. Five years later, in another sad postscript, his forty-eight-year-old son, Philip Jr., was killed in a traffic accident.[22]

Johnny Jenkins, even as he fell from the public eye and had his struggles with alcohol, retained a loyal following and some noted admirers, including guitarist Jimi Hendrix, who had relatives in the Macon area, where he remained. The two performed together occasionally in the late 1960s at the Scene, a trendy New York club. Phil Walden, who was still booking for him, would paint Jenkins as a funk-acid-rock forefather. "They both played the same way: [with the guitar] upside down. Johnny was playing the guitar behind his head and with his teeth back in 1958," an affectation that Hendrix of course became famous for.[23] Jenkins cut a well-received album, in 1970, *Ton-Ton Macoute!*, which featured slide guitarist extraordinaire (and Walden client) Duane Allman. He released two more albums in the early 2000s, recorded at Muscle Shoals, but hated that he was mainly known as the guy who was passed over by Stax for Redding; he even swore that Steve Cropper had stolen his guitar style. He died in 2006, all but unknown and a testament to what might have been, at age sixty-seven.

Meanwhile, in Macon, Bobby Smith, the man who had unwittingly lost Redding when he sent him to Stax in a station wagon, grew progressively more steamed about being left holding the bag, and seven hundred dollars, while Walden and Stewart made millions. Smith never made more than tipping money from the Redding link. And though he never blamed Redding, Smith loathed Walden, bridling whenever he read Walden taking credit for Redding's rise. Shortly before he died in 2012, Smith said of Walden, "I am a little disturbed at how people don't tell the truth."[24] The only Redding holding he had was "Shout Bamalama," which he put out again with King after Redding's death.

Sadly, the entire nexus of Southern soul and its symbiotic marriage of convenience and profit with Northern overlords had already begun to unravel right after Otis's death and soon would end with an avaricious Atlantic selling its soul, literally, to Warner. In the shakeout, which saw Atlantic transition to rock and roll, reeling in the Rolling Stones' American distribution rights, the vital center of soul seemed to shift overnight, recast in the harder, socially aware groves of the new Motown, and the smoother, more elegant "Sound of Philadelphia." Atlantic would have no place in this new soul galaxy, nor care to. But they did own all the Redding masters from Stax/Volt and wasted little time getting posthumous Redding product out on the market, most of which, wrote Robert Christgau in his review of one of the albums, was "obviously scraping bottom on Otis . . . nothing to prove he was the greatest soul singer who ever lived," even if "almost every track offers some special moment. . . . And even when he's got-ta got-ta got-ta do his shtick he's one of a kind."[25]

●

AT THE reinvented Stax Records, all functional decisions were being made by Al Bell, who in the deal with Paramount was elevated to executive vice-president. Still, Bell was in an impossible situation. The company was again broke and, he said, "Otis was dead, Sam and Dave were taken away from us, there was no catalog, Booker T. had left to go live in California. People were saying Stax was dead, and we *were*." Looking for anything that might work, he had Steve Cropper rummage through the vault. From what he found, Bell, as a last gasp, released an old Booker T. and the MG's tune called "Soul Limbo," which became a hit. Going back into what had been an abandoned studio, Cropper produced an even bigger hit for the

MG's, "Time Is Tight," cribbing the Motown bass line Otis had appropriated on "I Can't Turn You Loose," and, this time, allowing Cropper his writing credit for the copycat song.

But the company roster was dwindling. Stax induced Hayes and Porter to stay by finally breaking the prohibition on individual production credits. Rufus Thomas's 1967 "Sophisticated Sissy," for example, read: "Produced by David Porter and Isaac Hayes," who also co-wrote the song, one much-sampled in future years. Cropper was also receiving production credits. However, after years of being regarded as "Jim's pet" by fellow musicians, Cropper was about to take a fall. He had for years also been the company's director of A&R, or top decision-maker on what to record, and the publicity he—a white man—got became a problem. During the Revue's stay in London, Bell had called Cropper to his hotel room and, according to witnesses, tore into him for having a "big head." Cropper, by one account, left Bell's room "looking like a whipped dog."[26]

While Bell insists the flap was "a personal thing, man to man," Cropper would later recall that "I was given [an order] in no uncertain terms: change your ways or else," and that "there were some bad feelings that I never, ever got over."[27] The two maintained an uneasy peace thereafter, and even co-wrote the MG's song "Hip Hug-Her." But when Bell was permitted by Stewart to hire an industry guy named Don Davis to oversee the direction of the music, Cropper again felt slighted, punished for what others took as self-promotion. "They seemed to take it like I was in it for myself [even though] I was the only one that's been fighting for the team, that's trying to keep the team together . . . all of a sudden I wasn't A&R director anymore. My stick was taken away and given to Al Bell." Bell denied he did any such thing. "I hired Don as head of creative. I never took anything away from Steve." Still, there was a new reality at the company. "I had to make changes, come up with a different sound, because there was no Stax Sound anymore, it died with Otis. But I did everything I could to keep our family together. I had given raises to what I called the 'big six'—Booker T. and the MG's and the Memphis Horns—to $250 a week. I gave the producers access to a pool I set aside from Atlantic's royalty payments, to keep working. I felt I owed it to them. But I never had any authority to fire Steve from anything. Jim Stewart made those decisions. Jim took the A&R job from Steve to shield him from all the criticism. I don't know why Steve blamed me, that hurt."

Cropper, feeling marginalized, joined a mass exodus of Stax session men, which in 1969 included Duck Dunn, Andrew Love, and Wayne Jackson—"It just didn't feel the same," he later recalled. Dunn, Jones, and Al Jackson eased into Al Green's house band at the crosstown Hi Records, and Jackson and Love copyrighted the Memphis Horns name for themselves for acquiring session work and live gigs. Bell's rise also foreshadowed the end for Jim Stewart. After Stewart had severed ties with Atlantic, his life revolved not around music but endless negotiations with outside lenders to keep the company afloat, a necessity given Warner/Gulf and Western's near total apathy about Stax. Bell, meanwhile, completely altered the Stax profile, junking the old Memphis horn sound for less formulaic songs by a new crop of acts such as the Staples singers, the Soul Children, Mel and Tim, and the Dramatics. He wore out a lot of shoe leather putting together a network of small distributors, and kept giving Stax a harder racial edge, progressively eclipsing Stewart. He hired a communications consultant from SCLC and Jess Jackson's Operation Breadbasket to help with the company's marketing strategies, the better for Stax to identify with black people, an amazing requirement for the label of black "purity."[28]

•

IN RE-ESTABLISHING Stax, Bell had in 1968 set a goal of releasing twenty-eight albums and thirty singles, a ratio radically different from the one used by Stewart. "People thought I was crazy," Bell remembered, but Johnnie Taylor scored a huge hit with "Who's Making Love." Songs were also released with socially conscious lyrics, some in Swahili. Stax produced commercials for Afro-Sheen, the pomade that buffed up the in-vogue Afro hairdos. Stewart also sunk a good deal of Stax money, and his own, into Jackson's Operation PUSH campaign, such contributions now not regarded as extortion but, in a more political era, a matter of survival.

Estelle Axton, the grand matriarch of Southern soul, had already left Stax in 1970, by mutual agreement with her brother, who gave her a sweet buyout, with which she began her own label, Fretone Records, whose biggest crime—er, hit—was "Disco Duck." Jim Stewart then got the same itch to move on, usually after seeing whoever Bell's latest hire was. One, the redoubtable Johnny Baylor, a big, burly man who had been Sugar Ray Robinson's sparring partner before becoming a record promoter and talent manager, and who was generally considered to be a seriously fearful guy, came aboard in 1970. For Bell, hiring him had a side benefit—distributing Baylor's small label, Koko Records, and bringing under the Stax roof Koko's top client, plaintive soul singer Luther Ingram; in 1972, Ingram would reap a bonanza, his recording of "(If Loving You Is Wrong) I Don't Want to Be Right," written by Stax staff writers Homer Banks, Carl Hampton, and Raymond Jackson, hit number 1 on the soul chart, number 3 on the pop, and sold four million copies. Two years later, Baylor produced a cover of the song by Millie Jackson on Koko, which earned two Grammy nominations.

Bell and Stewart did combine to swing a deal to repurchase Stax from Gulf and Western. But Stewart's heart was not in it anymore. "The day Otis Redding died," he told Rob Bowman, "that took a lot out of me. I was never the same person. The company was never the same to me after that. Something was taken out and was never replaced. The man was a walking inspiration. He had that effect on everyone around him."[29] With the cash, Bell instead bought out a willing Stewart, though Jim would for five years still be listed as part owner. Bell, now alone in the driver's seat, then embarked on an ambitious attempt to produce what he called a "soul explosion," his intention underlined by the original Stax finger-snapping logo being changed—the fingers were now brown. Baylor took charge of protection and of relations with radio stations and stores, a duty he often discharged through threats, with a gun in his hand—"Actually," smiles Bell, "he never pulled his gun, he would unbutton his jacket, let it fly open, and there it would be, in his belt"—something he continued doing at the office, unnerving Stax employees.

Bell believed in black economic power, and delivered. From the ashes of the Atlantic double-cross, Stax by the early '70s had become one of the most successful black-run businesses in the nation. Its new star was someone whose image would have been anathema in the '60s—Isaac Hayes, who stormed from the shadows in the early 1970s as a pop/funk icon, composing albums such as *Hot Buttered Soul* and *Black Moses* that sold millions. Hayes also wrote, performed, and produced the soundtrack for *Shaft*, the title track of which was an enormous hit—with Willie Hall, who had been in the post-1967 reconstruction of the Bar-Kays, repeating the cymbal ruffle from "Try a Little Tenderness." This now-much-parodied song at the time defined a new model of seventies soul men who were "super fly," whether they were "private dicks" who were "sex machines to all the chicks" or respectable pimps and drug dealers who were good men done wrong by a white world.

In 1972, Stax produced the Wattstax concert in the L.A. Coliseum, marking the seventh anniversary of the Watts riots. Headlined by Hayes, and including a set by the Bar-Kays, in which Ben Cauley and James Alexander still played, the event was billed as the "black Woodstock." At one point Jesse Jackson came onto the stage and he and Bell stood side by side, fists clenched in a black power salute. A successful Stax movie of the concert portrayed it as the seventies' version of Monterey, with soul as the dominant music form in America. Hayes became the first black musician to win an

Oscar for best original song. By mid-decade, Stax was the fifth-largest black-owned corporation in America, after Motown.[30] Bell was so grateful he gave Hayes a gift—a peacock-blue Cadillac with gold trim and fur lining. Hayes rode his fame a long way, with an in-your-face attitude about race that included wearing slave chains on his usually bare chest, described in one press story as "emancipatory bling."[31]

However, as if such impudent racial pride had somehow gone too far in an era still light-years from the defiant hip-hop/rap climate of the late 1980s, after Stax made a distribution deal in 1973 with CBS Records, presaging a new golden era of soul, Memphis soul took another kick to the groin. The deal was brokered by Clive Davis, CBS's president, who wanted to get into the soul derby after having made the label the world's biggest by signing the likes of Janis Joplin, the Grateful Dead, Bruce Springsteen, Pink Floyd, Aerosmith, and Billy Joel. However, the puckish Davis was fired only days later for allegedly bilking the company out of $94,000 in personal expenses.[32] Davis would land on his feet, making Arista Records even bigger than CBS Records. But Stax was again down for the count, with CBS seemingly wanting to loot the company, as had Atlantic.

In 1975, Stax suddenly found itself under investigation by the IRS, and the corporation's bank, Union Planters—with mordant irony, where Jim Stewart and Estelle Axton had once worked—filed a bankruptcy petition against the little Memphis label. Armed guards were dispatched to the old theater one day. Entering Al Bell's office, according to reports, they told him, "You got fifteen minutes to get out of the building."[33] Bell, however, says it was much worse. "They came to physically kill me," he says, with no wavering. "It was December 19, 1975, between 11:30 and 11:45 P.M. One was ex-CIA, another ex-FBI, both were black. They were from a private security firm and CBS got a judge to federalize them so that white men wouldn't be killing a black man in Memphis. I am alive today only because a black federal marshal happened to be there when they came in. That marshal saved my life."

Soon Bell was indicted for conspiring to defraud the bank. His trial was a cause célèbre, attended by Revs. Jesse Jackson and Ralph Abernathy. Bell was acquitted, but the damage was done and he had to sell the company at a loss—to the same bank that had made life miserable for him. It was a humiliating, heartbreaking demise that, for some, smacked of a racial contract killing. "In its own way," said one of the label's officials, "Stax Records was fighting the same fight as Dr. King, and Stax Records was assassinated too." Said Bell: "I didn't feel broken—I'm a fighter—but I did experience the low lows. ... I went from a man that owned a company whose masters were valued by Price Waterhouse at sixty-seven million dollars to a man that could scrape together fifteen cents from time to time."[34] As for the company he led through glory and agony, its denouement was when a bankruptcy trustee named A. J. Calhoun placed a notice in *Billboard*, reading: SALE, STAX RECORDS. Among the assets to be sold off were 1,500 master recordings, "200,000 pieces of finished record product, including singles, albums, and tapes," 16-track recording equipment, office furniture, typewriters, calculators, and "various stereo component sets."[35] Months before, a headline in a Memphis paper seemed to say it all: STAX RECORDS: THE DREAM THAT DIED. [36]

•

IN THEIR post-Stax lives, Steve Cropper, Duck Dunn, and Booker T. Jones (Al Jackson was murdered in his home in 1975) had no trouble getting gigs with high-profile artists. Nor did they have any objection to riding their own coattails as soul legends, sort of acting while playing themselves (as did Willie Hall) for John Landis's 1980 movie *The Blues Brothers*, which was designed to salute and reanimate the Stax sound. Cropper and Dunn, who had become something like a buddy act over the years, further prospered when the John Belushi–Dan Aykroyd note-for-note cover of "Soul Man" became, like the flick, a huge hit. Belushi even recycled Sam Moore's "Play it, Steve!" exhortation.

As for the eternal flame that is Otis Redding, he received his due in March 1989, elected to the third class of the Rock and Roll Hall of Fame, and though it was another in the contrived rites of a self-glorifying industry and self-important rock media, it was the least the industry could do for him. The induction speech was given, aptly, by a still-resplendent Little Richard—who crowed, accurately, "I'm still here and I'm still decent"—and in a nifty role reversal did an impeccable impression of Otis on "I Can't Turn You Loose," including the "got-ta got-ta's," "Dock of the Bay," "I've Been Loving You Too Long," and "Fa-Fa-Fa-Fa-Fa." In a wonderful and hysterical elegy, Richard anointed Otis as "the pillar of rock and roll," and added that he "should have been in the Hall of Fame before me, 'cause he's gone." He pointed out a strange but true fact: He had never met or seen Otis in Macon. The first time they met, he said, was in a New York Hotel when Richard gave him fifty dollars. "I wanted him to come into my room," he said, "but he was scared to come in there by himself. I said, 'Otis, I need to talk to you' He said, 'I'll be back.' *Whoooo!* He didn't want me to lock the door. I wasn't gonna do nothin'. I just wanted to hear him sing . . . by myself."[37]

He then introduced Zelma—calling her "Zelda"—who came out in a black dress, looking small and brittle. Fighting back tears, she said, "It's been twenty-one years now but it doesn't seem that long. We can't forget his music, it was so great." She then took her leave, quietly, barely acknowledged on a night when more attention was vested on the night's other inductees, the Rolling Stones, the Temptations, Stevie Wonder, and Phil Spector. But Redding, like them, was more than a rock legend; he was an influence deeply ingrained in soul and, by extension, the music rooted in blues and R&B. And in that light, an essentially empty confection like the Rock and Roll Hall of Fame was practically irrelevant.

•

BELYING THE image of her that night, that same tiny, bespectacled woman guarded Redding's legacy like a hawk. Widowed at the age of twenty-two with three small children to raise, Zelma Atwood Redding adopted a second daughter soon after Otis's death. Still, Zelma never remarried, and, with his remains only feet from the front door, sees no need to. "I'm still married," she has said. "I just don't see him here with me. When it seems like a long time, I just put on Otis Redding, and I just listen to him and it seems like yesterday. It's like he's talking to me. It's conversation."[38] Sentimentally, even eerily, there is the long black leather coat that is ceremonially draped over a chair in the house.

"This jacket is so special to me," Zelma once explained, without blanching. "He was killed in this jacket."

She forged ahead on her own, needing to exercise the legal or implied authority she had as Redding's widow. At first, it seemed she would have no say at all. After Redding's death, the Redding corporate entities were subsumed to Walden Artists and Promotions, which would go on receiving all publishing and writing royalties accrued from Redding's records, and though Walden quickly and properly transferred Otis's splits to Zelma, Walden still had all the decision-making powers.

Unlike older performers whose wills provided for their families—Ray Charles, for one, who was reported to be broke when he died, in reality left each of his ten children, ranging from age sixteen to fifty, one million dollars, something he revealed to them a few days before he died[39]—Otis did not leave a will, and Zelma had to fight in probate court for every nickel and for status as executor of his estate. Eventually, after years of lawsuits, and as Walden's personal travails drained him, she gained complete dominion of the estate. At the same time, she had to start a career of her own. In 1972, she opened the Redding Theatrical Agency and the Big O Record Shop in

Macon, and did some booking for Phil Walden's Paragon agency. In 1977 she tried her hand as an entrepreneur, buying a nightclub called New Directions. She managed the briefly successful soul/funk trio formed in the '80s by her two sons called the Reddings, with Dexter on vocals and Otis III on guitar, which had a couple of high-charting disco hits—including a cover of "Dock of the Bay." In the 1990s, Zelma owned a shoe store named after her daughter Karla and was a partner in two Zaxby's food franchises in Jacksonville, Florida.

An accomplished woman, she also earned a business degree from Crandall Business College and served as a director of Piedmont Community Bank Group. But her existence gradually became centered on the increasingly big business of the Redding estate and the grants made by the Otis Redding Memorial Fund. While the Universal Music Publishing Group owns the catalog Atlantic acquired in the '60s, nothing can be used without permission from Zelma.

Not that Zelma herself wasn't a bit overwhelmed by the enduring hold a man gone so long could have on the culture. She was amazed that when she would walk outside of the manor house at the Big O Ranch, gawkers would be congregated outside the gate. In the late '90s, she opened the gate so that she could host tours of the grounds, during which fans would linger at the mausoleum where his body is interred. When she would take them through the den, where Otis memorabilia and gold records hang from the walls, she said, "They act like they're walking through the White House." And, rather than graybeards, "these are kids twenty-four, twenty-five years old, who weren't even born when Otis was alive. They'll just stand there and they just cry and cry."[40]

•

ZELMA FOUND herself in a situation not unlike in *Casablanca* where everybody came to see Rick; in the matter of Otis Redding, everybody came to see Zelma. By the nineties, the ranch was a rock and culture landmark in the manner of, but far less crass, garish, opulent, and commercial than the sprawling donjon where Elvis took his last breath—"This is not Graceland," Zelma has said. "This is my home."[41] Reflecting Otis's down-home ethos, pilgrims here are anything but the kind of crazed ghouls who attempted to dig up Elvis's body when it was buried at Graceland, leading the Presley estate to relocate his remains to a secure cemetery in Memphis. Redding's stately crypt, lit by an eternal flame and a simple plaque reading, TEN THOUSAND MILES I ROAMED JUST TO MAKE THIS DOCK MY HOME. YOUR SPIRIT LIVES ON WITHIN US,[42] seems to inspire more quiet reflection than ghoulish impulses.

The problem for Zelma was that ghoulishness could take different forms, one being that certain pilgrims sought to honor Otis by enriching themselves. For her, that is a form of grave-robbing in itself. "To this day everybody has trouble with songwriters, record companies, and the like," she once said. "You've got to stay on top of your game. Back then they weren't making as much money as they do today, so you got to fight, to maintain and stay strong and believe he lost his life for this—and I'm not just going to let it go away. And that's what I'm going to do—some people say I'm a little bit crazy, but I have to get my point across."[43]

Dennis Wheeler, who could never be called a grave robber, found that out. Early in the new millennium, he had planned to release an album of the old Confederate/Orbit catalog. Having been given Redding's master tapes by Smith before he died, Wheeler wanted to include "Shout Bamalama" and "Fat Gal." Then, he says, "I found out that 'Fat Gal' somehow had been claimed by Redwal Music, and Zelma refused to let us release the song on the Confederate label again. I thought that was petty. It was Bobby who launched Otis. And even in the weeks just before the plane crash, Otis still would come by the studio and spend time with Bobby and me. We would jam or go out to clubs or the pool hall or just do some jive talkin'. And now we couldn't use a song on an album?"[44]

Zelma Redding clearly isn't crazy, though when riled she can be fierce, such as when Scott Freeman's book *Otis! The Otis Redding Story* appeared in 2001. Zelma was incensed by its supermarket tabloid-style scuttlebutt that, among other things, alleged that when Otis died, he was about to divorce Zelma and take up with Carla Thomas.[45] Phil Walden also felt tarred by the book's breezy suggestion that he was somehow involved with mobsters "in black suits"[46]—and worse, preposterously so, that Walden might have actually "sabotaged" Otis's plane to collect on that million-dollar insurance policy before Otis could sack him in a general reformation of his business affairs.[47] Rather than laughing off these nothing but absurd claims, Zelma and Walden jointly sued Freeman for $15 million,[48] settling out of court for an undisclosed sum, and because of Zelma's objections the book was banned in several venues around Macon, and in the now-extinct Georgia Music Hall of Fame.[49]

That hardly settled the matter for Zelma, who still is prone to open a paper or browse the Internet and see headlines such as, on a British tabloid site, EXCLUSIVE: SOURCE CLAIMS OTIS REDDING HAD LOVE CHILD WITH QUEEN OF MEMPHIS CARLA THOMAS.[50] But if Zelma was prepared to go to fight for his name, she was just as hard-knock with industry movers. While denying Wheeler, she did in the new millennium give permission for Concord Music Group to lease to Rhino Records—a division of Time Warner then and thus the property-holder of the vintage Stax catalog—masters of the full set of Whisky a Go Go tapes, and to European distributors to release the massive 2010 five-CD box set import *100 Hits: Legends—Otis Redding*. She has also given her assent to the remains of the Beechcraft being put on display at the Rock and Roll Hall of Fame (another piece is displayed at the Hard Rock Cafe in Las Vegas). But, not far from her down in Macon, Dennis Wheeler waits, not knowing why a man who personally knew and was tight with Otis for years stands excommunicated.

●

STAX RECORDS became a loss leader for Union Planters Bank, and in 1977 was sold to Saul Zaentz's Fantasy Records as part of the company's acquisition of jazz, soul, and country blues labels to go along with its big act, the remains of Creedence Clearwater Revival. For all intents and purposes, Stax was no more than a reissue label with no new acts. In 1981, the famous old theater on East McLemore was deeded to the Southside Church of God in Christ for ten dollars, prefacing the church razing it, which was finally done in 1989. Bell's long road back began after a decade of lying low in Little Rock, when he became head of the Motown Records Group during its restructuring and incipient sale to MCA and Boston Ventures Group. Having focused on hip-hop acts, in the '90s he formed his own label, Bellmark Records, signing the group Tag Team, whose 1993 novelty hip-hop song "Whoomp! (There It Is)" went to number 2 on the Hot 100 chart, number 1 R&B, and became a standard play at sports events. He also released Prince's "The Most Beautiful Girl in the World." In 1994 he was named Record Executive of the Year, before turning to radio and Internet ventures. But, walking through the vacant lot on trips to Memphis, he recalls, "I'd see beer bottles and paper bags and all that. And I would cry."

In 2004, Concord Records purchased the Fantasy label and in December 2006 announced the reactivation of Stax. The first acts signed to the new Stax included Isaac Hayes, two years before his death. Meanwhile, Al Bell, a member of the Memphis chamber of commerce, helped gain the city's blessing and the funds to restore Stax's old home as a museum. Yet for all his work, his prosecution still stings, and sometimes the only thing that can soothe the wound is when he's asked to talk about the good times, when Otis Redding ruled the kingdom.

●

KARMA MAY explain what befell Atlantic Records. In knifing Stax in the back while seeking more lucrative piggybacking, the Erte- guns overplayed their hand—and, as it would turn out, Stax had the last laugh, its severing from Atlantic reducing the latter's value. In its corporate expansion, Atlantic initially soared as a rock depot for Brit superbands and their American analogs. However, while Erte- gun enjoyed this new turn, Wexler never really got with what he dismissively called "white rock" and music by "rockoids."[51] He had scored another triumph bringing the smoky British songbird Dusty Springfield to record in Memphis, but in the seventies, as Aretha Franklin's crossover popularity became sporadic, he had less to do. When Warner expanded into the larger, more corporate and face- less Warner-Elektra-Atlantic, his authority was diluted; in 1975, he walked, though not far, to Warner Brothers Records, producing Bob Dylan's *Slow Train Coming* in Muscle Shoals.

Jerry Wexler had once said he and Ertegun had run Atlantic as a den of "utmost despots." But they had not been immune to bad decisions. One was their releasing in 1993 of Redding's *Whisky a Go Go* live album. Because of an oversight, they didn't know that the rights to those tapes had reverted back to Stax in 1972; now, Al Bell had *them* by the balls, and received a settlement for—of all things— *copyright infringement*. It became clear, as well, that Atlantic had lost millions by selling itself so cheaply to Warner in 1967. And after Wexler was gone, Ertegun, elevated to chairman of his label when Warner became Time Warner, had so many power struggles within the corporation jungle that he took his eye off the ball, los- ing Led Zeppelin and the Stones, and Peter Gabriel just before he had his 1987 breakthrough solo hit "Sledgehammer," a song Gabriel cut with the Memphis Horns, calling it his "chance to sing like Otis Redding."[52]

Like Otis Redding, all the Atlantic lions are gone now, their glo- ries and their names codified in the Rock and Roll Hall of Fame that Ahmet Ertegun co-founded. Nesuhi Ertegun died in 1989, Tom

Dowd in 2002, Ahmet in 2006 (after striking his head in a fall after a Rolling Stones concert at the Beacon Theater), Wexler in 2008. The sacred Stax catalog they looted from Jim Stewart has made millions in repackaged albums, but by the 1990s it too was being bandied around like a shuttlecock in more mergers and reformations. Atlantic's enormous role in the evolution of soul music was now past tense. But Stax lingered on, if only as another grand old independent label buried in deep, suffocating corporate shadows, the same fate as Motown. Still, Stax and Motown represent a continuum of the history they made. As such, like Redding they will never really die, and can be as easily claimed as a staple in both black and white culture. In 1989, Sam Moore and Percy Sledge agreed to sing at the inauguration of President George H. W. Bush, sharing the stage with Lee Atwater, the sneering, guitar-playing campaign manager who had created the borderline racist Willie Horton ad, something Moore knew little of. Soul singers could still be confounding in that way, and upset assumptions about black political opinion, witness James Brown. Though there was a certain symmetry when in 2013, Moore, Booker T. Jones, Eddie Floyd, and Steve Cropper (Duck Dunn had died the year before) performed for President Barack Obama at the White House in a tribute to Memphis soul. *That* was more like it.

•

LITTLE RICHARD, who forever soldered Macon to the soul tree, maintained icon status even as his life became a living death. By 1972 he was a cocaine addict, later lamenting that period by saying, "They should have called me Little Cocaine, I was sniffing so much of that stuff!" He also became addicted to heroin and PCP, and had atrophied to 115 pounds. Dealers were threatening to kill him for unpaid drug debts. Once more, Richard returned to the ministry, with a lingering bitterness about never achieving all that seemed to be rightfully his in the industry—partly because, unlike his famous protégés, he had played down his racial identity. "If I'd been a black attraction, like James Brown or Otis Redding," he said, "it would have been different. I think I scared them. I would have had the same stature as the Beatles."[53] Having split from Macon early, he makes his home in Lynchburg, Tennessee. When last heard from, he, like so many other soul men of his generation, was suing the rights holder of his own priceless catalog for back royalties.

The other third of the Macon soul trinity, James Brown, did reach Beatles-like levels in the soul arc. Yet it hardly helped him with his primary audience that, after endorsing Richard Nixon for president in 1968, he came to praise people like the segregationist South Carolina Senator Strom Thurmond, who he said was "like a grandfather to me" after Thurmond in 1991 helped spring Brown from one of his several stays in jail on drugs and weapons charges. In 2003, Brown was pardoned by South Carolina for past crimes, though this did not stop his habitual domestic violence, for which he was arrested four times. On Christmas Day, 2006, the Godfather of Soul died of congestive heart failure, his last words being "I'm going away tonight."[54]

●

LIFE MOVES slowly on, but after it moves one day at a time for long enough, eventually you look up and nearly half a century has gone by. Stax is a museum and the Big O Ranch is, well, a ranch. Fannie Mae Redding, who lived out her life in rustic splendor in old Confederate country, died on April 30, 1989, at seventy-two in the log cabin at the Big O, only weeks after her son entered the Rock and Roll Hall of Fame. She had lived a full life, comforted by her religion, singing in the choir every Sunday at the deacon's old Vineville Baptist Church and joined various women's leagues, as well as managing Edwells Trick Novelty Shop. But she never could quite accept the fact that the Lord had taken both the man she married and the son given his name so soon.

Otis Ray Redding Jr. of course is still a thing, a commodity. His records are gifts that keep on giving, like those of Hendrix, Morrison, Lennon, et al. Legends on the order of Redding have a carryover popularity, go through a lull, then are rediscovered when each new generation comes of age. This explains why an album like, say, 1987's *The Dock of the Bay: The Definitive Collection* went double platinum, and why 1992's *The Very Best of Otis Redding* also went double platinum, and often ranks on Amazon.com as the number one album in the Southern soul, Memphis soul, and blues categories. And why in June 1993, *Essence* published the results of a listener poll conducted by a Newark radio station that asked listeners to name their favorite R&B classics, and the only artist to have two singles in the Top Ten was Otis Redding, "Try a Little Tenderness" being number one and "These Arms of Mine" number nine.[55]

Whatever corporate entity owns his catalog, a catalog of riches, to be sure, his permanence is that almost wherever one looks in popular music, there is still someone waiting, as Peter Gabriel did, to have a chance to sing like Otis Redding, even if each passing year solidifies the universal law that no human ever will.

Nowhere is this more infallibly ingrained as fact than in Memphis, where the coolest guy in town stands under that big neon STAX sign looming over East McLemore.

"Yeah, you can still feel him around, and for a minute, you know, you get that old feeling we used to have around here," says Wayne Jackson.[56] "But I can understand what Jerry Wexler means when he talks about hearing 'Dock of the Bay.' Because when Andrew called me—God, it's so long ago now—and told me Otis was gone, I knew something had ended. Something that happened so fast and lasted only a few years and was on borrowed time, like it was only supposed to be for a little while. We all wanted it to go on forever, but that day the light went off and it ain't never gonna go back on again."

ACKNOWLEDGMENTS

For a student of music history "(Sittin' On) The Dock of the Bay" is indelibly a dreamy, two-minute transport to a far-off place and time, both within the history of the song and the man who wrote and sang its lyrics of lonely isolation in a voice cleaved from the heart. For a biographer of a legendary wraith like Otis Redding, the song is also a road map with daunting challenges. The main challenge being to find the clues and the answers to the question: Why *was* he so lonely and alienated? This mystery has never been satisfactorily resolved, if even given much thought. Redding, after all, lived and died just before solving such mysteries became a common objective in what was fancifully called the "rock and roll press." Thus, his legend was carved mainly on the raw power and deep personal emotion of his songs, allowing him to run down the road to fame with no more than a sheaf of PR releases and a few knowing pieces in the upscale newspapers that bridged the gap between black and white forms in popular music.

Of course, it was mandatory that journalists would take a shot ex post facto at piecing together who Otis Redding really was, but the fact that so little had been written about him in real time was a problem only compounded by the fact that his widow zealously guarded the vaults to her husband's inner soul, and only fleetingly cooperated with those seeking to swing the door open. Not even the town's newspaper the *Telegraph*, or the curators of the considerable music heritage of Redding's hometown of Macon, the Washington Memorial Library, were trusted to keep the Redding image spotless. As Charlotte Bare, the *Telegraph*'s librarian told me, "His family holds everything belonging to him. They have not turned over anything to any archives." Indeed, while the staff at both locations were most helpful to me in combing through decades of clippings and other material they did have, they were contrite about what they *didn't*. I am also grateful to folks at the Rock and Roll Hall of Fame, and in particular researcher Jennie Thomas, for extracting from the teeming archives a bountiful cache of Redding-related artifacts they've managed to amass, including a chilling credit card receipt for the purchase of the oil that filled Redding's doomed airplane before it took off on its final flight and, with no fuel apparently left in its engines, wound up at the bottom of an icy lake in Wisconsin.

While for most Redding biographers, the challenges posed by his family's idea of proprietorship led to either reflexive hagiography of a saintly man who never claimed to be one or acted like one, or a reliance on sources with questionable claims—the transmission of which landed one biographer in legal hot water when Redding's widow took grave offense—these pages offer no legitimacy to such claims, nor any laying on of hands for Redding's sainthood beyond the holiness of his music. The research was exhaustive and sources were chosen not for the prospect of sensationalism but for an ability to fill in the gaps of Redding's previously untraced steps, undissected songs, and unexplained tortured soul. All added something vital and trenchant about a man of flesh and blood and pain who defies easy analysis, no more so than Al Bell, the closest thing to a shaman in Reddingology. Bell, who lights up these pages the way the Stax marquee used to light up the Memphis night sky, went through heaven and hell at Stax, building the Redding legacy as the fulcrum of the company's own legacy and that of soul music itself, and knew Otis like few in a white-controlled industry they both were greatly suspicious of, with cause. Survivor that he is, he has retained his infectious, hipper-than-hip persona, and his sharp memory, and for his time I am indebted.

Trolling through the now-gone landscape of Southern soul offered me the opportunity to pick the brains and thoughts of the people most overlooked during rock's evolution but who made it possible, and shaped its heritage—the studio musicians who turned idle ideas and chaotic chords into sweet, sweet music. Having previously spent precious time with men who had been foot soldiers in Phil Spector's L.A.-rooted Wrecking Crew and Motown's Funk Brothers, it was another personal thrill to be able to do the same with two of the most distinguished members of the Memphis Horns, Wayne Jackson and Floyd Newman, whose work can be heard on almost every song ever recorded by Otis Redding, and carved a whole genre with those hard-blowing riffs. A big shout-out to Wayne's wonderfully cheerful and helpful wife, Amy, for sitting Wayne down long enough to spill out his thoughts.

My appreciation cannot be stated enough for the contributions of Dennis Wheeler and James McEachin, each of whom walked with Redding on his early paths in Macon and L.A. and shared memories still vivid in their minds of long-ago days and nights. As the Redding story moved into high gear, the business end of the Otis Redding phenomenon took on a fascinating history of its own thanks to the enthusiasm and detail offered by Alan Walden and Alex Hodges, two of the most important figures in the Southern rock arc, something that is still the case for Alex, who took much time from his work as one of the world's biggest entertainment promoters to look back on the manic rise and awful tragedy of life with Otis. Many thanks, as well, go to one of my all-time favorite people, the "other" Otis in sixties soul, the Temptations' founder Otis Williams—who's still out there on the road with the immortal group looking and sounding friskier than ever—for his keen insight about Redding and the critical sonic, textural, and contextual differences between Motown and Stax.

For tying up loose ends and giving me essential background information and thematic guidance without fear or favor, as they say, and for that unbelievable nighttime photo of the great old Stax marquis—an image that is something like a visual B-12 shot—I tip my tattered Mets cap to Tim Sampson, head of promotions for the amazingly reconstituted Stax Museum of American Soul Music, where the marquee again lights up the sky in Memphis with the spirit of days long ago. I owe more gratitude than I can express to Jennie Thomas and Laura Moody, the gatekeepers of the seemingly endless archival treasures under the roof of another modern-day rock museum, the biggest of them all, the Rock and Roll Hall of Fame in Cleveland, for pieces of information large and small, and always fascinating, about Otis. And for uncovering a similar raft of material from the now-dusty vaults of microfilm from the sacred archives of the *New York Times*, I was blessed to be able to work with Paul Friedman, who delivered likely every word of every article ever carried in the pages of the Gray Lady about Redding, which stretched out to—gulp—over seven *hundred* document files, with not a word of objection. Profound kudos to you all.

This book was a group effort in every imaginable way, right from the start when the idea for it came as the result of a team mission to wrap pop culture and social history around the most indelible music, and musician, that lay at its core. In many ways, Otis Redding *was* the music that brought groove and meaning to, and reflected the angst and loneliness of, a generation finding its way beyond the racial and political conditioning of its forebears, and this is the overriding story of rock and roll, a homeless creature born out of confusion and bold ideas that gave full-throated ignition to soul music. I cannot be more proud that my editor Phil Marino at Liveright and my agent Jim Fitzgerald, president of the James Fitzgerald Agency, saw these broad parameters and the need for the story to be connected to and anchored by Redding, and that they had the confidence that I could deliver the goods. I hope that, between these covers, I have repaid that trust.

NOTES

INTRODUCTION: THE BIG O

1. *New York Amsterdam News*, November 4, 1967, p. 21.
2. Deborah Norville, *The Power of Respect: Benefit from the Most Forgotten Element of Success* (Nashville: Thomas Nelson, 2009), p. 18.
3. "By the Numbers: 10 Greatest Jukebox Hits of All Time," *Los Angeles Times*, March 12, 1990.
4. Robert Hilburn, "Ole King Soul," *Los Angeles Times*, February 9, 1997.
5. Roni Sarig, "Redding in the Face," Sharp Notes, CreativeLoafingAtlanta.com, November 27, 2002, http://clatl.com/atlanta/sharp-notes/Content?oid=1239433.
6. Jack Barlow, "Otis Redding's Widow: 'I Always Thought Everything He Sang, He Sang for Me,'" August 18, 2013, *Salon*, http://www.salon.com/2013/08/18/otis_reddings_widow_i_always_thought_everything_he_sang_he_sang_for_me/.
7. Doug Moe, "The Riddle of Otis Redding," in *Surrounded by Reality: The Best of Dog Moe on Madison*, (Madison, WI: Jones Books, 2005).
8. Ibid.
9. Barlow, "Otis Redding's Widow: 'I Always Thought Everything He Sang, He Sang for Me.'"

10. William Clark, Joe Cogan, *Temples of Sound: Inside the Great Recording Studios* (San Francisco: Chronicle, 2003), pp. 74, 79.

11. Paul Grein, "Week Ending July 17, 2011, Kanye West Album & Song Chart History: Hot R&B/Hip-Hop Songs," Yahoo! Music, https://music .yahoo.com/blogs/chart-watch/week-ending-july-17-2011-songs-demis-breakthrough.html.

12. Wayne Jackson, *In My Wildest Dreams—Take 3* (Memphis: Wayne and Amy Jackson, 2013), pp. 27–28, 37.

13. "JEF_AEROSOL_Galerie XIN ART_La Rochelle_Fresque Ray Charles & Otis Redding," YouTube video, 5:22, posted by PLANAS Alexandra, October 10, 2012, https://www.youtube.com/watch?v=CrJ14VXMcIA.

14. Clair MacDougall, "Too Small to Succeed? Liberia's New Army Comes of Age," AlJazeeraAmerica.com, March 4, 2014, http://america.aljazeera .com/articles/2014/3/4/too-small-to-succeedliberiasnewarmycome-sofage.html.

15. Booker T. Jones, "100 Greatest Singers: Otis Redding," Rolling-Stone.com, http://www.rollingstone.com/music/lists/100-greatest-singers-of-all-time-19691231/otis-redding-20101202.

16. Steve Cropper, "100 Greatest Artists: Otis Redding," RollingStone .com, http://www.rollingstone.com/music/lists/100-greatest-artists-of-all-time-19691231/otis-redding-20110420#ixzz2qzHLPG2O.

17. Jim Delehant, "Otis Redding: Soul Survivor," *Hit Parader*, August 1967.

PROLOGUE: "IT WAS *MUSIC*"

1. Robert Palmer, "Pop and Jazz Guide," *New York Times*, July 24, 1987, p. C28.

2. Author's interview with Wayne Jackson.

3. Author's interview with Tim Sampson.

4. Russ Bynum, "Redding's Legend Lives On," Associated Press, December 7, 1997.

CHAPTER 1: SON OF A PREACHER MAN

1. "Martin Luther King and the Global Freedom Struggle," http://mlk-kpp01 .stanford.edu/index.php/encyclopedia/encyclopedia/enc_davis _benjamin_jefferson_jr_1903_1964.

2. Scott Freeman, *Otis! The Otis Redding Story* (New York: St. Martin's Press, 2001), p. 6.

3. Ibid.

4. Edwin S. Redkey, "Bishop Turner's African Dream," *The Journal of American History* (September 1967), pp. 271–90.

5. A. L. Glenn, Sr., *History of the National Alliance of Postal Employees, 1913–1955* (Cleveland, OH: Cadillac Press Co., 1957), pp. 17, 38.

6. Macon, Georgia Visitor, Information, http://www.maconga.org/about/culture-and-heritage/african-american/#sthash.1g1Jsvqa.dpuf.

7. Andrew Michael Manis, *Macon Black and White: An Unutterable Separation in the American Century* (Macon: Mercer University Press and the Tubman African American Museum, 2004).

8. Robert Chalmers, "Legend: Little Richard," British *GQ* online, November 1, 2010, http://www.gq-magazine.co.uk/men-of-the-year/home/winners-2010/gq-men-of-the-year-2010-little-richard-legend.

9. Peter Guralnick, *Sweet Soul Music: Rhythm and Blues and the Southern Dream of Freedom* (New York: Back Bay Books, paperback edition, 1999), p. 134.

10. Geoff Brown, *Try a Little Tenderness* (Edinburgh, Scotland: MOJO Books, 2001), p. 9.

CHAPTER 2: HEEBIE JEEBIES

1. Robert Chalmers, "Legend: Little Richard," British *GQ* online, November 1, 2010, http://www.gq-magazine.co.uk/men-of-the-year/home/winners-2010/gq-men-of-the-year-2010-little-richard-legend/page/3.

2. Charles White, *The Life and Times of Little Richard: The Quasar of Rock* (New York: Harmony Books, 1985), p. 231.

3. "Online Etymology Dictionary," http://www.etymonline.com/index.php?term=soul.

4. Scott Freeman, *Otis! The Otis Redding Story* (New York: St. Martin's Press, 2001), p. 22.

5. Phillip Ramati, "Famed 'Three Horsemen' to Be Inducted into Ga. Radio Hall of Fame," *The Telegraph* (Macon), March 29, 2012, http://www.macon.com/2012/03/29/1967594/famed-three-horsemen-to-be-inducted.html#storylink=cpy.

6. "Hello Mr. Soul: Otis Redding Speaks," *Hit Parader*, August 1967.

7. Jane Schiesel, *The Otis Redding Story* (New York: Doubleday, 1973), p. 16.

CHAPTER 3: ROCKIN' REDDING

1. Richard Harrington, "'A Wopbopaloobop,' and 'Alopbamboom,' as Little Richard Himself Would Be (and Was) First to Admit," *Washington Post*, November 12, 1984.
2. Scott Freeman, *Otis! The Otis Redding Story* (New York: St. Martin's Press, 2001), p. 27.
3. Ibid., p. 39.
4. Ibid., p. 136.
5. Robert Chalmers, "Legend: Little Richard," British *GQ* online, November 1, 2010, http://www.gq-magazine.co.uk/men-of-the-year/home/winners -2010/gq-men-of-the-year-2010-little-richard-legend/page/2.
6. Bruce Pegg, *Brown Eyed Handsome Man: The Life and Hard Times of Chuck Berry* (New York: Routledge, 2006), p. 14.
7. Author's interview with Alex Hodges.
8. Phil Walden interview. Disc 2. *The Complete Monterey Pop Festival.* Directed by D. A. Pennebaker. (Criterion, 2001), DVD.

CHAPTER 4: "IT'S SOMETHING CALLED SOUL"

1. Phil Walden interview. Disc 2. *The Complete Monterey Pop Festival.* Directed by D. A. Pennebaker. (Criterion, 2001), DVD.
2. Scott Freeman, *Otis! The Otis Redding Story* (New York: St. Martin's Press, 2001) p. 48.
3. All Alex Hodges quotes in this chapter are from the author's interview.
4. Freeman, *Otis!*, pp. 49–50.
5. David Kirby, *Little Richard: The Birth of Rock 'n' Roll* (New York and London: Continuum, 2009), p. 59.
6. Otis Redding, *The Definitive Otis Redding*, Rhino Records, 1993, compact disc. Liner notes, Zelma Redding.
7. Author's interview with James McEachin.
8. Harvey Kubernik, "Otis Redding Was King of the Sunset Strip in 1966," Goldmine.com, June 28, 2010, www.goldminemag.com/article/otis-redding -was-king-of-the-sunset-strip-in-1966.

9. George Lipsitz, *Midnight at the Barrelhouse: The Johnny Otis Story* (Minneapolis: University of Minnesota Press, 2010), p. 43.
10. Stanley Booth, *Rhythm Oil: A Journey Through the Music of the American South* (New York: Pantheon, 1992), p. 76.

CHAPTER 5: "A LOUSY SINGER"

1. John Cohassey, "Otis Redding," *Contemporary Black Biography* (Gale Group, 1998).
2. "Alan Walden talks about the first recording studios in Macon Ga.," YouTube video, 6:39, posted by Tony Beazley/Rick Broyles, March 27, 2009, http://www.youtube.com/watch?v=03TKoDbzbWg.
3. All Alex Hodges quotes in this chapter are from the author's interview.
4. All Dennis Wheeler quotes in this chapter are from the author's interview.
5. "Effects of Marriage and Fatherhood on Draft Eligibility," Selective Service System, updated August 6, 2008, https://www.sss.gov/FSeffects.htm.
6. Bobby Smith, "The True Story of Confederate Record Co. and Otis Redding," http://confederaterecordco.tripod.com.
7. Peter Guralnick, *Sweet Soul Music: Rhythm and Blues and the Southern Dream of Freedom* (New York: Back Bay Books, paperback edition, 1999), p. 73.
8. Jerry Wexler and David Ritz, *Rhythm and the Blues: A Life in American Music* (New York: Knopf, 2012), p. 194.
9. "Johnny Jenkins, Guitarist Who Influenced Hendrix," *The Independent*, July 1, 2006.
10. Wexler and Ritz, *Rhythm and the Blues*, p. 194.
11. Scott Freeman, *Otis! The Otis Redding Story* (New York: St. Martin's Press, 2001) p. 75.

CHAPTER 6: "WAIT, WE GOT TIME FOR ANOTHER KID"

1. W. C. Handy, Arna Wendell Bontemps, *Father of the Blues: An Autobiography* (New York: Da Capo Press, 1991), p. 99.
2. *Respect Yourself: The Stax Records Story*, PBS documentary, August 2, 2007, produced by Tremolo Productions, Concord Music Group and Thirteen/WNET New York.

3. Mark Ribowsky, *Ain't Too Proud to Beg: The Troubled Lives and Enduring Soul of the Temptations* (Hoboken, NJ: Wiley, 2010), p. 58.

4. Elsa Dixler, "Sweet Soul Music: Robert Gordon's 'Respect Yourself,' *New York Times*, December 6, 2013.

5. Author's interview with Wayne Jackson.

6. Rob Bowman, *Soulsville, U.S.A.: The Story of Stax Records* (New York: Schirmer Trade Books, 2000), p. 40.

7. *The Ronnie Wood Show*, Sky Arts 1 Television (UK), episode 5, August 13, 2013.

8. Author's interview with Floyd Newman.

9. Stanley Booth, *Rhythm Oil: A Journey Through the Music of the American South* (New York: Pantheon, 1992), p. 76.

10. Scott Freeman, *Otis! The Otis Redding Story* (New York: St. Martin's Press, 2001), p. 76.

11. Bowman, *Soulsville*, p. 42.

12. Booker T. Jones, "100 Greatest Artists: Otis Redding,"Rolling Stone.com, http://www.rollingstone.com/music/lists/100-greatest-artists-of-all-time-19691231/otis-redding-20110420#ixzz2qzHLPG2O.

13. Freeman, *Otis!*, p. 76.

14. Bowman, *Soulsville*, p. 42.

15. Freeman, *Otis!*, p. 84.

16. Ibid., p. 85.

17. Ibid., p. 75.

18. Author's interview with Dennis Wheeler.

19. Jerry Wexler and David Ritz, *Rhythm and the Blues: A Life in American Music* (New York: Knopf, 2012), p. 195.

CHAPTER 7: CHOPS LIKE A WOLF

1. Scott Freeman, *Otis! The Otis Redding Story* (New York: St. Martin's Press, 2001), p. 86.

2. Rob Bowman, *Soulsville, U.S.A.: The Story of Stax Records* (New York: Schirmer Trade Books, 2000), p. 11.

3. Author's interview with Alan Walden.

4. Denise Grollmus, "The Great Pretenders: They're Defrauding the Legends of Soul—and It's Perfectly Legal," Cleveland Scene.com, http://www.clevescene.com/cleveland/the-great-pretenders/Content?oid=1496687.

5. Phil Phillips entry, Black Cat Rockabilly.com, http://www.rockabilly.nl/references/messages/phil_phillips.htm.

6. Author's interview with Alex Hodges.

7. Author's interview with Wayne Jackson.

8. Author's interview with Floyd Newman.

9. "Atlantic to Record Stars on Apollo Stage Saturday," *New York Amsterdam News*, November 16, 1963, p. 16.

10. Peter Guralnick, *Sweet Soul Music: Rhythm and Blues and the Southern Dream of Freedom* (New York: Back Bay Books, paperback edition, 1999), p. 143.

11. Jane Schiesel, *The Otis Redding* Story (New York: Doubleday, 1973), pp. 58–59.

12. Jerry Wexler and David Ritz, *Rhythm and the Blues: A Life in American Music* (New York: Knopf, 2012), p. 195.

13. "Otis Redding: Live at the Apollo November 1963," BrownEyedHandsomeSoul.com, http://browneyedhandsomeman.blogspot.com/2006/05/otis-redding-live-at-apollo-november.html.

14. Ibid.

15. Guralnick, *Sweet Soul Music*, p. 143.

16. Wexler and Ritz, *Rhythm and the Blues*, p. 196.

CHAPTER 8: TURNING THE KNIFE

1. Author's interview with Dennis Wheeler.

2. Bob Lamb, "Macon's Own Otis Redding Returns Home," *The Telegraph* (Macon), July 11, 1965.

3. Peter Guralnick, *Sweet Soul Music: Rhythm and Blues and the Southern Dream of Freedom* (New York: Back Bay Books, paperback edition, 1999), p. 328.

4. Author's interview with Floyd Newman.

5. Booker T. Jones, "100 Greatest Singers: Otis Redding," Rollingstone.com, http://www.rollingstone.com/music/lists/100-greatest-singers-of-all-time-19691231/otis-redding-20101202.

6. John A. Warnick, "More Lessons from the Life of Ray Charles," Seedlings: The Blog of John A. Warnick, August 2010, http://johnawarnick.typepad.com/seedlings/2010/08/more-lessons-from-the-life-of-ray-charles.html.

7. Author's interview with Otis Williams.

8. "500 Greatest Songs of All Time: 'I've Been Loving You Too Long (to Stop Now),'" Rolling Stone.com, http://www.rollingstone.com/music/lists/the-500-greatest-songs-of-all-time-20110407/otis-redding-ive-been-loving-you-too-long-to-stop-now-20110526#ixzz2wVK3Ngse.

9. Scott Freeman, *Otis! The Otis Redding Story* (New York: St. Martin's Press, 2001), p. 117.

10. Author's interview with Al Bell.

11. Rob Bowman, *Soulsville, U.S.A.: The Story of Stax Records* (New York: Schirmer Trade Books, 2000), p. 55.

12. Press releases from Phil Walden Artists and Promotions, 1963 and 1964, courtesy of the Rock and Roll Hall of Fame.

CHAPTER 9: THE KING OF SOUL

1. All Alex Hodges quotes in this chapter are from author's interview.

2. Press release from Phil Walden Artists and Promotions, 1964; courtesy of Rock and Roll Hall of Fame.

3. Rob Bowman, *Soulsville, U.S.A.: The Story of Stax Records* (New York: Schirmer Trade Books, 2000), p. 64.

4. *Respect Yourself: The Stax Records Story*, PBS documentary, August 2, 2007, produced by Tremolo Productions, Concord Music Group and Thirteen/WNET New York.

5. Louis Robinson, "The Tragic Death of Sam Cooke," *Ebony*, February 1965, pp. 92–96.

6. Peter Guralnick, *Dream Boogie: The Triumph of Sam Cooke* (New York: Little, Brown and Company, 2005), p. 264.

7. "Otis Redding, King of Soul—Still Ruling Forty-Seven Years After His Passing," SoulandJazzandFunk.com, http://www.soulandjazzandfunk.com/interviews/2593-otis-redding-king-of-soul-still-ruling-forty-seven-years-after-his-passing.html?start=1.

8. Peter Guralnick, *Sweet Soul Music: Rhythm and Blues and the Southern Dream of Freedom* (New York: Back Bay Books, paperback edition, 1999), p. 146.

9. All Dennis Wheeler quotes in this chapter are from the author's interview.

10. Alan Walden, "Remembering Otis Redding," http://jpp-product.perso.sfr.fr/nouvellepage1.htm.

11. Jon Pareles, "Of Rasps, Yowls and Din," *New York Times*, June 14, 1987, section II, page 30.

12. Robert Shelton, "Otis Redding: A Major Loss," *New York Times*, March 3, 1968.

13. Otis Redding, *The Definitive Otis Redding*, Rhino Records, 1993, compact disc. Liner notes, Booker T. Jones.

14. *Respect Yourself: The Stax Records Story*, PBS documentary, August 2, 2007, produced by Tremolo Productions, Concord Music Group and Thirteen/WNET New York.

15. Robert Gordon, *Respect Yourself: Stax Records and the Soul Explosion* (New York: Bloomsbury, 2013), p. 82.

16. Jerry Wexler and David Ritz, *Rhythm and the Blues: A Life in American Music* (New York: Knopf, 2012), p. 194.

17. Baseball Almanac.com, http://www.baseball-almanac.com/quotes/quojckr.shtml.

18. Johnny Black, *Classic Tracks Back to Back Singles and Albums* (Charlotte, NC: Thunder Bay Press, 2008), p. 71.

19. Guralnick, *Sweet Soul Music*, p. 15.

20. Ian Crouch, "Otis Redding vs. Reading," *The New Yorker*, March 14, 2014.

21. "Hello Mr. Soul: Otis Redding Speaks," *Hit Parader*, August 1967.

22. Jann Wenner, "The Rolling Stone Roundtable: Booker T. and the MG's," *Rolling Stone*, August 24, 1968.

23. "500 Greatest Albums of All Time: Otis Redding, *Otis Blue*," Rolling Stone.com, http://www.rollingstone.com/music/lists/500-greatest-albums-of-all-time-20120531/otis-redding-otis-blue-20120524.

24. Robert Christgau, "Otis Redding: *Otis Blue—Otis Redding Sings Soul*," http://www.robertchristgau.com/xg/bl/redding-08.php.

25. Jack Doyle, ". . . No Satisfaction," The Pop History Dig, July 11, 2011, http://www.pophistorydig.com/topics/%E2%80%9C-no-satisfaction%E2%80%9D1965-1966/.

26. Harvey Kubernik, "Otis Redding Was King of the Sunset Strip in 1966," Goldmine.com, June 28, 2010, http://www.goldminemag.com/article/otis-redding-was-king-of-the-sunset-strip-in-1966.

27. Atlantic Records internal memo, June 18, 1965, courtesy of the Rock and Roll Hall of Fame.

28. "500 Greatest Albums," RollingStone.com.

29. Scott Freeman, *Otis! The Otis Redding Story* (New York: St. Martin's Press, 2001), p. 111.

30. Alan Walden, "Remembering."

31. Author's interview with Dennis Wheeler.

CHAPTER 10: JUST ONE MORE DAY

1. Rob Bowman, *Soulsville, U.S.A.: The Story of Stax Records* (New York: Schirmer Trade Books, 2000), p. 64.

2. Author's interview with Floyd Newman.

3. Robert Gordon, "The Rise of Stax Records: The Tragic Tale of Otis Redding and the Legendary Label He Helped Build," *Daily Mail* online, January 18, 2014, http://www.dailymail.co.uk/home/event/article-2540752/Otis-Reddings-death-The-rise-Stax-Records-The-tragic-tale-Otis-Redding-legendary-label-helped-build.html.

4. Jerry Wexler and David Ritz, *Rhythm and the Blues: A Life in American Music* (New York: Knopf, 2012), p. 194.

5. "Hello Mr. Soul: Otis Redding Speaks," *Hit Parader*, August 1976.

6. *Respect Yourself: The Stax Records Story*, PBS documentary, August 2, 2007, produced by Tremolo Productions, Concord Music Group and Thirteen/WNET New York.

7. All Al Bell quotes in this chapter are from the author's interview.

8. Otis Redding, *The Definitive Otis Redding*, Rhino Records, 1993. Liner notes.

9. Author's interview with Otis Williams.

10. "Otis Redding: Otis Blue," *Record Mirror*, February 12, 1966, http://www.rocksbackpages.com/Library/Article/otis-redding-iotis-bluei-atlantic-atl-5041-.

11. Scott Freeman, *Otis! The Otis Redding Story* (New York: St. Martin's Press, 2001), p. 139.

12. Ibid., p. 140.

13. Booker T. Jones, "100 Greatest Singers: Otis Redding," Rolling Stone.com, http://www.rollingstone.com/music/lists/100-greatest-singers-of-all-time-19691231/otis-redding-20101202.

14. *Billboard*, Rhythm and Blues chart, October 22, 1966, p. 64.

15. Author's interview with Dennis Wheeler.

16. *The Telegraph* (Macon), July 17, 1966.

17. Alan Walden, "Remembering Otis Redding," http://jpp-product.perso.sfr.fr/nouvellepage1.htm.

18. Bibb County Superior Court, civil cases: *David McGee vs. Otis Redding, Willie McGee vs. Otis Redding*; Freeman, *Otis!*, pp. 109–10.

19. Freeman, *Otis!*, p. 134.

20. Ibid., pp. 232–33.

21. Author's interview with Dennis Wheeler.

22. Author's interview with Al Bell.

CHAPTER 11: CROSSING OVER

1. All Al Bell quotes in this chapter are from the author's interview.

2. Rob Bowman, *Soulsville, U.S.A.: The Story of Stax Records* (New York: Schirmer Trade Books, 2000), p. 4.

3. Ibid., p. 59.

4. Chester Higgins, "Eyewitness Tells of Otis Redding's Violent Death," *Jet*, December 28, 1967, p. 56.

5. Stanley Booth, *The True Adventures of the Rolling Stones* (Chicago Review Press, 2000), p. 210.

6. Author's interview with Alan Walden.

7. All Dennis Wheeler quotes in this chapter are from the author's interview.

8. Author's interview with Floyd Newman.

9. Bowman, *Soulsville, U.S.A.*, pp. 66-69.

10. Ibid., p. 88.

11. Wayne Jackson, *In My Wildest Dreams, Take 1* (Memphis: Wayne and Amy Jackson, 2005), p. 173.

CHAPTER 12: THE WHOLE DAMN BODY

1. "Otis Redding Live on the Sunset Strip," The Ripple Effect, http://ripplemusic.blogspot.com/2010/07/otis-redding-live-on-sunset-strip.html.

2. Gustavo Turner, "Complete 1966 Otis Redding Show Live on the Sunset Strip to Be Released," *LA Weekly*, April 2, 2010, http://www.laweekly.com/westcoastsound/2010/04/02/complete-1966-otis-redding-show-live-on-the-sunset-strip-to-be-released; Harvey Kubernik, "Otis Redding Was King of the Sunset Strip in 1966," Goldmine.com, June 28, 2010, http://www.goldminemag.com/article/otis-redding-was-king-of-the-sunset-strip-in-1966.

3. Randy Lewis, "Album Review: 'Otis Redding Live on the Sunset Strip,'" Pop and Hiss, May 18, 2010, http://latimesblogs.latimes.com/music_blog /2010/05/album-review-otis-redding-live-on-the-sunset-strip.html.

4. "Otis Redding in Person at the Whiskey a Go Go," AllMusic.com, http:// www.allmusic.com/album/in-person-at-the-whiskey-a-go-go-mw00000 78246.

5. David McGee, "Flat Right: The Bluegrass Special, May 2008," TheBlue-grassSpecial.com, http://www.thebluegrassspecial.com/archive/2008/ may2008/otisredding.php.

6. Kubernik, "Otis Redding Was King."

7. "Tag Archives: Robbie Robertson," The Blues Mobile, May 17, 2014, http:// thebluesmobile.com/tag/robbie-robertson/.

8. Author's interview with Alex Hodges.

9. Bill Graham and Robert Greenfield, *Bill Graham Presents: My Life Inside Rock and Out* (New York: Doubleday, 1992), p. 153.

10. Kubernik, "Otis Redding Was King."

11. Graham, *My Life*, p. 173.

12. Ibid., p. 174.

13. Author's interview with Dennis Wheeler.

14. Peter Guralnick, *Sweet Soul Music: Rhythm and Blues and the Southern Dream of Freedom* (New York: Back Bay Books, paperback edition, 1999), p.183.

15. The Hit Parade Blog, http://thehitparade.blogspot.com/2008/11/number-23-otis-redding.html.

16. Author's interview with Al Bell.

17. "500 Greatest Songs of All Time: 'Try a Little Tenderness,'" Rolling Stone.com,http://www.rollingstone.com/music/lists/the-500-greatest-songs-of-all-time-20110407/otis-redding-try-a-little -tenderness-20110527#ixzz2wVCmyG1j.

18. Otis Redding, *Complete & Unbelievable: The Otis Redding Dictionary of Soul*, 1993, CD rerelease. Liner notes, Jon Landau.

CHAPTER 13: MAKING THE WHITE FEEL BLACK

1. "Ray Charles Gets 5-Year Probation, $10,000 Fine," *Jet*, December 8, 1966.

2. Rob Bowman, *Soulsville, U.S.A.: The Story of Stax Records* (New York: Schirmer Trade Books, 2000), p. 96.

3. Bill Millar, "Otis Redding at Tiles," *Soul Music Monthly*, October 1966.

4. Geoff Brown, *Try a Little Tenderness* (Edinburgh: MOJO Books, 2001), p. 117.

5. Author's interview of Floyd Newman.

6. *Otis Redding Live: Ready Steady Go! Special Edition*, aired September 16, 1966 (Sony video, 1985), VHS.

7. "Otis Redding: Mr Cool and the Clique from Memphis," *Melody Maker*, September 17, 1966.

8. Masco Young, "Negro Rock & Roll 'Big' in London," *Philadelphia Tribune*, December 24, 1966, p. 13.

9. Walden Artists and Promotions press release, 1968, courtesy of the Rock and Roll Hall of Fame.

10. Jerry Wexler and David Ritz, *Rhythm and the Blues: A Life in American Music* (New York: Knopf, 2012), p. 196.

11. Scott Freeman, *Otis! The Otis Redding Story* (New York: St. Martin's Press, 2001), p. 152.

12. Author's interview with Al Bell.

13. Author's interview with Alan Walden.

14. "Hello Mr. Soul: Otis Redding Speaks," *Hit Parader*, August 1967.

15. Bill Graham and Robert Greenfield, *Bill Graham Presents: My Life Inside Rock and Out* (New York: Doubleday, 1992), p. 173.

16. Ibid., p. 274.

17. Author's interview with Alex Hodges.

18. Graham, *My Life*, p. 175.

19. Ibid.

20. Bill Lane, "The Inside Story," *Los Angeles Sentinel*, December 29, 1966, p. A3.

CHAPTER 14: "THE ONLY SON-OF-A-GUN THIS SIDE OF THE SUN"

1. Robert Shelton, "Otis Redding: A Major Loss," *New York Times*, March 3, 1968.

2. All Alex Hodges quotes in this chapter are from the author's interview.

3. Rob Bowman, *Soulsville, U.S.A.: The Story of Stax Records* (New York: Schirmer Trade Books, 2000), p. 110.

4. Robert Christgau, "Otis Redding and Carla Thomas: *King & Queen*," http://www.robertchristgau.com/get_artist.php?id=4673&name=Otis+Redding+%26+Carla+Thomas.

5. All Al Bell quotes in this chapter are from the author's interview.

6. Otis Redding and Carla Thomas, *King & Queen*. Liner notes, Howard Baker.

7. "Eddie Floyd: 'Knock on Wood,'" Allmusic.com, http://www.allmusic .com/song/knock-on-wood-mt0012027635.

8. *Billboard*, Rhythm and Blues chart, October 22, 1966, p. 64.

9. Author's interview with Floyd Newman.

10. Mike Boone, "Otis Redding," ChancellorofSoul.com, August 2004, http:// chancellorofsoul.com/redding.html.

11. Peter Guralnick, *Sweet Soul Music: Rhythm and Blues and the Southern Dream of Freedom* (New York: Back Bay Books, paperback edition, 1999), p. 214.

12. Chester Higgins, "Eyewitness Tells of Otis Redding's Violent Death," *Jet*, December 28, 1967, p. 50.

13. Michael Buffalo Smith, "Skynyrd, the Allmans and Otis: Alan Walden's Career in Rock and Soul," Swampland.com, January 2002, http://www .swampland.com/articles/view/title:alan_walden.

14. "Inside the Rock Era: The Top 200 Songs of the '60s," July 14, 2014, http:// top5000-rocketman5000.blogspot.com/2014/07/the-top-200-songs-of-60s-70-61.html.

15. "500 Greatest Songs of All Time," Rolling Stone.com, http://www .rollingstone.com/music/lists/the-500-greatest-songs-of-all-time-20110407.

16. Robert Palmer, "Pop and Jazz Guide," *New York Times*, July 24, 1968, p. C28.

17. "Hello Mr. Soul: Otis Redding Speaks," *Hit Parader*, August 1967.

18. Shelton, "A Major Loss."

19. Loretta Williams Handy, *Woman Who Lived Twice: Her Story of the Late Great Otis Redding* (Bloomington, IN: Trafford, 2007), p. 83.

CHAPTER 15: LONDON CALLING

1. "Seven Seconds of Fire," *The Economist*, December 17, 2011, http://www .economist.com/node/21541707.

2. Chuck McPhilomy, "Mississippi Writers and Musicians: Jaimoe and the Allman Brothers Band," http://mswritersandmusicians.com/musicians/ jaimoe.html.

3. Loretta Williams Handy, *Woman Who Lived Twice: Her Story of the Late Great Otis Redding* (Bloomington, IN: Trafford, 2007), p. 94; quotations in this chapter are from pp. 95, 102, 104, 114–17, 120–23, and 130.
4. Ibid., p. 116.
5. Ibid., pp. 120–21.
6. Ibid., p. 123.
7. Author's interview with Alex Hodges.
8. All Al Bell quotes in this chapter are from the author's interview.
9. Alan Walden, "Remembering Otis Redding," http://jpp-product.perso .sfr.fr/nouvellepage1.htm.
10. All Wayne Jackson quotes in this chapter are from the author's interview.
11. Rob Bowman, *Soulsville, U.S.A.: The Story of Stax Records* (New York: Schirmer Trade Books, 2000), p. 117.
12. BBC Radio 4, "Hit the Road Stax," September 25, 2007, http://www.bbc .co.uk/programmes/b00776mx.
13. Miranda Ward, "Otis Redding in London," *Hit Parader*, February 1967.
14. "A History of the Rainbow Theatre," http://www.rainbowhistory.x10 .mx/.
15. Peter Guralnick, *Sweet Soul Music: Rhythm and Blues and the Southern Dream of Freedom: Rhythm and Blues and the Southern Dream of Freedom* (New York: Back Bay Books, paperback edition, 1999), p. 312.
16. *Respect Yourself: The Stax Records Story*, PBS documentary, August 2, 2007, produced by Tremolo Productions, Concord Music Group and Thirteen/WNET New York.
17. Scott Freeman, *Otis! The Otis Redding Story* (New York: St. Martin's Press, 2001), p. 172.
18. Ibid., p. 191.
19. Author's interview with Dennis Wheeler.
20. Freeman, *Otis!*, p. 189.
21. Guralnick, *Sweet Soul Music*, p. 314.
22. Ibid., p. 317.

CHAPTER 16: PEACE, LOVE, AND OTIS REDDING

1. All quotes by Al Bell in this chapter are from the author's interview.
2. Scott Freeman, *Otis! The Otis Redding Story* (New York: St. Martin's Press, 2001), p. 180.

3. "Little Richard," RollingStone.com, http://www.rollingstone.com/music/lists/100-greatest-singers-of-all-time-19691231/little-richard-20101202.

4. All quotes by Wayne Jackson in this chapter are from the author's interview.

5. Phil Walden interview. Disc 2. *The Complete Monterey Pop Festival*. Directed by D. A. Pennebaker. (Criterion, 2001), DVD.

6. Freeman, *Otis!*, p. 187.

7. Geoff Brown, *Try a Little Tenderness* (Edinburgh: MOJO Books, 2001), p. 1.

8. Robert Christgau, "Anatomy of a Love Festival," *Esquire*, January 1968.

9. Phil Walden interview, *Monterey Pop Festival*.

10. Ibid.

11. Renata Adler, "Monterey Pop (1968), Screen: Upbeat Musical: 'Monterey Pop' Views the Rock Scene," *New York Times*, December 27, 1968.

12. Robert Christgau, "Christgau's Reviews," http://www.robertchristgau.com/get_artist.php?id=3542&name=Otis+Redding%2FThe+Jimi+Hendrix+Experience.

13. Peter Guralnick, *Sweet Soul Music: Rhythm and Blues and the Southern Dream of Freedom* (New York: Back Bay Books, paperback edition, 1999), pp. 320–21.

14. Jim Delehant, "Otis Redding: Soul Survivor," *Hit Parader*, August 1967.

15. Nik Cohn, *Awopbopaloobop Alopbamboom: The Golden Age of Rock* (New York: Grove Press, paperback edition, 2001, originally published in 1970), p. 123.

16. Robert Greenfield, *The Last Sultan: The Life and Times of Ahmet Ertegun* (New York: Simon & Schuster, 2011), p. 184.

17. Ibid.

18. Phil Walden interview, *Monterey Pop Festival*.

19. Robert Shelton, "Blues Look Lively," *New York Times*, August 28, 1966.

20. Rob Bowman, *Soulsville, U.S.A.: The Story of Stax Records* (New York: Schirmer Trade Books, 2000), p. 124.

21. Otis Redding, *The Complete Stax/Volt Singles, 1959–1968*, Atlantic Records, 1991. Liner notes, Rob Bowman.

22. Sausalito Historical Society: "Sittin' at which 'Dock of the Bay'?" August 3, 2010, http://www.marinscope.com/sausalito_marin_scope/opinion/article_9ae6cf2a-3f5f-57bb-b57e-0709d4e4b994.html.

23. Guralnick, *Sweet Soul Music*, p. 321.

24. Peter Guralnick, "Otis Redding Was His Name," *Georgia Music Magazine*, Summer 2007, http://georgiamusicmag.com/otis-redding-was-his-name.

25. "Otis Redding Stars in 2 Park Concerts," *New York Times*, August 18, 1966, p. 28.

26. Concert receipts of Redding tour, courtesy of the Rock and Roll Hall of Fame.

27. Author's interview with Alex Hodges.

28. David J. Krajicek, "Lord He's a Stabbin', Ramblin' Man! Allman Brothers Tour Manager Spends Only 18 Months in Jail After Argument with Club Owner Turns Deadly," *New York Daily News*, May 11, 2013.

CHAPTER 17: HARD TO HANDLE

1. All Al Bell quotes in this chapter are from the author's interview.

2. Scott Freeman, *Otis! The Otis Redding Story* (New York: St. Martin's Press, 2001), p. 192.

3. Ronald E. Franklin, "How Otis Redding Got to 'The Dock of the Bay,'" Hubpages.com, http://ronelfran.hubpages.com/hub/How-Otis-Redding-Got-To-The-Dock-of-the-Bay.

4. Robert Greenfield, *The Last Sultan: The Life and Times of Ahmet Ertegun* (New York: Simon & Schuster, 2011), p. 249.

5. Jann Wenner, "Phil Spector: The Rolling Stone Interview," *Rolling Stone*, November 1, 1969; rollingstone.com/music/news/the-rolling-stone-interview-phil-spector-19691101#ixzz3HTZcS000.

6. Jerry Wexler and David Ritz, *Rhythm and the Blues: A Life in American Music* (New York: St. Martin's Press, 1994), p. 196.

7. James Brown, *James Brown: The Godfather of Soul* (New York: Da Capo, 2003), p. 176.

8. William Ott, "Home Forever," *The Telegraph* (Macon), December 18, 1967.

9. John Sibley Butler, "African Americans in the Vietnam War," *The Oxford Companion to American Military History* (Oxford: Oxford University Press; 1st edition, 2000); http://www.english.illinois.edu/maps/poets/s_z/stevens/africanamer.htm.

10. *New York Amsterdam News*, November 4, 1967, p. 21.

11. Russ Bynum, "Redding's Legend Lives On," Associated Press, December 7, 1997.

12. Wexler and Ritz, *Rhythm and the Blues*, p. 201.

13. Ibid.

14. Freeman, *Otis!*, p. 195.

15. Peter Guralnick, *Sweet Soul Music: Rhythm and Blues and the Southern Dream of Freedom* (New York: Back Bay Books, paperback edition, 1999), p. 318.

16. Letter from Redding, courtesy of the Rock and Roll Hall of Fame.

17. Stanley Booth, *Rhythm Oil: A Journey Through the Music of the American South* (New York: Pantheon, 1992), p. 75.

18. Freeman, *Otis!*, p. 198.

19. *The Ronnie Wood Show*, Sky Arts 1 Television (UK), episode 5, August 13, 2013.

CHAPTER 18: "SO I GUESS I'LL REMAIN THE SAME"

1. Author's interview with Floyd Newman.

2. Rob Bowman, *Soulsville, U.S.A.: The Story of Stax Records* (New York: Schirmer Trade Books, 2000), p. 132.

3. Marc Myers, "Then I Watch 'Em Roll Away Again," *Wall Street Journal*, January 3, 2013.

4. Ibid.

5. Geoff Brown, *Try a Little Tenderness* (Edinburgh: MOJO Books, 2001), p. 135.

6. Author's interview with Wayne Jackson.

7. Bowman, *Soulsville*, p. 132.

8. Author's interview with Al Bell.

9. Lydia Hutchinson, "Otis Redding's "(Sittin' On) The Dock of the Bay," PerformingSongwriter.com, September 9, 2012, http://performingsong writer.com/otis-redding-sittin-dock-bay/.

10. Stanley Booth, *Rhythm Oil: A Journey Through the Music of the American South* (New York: Pantheon, 1992), p. 79.

11. "'(Sittin' On) The Dock Of the Bay,'" NPR.org, September 17, 2000, http://www.npr.org/2000/09/17/1082281/-sittin-on-the-dock-of-the-bay.

12. Author's interview with Alan Walden.

13. Jerry Wexler and David Ritz, *Rhythm and the Blues: A Life in American Music* (New York: St. Martin's Press, 1994), p. 202.

14. "Otis Redding's Last Day in Cleveland," Rockhall.com, http://rockhall .com/blog/post/7045_otis-reddings-last-day-in-Cleveland/.

15. Scott Freeman, *Otis! The Otis Redding Story* (New York: St. Martin's Press, 2001), p. 217.
16. James Brown, *James Brown: The Godfather of Soul* (New York: Da Capo, 2003), p. 177.
17. Chester Higgins, "Eyewitness Tells of Otis Redding's Violent Death," *Jet*, December 28, 1967, p. 56.
18. Purchase receipt, courtesy of the Rock and Roll Hall of Fame.
19. Michael Buffalo Smith, "Skynyrd, The Allmans and Otis: Alan Walden's Career in Rock and Soul," Swampland.com, January 2002, http://www .swampland.com/articles/view/title:alan_walden.
20. Mark Myers, "Then I Watch 'Em Roll Away Again," *Wall Street Journal*, January 3, 2013.

CHAPTER 19: AMEN

1. Scott Freeman, *Otis! The Otis Redding Story* (New York: St. Martin's Press, 2001), p. 205.
2. Chester Higgins, "Eyewitness Tells of Otis Redding's Violent Death," *Jet*, December 28, 1967, p. 56.
3. Marc Myers, "Then I Watch 'Em Roll Away Again," *Wall Street Journal*, January 3, 2013.
4. Author's interview with Al Bell.
5. Todd Leopold, "The Legacy of Otis Redding," CNN Entertainment, December 14, 2009, http://www.cnn.com/2009/SHOWBIZ/Music/12/10/ otis.redding.legacy/.
6. Robert Greenfield, *The Last Sultan: The Life and Times of Ahmet Ertegun* (New York: Simon & Schuster, 2011), p. 184.
7. Author's interview with Floyd Newman.
8. All Dennis Wheeler quotes in this chapter are from the author's interview.
9. Author's interview with Wayne Jackson.
10. Doug Moe, "45 Years Later, Questions Still Remain over Otis Redding's Plane Crash," *Wisconsin Journal*, December 10, 2012.
11. Doug Moe, "The Bar-Kays at 50," *Wisconsin State Journal*, April 16, 2014.
12. Doug Moe, "The Riddle of Otis Redding" in *Surrounded by Reality: The Best of Dog Moe on Madison* (Madison, WI: Jones Books, 2005), p. 3.
13. Jann S. Wenner, "Otis Redding: The Crown Prince of Soul Is Dead," *Rolling Stone*, January 20, 1968.

14. Loretta Williams Handy, *Woman Who Lived Twice: Her Story of the Late Great Otis Redding* (Bloomington, IN: Trafford, 2007), p. 130.

15. Rob Bowman, *Soulsville, U.S.A.: The Story of Stax Records* (New York: Schirmer Trade Books, 2000), p. 141.

16. Peter Guralnick, *Sweet Soul Music: Rhythm and Blues and the Southern Dream of Freedom* (New York: Back Bay Books, paperback edition, 1999), p. 328.

17. Melissa Limoncella, "Fa-fa-fa-fa-fa," Vice.com, December 1, 2000; http://www.vice.com/en_uk/read/arthur-conley-v7n10.

18. Jerry Wexler and David Ritz, *Rhythm and the Blues: A Life in American Music* (New York: St. Martin's Press, 1994), p. 201.

19. Limoncella, "Fa-fa-fa-fa-fa."

20. David Dalton and Lenny Kaye, *Rock 100* (New York: Grosset & Dunlap, 1977).

21. Higgins, "Eyewitness."

22. Moe, *Surrounded by Reality*.

23. Author's interview with Otis Williams.

24. Moe, *Surrounded by Reality*.

25. Freeman, *Otis!*, p. 210.

26. National Transportation Safety Board, "Lessons Learned and Lives Saved," 1967–2007, April 27, 2007, http://www.ntsb.gov/doclib/reports /2007/sr0701.pdf, p. 10.

27. "Otis Redding: The NTSB Report," http://www.planecrashinfo.com/1967 /1967-88.htm.

EPILOGUE: "WOULDN'T THAT HAVE BEEN SOMETHIN'?"

1. Jeff Cochran, "Poor Otis, Dead and Gone," *Like the Dew: A Journal of Southern Culture and Politics*, January 31, 2012,http://likethedew .com/2012/01/31/poor-otis-dead-and-gone/.

2. Rob Bowman, *Soulsville, U.S.A.: The Story of Stax Records* (New York: Schirmer Trade Books, 2000), p. 134.

3. Jerry Wexler and David Ritz, *Rhythm and the Blues: A Life in American Music* (New York: St. Martin's Press, 1994), p. 201.

4. "'(Sittin' On) The Dock of the Bay,'" September 17, 2000, NPR.org, http://www.npr.org/2000/09/17/1082281/-sittin-on-the-dock-of-the-bay.

5. Russ Bynum, "Otis Redding Still Drawing Fans," AP News Archive,

December 5, 1997; http://www.apnewsarchive.com/1997/Otis-Redding-Still-Drawing-Fans/id-a14f55f7b1c9377c5a8cb218528163b4.

6. All Al Bell quotes in this chapter are from the author's interview.

7. Nik Cohn, *Awopbopaloobop Alopbamboom: The Golden Age of Rock* (New York: Grove Press, paperback edition, 2001), p. 124.

8. BMI.com, "BMI Announces Top 100 Songs of the Century," December 13, 1999; http://www.bmi.com/news/entry/232893.

9. RollingStone.com, "Artists"; http://www.rollingstone.com/music/artists/otis-redding/albumguide.

10. Barry Dean Kernfield, *New Grove Dictionary of Jazz* (New York: Macmillan, 1988), p. 544.

11. Doug Bradley, "The Legacy of Otis Redding's 'Dock of the Bay,'" HuffingtonPost.com, January 1, 2013; http://www.huffingtonpost.com/doug-bradley/otis-redding-dock-of-the-bay_b_2435220.html.

12. Wexler and Ritz, *Rhythm and the Blues*, p. 202.

13. *Variety*, December 20, 1967, p. 44.

14. Bowman, *Soulsville*, p. 359.

15. Author's interview with Floyd Newman.

16. Harvey Kubernik, "Otis Redding Was King of the Sunset Strip in 1966," Goldmine.com, June 18, 2010, http://www.goldminemag.com/article/otis-redding-was-king-of-the-sunset-strip-in-1966.

17. Robert Greenfield, *The Last Sultan*: *The Life and Times of Ahmet Ertegun* (New York: Simon & Schuster, 2011), p. 191.

18. Ibid. p. 192.

19. Peter Guralnick, *Sweet Soul Music: Rhythm and Blues and the Southern Dream of Freedom* (New York: Back Bay Books, paperback edition, 1999), p. 357.

20. Greenfield, *The Last Sultan*, p. 189.

21. Author's interview with Alan Walden.

22. Philip Walden Jr. obituary, *Atlanta Journal-Constitution*, June 7, 2011.

23. *Los Angeles Daily News*, August 28, 1996.

24. "Bobbie Smith's First Recording Studio—Otis Redding and Confederate Records," YouTube video, 2:41, uploaded by Sarah Barnes, November 30, 2013, http://www.youtube.com/watch?v=29ZSP9Es6H8.

25. Robert Christgau, "Otis Redding," http://www.robertchristgau.com/get_artist.php?name=Otis+Redding.

26. Bowman, *Soulsville U.S.A.*, p. 121.

27. Guralnick, *Sweet Soul Music*, p. 314.

28. Bowman, *Soulsville U.S.A.*, p. 193.

29. Ibid., p. 134.

30. "Museum of American Soul Music: Stax lives! The other soul record label celebrates 50 years at SXSW after tumultuous Memphis history"; http://www.staxmuseum.com/events/news/view/stax-lives-the-other-soul-record-label-celebrates-.

31. *Respect Yourself: The Stax Records Story*, PBS documentary, August 2, 2007, produced by Tremolo Productions, Concord Music Group and Thirteen/WNET New York.

32. Deborah Sontag, "Out of Exile, Back in Soulsville," *New York Times*, August 14, 2009.

33. "Let C.B.S. Tell Its Own Ugly Story," *The New York Times*, June 22, 1973.

34. Sontag, "Out of Exile."

35. Stax Photo Museum, http://staxrecords.free.fr/bankrupcy_l.jpg#bankrupcy_l.jpg.

36. *Memphis Commercial Appeal*, February 8, 1976.

37. "Little Richard Inducts Otis Redding into the Hall of Fame," YouTube video, 15:56, uploaded by Rock and Roll Hall of Fame and Museum, May 21, 2012, https://www.youtube.com/watch?v=YUvHBirr1PI.

38. Russ Bynum, Associated Press, "Redding's Legend Lives On," December 7, 1997.

39. John A. Warnick, "More Lessons from the Life of Ray Charles," Seedlings: The Blog of John A. Warnick, August 2010, http://johnawarnick.typepad.com/seedlings/2010/08/more-lessons-from-the-life-of-ray-charles.html.

40. Bynum, "Redding's Legend Lives On."

41. Ibid.

42. "Stairway to Heaven," *People*, June 17, 1996.

43. Ibid.

44. Author's interview with Dennis Wheeler.

45. Scott Freeman, *Otis! The Otis Redding Story* (New York: St. Martin's Press, 2001), p. 188.

46. Ibid., p. 191.

47. Ibid., p. 217.

48. Roni Sarig, "Redding in the Face," Sharp Notes, CreativeLoafingAtlanta.com, November 27, 2002, http://clatl.com/atlanta/sharp-notes/Content?oid=1239433.

49. Jack Barlow, "Otis Redding's Widow: I Always Thought Everything

He Sang, He Sang for Me," August 18, 2013, *Salon*, http://www.salon.com/2013/08/18/otis_reddings_widow_i_always_thought_everything_he_sang_he_sang_for_me/.

50. Derick Jacobs, "Source Claims Otis Redding Had Love Child with Queen of Memphis Carla Thomas," July 25, 2013, http://www.bazaardaily.co.uk/2013/05/07/exclusive-source-claims-otis-redding-had-love-child-with-queen-of-memphis-carla-thomas/.

51. Dorothy Wade and Justine Picardie, *Music Man: Ahmet Ertegun, Atlantic Records and the Triumph of Rock & Roll* (New York: W. W. Norton, 1990), p. 64.

52. "Peter Gabriel—So Special Edition," Henri Strik (edited by Peter Willemsen), BackgroundMagazine.nl, http://www.backgroundmagazine.nl/Cdreviews/PeterGabrielSoSpecialEdition.html.

53. Charles White, *The Life and Times of Little Richard: The Quasar of Rock* (New York: Harmony Books, 1985), p. 167.

54. "James Brown, the 'Godfather of Soul,' Dies at 73," HighTimes.com, December 25, 2006, http://www.hightimes.com/read/james-brown-godfather-soul-dies-73.

55. *"The Definitive Otis Redding* (Rhino Records, 1993). Liner notes.

56. Author's interview with Wayne Jackson.

INDEX

Redding, Otis, songs and albums of:
- "Amen," 95, 256, 284
- "Any Ole Day," 168
- *Apollo Saturday Night*, 92–93
- "Baby Cakes," 201
- "Baby I Need Your Lovin'," 95
- "Baby Scratch My Back," 169, 192
- "Backdoor Santa," 253
- "Chained and Bound," 98–99, 105
- "Chain Gang," 169
- "Champagne and Wine," 256
- "Change Is Gonna Come, A," xiv, 112, 113, 120, 138
- "Cigarettes and Coffee," 169
- "Come to Me," 95, 98, 105, 256
- *Complete & Unbelievable: The Otis Redding Dictionary of Soul*, 170–71, 173, 174, 175, 191–92
- "Danny Boy," 162
- "Day Tripper," 171, 175, 192, 209, 213
- *Definitive Otis Redding, The*, 49, 53–54, 93
- "Demonstration," 256
- "Direct Me," 256
- *Dock of the Bay: The Definitive Collection, The*, 284
- "Dog, The," 94
- "Don't Mess with Cupid," 168
- "Down in the Valley," 112
- "Dream Girl," 97
- "Fa-Fa-Fa-Fa-Fa (Sad Song)," xxvi, 169–70, 173, 181, 213, 215, 219, 253, 254, 300
- "Fat Gal," 60, 303
- "Fool for You, A," 256
- "For Your Precious Love," 43, 106
- "Gamma Lama," 51, 52, 54, 59
- "Gee Whiz It's Christmas," 253
- "Gettin' Hip," 51, 54
- "Good to Me," 168
- *Great Otis Redding Sings Soul Ballads, The*, 105–8, 111–12
- "Happy Song (Dum-Dum), The," 254, 284
- "Hard Day's Night, A," 162
- "Hard to Handle," 255, 281, 284
- "Hey Hey Baby," 77, 80
- *History of Otis Redding*, 253, 283–84
- *Hit the Road Stax*, 219
- "Home in Your Heart," 106
- *How Strong My Love Is*, 106–7
- "Huckle-Buck, The," 251
- "I Can't Turn You Loose," 136–37, 163, 164, 178, 213, 253, 286, 294, 300
- "I Feel Good," 162
- "If I Had a Hammer," 162
- "I Got to Go Back (and Watch That Little Girl Dance)," 254
- "I Love You More Than Words Can Say," 211–12, 221–22
- *Immortal Otis Redding, The*, 284
- "I'm Sick Y'all," 172
- "I Need Your Lovin' (Part 2)," 94–95
- *In Person at the Whiskey a Go Go*, 160–65
- "It's Growing," 169
- "It's Too Late," 106
- "It Takes Two," 188
- "I've Been Loving You Too Long (To Stop Now)," xviii, xx, 103–5, 112, 122, 133–34, 164, 213, 252, 253, 300
- "I've Got Dreams to Remember," xxii, xxv, 255, 281, 284

ABOUT THE AUTHOR

Mark Ribowsky has written thirteen highly acclaimed books encompassing a wide range of pop culture topics, including the definitive biographies of the legendary sportscaster Howard Cosell (*Howard Cosell*) and Negro League legends Satchel Paige (*Don't Look Back*) and Josh Gibson (*The Power and the Darkness*), maverick Oakland Raiders owner Al Davis (*Slick*), controversial music producer Phil Spector (*He's a Rebel*), and a trilogy of Motown biographies about the Supremes (*The Supremes: A Saga of Motown Dreams, Success, and Betrayal*), Stevie Wonder (*Signed, Sealed, and Delivered*), and the Temptations (*Ain't Too Proud to Beg*). He has also written the exhaustive *A Complete History of the Negro Leagues*, *The Complete History of the Home Run*, and the autobiography of eccentric real estate baron Abe Hirschfeld (*Crazy and in Charge*), as well as hundreds of articles for national magazines including *Playboy*, *Penthouse*, *Sport*, *Inside Sports*, and *TV Guide*, his subjects including Eddie Murphy, David Letterman, Kareem Abdul-Jabbar, Larry Bird, Magic Johnson, Peyton Manning, Charles Barkley, Alex Rodriguez, and O. J. Simpson. He lives in Florida.